The History of the CATHOLIC CHURCH

The History of the CATHOLIC CHURCH

Ave Maria Press AVE Notre Dame, Indiana

The Subcommittee on the Catechism, United States Conference of Catholic Bishops, has found that this catechetical high school text, copyright 2020, is in conformity with the *Catechism of the Catholic Church* and that it fulfills the requirements of Elective Course B of the *Doctrinal Elements of a Curriculum Framework for the Development of Catechetical Materials for Young People of High School Age*.

Nihil Obstat: Reverend Monsignor Michael Heintz, PhD
Censor Librorum

Imprimatur: Most Reverend Kevin C. Rhoades
Bishop of Fort Wayne–South Bend
Given at: Fort Wayne, Indiana, on 21 May 2018.

The *Nihil Obstat* and *Imprimatur* are official declarations that a book or pamphlet is free of doctrinal or moral error. No implication is contained therein that those who have granted the *Nihil Obstat* or *Imprimatur* agree with its contents, opinions, or statements expressed.

Catechetical Writing Team
Justin McClain
Michael Amodei

Theological Consultant
Troy Stefano, PhD
Associate Professor of Systematic and Historical Theology
St. Vincent de Paul Regional Seminary
Boynton Beach, Florida

Pedagogical Consultant
Michael J. Boyle, PhD
Director, Andrew M. Greeley Center for Catholic Education
Loyola University Chicago

---

www.avemariapress.com

Founded in 1865, Ave Maria Press is a ministry of the United States Province of Holy Cross.

Engaging Minds and Hands for Faith® is a trademark of Ave Maria Press, Inc.

Paperback: ISBN-13 978-1-59471-711-6

E-book: ISBN-13 978-1-59471-712-3

Cover images © Getty Images, Superstock.

Cover and text design by Andy Wagoner.

Printed and bound in the United States of America.

ENGAGING MINDS, HEARTS, AND HANDS FOR FAITH

An education that is complete is the one in which hands and heart are engaged as much as the mind. We want to let our students try their learning in the world and so make prayers of their education.

Bl. Basil Moreau
Founder of the Congregation of Holy Cross

In this text you will

explore the Church's enduring presence and contribution to world history as she shares the Gospel of Christ to the ends of the earth.

prayerfully acknowledge that only in faith can you recognize the Church's place in history as the bearer of divine life.

be encouraged to actively participate in the mission of the Church to love as Jesus did, especially in the service of the poor and those with special needs.

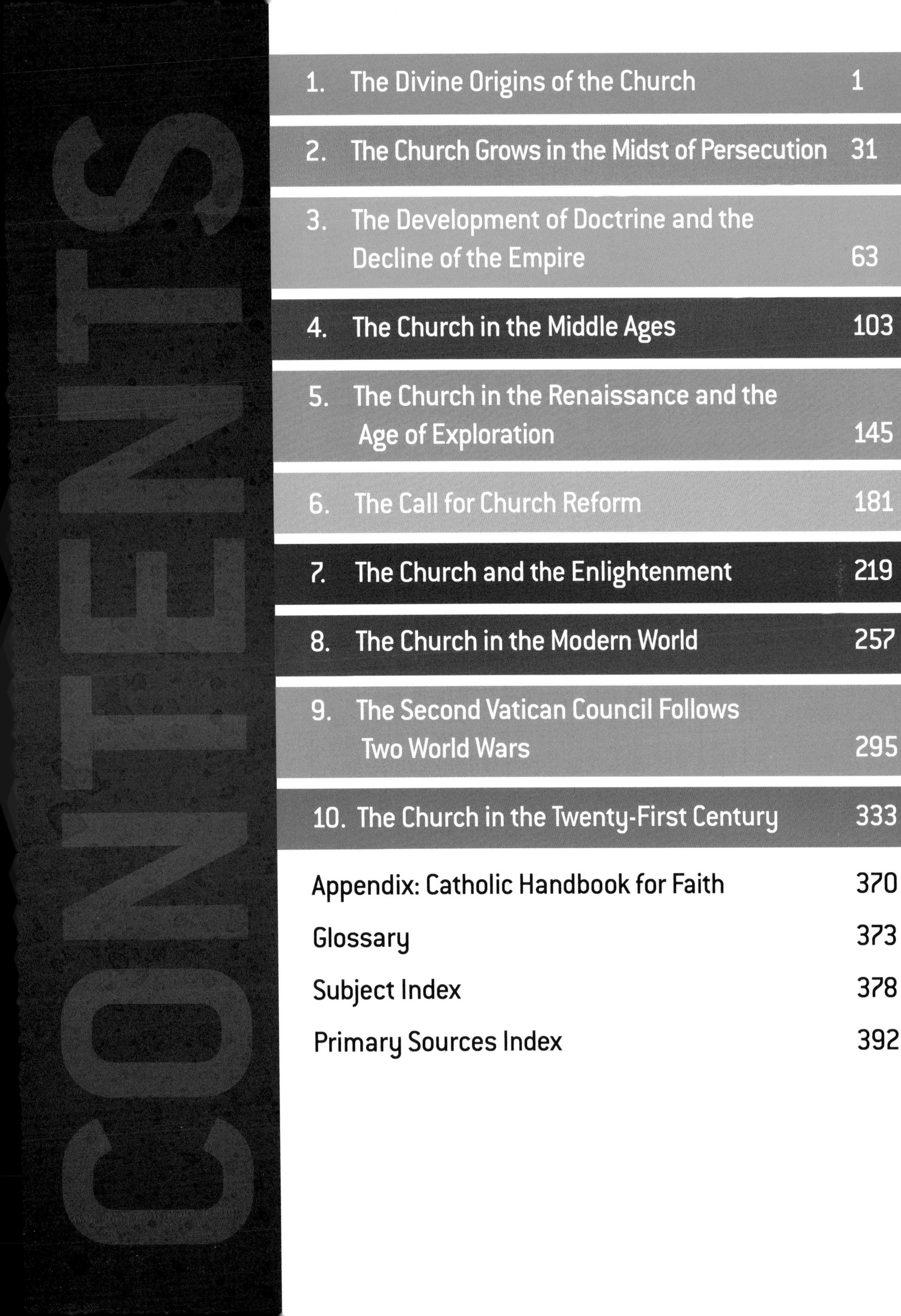
CONTENTS

THE DIVINE ORIGINS OF THE CHURCH

VATICAN DISPLAYS THE RELICS OF ST. PETER FOR THE FIRST TIME

St. Peter's Basilica at the Vatican in Rome was built between 1506 and 1626 on the site where tradition held that St. Peter had been entombed. (Peter was martyred in about AD 65 [around the same time as St. Paul, his collaborator in the faith] during the reign of the Roman emperor Nero.) But it was not until the mid-twentieth century that a series of excavations beneath the altar of St. Peter's unearthed human skeletal remains in such a location that archaeologists believed that they could only be those of Peter. Subsequently, a team of scientists determined that the bones were approximately two thousand years old, and genetic testing revealed that they indeed belonged to a Middle Eastern man in his sixties. These observations, along with other factors, pointed to the conclusion that the bones belong to Peter, and they were definitively declared authentic by Pope Paul VI in 1968.

In 2013 the Vatican decided to put the *relics*, or earthly remains, of St. Peter on public display for the first time. This exposition of Peter's relics was organized to coincide with the conclusion of the Church's liturgical "Year of Faith," which Pope Benedict XVI had opened on October 11, 2012, and which Pope Francis concluded on November 24, 2013.

Pope Francis holds relics of St. Peter the Apostle.

FOCUS QUESTION

What is the Church's **DIVINE ROLE** within **SALVATION HISTORY**?

Chapter Overview

INTRODUCTION

Studying Church History

MAIN IDEA
The Church is the continuation of the Incarnation in the world. The Church is the intimate connection between Christ and the world.

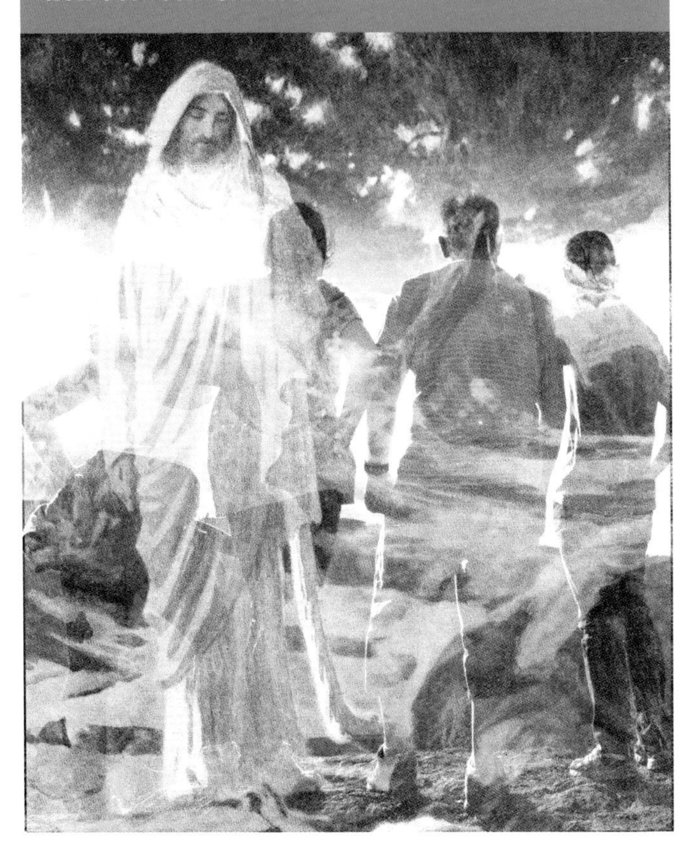

You've learned the value of studying history from other history courses you have taken in school. Historians look back at evidence and written records from a particular time and attempt to determine what they meant to the people of that period, as well as whether they can explain certain developments such as war, the collapse of an empire, economic prosperity, or the flourishing of the arts. Historians also endeavor to show that understanding past events can help people understand occurrences today as well as what might happen in the future.

This course is a history course. It is the study of the history of the Catholic Church. The Church has a long, traceable history of almost two thousand years that has paralleled the history of the great Roman Empire, the Renaissance, the Age of Exploration of the New World, the era of the Enlightenment, the Industrial Revolution, and the accelerating technological advances of the twentieth century through today.

The Church is certainly a human institution made up of a community of people and a hierarchy of structure. Elements of a historical study of the Church are similar to those you would find in other historical studies (e.g., uncovering written records and artifacts such as the remains of St. Peter). But studying the history of the Church is also much different from

NOTE TAKING

Synthesizing Information. After you read the text section, write a sentence that might persuade a friend of what you believe to be the value of studying the history of the Catholic Church. You may use one of the following to sentence starters.

It is important to study the history of the Catholic Church because . . .

For me, the value in studying Church history is . . .

Jesus is present in the lives of the people who make up the Church and especially in the consecrated gifts of bread, shown here in a Eucharistic procession.

studying about any other long-standing human institution, such as a nation or government. When God the Father created the whole universe and then created humans to share in his divine life, he had the Church in mind. She is truly "a plan born in the Father's heart" (*CCC*, 759), foreshadowed or "already present in figure at the beginning of the world" (*Lumen Gentium*, 2).

The Church is the place where Jesus Christ, the Son of God, remains present. She is the place where God continues to share his Revelation to the world. This means that although the Church is in historical time, she also transcends history. The Church both takes part in human history and surpasses human comprehension. Through the years and generations, the Church has been and remains the bearer of the divine life even as she takes her place in human history. That's what makes a course on Church history different from other history courses you take in school.

What Is the Church?

St. Joan of Arc once described the Church this way: "About Jesus Christ and the Church, I simply know they are just one thing, and we shouldn't complicate the matter." Most people today—Catholics and non-Catholics alike—understand that there is a connection between Jesus Christ and the Church. But many people also seem to believe that Christian faith and participating in the Church can be separated. It is not uncommon to hear people say things such as:

- "I believe in God, but I have no use for the Church"; or
- "As long as you accept Jesus, the question about whether or not you belong to a church is irrelevant"; or even
- "Don't commit yourself to any church. Churches get in the way of real faith."

These perspectives are false. The Christian faith cannot be separated from a relationship with the Church because where the Church is, God is.

The Catholic Church is rooted in faith in God, who became incarnate in history in the Divine Person of Jesus of Nazareth. In Jesus, people were able to touch, listen to, and speak to God directly. In Jesus, people came to know God's healing and forgiveness in an immediate way. In Jesus, God's offer of salvation and fullness of life became a tangible reality. Following Jesus' **Paschal Mystery**, salvation and fullness of life became accessible to all people through the Church. Jesus breathed his Spirit into the Church so that the Church could be his Body on earth. From this time on, "the mission of Christ and the Spirit becomes the mission of the Church" (*CCC*, 730).

The Church is indeed in history, but she also transcends history. Only "with the eyes of faith" can you see both the visible reality and spiritual reality of the Church (see *CCC*, 770). If the Church is both the visible reality and spiritual reality of God's life on earth, then it is obvious that people cannot separate their response to God's call from their relationship to the Church.

The very word *church* reveals the connection between answering God's call and being part of a community: the Greek word used in the New Testament is *ekklésia*, meaning "those called out of." *Ekklésia* was commonly used to refer to a legislative assembly; when it was used in Scripture, it referred to the community called out of the world by God to live and act in a way that was different from others. But God does not call you to the Church as an isolated individual. The meeting place is not a private dinner with God. Rather, God's call resounds through all creation, summoning those who hear to gather in an assembly and to act together on behalf and in the name of God. God's call is a call to be united with Christ, to be part of his body. In other words, God's call to faith is a call to be Church. Only in faith can you recognize the Church's place in history along with its role in bearing God to the world.

Paschal Mystery The redemptive Passion, Death, Resurrection, and glorious Ascension of Jesus Christ, through which Jesus not only liberated humans from sin but also gave them new life.

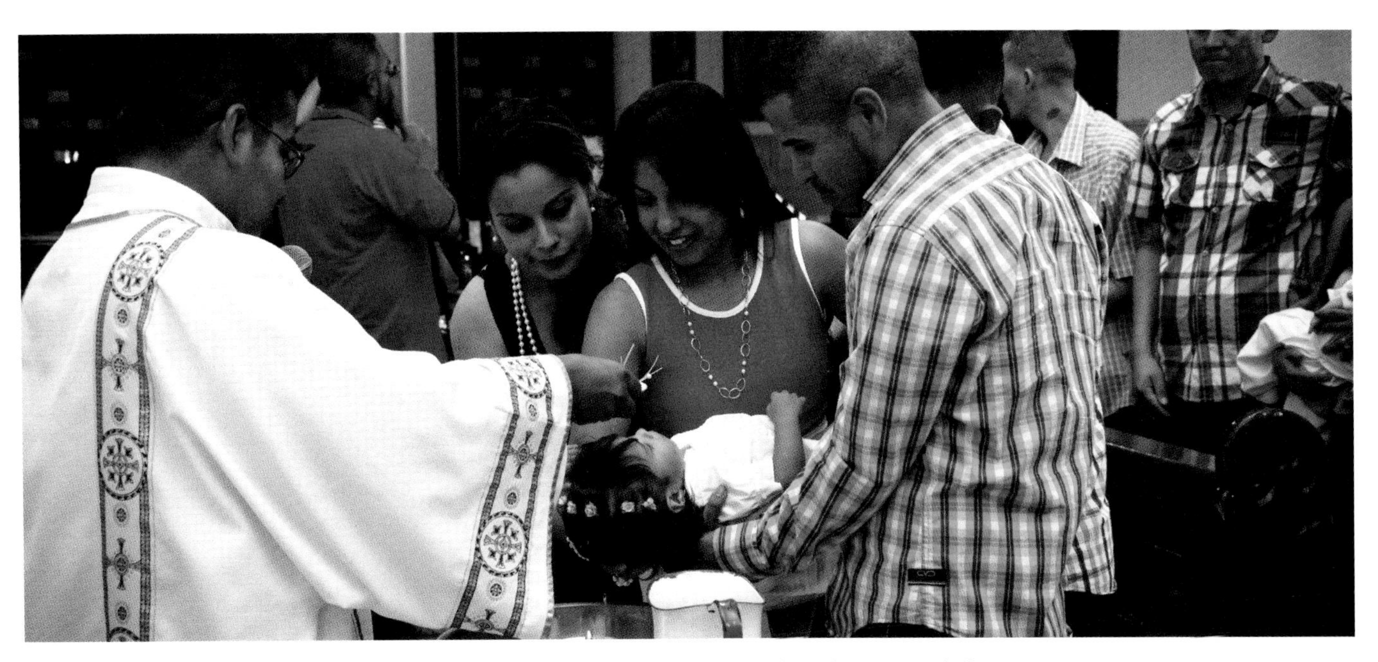

Baptism is the sacrament that incorporates a person into the Church. It is usually celebrated at Mass with the community present.

SECTION ASSESSMENT

NOTE TAKING

Use the sentence you constructed as part of the Note Taking assignment to help you answer the following questions.

1. What is the difference between studying Church history and studying the history of any other human institution?
2. What one question do you have about the Church that you would like this course to answer?

COMPREHENSION

3. Fill in the blank: The Church is historical in time, but it also _______ history.
4. How did St. Joan of Arc describe the Church?
5. How does the meaning of the Greek term for Church—*ekklésia*—relate to the dual nature of the Church as a human and divine institution?

VOCABULARY

6. What does the *Paschal Mystery* refer to?

APPLICATION

7. How do you imagine your study of Church history will help you to grow closer to Jesus Christ?

SECTION 1

The Need for Faith

MAIN IDEA

When you respond to God's gift of faith, you are then able to experience the fullness of faith present in the Church. Your faith is deepened and fortified by the faith of the Church.

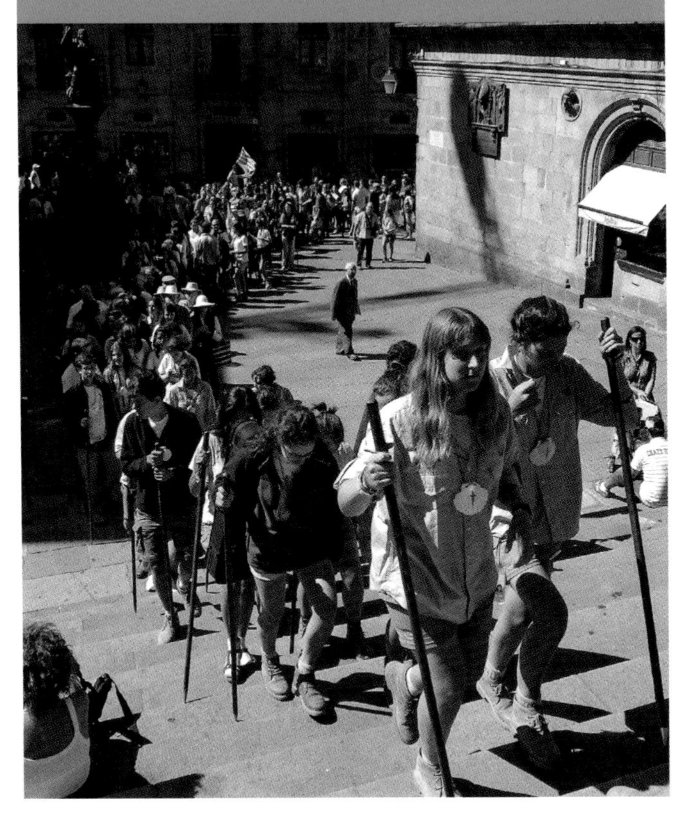

In order for you to accept your role in the Body of Christ, the Church, you need **faith**. In his encyclical *Redemptoris Mater* (*Mother of the Redeemer*), Pope John Paul II wrote that faith is "contact with the mystery of God" (17). Faith is a free gift from God, and without God's help you could not believe. But faith is also an authentically human act. It is your response to God's gift, a surrendering of yourself to God. When you believe in God, or surrender yourself to the mystery of God that has been revealed to you, your faith is deepened. Before you can act as a member of the Body of Christ, the Church, God must touch you with the gift of faith and you must respond. Only then will you experience the fullness of unity with Christ, the "head of the body, the church" (Col 1:18).

Each member of the Church needs to believe in Christ if he or she is going to act on behalf of Christ in the world. To believe in Christ means to abandon yourself to him, to be shaped by him, and to let go of the things that prevent you from listening to and following him. You cannot act as a part of the Body of Christ unless you have a faith that connects you to Christ.

NOTE TAKING

Sketching to Remember. Draw sketches to represent some of the lessons on faith presented in this section. For example:

- Faith is a gift from God.

- Faith is a human act.
- Your faith is united to the faith of the Church.
- The Church preserves faith in formal structures.
- The Church is a model of faith.

faith Both a gift from God that can only exist with God's preceding grace and an act of a person's intellect, an assenting to the divine truth by command of the will that has been moved by that grace. Though only possible by grace and the interior helps of the Holy Spirit, faith is truly a human action. "Trusting in God and cleaving to the truths he has revealed are contrary neither to human freedom nor to human reason" (*CCC*, 154).

No one acting alone can be the Body of Christ. Each person is only a single member of that body. A true disciple of Christ must join with others. Hence, statements such as "As long as you accept Jesus, the question about whether or not you belong to a church is irrelevant" are not accurate. Your faith must be communal as well as personal. You must believe in Christ not only as an individual but also as a part of groups—with your family, with your friends, with your parish, and with the Church at large. In other words, you cannot really answer God's call unless you participate in Christ's Church.

Your Faith and the Church

Your personal faith is deepened and fortified by the Church's faith. The Church's faith also makes it possible for you to do what God calls you to do: to know and love him more fully and to live not in isolation but as a member of the one Body of Christ. This community of faith exists wherever two or more people gather to share their faith, pray, or support and encourage one another out of love rooted in love for God. For this reason the Church needs to maintain *formal structures* that help preserve essential truths. These formal structures include creeds, doctrines, and rituals. The formal aspects of Catholicism have ensured that the faith revealed by Jesus Christ has survived even when members of the Church have sinned.

The formal structures help you maintain your identity as an individual believer and help the Church maintain her identity as a model of faith. The formal structures make the communal relationships with God among Catholics visible and tangible. The task of defining and interpreting these formal structures is carried out by the Church's **Magisterium**. The Magisterium comprises the bishops in communion with the pope, who is the successor of St. Peter. Unless you commit yourself to the formal structures of the faith of the Church, you may find you are cobbling together an individualistic and perhaps narcissistic type of faith that is not in your best interest either now or for eternity. If you reject the formal structures of the Church's

Magisterium The bishops, in communion with the pope (the successor of St. Peter), who are the living and teaching office of the Church. The Magisterium authentically interprets the Word of God in the forms of both Sacred Scripture and Sacred Tradition.

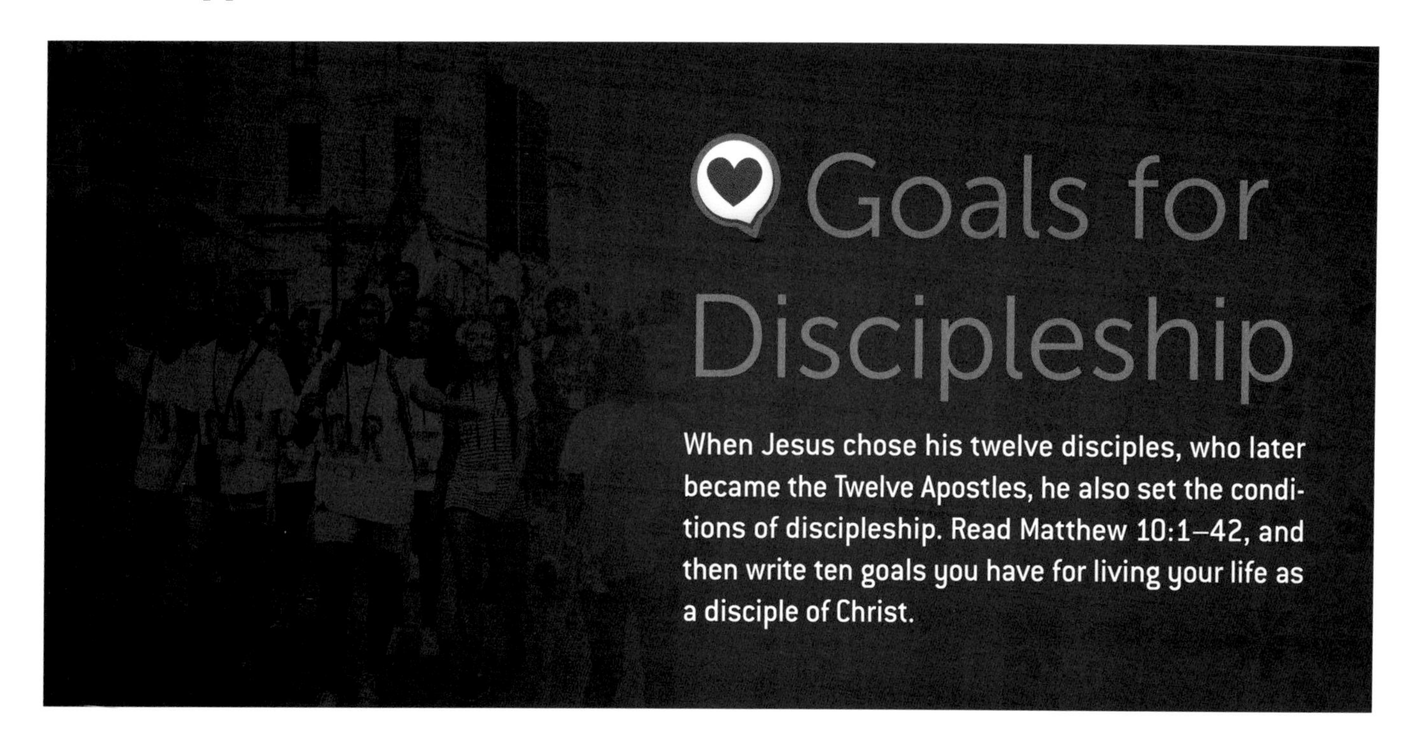

Goals for Discipleship

When Jesus chose his twelve disciples, who later became the Twelve Apostles, he also set the conditions of discipleship. Read Matthew 10:1–42, and then write ten goals you have for living your life as a disciple of Christ.

faith, you will probably end up selecting those parts of faith that demand the least of you and that are most in keeping with the secular culture in which you live.

The Church's catholicity depends in part on the continuity of her teaching with that of the past. The **Deposit of Faith** of the Church contains God's Revelation—all that Catholics believe is divinely revealed. The Deposit of Faith is transmitted in two ways: through Sacred Tradition and through Sacred Scripture. A great gift of being a member of the Catholic Church is that you are able to build your faith on the understanding of generations that came before you, secure in the knowledge that the Holy Spirit, the Spirit of Truth, ensures that the Church never loses what the Father revealed through Jesus, his Son.

Deposit of Faith "The heritage of faith contained in Sacred Scripture and Sacred Tradition, handed down in the Church from the time of the Apostles, from which the Magisterium draws all that it proposes for belief as being divinely revealed" (*CCC*, Glossary).

SECTION ASSESSMENT

NOTE TAKING

Use the sketches you created to help you answer the following questions.

1. What does it mean to say that without God's help you could not believe?
2. How is personal faith fortified by the Church's faith?
3. What is the risk of not committing yourself to the formal structures of faith found in the Church?

COMPREHENSION

4. How is the Deposit of Faith transmitted?

VOCABULARY

5. Define *Magisterium*.

APPLICATION

6. How can remaining open to deepening your faith help to make this course more productive?

SECTION 2

Christ Instituted the Church

MAIN IDEA
The Church was foreshadowed from the world's beginning, remotely prepared for through a series of covenants, and instituted by Christ through his words and actions as part of his public ministry.

The call to be an active participant in the Church highlights God's invitation to you to enter into dialogue with him. In the Church, you are invited to relate to the Father as his son or daughter. The call to participate in the Church is an incredible gift and an incredible trust. The Church is the summation of all of God's gifts to the world throughout history. Despite human weakness and failings, God has never abandoned the human race. Despite the many times that people have violated God's trust, God has offered humanity the most precious gift of the Church. In order to better understand this, it is helpful to consider some of the other ways that God has invited and trusted humanity throughout the course of salvation history.

Tracing Salvation History

At the beginning of human history, God invited man and woman to be cocreators with him by giving Adam and Eve, in the name of all humanity, dominion over the earth (see Genesis 1:28). God has invited all people throughout history to use their own talents and efforts to perfect and complete the work of creation. Even after sin entered the world, God never took away from humanity the role of cocreator or caretaker of the world.

Later, God invited a particular people to do more than care for the earth. As part of his remote preparation for the founding of the Church, God called the Israelites (the Chosen People, later known as the Jews)

NOTE TAKING

Timeline of Key Events. Create a timeline that highlights key events in the formation of the Church from the beginning of time to the birth of Jesus.

Beginning of time ———————————————— Birth of Jesus

to enter into a mutually binding **covenant** relationship with him. God willingly bound himself forever to this group of people and gave them a pivotal role in his plan for the world. Although the Israelites broke the covenant over and over again, God never gave up on them or abandoned them. In fact, God trusted them as people of faith from which his own Son, Jesus, would be born.

When the time was right, God himself became a member of that Chosen People. Jesus, the Son of God, was born as a helpless baby completely dependent upon the love, support, and care of the people around him. God the Father entrusted his own Son, his very self, to human beings. What is more, in the Divine Person of Jesus, God chose to bind the divine nature with human nature so that the two became one.

"The world was created for the sake of the Church" (quoted in *CCC*, 760). This phrase was used by Christians of the first centuries to express their understanding of the role of the Church in God's plan for the world. The Church is the culmination of **salvation history**. From the creation of the world, God has intended for human beings to share in divine life. In the Church this sharing finally becomes a reality.

It is Jesus who instituted the Church. "The Lord Jesus inaugurated his Church by preaching the Good News, that is, the coming of the Reign of God, promised over the ages in the scriptures" (*Lumen Gentium*, 5, quoted in *CCC*, 763). Through the Incarnation of Jesus, the **Kingdom of God** broke into human history. The barrier between the divine and the human, which had been in place since Adam and Eve caused the fall of humanity, was shattered. The Kingdom of God, the realm in which God's will is done, was opened to humanity. Through Jesus' Death and Resurrection, earthly life was permanently linked to God's Kingdom; but no one on earth will fully experience the Kingdom until Jesus' **second coming**. The Church is the focal point of the Kingdom's presence on earth. The Church is also the place where people are most acutely aware of the fact that the fullness of the Kingdom is still to come.

Jesus had a relatively short public ministry, spanning about three years. During this time he undertook actions that were oriented to the Kingdom of God, such as performing miracles (healings, exorcisms, nature miracles, and raising the dead), giving moral teachings, praying, and preaching the Good News of his offer of salvation and redemption.

Jesus established the basic structure for the Church when he chose twelve disciples, who would later be known as **Apostles**. Because of human limitations, some followers were bound to know Jesus and his message more intimately than others. Jesus specifically

covenant The partnership between God and humanity that God has established out of his love. The New Covenant is offered through Christ; the blood that Christ shed on the Cross is a sign of the New Covenant.

salvation history The story of God's action in human history. Salvation history refers to the events through which God makes humanity aware of and brings humanity into the Kingdom of God. It began with the creation of the world and will end with the second coming of Christ.

Kingdom of God The reign or rule of God. The Kingdom of God began with the coming of Jesus. It will exist in perfect form at the end of time.

second coming The final judgment of all humanity when Christ returns to earth. It is also known by its Greek name, *Parousia*, which means "arrival."

Apostles Jesus' twelve specially chosen and commissioned disciples, as well as other figures such as St. Paul; they earned this designation when they were sent forth to evangelize. The word *apostle* originates from the Greek for "to send forth."

selected some with whom he would share the most of his ministry, and he made it clear that this selection came with responsibilities. Jesus gave the Apostles authority to teach and baptize in his name. He also made it clear that this authority was to be used not to gain power but to serve others and to help them grow spiritually. For all of these reasons, it can be clearly stated that Jesus himself instituted the Church.

Given the power from Jesus to act in his name, the Apostles passed on to their successors their knowledge of Jesus, their authority from him, and their commitment to service in his name. In this way, the hierarchical structure of the Church was permanently established. This is what Jesus intended. When Jesus commissioned the Apostles, he promised that he would be with them to the end of time (see Matthew 28:20). He would guide their teaching and whom they baptized. Since the Apostles themselves did not live until "the end of the age," the Church understands this promise to mean that Jesus will guide those who succeed the Apostles to the end of time. Bishops, in union with the pope and with priests as their coworkers, have the responsibility of carrying on this role, a role that is directly guided by Jesus.

SECTION ASSESSMENT

NOTE TAKING

Use the timeline you created to help you answer the following questions.

1. "From the creation of the world, God has intended for human beings to share in the divine life." How does this statement point to the beginning of the Church?
2. Explain the role of the Israelites in the Church's history.
3. What does it mean to say that "Christ instituted the Church"?

COMPREHENSION

4. How did Christ inaugurate the Church?
5. When will the Kingdom of God be fully experienced by people on earth?

VOCABULARY

6. Explain the duration of *salvation history.*
7. Define *Apostles.*

CRITICAL THINKING

8. What does it mean to say that "the world was created for the sake of the Church"?

SECTION 3

Pentecost and the Growth of the Church

MAIN IDEA

The Church was revealed by the Holy Spirit at Pentecost and, with the gifts bestowed on her by Christ, faithfully carried out his command to share the Good News with all people in all ages.

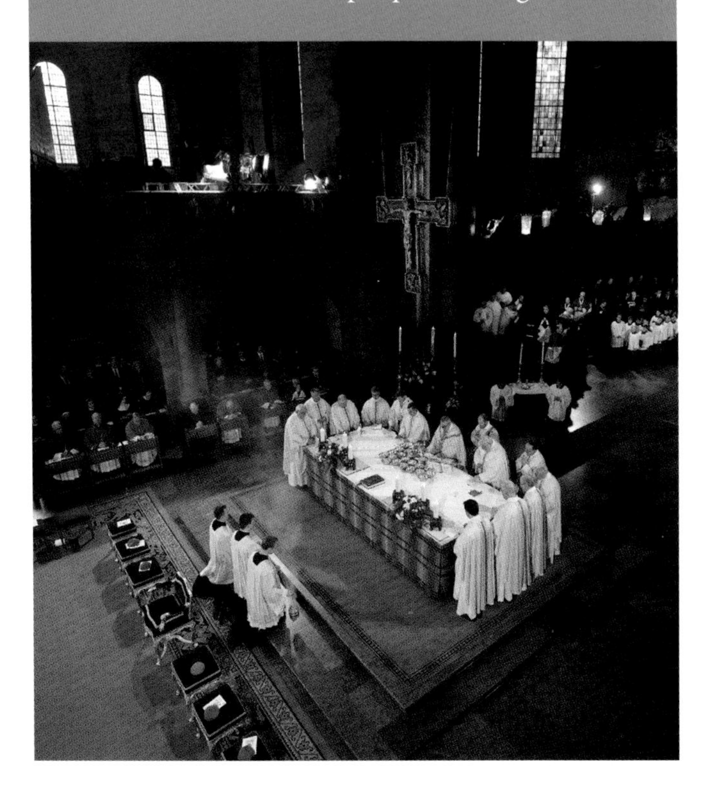

Even the union of human nature and divine nature in the Divine Person of Jesus Christ was not the final gift of God to humanity, nor was it God's final effort to unite humanity in partnership with God. Even after becoming human—even after living, suffering, and dying as a human for the sake of humanity—God still had more to offer. The depth and breadth of God's love for humanity and trust in humanity is revealed beyond Christ's Death—and even beyond his Resurrection—in the gift of the Holy Spirit to the Church.

Following his Resurrection, Jesus returned to the Father, but his **Ascension** did not mark the end of God's tangible involvement in history. The day of **Pentecost**, less than two weeks later, marked the beginning of a new era in God's relationship with humanity. On that Pentecost, the Father and the Son gave the Holy Spirit to the Church so that the Church could continue the work of Christ in proclaiming and establishing the Kingdom of God.

The word *Pentecost* is a Greek term that means "fiftieth day"; it marks a Jewish harvest feast that occurs fifty days after Passover. Jesus' disciples were among those gathered in Jerusalem for this feast ten days after Jesus' Ascension. The Acts of the Apostles records the details of this first Christian Pentecost:

> When the time for Pentecost was fulfilled, they were all in one place together. And suddenly

NOTE TAKING

Sequencing. Put the following terms and concepts in correct sequential order, and write a sentence for each explaining what it had to do with the spread of the Church.

- Gentile converts
- Pentecost
- Jewish Christians
- Ascension
- apostolic succession

Ascension The event that "marks the definitive entrance of Jesus' humanity into God's heavenly domain" (*CCC*, 665). It is from heaven that Christ will come again.

Pentecost From the Greek for "fiftieth day," a Jewish harvest feast occurring fifty days after Passover; the first Pentecost for Christians was when the Holy Spirit appeared to the Apostles in the form of wind and fire fifty days after Jesus' Resurrection.

there came from the sky a noise like a strong driving wind, and it filled the entire house in which they were. Then there appeared to them tongues as of fire, which parted and came to rest on each one of them. And they were all filled with the Holy Spirit and began to speak in different tongues, as the Spirit enabled them to proclaim. (Acts 2:1–4)

The images of fire and wind are symbolic of the presence of the Holy Spirit. As the Holy Spirit inspired the disciples to speak in various languages, they finally began to understand their role as Apostles: to bring the Good News of Jesus Christ out into the world.

It is worthwhile to note that the disciples were not originally seen as convincing leaders within their community. Prior to Pentecost, they were not persuasive public speakers. At Pentecost, the Holy Spirit gave them the courage and resourcefulness to be able to evangelize without fear or reservation. In fact, Peter, who had formerly been so afraid that he denied Jesus three times leading up to his Crucifixion (see Matthew 26:69–75), now had such fortitude that he went among the Jews gathered for the festival and preached boldly, baptizing around three thousand people in the process (see Acts 2:14–41). Because of this significant feat of evangelization, Pentecost is often considered the "birthday of the Church." Before Pentecost, the spreading of the Gospel was carried out by one person: Jesus Christ. However, following Pentecost, evangelization became a collective activity undertaken by an organized group—the Apostles.

The Church Shares the Essential Christian Message

Acts of the Apostles shows just how closely Jesus and his Church are connected. Acts was probably written by the same author as the Gospel of Luke, which provides a rather detailed sequence of Jesus' life and ministry, beginning with the infancy narratives. Acts presents the earliest Christians as at first believing that Jesus would return during their lifetimes and then beginning to realize that this might not be so. One thing this realization led to was a need for the Church to record the essentials of Christ's message in written form—that is, in the Gospels and epistles (letters) that would eventually make up the New Testament.

The heart of the Good News preached by the Apostles centered on the love of the Father poured out for the world in the gift of his Son. Core Gospel teachings that remain essential for you and all Catholics today include the following:

- **Jesus frees you from your sins.**
- **You must have unwavering trust in God.**
- **Your heart must undergo a constant conversion to the Lord's will.**
- **You should celebrate that you are a son or daughter of the Father.**
- **You must serve and minister to your neighbors.**
- **You should evangelize and work for the Kingdom of God.**

The Apostles understood that the Church herself is the Body of Christ on earth and each member of the Church is a member of that Body. Now, as then, it is primarily through the Church that God chooses to be made known, present, and tangible. It is primarily through the Church that God communicates truth and grace.

"At the Last Supper, . . . our Savior instituted the Eucharistic sacrifice of his Body and Blood" (CCC, 1323).

The Structure of the Early Church

The Apostles eventually realized that they might not see Jesus' return during their lifetimes. This meant that, for the spiritual well-being of successive generations, they had to consider how the Church would function into the future. Thus, they began to make various practical resolutions regarding such matters as the definition of roles within the Church, ways to resolve conflicts that could arise, and how to determine the authenticity and inspired nature of the Gospel.

Regarding the approval of Scripture, over time a universally accepted *canon*, or list of approved Scripture, was developed. Furthermore, around AD 150 the Church compiled the basic outline of the Apostles' Creed as a summary of the beliefs that any person seeking Baptism must affirm. Also, this was the period when the understanding of **apostolic succession** developed. To counteract false witnesses who claimed the authority to teach, the Church taught that her authority was given by Christ to his Apostles. Through this position of authority, the Apostles passed on through apostolic succession authority to bishops whom they ordained through the laying on of hands. Apostolic succession maintains the office, teaching, and mission of the Apostles as entrusted to them by Christ (see *CCC*, 857–862). Apostolic succession requires that no bishop teach anything that is contrary to what has been handed down to him by his predecessors. Apostolic succession protects the Church against the influx of ideas that are antithetical to Christianity.

apostolic succession The handing on of the teaching, preaching, and office of the Apostles to their successors, the bishops, through the laying on of hands.

It is important to note that during the earliest days of the Church, Jesus' followers did not view themselves as being of a different faith from the other Jews to whom they were evangelizing. Their efforts at sharing the Christian Gospel with their Jewish neighbors led them to defend Christ and his message based on their foundation in the Mosaic Law and Jewish traditions. As such, Jesus' followers did not refer to themselves in any distinctive way, such as using the term *Christian* extensively. In fact the term *Christian* appears only three times in the New Testament, in Acts 26:28, 1 Corinthians 9:5, and 1 Peter 4:16.

Since many early Christians were also practicing Jews, the structure of the early Church reflected Jewish worship. For example, these first Jewish Christians made pilgrimages to the Temple in Jerusalem, attended services at their local synagogue, shared meals in their neighbors' homes, and followed the Mosaic Law. Jesus' followers, however, had a practice that distinguished them from other Jews: when they broke bread during meals, this was in keeping with Jesus' command to them at the Last Supper to "do this in memory of me" (Lk 22:19b).

The early Christians' celebration of the Eucharist, which recognized their shared belief in Jesus Christ as Lord and Savior, allowed them to remain unified. Also, the Apostles shared everything in common: money, possessions, food, and other belongings, all of which they shared with the needy as well. These community living practices, too, would be foundational for the Church, and they remain in practice today, especially through the Church's large mission of social outreach to the poor. Likewise, there were men and women in the early Church who set out to follow Christ more closely by practicing the **evangelical counsels**. These Christians would be the forerunners of hermits and the founders and members of religious communities that arose in later centuries and whose practices also remain part of the Church to this day.

evangelical counsels Vows of personal poverty, chastity (understood as lifelong celibacy), and obedience to a bishop or superior of a religious community.

Sharing the Story of Your Faith

All Catholics are called to witness to their faith and to share the Good News of Jesus Christ with others. Prepare a ten-minute talk explaining how you came to the faith and something about the current stage of your faith journey. Your talk may include the following:

- your family's history as Catholics
- your reception of the sacraments
- a time you became aware of Christ's presence in your life
- how you plan to share the Lord with others in the future

If you have yet to experience any of the faith milestones listed above, plan a similar talk based on the experience and model of a Catholic you know. Include in your talk some life lessons you have learned from that person.

Plan to share your talk with your classmates, either live or as a recorded presentation.

The Holy Spirit Forms the Church

The presence of the Holy Spirit gives life to the Church, builds up the Church, and sanctifies the Church. The Holy Spirit forms the Church, which is the very Body of Christ and the Temple of the Holy Spirit. The Holy Spirit uses the Church to draw you to Christ, to reveal the good things Christ has done for you, and to make present the Paschal Mystery of his love in your life. This is done most clearly in the Holy Eucharist, in which you share in God's own life.

The Holy Spirit showers many gifts on the Church that help Catholics live like Jesus Christ. These gifts build up the Church. They include:

- *Gifts that make the Church holy.* These seven gifts of the Holy Spirit are those that the prophet Isaiah said would identify the Holy Spirit (see Isaiah 11:2–3). They are: wisdom, understanding, counsel (right judgment), strength (fortitude or courage), knowledge, piety (reverence), and fear of the Lord.
- *Gifts that serve the Church.* St. Paul lists other gifts that are meant to build up the Body of Christ in 1 Corinthians 12:4–11. Each of these special gifts is known as a **charism**. They include wisdom, knowledge, faith, healing, miracle working, prophecy, discernment, speaking in tongues, and interpreting tongues.

charism A special gift or grace of the Holy Spirit that directly or indirectly builds up the Church, helps a person live a Christian life, or serves the common good.

- *Gifts that result in spiritual fruit.* Also, St. Paul named some fruits of the Holy Spirit that result from the Holy Spirit living in you. These are the first fruits of your eternal glory and are love (charity), joy, peace, patience, kindness, generosity, faithfulness, gentleness, and self-control (see Galatians 5:22–23).

All of the gifts of the Holy Spirit are related to one another. When these gifts are present in the Church, they show that the Church is one with Jesus, the true vine described in John 15:1. The Holy Spirit is the spirit of love, God's great gift to the Church through Christ:

> "God is Love" and love is his first gift, containing all others. "God's love has been poured into our hearts through the Holy Spirit who has been given to us." (*CCC*, 733, quoting 1 John 4:8, 16; Romans 5:5)

Of all the gifts of the Holy Spirit, love is the greatest of all (see 1 Corinthians 13:1–13). God's love is given to you freely. It cannot be earned. It is a pure gift. God does not give love to you because you are good; you are good because God loves you and lives in you.

Assignments

- Read and summarize paragraph 4 of *Lumen Gentium* (*Dogmatic Constitution on the Church*) on the role of the Holy Spirit in the Church.
- Think about a Catholic you know who exemplifies in a powerful way one of the charisms of the Holy Spirit. Write a three-paragraph profile of this person and how he or she uses this charism for the benefit of others.

The Christian Faith's Appeal to Gentiles

People with Jewish ancestry were not the only followers of Christ; *Gentiles* (non-Jews) were also attracted to the Christian Gospel. By the first century AD, many Jews lived outside of the region of Palestine and therefore had many interactions with Gentiles. Many of these Gentiles had already acquired a great respect for the moral teachings of Judaism but understood they were generally not allowed to convert to the Jewish faith. Also, many Gentiles were attracted to *monotheism*, the belief in one God held by both Jews and Christians. This attraction was due, in part, to their opposition to the oppressive Roman government, which required belief in many state-sponsored gods. And the newness of the Christian faith, along with Jesus' words of welcome to the poor and oppressed—to all people—appealed to many Gentiles. The main attraction to the Gentiles was that God had come to earth and revealed himself as a historical person. This was the main scandal and claim in a time when there was so much diversity of views about God.

The Church had several decisions to make about whether or not to admit Gentiles to this Jewish-rooted faith. Foremost among those eventually reaching out to the Gentiles was St. Paul, a Pharisaic Jewish convert to Christianity who became known as the "Apostle to the Gentiles." The next section provides details about his missionary efforts.

SECTION ASSESSMENT

NOTE TAKING

Use the notes you kept of the sequencing of major events in the early Church to help you complete the following item.

1. Write a paragraph that explains the history of the early years of the Church and the spread of Christianity and uses the following terms: Gentile converts, Pentecost, Jewish Christians, Ascension, apostolic succession.

COMPREHENSION

2. What caused Jesus' disciples to be more bold and unafraid to share the Good News after Pentecost?
3. What are some of the things the Apostles did when they realized Jesus might not return in their lifetimes?
4. What was a significant distinction between the religious practice of early Jewish Christians and traditional Jewish practice?

VOCABULARY

5. Explain the importance of *apostolic succession* in the Church.

APPLICATION

6. Choose one of the essential teachings of the Apostles (see "The Church Shares the Essential Christian Message" in this section), and write a practical way you are following this teaching in your own life.

SECTION 4

St. Paul: Apostle to the Gentiles

MAIN IDEA

In the first century AD, the Apostles, eventually joined by St. Paul and other converts to Christ, spread the Good News beyond Jerusalem, including to the Gentiles.

In the early Church, disputes soon arose regarding not only how to evangelize but also whom to evangelize. Prior to the evangelization of the Gentiles, the general religious understanding of the time was that what the Gentiles believed and practiced was unsuited to being associated with Jewish beliefs and practices. For example, observant Jews could not even eat with Gentiles. However, a vision Peter had and his encounter with Cornelius (see Acts 10) gave Peter the impetus to evangelize the Gentiles, ushering in a distinct and lasting division between Judaism and Christianity.

Peter's vision and subsequent baptism of Cornelius, a Gentile, did not entirely decide the issue of whether to admit Gentiles into the Church. It was left to the Council of Jerusalem, which took place around AD 50 and is recounted in Acts 15:1–29, to more completely resolve the matter. The Council of Jerusalem determined particulars such as whether Gentile converts had to comply with Jewish dietary laws and whether Gentile males had to be circumcised upon entering the faith. The final decision is detailed in Acts 15:28–29.

NOTE TAKING

Identifying Key Events. Create a two-column chart like the one below to help you organize the key events covered in this section. As you read the text, fill in the second column with further details about the event.

KEY EVENTS	DESCRIPTION OF EVENT
Outreach to Gentiles	
Council of Jerusalem	
Paul's conversion	
Paul's missionary journeys	

Baptism of St. Paul *at St. Paul Chapel in Bab Kissan, Damascus*

Paul's Conversion and Evangelization

As a Pharisee, Paul, then known as Saul, was a strict follower of the Mosaic Law, which he had been formally taught in Jerusalem. Saul was also a harsh persecutor of the earliest Christians. He had even consented to the death of St. Stephen, the first martyr for Christ (see Acts 7:54–60, 8:1–3).

Saul was on his way to Damascus to harass and arrest more Christians when the Risen Jesus appeared to him:

> On his journey, as he was nearing Damascus, a light from the sky suddenly flashed around him. He fell to the ground and heard a voice saying to him, "Saul, Saul, why are you persecuting me?" He said, "Who are you, sir?" The reply came, "I am Jesus, whom you are persecuting. Now get up and go into the city and you will be told what you must do." (Acts 9:3–6)

After Saul's conversion, he was baptized by Ananias (see Acts 9:10–19) and immediately began spreading the Gospel through his preaching and his example. This incident of conversion—in which Saul was called and sent forth on a mission—defines the very meaning of apostleship. St. Paul referred to himself often as an Apostle and later defended his apostleship in 1 Corinthians 9:1–2.

Since Saul had been a Pharisee before his conversion, he was very knowledgeable about the Hebrew Scriptures and their references to a **Messiah**. Saul had grown up in Tarsus (in what is now Turkey), so he was likewise a Roman citizen and was familiar with the Gentile world. These two factors—knowledge of the

Messiah From the Hebrew for "the Chosen One" or "the Anointed One"; the role that Jesus filled.

Mosaic Law and familiarity with Gentile practices—made Saul an ideal candidate to bridge the two worlds as he brought the Good News beyond Jerusalem. As he evangelized, Saul began using his Greco-Roman name, Paul, leaving behind his Hebrew name of Saul. St. Paul is also known as the "Apostle to the Gentiles."

Paul's Missionary Journeys

Paul was a tentmaker and may have been adept at traveling the widely developed Roman highway system to support himself in this occupation. Following his conversion, he undertook three missionary journeys, each of which is described in Acts of the Apostles, prior to his fourth—and final—journey, which ended in Rome. During Paul's first missionary journey, he visited such locations as Cyprus and Turkey. During the second, he visited Syria, Greece, and Jerusalem. During the third, he visited Turkey, Lebanon, and Jerusalem. Along the way, Paul steadfastly evangelized those who had not yet heard the Gospel and also reinvigorated the faith of those who had.

Paul's Letters in the New Testament

During Paul's missionary journeys (including his occasional periods of captivity) throughout the Mediterranean world, he wrote letters to many of the local Church communities in order to stay in touch with them and offer them encouragement and further Christian instruction. The issues that Paul addressed with these communities provide a glimpse into the earliest Christian communities, along with a realization that the Church in modern times faces many of the same questions and situations. Some of the central theological themes in the Pauline letters include the following:

- There is only one God, the Father of Jesus Christ.
- Salvation takes place through Jesus Christ.
- The Death and Resurrection of Christ are at the heart of the Gospel.
- Christ's Resurrection is for all people.
- Salvation is a gift from God. It cannot be earned. It requires faith.
- The Church is one Body, of which Christ is the head.
- Disciples become sons and daughters of the Father in union with Jesus and through the power of the Holy Spirit.
- The Holy Spirit enables believers to call God "Father."
- Everyone has dignity and should be loved and treated as a brother or sister in Christ.
- To be a disciple of Jesus requires a willingness to suffer for him.

St. Paul's letters have influenced Christian thinking about Jesus Christ more than any other theologian in history.

Paul's Final Years

In approximately AD 58, after Paul's three missionary trips throughout the Mediterranean region, he returned to Jerusalem, where he was arrested and remained in prison for two years. Since he was a Roman citizen, he had the legal right to appeal to the emperor in Rome for judgment. He was taken to Rome

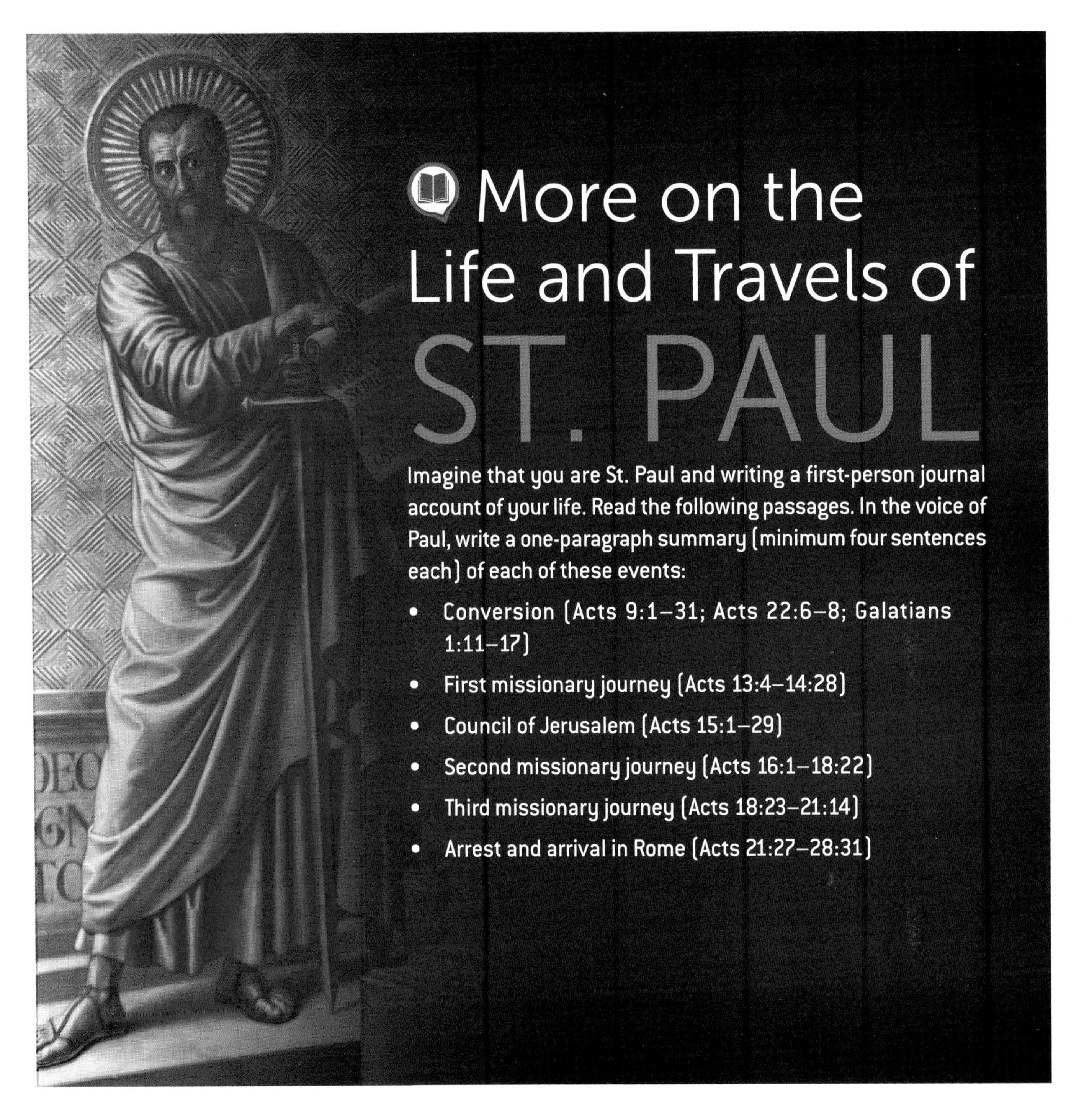

around 61, and remained imprisoned there for two more years. St. Paul was martyred in about 65, around the same time as St. Peter, during the emperor Nero's ruthless persecution of Christians in Rome.

Paul's missionary efforts led to the spread and growth of the Church throughout the Mediterranean, and those inspired by his preaching took his message as far as Spain. It is for good reason that Paul is referred to as the "Apostle to the Gentiles," because he bridged the gulf between the Jews and the Gentiles, showing that Jesus was the Messiah who came to offer salvation and redemption to all of humanity. St. Paul ushered in an era of courageous evangelization that allowed the Church to extend even farther over the course of the remainder of the first century and beyond.

SECTION ASSESSMENT

NOTE TAKING

Use the notes you made to help you answer the following questions.

1. What was the objective of the Council of Jerusalem?
2. List three facts about St. Paul.
3. What two factors made Paul an ideal candidate to evangelize the Gentiles?

COMPREHENSION

4. How does St. Paul fit the definition of an Apostle?
5. Why did Paul have the right to a trial in Rome?

CRITICAL THINKING

6. Which of Paul's theological themes do you have the most difficulty understanding? Name two questions you have about it.

Section Assignments

Focus Question

What is the Church's divine role within salvation history?

Complete one of the following:

→ Christ fulfilled many Old Testament prophecies of the Messiah. For example, Isaiah 7:14 ("Therefore the Lord himself will give you a sign; the young woman, pregnant and about to bear a son, shall name him Emmanuel") is fulfilled in Luke 1:30–31 ("Then the angel said to her, 'Do not be afraid, Mary, for you have found favor with God. Behold, you will conceive in your womb and bear a son, and you shall name him Jesus.'") Make a chart and list ten messianic prophecies from the Old Testament that Christ fulfilled in the New Testament. These can be discovered in the footnoted references on the pages of the Gospels in the *New American Bible Revised Edition* and other approved translations as well.

→ Read the account of the Apostle Thomas ("doubting Thomas") in John 20:24–29. Why do you think Thomas responded to Jesus with his proclamation in verse 28? How does this answer relate to the first verse of John's Gospel? What is the significance of verse 29 for Catholics today? What does this verse say about Christ's presence in the Church? Write a one-page reflective paper that responds to these questions.

→ In a one-page essay or a five-minute audio presentation, list specific actions that you can do within the next few years to help the Church further her mission

- to more effectively spread her message;
- to build up Christian community; and
- to serve the needy.

INTRODUCTION

Studying Church History

Read Christ's words to Simon Peter in Matthew 16:18. In a short paragraph, use your own words to describe what takes place, and what Christ promises about the Church.

SECTION 1

The Need for Faith

Tell several ways that groups you belong to—family, friendships, and parish—are shaped by Christ.

SECTION 2

Christ Instituted the Church

Name and give examples from the recent news in which the Church had to speak out because a situation was not compatible with the Gospel and total surrender to Jesus Christ.

SECTION 3

Pentecost and the Growth of the Church

Choose one of the original Twelve Apostles (recall that St. Matthias replaced Judas Iscariot). Research and report on traditional biographical information on the Apostle, including his date and place of death and information about his patronage.

SECTION 4

St. Paul: Apostle to the Gentiles

Read 1 Corinthians 9:19–27. How did these words of St. Paul translate to a style of evangelization? How would you utilize this style in your own life? Give at least one example.

Chapter Assignments

Choose and complete at least one of the three assignments to assess your understanding of the material in this chapter.

1. Tracing God's Revelation through Covenants

The Old Testament is marked by increasingly important covenants between God and humankind, leading to the New Covenant established by Jesus. Read about and write a summary of each of the following covenants. In your summary, tell what each of the covenants promised.

- Adam (Gn 1:26–30, 3:16–19)
- Noah (Gn 8:21–22)
- Abraham (Gn 12:1–3)
- Moses/Sinai (Ex 19–24, particularly 20:1–17)
- David (2 Sm 7:8–16)
- Jesus/New Covenant (Jer 31:31–34; Mt 5:17; Mk 14:24; Lk 22:20; Rom 7:6)

2. One Body, Many Parts in Christ

The image of a body is presented in 1 Corinthians 12:12–26 to explain Christ's relationship with believers in the Church. Slowly and carefully read this passage. Draw (e.g., using watercolors, chalk, colored pencils) a symbolic representation of the Church as a diversity of people having different gifts integrated into one organism with Christ as its head. (Other options: Write a poem or song lyrics that represent this passage. Record a reading or performance to turn in to your teacher.) You may wish to use images from the following passages for your artistic representation as well: Romans 12:4–5; 1 Corinthians 10:17; Ephesians 2:14-22; and Colossians 3:15.

3. Mapping the Pauline Letters

Review the following list of Pauline letters:

- Letter to the Romans
- First Letter to the Corinthians
- Second Letter to the Corinthians
- Letter to the Galatians
- Letter to the Ephesians
- Letter to the Philippians
- Letter to the Colossians

- First Letter to the Thessalonians
- Second Letter to the Thessalonians
- First Letter to Timothy
- Second Letter to Timothy
- Letter to Titus
- Letter to Philemon

Using a large, blank map of the Mediterranean region, indicate *where* each letter was written (or to which local Church community) and *when* it was written. In the margins of the map, write one paragraph about each letter, explaining the main topics that Paul covered within it.

Prayer

A Novena Prayer to St. Peter

O holy Apostle,
because you are the Rock
upon which Almighty God has built his Church;
obtain for me; I pray you,
lively faith, firm hope and burning love;
complete detachment from myself,
contempt of the world,
patience in adversity,
humility in prosperity,
recollection in prayer,
purity of heart,
a right intention in all my works,
diligence in fulfilling the duties of my state of life,
constancy in my resolutions,
resignation to the will of God,
and perseverance in the grace of God even unto death;
that so, by means of your intercession
and your glorious merits,
I may be worthy to appear
before the chief and eternal Shepherd of souls,
Jesus Christ,
who with the Father
and the Holy Spirit
lives and reigns forever.
Amen.
—Courtesy of Catholic Doors Ministry

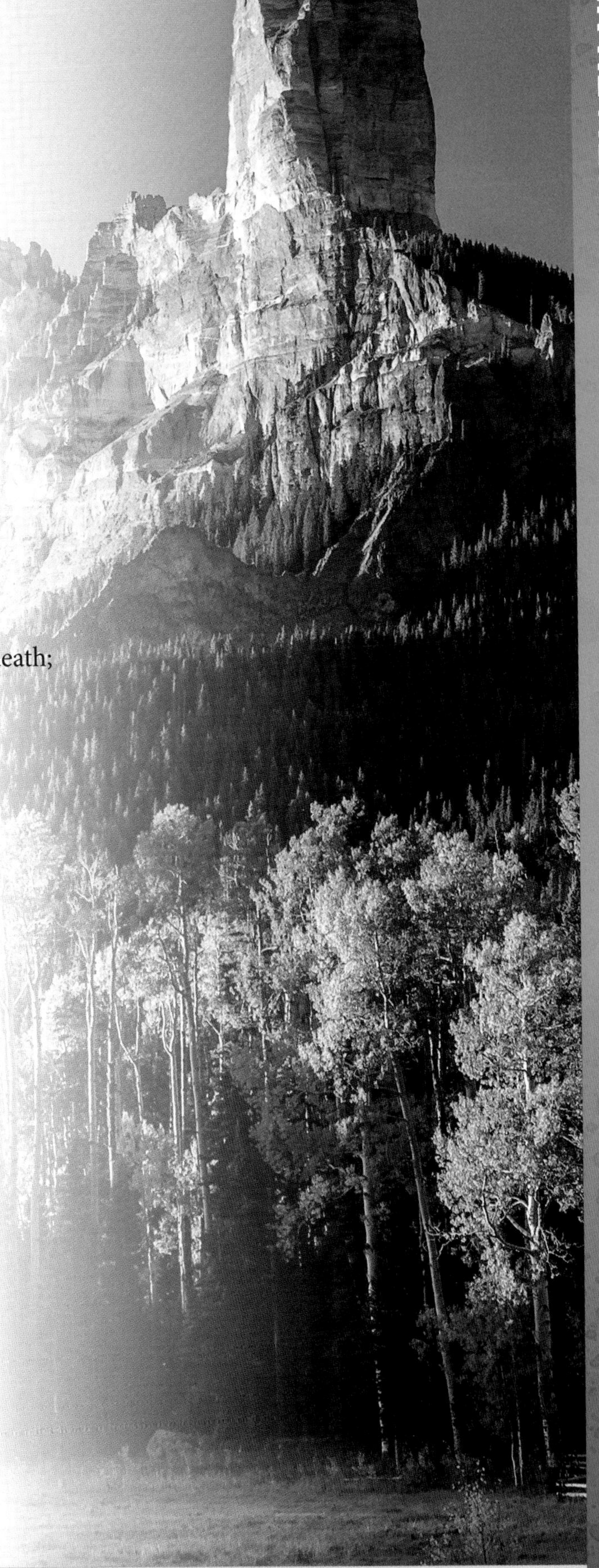

2

THE CHURCH GROWS IN THE MIDST OF PERSECUTION

Melkite archbishop Jean-Clement Jeanbart of Aleppo and Chaldean archbishop Bashar Warda of Erbil discussing the plight of Middle Eastern Christian refugees

ARCHBISHOP SPEAKS OUT against the Brutal Persecution of Christians in the Middle East

In April 2015, Archbishop Bashar Warda of Erbil, Iraq, which is one of the areas in the Middle East that has been the most brutalized by the terrorist network ISIS (the Islamic State of Iraq and Syria), spoke to the global community. Archbishop Warda spoke at an international conference in Madrid, Spain, titled "We Are All Nazarenes." *Nazarene* is a term that ISIS has used for Christians; it stems from the fact that Jesus was from Nazareth and was therefore a Nazarene. The archbishop spoke about how deadly and destructive ISIS had been to both Christians and other religious minorities in the region and also stated that a significant way to combat ISIS's onslaught was through greater education within the regional and global communities.

Archbishop Warda went on to explain that the mindset of ISIS was nothing particularly new within the region; rather, it reflected the chaos that had already been so widespread in areas around the border of Syria and Iraq. As a possible path to a solution, he suggested building schools that would be open to children of all faiths. In fact, in 2004, after his own parish had been bombed and many of his parishioners called for the construction of a barrier wall to protect their church, Bishop Warda responded by building a school instead. Students of all different faiths now attend the school.

Archbishop Warda, Pope Francis, and many other Church leaders have called on the global community to pray for an end to the strife that Christians face in the Middle East. The future of Christianity in the Middle East remains uncertain, but it is evident that education, as Bishop Warda has emphasized, will continue to serve as a means of informing the population about how to contribute to a world in which there is more respect and dialogue.

FOCUS QUESTION

How did the early Church continue to **GROW AND EXPAND**, even in the midst of harsh persecutions?

Chapter Overview

INTRODUCTION

The Church under Roman Rule

MAIN IDEA

The Church faced a challenging beginning, beset by both physical threats and threats against her core beliefs.

In the first three centuries of the Church, the vast majority of Christians lived under a Roman government that had deemed Christianity illegal. During this period, even when faced with harsh treatment by Roman society, the Church continued to grow and develop. In the increasingly unified Church, courageous Christian heroes inspired their fellow Christians by remaining steadfast through persecution, and many became **martyrs** for the Faith.

By the fourth century—when Christianity had become widespread and had a considerable presence in the Roman Empire—Christianity was finally not only tolerated but legalized. The greater openness to Christianity allowed the Church to further develop both her hierarchical structure and her liturgical practice. Christian **apologists** helped to defend and explain Christianity to nonbelievers.

martyrs The word *martyr* literally means "witness" in Greek. Martyrs are witnesses to the truth of faith who endure even death to be faithful to Christ.

apologists Christian writers who defend the Church against anti-Christian writings or heresies through the use of reason and intellectual defenses. An apologist "speaks in one's defense."

NOTE TAKING

Gauging Understanding. Make a table like the one below. Before you read the glossary definitions in the Introduction, write your own definition of the terms below.

TERMS	MY DEFINITION	GLOSSARY DEFINITION
Martyrs		
Apologists		

SECTION ASSESSMENT

NOTE TAKING

Go back and complete the chart by adding the glossary definitions of *martyrs* and *apologists*. Answer the following questions.

1. Who can you describe as a Christian hero? Your example can be someone from the past or from today.
2. How does the root of the term *apologist* help you to understand its meaning?

SECTION 1

Christianity Is Made Illegal in the Roman Empire

MAIN IDEA

The Church grew in the first and second centuries even though Christians living under Roman rule suffered intense and brutal persecution.

The Council of Jerusalem (AD 50) determined that Gentiles could be accepted into the Church, thereby reflecting the mission and ministry of St. Paul. After the council, the early Christians distinguished themselves from those Jews who did not view Jesus as the Messiah and Lord by their religious practices and by their outreach to Gentiles.

Judaism was permitted in the Roman Empire (consider that Paul was a Roman citizen), but once Christianity started to gain more followers among the Gentiles, the Roman government declared Christianity to be illegal. After all, most Romans were Gentiles, and the Roman leaders felt that they had to maintain control over them. This was a flawed rationale, but one that persisted.

Some historical events exacerbated the persecution of Christians by the Romans. In AD 64, a fire swept through Rome, destroying much of the city. The emperor Nero was quick to blame the fire on Christians, and the local Christian population in the city of Rome was so small at the time and lacking in power or influence that it was unable to effectively defend itself against these accusations. (The historian Tacitus, five decades later, reported that Nero started the fire

NOTE TAKING

Naming Key Concepts. As you read this text section, create a graphic organizer like the one on the right to keep a numbered list of reasons Christians were persecuted under Roman rule in the first three centuries AD. Add as many reasons (and rectangles) as needed and as much detail as necessary for each reason.

1. Christians were now viewed as apart from Judaism.	2.
3.	4.

himself.) Thus, an intense persecution of Christians began in 64 and lasted until 67. It was during this persecution that Paul and Peter met their martyrdom. According to tradition, Peter was crucified upside down on a cross, and Paul was beheaded.

In the years that followed, Christianity was increasingly viewed by the Romans as subversive and unwilling to adjust to Roman standards of conduct and make sacrifices to the emperor. Christians were accused of having "secret" meetings in which they would undertake sacrifices. Of course, these secret meetings were actually the celebration of the Lord's Supper, or Sacrament of Holy Eucharist, in keeping with Christ's command to "do this in memory of me" (Lk 22:19).

Also, Christians supported family life and spoke out against societal instability that harmed the unity of families. Christians were vocal against various immoral practices—such as prostitution, fornication, adultery, and homosexual acts—that were incompatible with the Christian faith. Christians also supported marginalized groups, including the poor, orphans, abandoned children, the homeless, and others who would not necessarily have support within the Roman Empire, especially from the wealthier members of the upper class.

Another factor that contributed to the spurning of Christians by Roman (and Greek) intellectuals was that they were considered unsophisticated. Roman culture had a rich heritage of classical writings, whereas the writings of the Christians, particularly the New Testament, were still in formulation and not considered as highly polished. Christians were also seen as irrational, because they professed belief in transcendent events such as the Incarnation, the Resurrection, and the Ascension, not to mention Jesus' other miracles, all of which are key tenets of the Christian faith. Effectively, the **pagan** Roman society was unwilling to entertain beliefs that were deemed unnatural and not aligned with reason. Similarly, Jesus' teachings, such as "love your enemies" (Mt 5:44), "you shall love your neighbor as yourself" (Mk 12:31), and "do to others as you would have them do to you" (Lk 6:31), were entirely foreign to the mindset of Romans, who lived in a society marked by selfishness, brutality, and vengeance. Christianity had a very challenging couple of centuries ahead.

Root of Conflicts between Christians and Rome

At a very basic level, the monotheism of Christians put them at odds with the polytheism of pagan Rome. In addition to the other gods in Rome's polytheistic belief system, Roman citizens were expected to worship the emperor. Christians spoke out against the worship of the emperor, not to mention the Romans' pagan belief in multiple gods. The refusal on the part of a Christian to worship the Roman emperor, typically in the form of burning incense to him, making a certain official proclamation, and so forth, often meant societal exclusion at best and a death sentence at worst. There were many martyrs during this era, but some Christians—known as *lapsi*—did renounce their faith.

Idol worship was also expected of Roman citizens. Idols took the form of statues large and small. Merchants sold idols, incense, and other materials used to worship the Roman gods (including the emperor). Christians refused to engage in idol worship since it violated the First Commandment: "You shall not have other gods beside me" (Ex 20:3).

The Roman authorities believed that Christians, through their refusal to worship the emperor and idols,

pagan In earlier times, a pagan exclusively referred to a person who was polytheistic. Today a broader definition refers to a person holding religious beliefs other than those of one of the major world religions or being polytheistic.

Temple service of the Vestals (priestesses of Vesta, goddess of the hearth) in ancient Rome. Early Christians were punished for their refusal to worship her and other Roman gods.

along with other practices they objected to, were not only disrespecting the Roman state but also resisting the rule of Roman law. During the second century, as the internal structure of the empire weakened, Roman persecution of Christians increased in intensity. The Roman government continued to imprison, exile, or execute Christians who dissented from Rome's positions. Yet Christianity expanded, reaching into the millions of adherents by the third century. Christianity grew at least in part because it

- offered hope to those who had lost faith in the material and military excesses of the Roman Empire;
- provided believers with the opportunity to have a personal relationship with God (whereas the false Roman **deities** did not have any promise for eternal life or salvation); and
- emphasized the human dignity of all people, including both men and women, young children, the rich and the poor, the homeless, and slaves.

deities Higher beings or gods based on the belief system of a particular religion.

Christianity spread to various segments of Roman society. Although it remained a religion primarily of those who lived in poverty, those of other social classes soon became Christian as well. The extensive Roman Empire permitted the Faith to spread to the far reaches of its boundaries, and it was possible for Christians in these faraway areas to practice their faith somewhat more openly. Nevertheless, Christianity remained officially illegal.

SECTION ASSESSMENT

NOTE TAKING

Use the notes from your chart to help you respond to these items.

1. Why was the Roman Empire suspicious of Christians?
2. In what ways were the lifestyles of some Romans unacceptable to Christians?

COMPREHENSION

3. What led to Christians being seen as a distinct group from the Jews?
4. Why did the Roman pagans consider Christians unsophisticated?

CRITICAL THINKING

5. Imagine you are hearing Jesus' teachings listed in the opening of this section for the first time. Which of these teachings would you find most radical and most difficult to keep? Explain why.
6. Why do you think Christianity appealed to Roman pagans even while the government tried to rid the empire of the practice of Christianity?
7. What are some similarities and differences between the lives of Christians in the Roman Empire and the lives of Christians in the twenty-first century? Before responding, briefly research the situation of Christians around the globe.

SECTION 2

Persecutions Lead to Martyrdom

MAIN IDEA

The Roman Empire did not persecute Christians continuously; rather, there were particular periods of brutal torment of Christians, during which many Christians were martyred.

It is important to note that although the persecution of Christians within the Roman Empire spanned the mid-first century to the early fourth century, it was not constant. Christianity was formally illegal during this period—beginning with the oppression of Christianity under the emperor Nero and ending with the legalization of Christianity (along with other faiths) in 313—but there were some periods during which the law against practicing Christianity was either not enforced or ignored. Here are the approximate years when certain persecutions began:

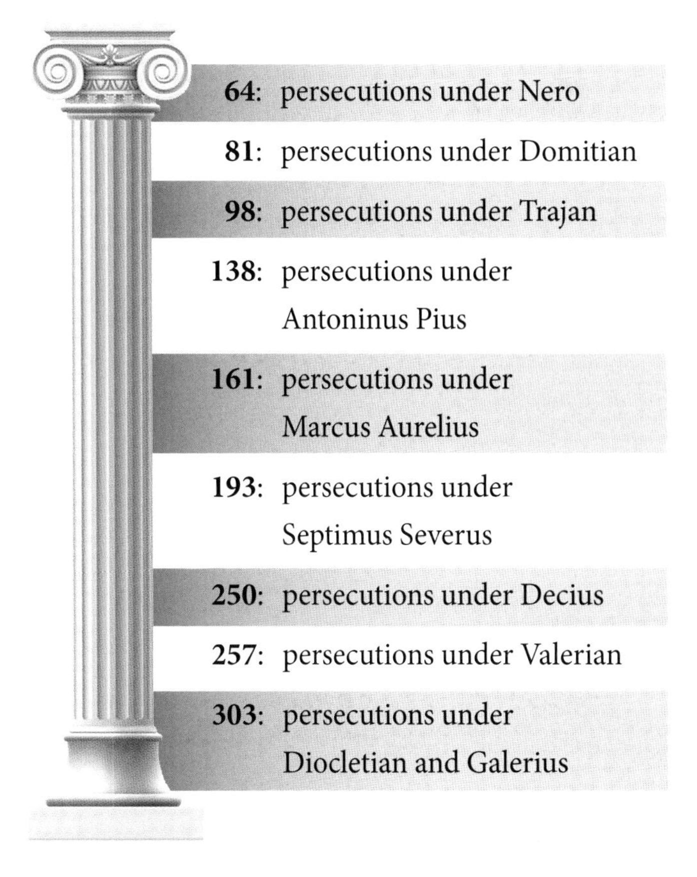

64: persecutions under Nero

81: persecutions under Domitian

98: persecutions under Trajan

138: persecutions under Antoninus Pius

161: persecutions under Marcus Aurelius

193: persecutions under Septimus Severus

250: persecutions under Decius

257: persecutions under Valerian

303: persecutions under Diocletian and Galerius

The Roman Empire during this time stretched over territories throughout Europe, North Africa, and the

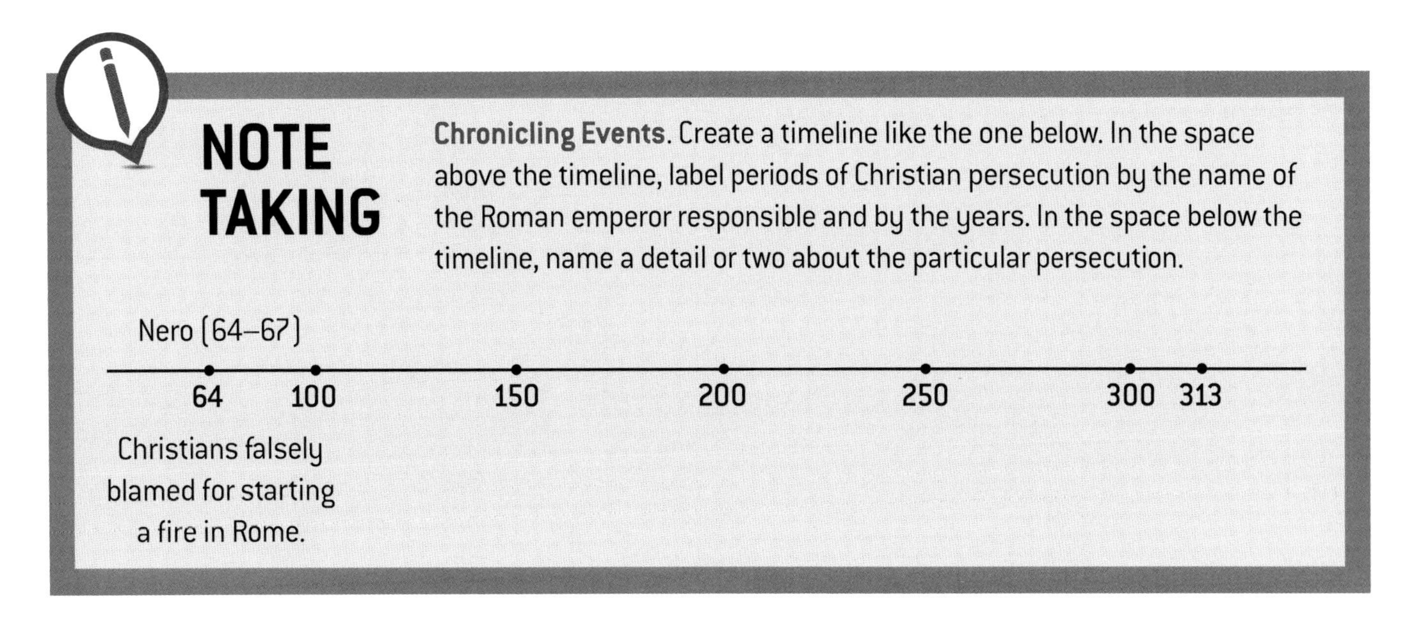

NOTE TAKING

Chronicling Events. Create a timeline like the one below. In the space above the timeline, label periods of Christian persecution by the name of the Roman emperor responsible and by the years. In the space below the timeline, name a detail or two about the particular persecution.

The Roman emperor Trajan at a public audience. Under Trajan, Christians were not sought out for persecution but were still punished if convicted of practicing their faith.

Middle East—almost two million square miles. Its population was between fifty-five and seventy million people, about one-fourth of the total world population. Christians were less likely to be harassed by the Roman authorities in the outlying areas of the empire away from the capital city of Rome. However, harsh treatment of Christians occurred more frequently in the highly populous areas, and it is a wonder that the Church was able to survive these periods of persecution. Survival was due to the witness of Christian men and women who held fast to their faith.

Tracing Major Periods of Persecution

Following the fire in Rome that Nero held Christians responsible for, the emperor Domitian began the first widespread persecution of Christians throughout the Roman Empire. His persecutions lasted from AD 81 to 96. Domitian's main charge against Christians was that they failed to address him as "master and god." The Book of Revelation was written during this period. It features messages to seven churches in the empire, written in coded language so that the author, who calls himself John, could criticize the emperor without risking further persecution. The Apostolic Father Pope Clement I also wrote of persecutions in the 90s.

In AD 98, the persecutions under the emperor Trajan began. In the midst of these persecutions, Pliny—a Roman governor—sent a letter to Trajan inquiring about how to treat Christians. Trajan responded by stating that Christians should not be driven out of their hiding places, but if they were reported and later convicted, they had to be punished in some way. Trajan also allowed for the opportunity for Christians to denounce their faith and be spared:

> These people are not to be sought for; but with this caution, that he who denies himself to be a Christian, and makes it plain that he is not so

by supplicating to our gods, although he had been so formerly, may be allowed pardon, upon his repentance. ("Trajan's Epistle to Pliny")

The emperor Decius (249–251) sponsored persecutions that began in 250. Under Decius, every Roman citizen had to worship the Roman gods in a public display. Those who did so received a paper certificate of sacrifice as evidence of their loyalty to Rome. Anyone who was discovered without this certificate could be tortured and/or killed (martyred) if he or she persisted in refusing to honor the false Roman deities. Later, when Christianity was legalized and the danger of persecutions was over, the Church had to decide how to welcome back, if at all, the *lapsi* ("lapsed" Christians who abandoned their faith in order to save their lives).

The last persecutions of Christians under the Roman Empire were ordered by Diocletian (284–305) and covered a ten-year period from 303 through the issuance of the Edict of Milan under the emperor Constantine in 313. Though rather brief, this period of persecutions was ferocious. Diocletian attempted to confiscate the property of Christians, destroy their churches and sacred books, banish them to hard labor, subject them to a host of tortures, and inflict the death penalty. After Diocletian's death in 305, Galerius continued his persecutions of Christians until 311. As with the other persecutions, the degree of enforcement varied from region to region.

There were some periods of peace in between these persecutions. For example, the years between 211 and the beginning of the persecutions under Decius in 250 were relatively peaceful. The same is true of the period between 260 and the beginning of Diocletian's persecutions in 303.

fortitude The courage that Christians are called to embrace and rely on in order to evangelize and live their faith openly; also, one of the four cardinal virtues (along with temperance, justice, and prudence).

Despite the verbal and physical hostility periodically aimed at Christians, not only were Christian converts religious, but in many places they were quite open about their Christian identity. These Christians wanted to conquer the prejudice and misinformation that abounded and make it clear through the witness of their lives that they could be good citizens. One example of this occurred in Asia Minor in the second century. When a governor began to persecute Christians from the poor and lower classes, all of the Christians of the region—including those in positions of power—paraded in front of his home. They wanted to make it clear that the Christian faith was not limited to a small group of social outcasts and that they were peaceful citizens.

Perception of Martyrs by Romans and Fellow Christians

The early Christians had a difficult balance to maintain: their faith compelled them to proclaim the Good News of Christ. However, they had to live with the constant knowledge that they could be martyred for proclaiming Christ publicly. This was seen as the ultimate price that Christians could pay for their fidelity to the Lord Jesus Christ. It was a time of courageous Christian witness but also great turmoil.

As the decades passed after the first persecutions in the Roman Empire under Nero, Christians did not go away. Romans were perplexed by the martyrs—men, women, and even children who felt so strongly about what they believed that they were willing to be subjected to awful tortures and grotesque executions rather than renounce their beliefs. The witness of these early Christians cannot be underestimated. Later Christians were inspired by the example of these martyrs, and they gained great **fortitude** from their example. The martyrs serve as witnesses to love, fidelity, and commitment to Jesus Christ, whose love for

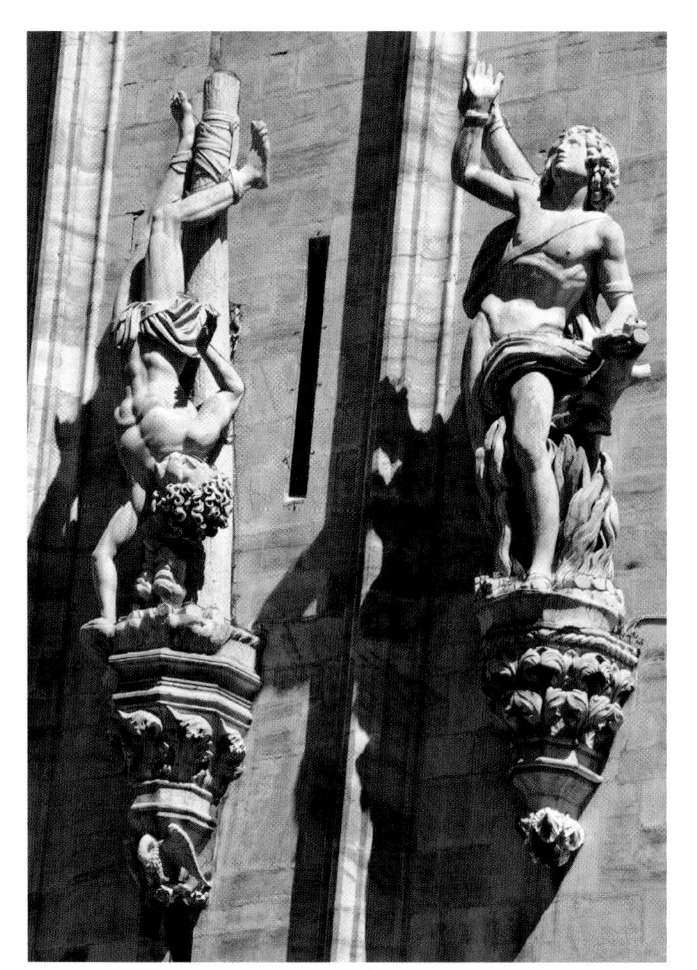

Two martyrs are depicted here on the facade of the Milan Cathedral, one being hanged upside down and the other being burned at the stake.

people extends even beyond death. Church Father Tertullian wrote that the "blood of martyrs is the seed of the Church" (*Apologeticus*, 50).

By the end of the third century, Christians were not being threatened as much as they had been before. But then a controversy erupted involving the military. Church leaders began to teach that Christians should not be part of the military. In approximately AD 295 a number of Christians were killed for refusing to join or attempting to leave the Roman army. The emperor Diocletian became convinced that the Christians were a threat to the army, and he ordered that all Christians should be expelled from the Roman legions. Rather than see their ranks dwindle, many officers tried to force Christian soldiers to abandon their faith. Those Christians who refused were executed.

Through all eras of persecution in the early Church, the martyrs gained a place of prominence among Christians because accounts of their heroism circulated quickly and enthusiastically. (Note the example of Sts. Perpetua and Felicity on the next page.) One way local churches recognized martyrs was by having a priest say Mass over their burial places if the location was known.

Many altars in Catholic churches throughout the world today still contain **relics** of martyrs from this time period. Martyrs also continue to be honored and celebrated in the Church's **liturgical year**. On a martyr's **feast day**, the entire Catholic Church commemorates the supreme sacrifice that these courageous figures made in order to further the Good News of Jesus Christ.

relic The physical remains or personal effects of a saint that are approved by the Church for veneration.

liturgical year Cycle of the liturgical seasons of Advent, Christmas Ordinary Time, Lent, Triduum, and Easter, organized around the major events of Jesus' life.

feast day The day on the liturgical calendar commemorating a saint's entry into heaven, typically celebrated on or close to the day when a saint died.

The Witness of
STS. PERPETUA and FELICITY

Two prominent martyrs from the days of the Roman Empire are Sts. Perpetua and Felicity, who lived during the third century. Perpetua was a young married woman from North Africa who had a slave named Felicity. The two women were arrested together while in the process of extensively preparing for Baptism. The two were placed under house arrest and were able to receive their Baptism before being transferred to a prison in Carthage.

Perpetua, who was a young mother of an infant son, kept a diary. She indicated that her father, who was not a Christian, encouraged her to burn incense to statues representing the Roman gods, which would have violated Perpetua's belief in Jesus Christ. She refused. While in prison, Perpetua's slave and fellow Christian Felicity gave birth to a baby girl. Days later, before her execution, she gave her daughter to a Christian woman to raise.

Perpetua and Felicity, as Christians who refused to renounce their faith, were thrown to the wild beasts in the arena in front of the emperor. The wild animals attacked them, but they survived. They were finally killed by gladiators—Perpetua actually guided the sword of a nervous gladiator to her throat. Her last words were to her brother and other witnesses: "Stand fast in the faith, and love one another. Do not let our sufferings be a stumbling block to you." They met their martyrdom in an embrace in the arena as they exchanged the sign of peace.

ASSIGNMENT

Along with Sts. Perpetua and Felicity, there are many other saints who were martyred by the Roman Empire. Briefly research one of the martyrs listed below. Write a three-paragraph biography, emphasizing his or her heroic virtue in the face of brutal persecution.

- St. Lawrence
- St. Agnes
- St. Agatha

SECTION ASSESSMENT

NOTE TAKING

Use the timeline of persecutions you created to help you answer the following questions.

1. What was Domitian's main charge against Christians?
2. Summarize Trajan's strategy for dealing with Christians.
3. What was the purpose of the certificate of sacrifice Decius provided to Roman citizens?
4. What were elements of Diocletian's particularly harsh persecutions?

COMPREHENSION

5. In what locations in the Roman Empire did most persecutions occur?
6. How did Sts. Perpetua and Felicity embrace the call to martyrdom?

VOCABULARY

7. How did Christian martyrs exhibit *fortitude*?
8. How is a martyr honored in the Church's *liturgical year* on a particular *feast day*?

CRITICAL THINKING

9. Describe how you would feel if you were a Christian living during a time of relative peace between eras of official persecution of Christians in the first three centuries AD.

SECTION 3

The Church Grows in the First Three Centuries

MAIN IDEA
Despite early persecution, the Church increased her membership and defined her teachings. Several aspects of contemporary life in the Roman Empire supported the Church's growth amid continued persecutions, and faithful apologists and others clarified Church teachings.

St. Luke concludes the Acts of the Apostles with Paul in Rome. This was the author's way of saying that the new religion had moved way beyond its Jewish roots in Jerusalem and into the political and cultural heart of the Roman Empire. Along the way, Christian churches sprang up throughout the empire as Christians transitioned their celebration of the Mass and sacraments from homes to more stately settings that allowed for more of a sense of God's transcendence. In spite of persecutions, the Church's enemies could not stamp out this new faith. Christianity grew steadily in numbers and influence. The following were central reasons for this astounding growth:

- *Jewish communities established in the Diaspora.* The *Diaspora* is the name for the dispersion of Jews outside of Jerusalem. When Jewish Christians such as Paul set out to preach the Gospel, they were able to use the synagogues as a home base. When Jews rejected the Gospel, the missionaries turned to local Gentiles who were more receptive.
- *Ease of communication and travel.* People in the empire spoke a common language—Greek at first, then Latin. There was a good system of roads and shipping. There was a common culture. These

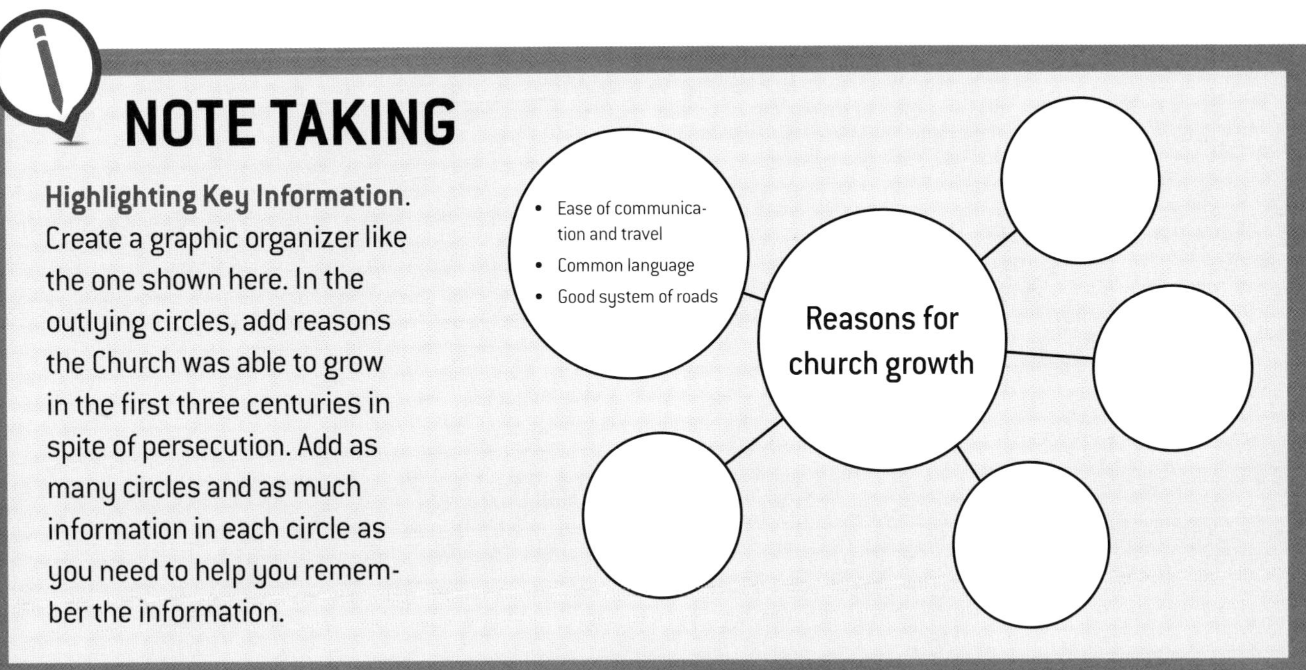

NOTE TAKING

Highlighting Key Information. Create a graphic organizer like the one shown here. In the outlying circles, add reasons the Church was able to grow in the first three centuries in spite of persecution. Add as many circles and as much information in each circle as you need to help you remember the information.

factors helped the missionaries preach everywhere and eased their travels around the empire.

- *Pax Romana.* The *Pax Romana* or "Roman peace" was a prosperous time of relative peace beginning twenty-five years after Jesus' birth. This stability—in which the empire was not under attack by outside enemies—lasted for two centuries during the time of the first Christian missionaries.
- *Words of love supported by action.* People of the day were searching for spiritual meaning. The new mystery religions and the philosophy of Stoicism helped some people, but they could not rival the appeal of Christianity, with its call to repentance and its inspiring moral code. Searching people experienced truth in the doctrines of a loving God, forgiveness, and Christian care for one another. And Christians backed up their words with actions. Christian love proved to be an irresistible magnet to people who were seeking more to life than Roman games and meaningless idol worship. Their care for the poor and orphans, plus their willingness to die for Jesus, greatly appealed to pagans. "See how they love one another" was the response of Roman citizens to the behavior of Christians, according to Church Father Tertullian.
- *Apostolic Fathers of the Church (those men who personally knew the Apostles) helped preserve and pass on the Faith.* Prior to the decriminalization of Christianity within the Roman Empire, it was quite a challenge for **catechumens** to learn about the Faith and be initiated into the Church. They had to do so in secret, out of fear of being discovered by Roman authorities. A catechetical document called the *Didache* ("Teaching") helped in this effort. It was written perhaps as early as AD 60 but more likely around 100. The author is unknown. The *Didache* mentions the Trinititarian formula, lists moral teachings, and explains the rites of Baptism and Eucharist.

catechumens People who are undergoing a period of study and spiritual preparation before receiving the Sacrament of Baptism.

Apologists and Church Fathers Refine and Defend Doctrine

The Church's first apologists, the second-century writers who defended and explained Christianity to nonbelievers, wrote primarily to convince Gentiles—especially the emperors, Roman officials, and Roman citizens in general—of the truth and high morals of Christians. The *First Apology* was written by the most famous Christian apologist of the second century, St. Justin Martyr (ca. 110–165). He was a convert from paganism, a philosopher, and a prolific writer. Only a few of his writings were preserved. St. Justin addressed his *First Apology* to Emperor Antoninus Pius (131–161), who, though persecutions were part of his reign, was among the most peaceful Roman emperors. He wrote:

> We who formerly delighted in fornication now cleave only to chastity. We who exercised the magic arts now consecrate ourselves to the good and unbegotten God. We who valued above all else the acquisition of wealth and property now direct all that we have to a common fund, which is shared with every needy person. We who hated and killed one another, and who, because of differing customs, would not share a fireside with those of another race, now, after the appearance of Christ, live together with them. We pray for our enemies, and try to persuade those who unjustly hate us that, if they live according to the excellent precepts of Christ, they will have a good hope

of receiving the same reward as ourselves, from the God who governs all. (*First Apology*, 14)

Church Fathers were theologians of the first eight centuries. The Church Fathers helped to write and form Church doctrine that has remained authoritative through the ages. Some of the early Church Fathers of the first three centuries—including St. Irenaeus of Lyons (ca. 130–202) and St. Clement of Alexandria (ca. 150–215)—argued against **heresies** and helped to define several Church teachings. Chapter 3 has more information about the Church Fathers.

The early Church was still in the process of articulating its central teachings in a way that was faithful to the gift of God's love in Christ and to the celebration of that gift in liturgical worship—all this while being cruelly persecuted. The need to give an account of what they believed and practiced to others outside the Church prompted early Christians to reflect more deeply on what God the Father did in Jesus Christ, which was made present and celebrated by liturgy. Early Christians took comfort in Jesus' own words:

> If the world hates you, realize that it hated me first. If you belonged to the world, the world would love its own; but because you do not belong to the world, and I have chosen you out of the world, the world hates you. Remember the word I spoke to you, "No slave is greater than his master." If they persecuted me, they will also persecute you. If they kept my word, they will also keep yours. (Jn 15:18–20)

This was a period of Church history when, under the inspiration of the Holy Spirit, God's Revelation was brought together in the Sacred Scriptures as an authoritative witness to the Faith. The Sacred Scriptures and other writings emerged from an oral tradition and served as catechetical manuals, witness statements, and liturgical guides.

St. Clement of Alexandria

Church Fathers Those men from the first through eighth centuries AD who were given this title based on their monumental contributions to the Church, especially their extensive teaching and writing about the Faith in order to help it grow and develop.

heresies Incorrect and otherwise errant understandings or teachings about certain doctrinal matters or dogmas; they are opposed to right teaching (orthodoxy).

PROFILING EARLY SAINTS

There were many saints who promoted and defended Christianity in the first three centuries. Some of these were Church Fathers and apologists for the Faith. The saints profiled here are among the most prominent.

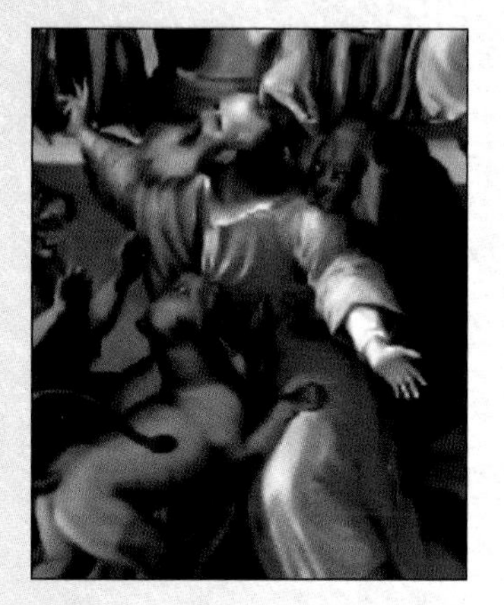

St. Ignatius of Antioch (CA. 35-107)

St. Ignatius of Antioch (in what is now Turkey) was a bishop who was eventually condemned to death based on his unrelenting promotion and defense of the Good News. He was a follower of the Apostle John. One tradition holds that John converted him. Under the reign of the emperor Trajan, Antioch's magistrates condemned Ignatius to death. While on the way to Rome for execution, Ignatius continued to preach the Faith. Along the way, he wrote seven letters to the churches he ministered to, reminding the faithful to be loyal to their bishops. He saw bishops as the symbols of unity in the Church. The earliest surviving reference to the Church as the "Catholic Church" is found in Ignatius's *Epistle to the Smyrnaeans*. Ignatius made it to Rome, where he was devoured by lions in the Flavian Amphitheater. His friends took his bones back to Antioch; today they rest in Rome.

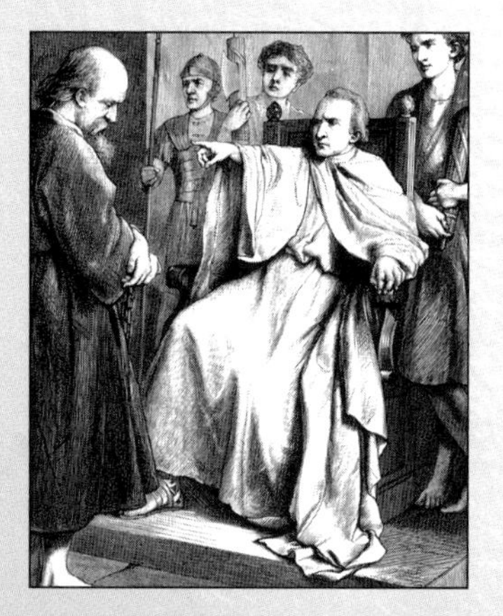

St. Polycarp of Smyrna (CA. 69-156)

St. Polycarp of Smyrna was the bishop of Smyrna, in what is now Turkey. He was a staunch defender against heresies that had sprung up in Asia Minor. His *Letter to the Philippians* survives today. In it, he quotes the Gospels of Matthew and Luke and other texts that would come to form the New Testament. These texts had a wide distribution early in the Church's history. In 155, Bishop Polycarp was arrested and told to renounce his "atheistic" behavior of refusing to worship the emperor and other Roman gods. Three times he was asked to renounce his belief in Jesus Christ, but the aged man replied, "Eighty-six years have I served him and he has done me no wrong. How can I blaspheme the King who saved me?" Eyewitness accounts of Polycarp's martyrdom report that he was set on fire, but his body was not consumed. They also describe his body in the fire "not like a human being in flames, but like a loaf baking in the oven," connecting his death to the Eucharist.

St. Justin Martyr (CA. 100-165)

St. Justin Martyr was born into a pagan family, and during his youth, he was formally educated based on the teachings of ancient Greek philosophers such as Socrates, Plato, and Aristotle. Justin's famous *Apology* (the title must be understood as it relates to the term *apologist*) was intended to show the Roman authorities that the Christian moral life is reinforced on the philosophical grounds of basic ethics and should therefore not be treated with contempt let alone persecution. He argued that Christianity is the truest and most intellectually satisfying philosophy because it is based on God's Revelation. Justin, who taught Christianity as the "true philosophy" in Rome after his conversion, caused so much turmoil that he was eventually sentenced to die along with some of his students.

St. Irenaeus of Lyons (CA. 130-200)

St. Irenaeus was the bishop of what is now the city of Lyons, France. Irenaeus was from the Eastern part of the Roman Empire, a Christian from childhood, and a follower of St. Polycarp. Irenaeus's most famous work is *Against Heresies*, in which he described and condemned various heresies, especially Gnosticism, which denied Jesus' divinity. Just as Ignatius of Antioch had done, Irenaeus supported the unity of bishops in terms of their role in defending orthodox teaching within the Church. He wrote, "Indeed, the tradition of the Apostles is clear to the whole world; it is possible to observe in every church, for those who wish to see the truth. We are prepared to enumerate those who were set up as bishops over the Church by the Apostles and their successors down to ourselves" (*Against Heresies*, III, 3). There is high probability he died of natural causes, not martyrdom.

St. Cyprian of Carthage (CA. 210-258)

St. Cyprian was the bishop of Carthage, in what is now Tunisia in northern Africa. After converting to Christianity, he soon distinguished himself as an influential writer by addressing various controversies within the Church. One such controversy involved how to treat Christians who had denied their faith in order to avoid persecution, the so-called *lapsi*. Cyprian eventually adopted a middle position between those who did not want any penalties at all for *lapsi* and those who wanted strict penalties (e.g., opposing readmission into the Church community for those who had denied their faith). Cyprian was the first bishop of Carthage to receive the crown of martyrdom.

How Can You SHARE THE FAITH?

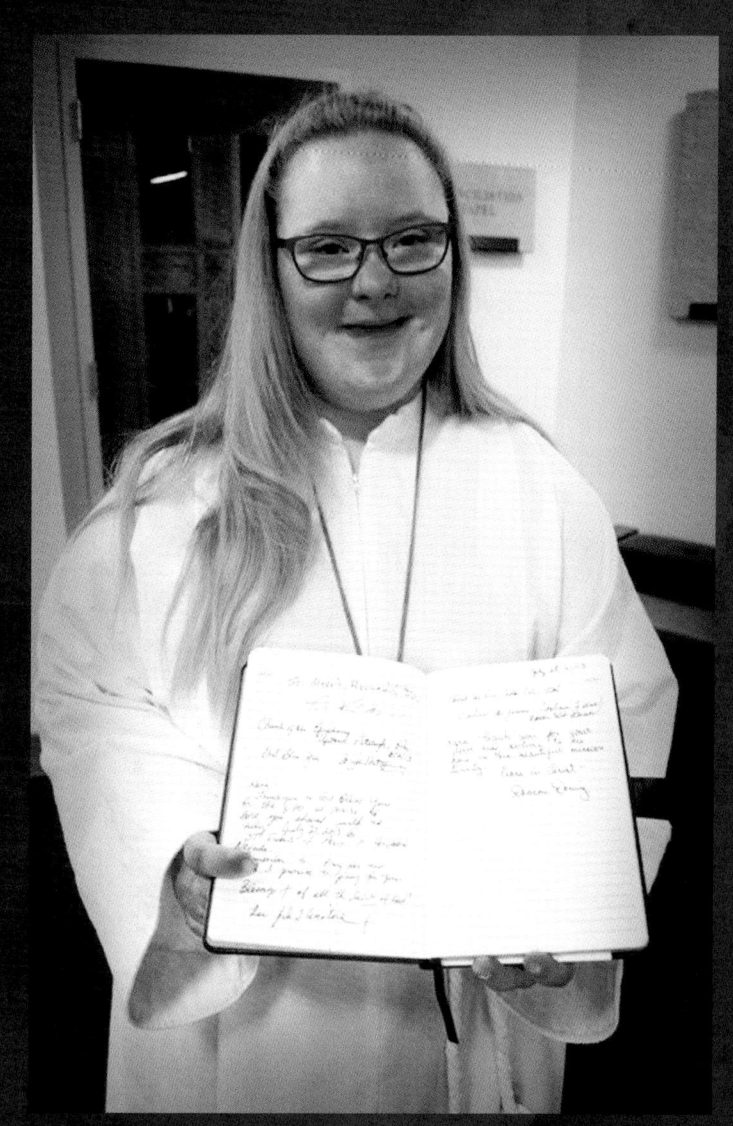

Kara Jackson's notebook is filled with messages from priests and documents her journey.

In 2013, eighteen-year-old Kara Jackson from Middleton, Ohio, began a quest to be an altar server at Mass in all fifty states. In 2015, Kara reached her goal after serving Mass in both Alaska and Hawaii.

Kara, who was born with Down syndrome, told her mom that God came to her in a dream one night and told her to begin her project of serving Mass in all fifty states. At first Kara's mom thought it was a crazy idea. But as finances allowed, the family followed her desire anyway. They would say a prayer and write a letter ahead to a parish in a new state and plan family trips around those occasions. Kara kept a notebook detailing her experiences at different parishes.

Kara began serving Mass at nine years old. She watched Mass on television each day to learn how to ring the bells. Why this goal? Kara's mom explained: "She tells me all I want to be is a saint."

ASSIGNMENT

Kara's goal to serve Mass in all fifty states was bold, unusual, dramatic, faith-filled, and committed. Brainstorm and list five similarly bold, unusual, dramatic, faith-filled, and committed things you could do to share your faith with others. Then choose one of your five ideas and write a three-paragraph explanation of how you could practically fulfill this goal.

SECTION ASSESSMENT

NOTE TAKING

Use the graphic organizer you created to help you answer the following questions.

1. What advantage did the Jewish synagogues in the Diaspora provide for Christian missionaries?
2. What were the common languages spoken in the Roman Empire?
3. How did the *Pax Romana* help Christianity to spread?
4. What did Tertullian name as a key example of Christian witness?

COMPREHENSION

5. Who was the first apologist to use the term *Catholic Church*?
6. How was St. Polycarp's death associated with the Eucharist?
7. What approach did St. Cyprian take toward *lapsi*?
8. What role did apologists play in spreading Christianity?

VOCABULARY

9. Why was it challenging to be a Christian *catechumen* in the first three centuries?

APPLICATION

10. Describe the most difficult situation you can imagine for your life today in which you would have to publicly choose between proclaiming Jesus Christ and renouncing your faith in him.

SECTION 4

The Development of Sacraments and Sacred Leadership

MAIN IDEA

Even while Christianity was still illegal, the Church developed liturgical practices around the Seven Sacraments and established her hierarchy of leadership.

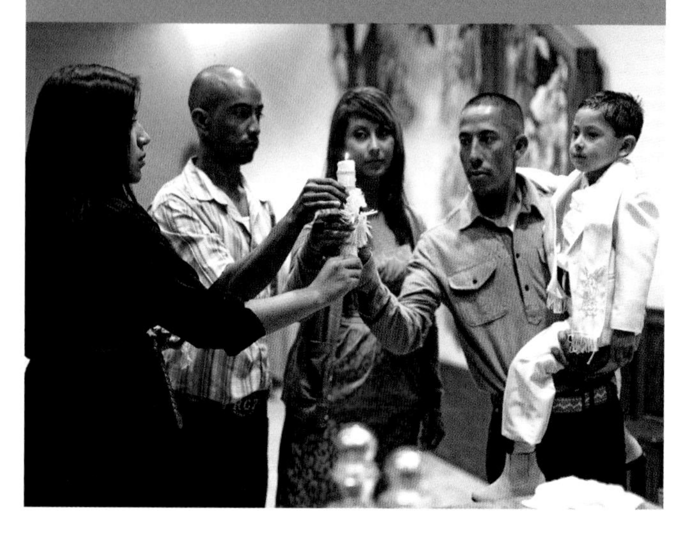

Christianity had become distinct from Judaism and other religions in the Roman Empire. Persevering through persecutions and other challenges, the early Christians increasingly developed into a recognizable Church. This community of faith crossed ethnic and racial lines to embrace all people. Common practices and beliefs of local churches throughout the Roman Empire included preaching the Gospel, public prayer, a ministry of care for each member, initiation rites, Eucharistic fellowship, and a common view of life and human destiny. Some specific Christian practices and beliefs of the early Church are discussed in this section.

Sacraments

The sacraments of the Church are rooted in the words and actions of Christ. The practice of the sacraments was present from the beginning of the Church. As it does today, Christian initiation in the early Church included the Sacraments of Baptism, Confirmation, and Eucharist. The period of preparation, known as the *catechumenate*, could take three years. During this time, the candidate for Baptism, usually an adult, would learn Christian teaching and the requirements for moral living. Becoming a Christian was serious business, so the candidate often had a sponsor who testified to the candidate's good behavior and renunciation of pagan ways. Initiation typically took place on Holy Saturday. The bishop would lay hands on the candidates, absolve their sins, breathe on them, and sign the cross on their foreheads, ears, and nostrils. Another anointing, the Baptism itself, and reception of first Holy Communion followed at a later date.

For the celebration of Sunday Eucharist, Christians gathered in each other's homes. Later, Christians met in donated houses or in enclosed places in gardens or cemeteries. However, by the middle of the third century, Christians began to build their own churches to worship in. Celebrants delivered homilies that showed how God brought the Old Testament to fulfillment in Jesus Christ and the meaning that had for them. The early Christians did "not receive these things as

NOTE TAKING

Asking Questions. Before reading the material in this section, write down in your notebook a central question you have about how the Church developed her practice of the sacraments and a second central question about how the Church established her structure of ordained leadership. For example:

- How was the Eucharist first celebrated?

common bread or common drink, but as Jesus Christ our Savior, who became incarnate by God's Word and took flesh and blood for our salvation" (St. Justin Martyr, *First Apology*, 61, 65–67).

The history of the Sacrament of Penance is complex. Baptism wipes away all sin, including mortal sin. However, due to their human nature, Christians commit mortal sin. The Sacrament of Penance is for sins committed after Baptism. St. Paul wrote that it is God who reconciled the world to himself in Christ and who gave the Apostles a "ministry of reconciliation" (2 Cor 5:18) so that they are truly "ambassadors for Christ" (2 Cor 5:20). The belief and practice developed that only the bishop could offer absolution from grave sins such as murder, adultery, divorce, and apostasy. This absolution could be offered only once and only after the penitent performed long, arduous penances. Being separated from the community of faith was a serious matter.

Ordained Leadership

Jesus established the basic organizational structure of the Church when he instituted the Twelve Apostles in the structure of a *college*, or permanent assembly, and singled out Peter, the rock of the Church, as the head of them. Though it took several centuries for Church ministries to develop into the forms recognizable today, even from ancient times clergy have been called bishops, priests, and deacons. The ministerial priesthood is different from the common priesthood of the baptized in that it confers a sacred power for the service of the faithful.

Peter and the other Apostles (including Matthias, who replaced Judas) were the eyewitnesses to Jesus' public life. Their chief tasks—carried on today by their successors, the pope and bishops—were to evangelize (preach the Gospel) and to witness to its truth. Their privileged role gave the Apostles supreme authority in the many churches they founded both within and outside Palestine.

From the earliest days *deacons*, or assistants, helped the Apostles in their work—for example, by taking up collections for the poor, visiting the sick, and distributing Communion. Widows—women of prayer and service—often helped, including by assisting women into and out of the baptismal pools of water.

"IT WOULD HAVE BEEN ENOUGH"

The *Dayenu* is a song that is part of the Jewish Passover. The word *Dayenu* translates to "it would be sufficient" or "it would have been enough for us." In fifteen stanzas, the song shares many of the graces God bestowed on his people. Take some time to write an adaptation of the *Dayenu* from a Christian perspective. Imagine each of your verses ending with the prayer statement "It would have been enough." For example:

- O Father, if you had loved us and called us your own but had not sent us Jesus, God-made-flesh, it would have been enough.
- If you had sent Jesus, God-made-flesh, but had not raised him from death to life, it would have been enough.

Write three of your own verses, focusing your statements on God's gift of the Church.

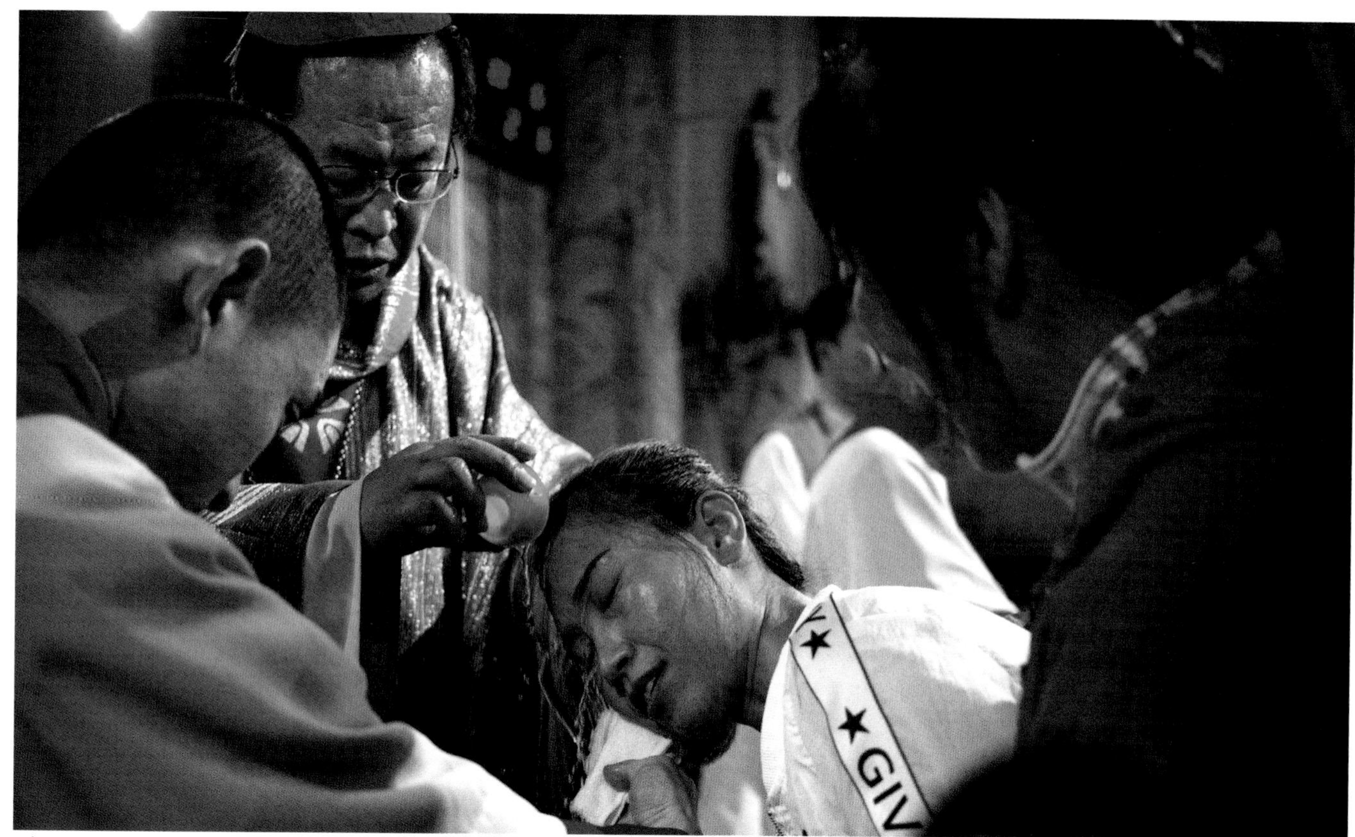

Christ instituted the Sacrament of Holy Orders. Bishops and priests are entrusted with the sacred power of ministry and service. They are "to serve in the person of Christ the Head in the midst of the community" (CCC, 1591).

Because the office of the bishop was instituted by Christ in all the Apostles and passed on by the Apostles to the bishops, the bishops took the place of the Apostles as the pastors of the Church. The main responsibilities of the *episkopoi* (bishops or overseers) were to preside at the Eucharist, baptize, and forgive sin.

At first there was little difference between bishops and the elders known as *presbyters* (priests). Some New Testament writings refer to them interchangeably. In the Jerusalem Church, for example, a council of elders served as a kind of senate. This council would meet with the Apostles to settle disputes. As the Church grew, the office of overseer (bishop) was more clearly distinguished from that of elder (priest).

By the mid-second century, the present-day order of the *hierarchy* (sacred leadership) took shape. At the top was the bishop, who served as the focus of unity in the local church. He also represented his church at regional meetings and wrote letters to other communities. Next were the priests; they presided at the Eucharist in place of the bishop, who could not attend all the liturgies around his growing diocese. Last were the deacons, who served the various needs of the local churches. Both priests and deacons were subordinate to the bishop.

The bishop of Rome, the man who is called pope today, held an increasingly important position among the bishops. He was the successor to Peter, the first bishop of Rome, and resided in the imperial capital, the place of Peter and Paul's martyrdom. Early on, Christians referred to the Church of Rome, led by the successor of Peter, as a measuring stick for measuring fidelity to apostolic teaching. Rome, as the center of the empire, was the ideal place for Christian leaders to defend the Church when she was under attack. Other bishops increasingly looked to the bishop of Rome for leadership when disputes arose. And many of them made sure that their own teaching was in line with his.

SECTION ASSESSMENT

NOTE TAKING

Copy the two central questions you wrote at the beginning of the section. Next, write answers to the questions based on the material you read in this section. If your questions were not answered, explain what additional information you will need to find their answers.

1.

2.

COMPREHENSION

3. Name the steps of Christian initiation that took place on Holy Saturday and the other steps that took place at a later date.

MATCHING

Match the following words associated with each form of leadership.

4. deacon	A. elder
5. bishop	B. overseer
6. priest	C. assistant

ANALYSIS

7. Explain how the current pope is a successor to St. Peter.

Section Assignments

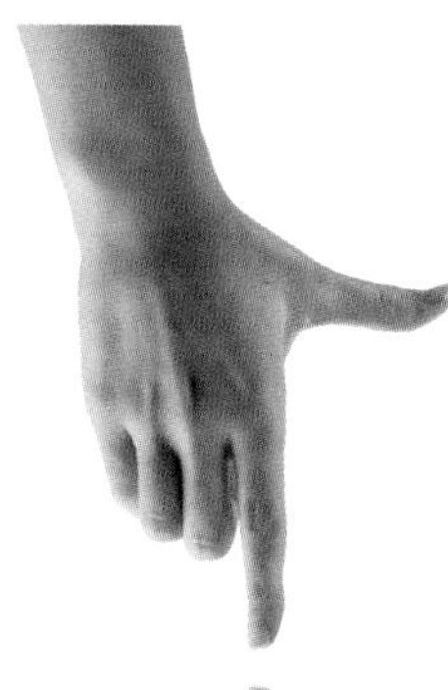

Focus Question

How did the early Church continue to grow and expand, even in the midst of harsh persecutions?

Complete one of the following:

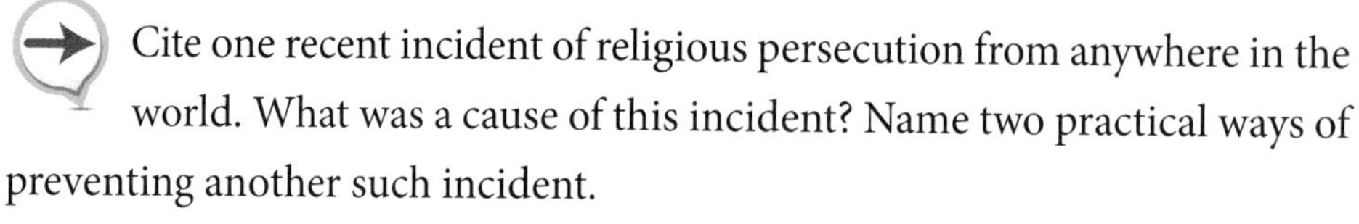

Cite one recent incident of religious persecution from anywhere in the world. What was a cause of this incident? Name two practical ways of preventing another such incident.

Read Luke 12:2–9. What do Christ's words mean for those who have given their very lives in the course of following him?

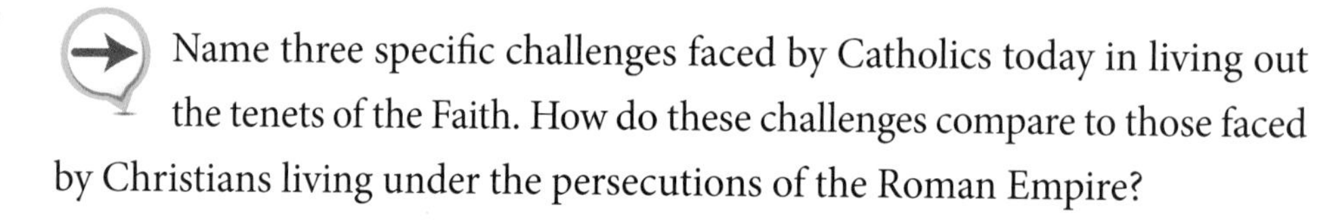

Name three specific challenges faced by Catholics today in living out the tenets of the Faith. How do these challenges compare to those faced by Christians living under the persecutions of the Roman Empire?

INTRODUCTION

The Church under Roman Rule

Search the New Testament letters for five sentences that contain the word "pray." Write about five things the early Church prayed for, the topic of those sentences. (*Hint*: See especially Ephesians 6:18–20.)

SECTION 1

Christianity Is Made Illegal in the Roman Empire

How do you find your life as a Christian to be countercultural among your peers, neighbors, and society at large? Share at least one example.

SECTION 2

Persecutions Lead to Martyrdom

Summarize a profile of a Christian martyr based on the definition of martyrdom in paragraph 2473 of the *Catechism of the Catholic Church.*

SECTION 3

The Church Grows in the First Three Centuries

In a broad sense, the term *apologetics* means "a form of defense." How is this so? Look up the term online in the *Catholic Encyclopedia* for a clue.

SECTION 4

The Development of Sacraments and Sacred Leadership

How are the bishops successors of the Apostles? Write a summary of paragraphs 861–862 of the *Catechism of the Catholic Church.*

Chapter Assignments

Choose and complete at least one of the three assignments to assess your understanding of the material in this chapter.

1. "Life for Christians in the Roman Empire" Group Video Project

Review what life was like for Christians living under Roman rule before 313. In particular, reflect on the difficulties Christians endured, including the harsh persecutions they underwent and the threats that came with attempting to live their faith openly.

Take on the role of a Christian living under Roman rule in the first three centuries. Prepare a twelve-minute video in which you share a particular part of your life as a Christian. Speak in the first person. Be as specific as possible, naming prayers, items, practices, and people who are part of the story. Choose one of the following scenarios as the theme of your presentation:

- how you celebrate a home Mass
- what it was like to prepare for Christian initiation
- your interview with Roman officials after being arrested for being a Christian
- how you witnessed your Christian faith to your pagan neighbors

2. The Development of the Sacraments of Initiation

Review the Sacraments of Initiation (Baptism, Confirmation, and Eucharist). Conduct further research on the development of these three sacraments, particularly in terms of how early Christians practiced them. Write a two-page report providing more details about how these sacraments were practiced in the first three centuries.

In your report, include details about such factors as

- the biblical basis for the sacrament (using specific scriptural passages and citations)
- the form and matter of the sacrament
- who administered the sacrament
- similarities and differences between how the sacrament is practiced today and how it was practiced in the early Church

Include at least two primary source quotations in your report: for example, what early Christian leaders (St. Irenaeus of Lyons, St. Justin Martyr, and others) wrote about these sacraments. You can review some biographical information about these leaders in Section 3 (see the feature "Profiling Early Saints") of this chapter.

3. Women in the Early Church

Because Jesus treated women with respect and had several female disciples, many women became part of the Church in her early history. Several women are named in the New Testament as active Christians. Create a multimedia presentation (e.g., PowerPoint, Prezi, Keynote) that highlights the roles some women named in the Scripture passages listed below played in the early Church. Include images from the period, Scripture quotations, and descriptions of their ministries or occupations. Use the *New American Bible Revised Edition* commentary to help you with your presentation.

- Acts 9:36–42 Tabitha
- Acts 16:14–15, 40 Lydia
- Acts 18:2, 18, 26 Priscilla/Prisca
  Romans 16:3–5
  1 Corinthians 16:19
  2 Timothy 4:19
- Romans 16:1–2 Phoebe
- Philippians 4:2–3 Euodia and Syntyche
- Colossians 4:15 Nympha

Prayer

Prayer for Persecuted Christians

O God of all the nations,
the One God who is and was and always will be,
in your providence you willed that your Church
be united to the suffering of your Son.
Look with mercy on your servants
who are persecuted for their faith in you.
Grant them perseverance and courage
to be worthy imitators of Christ.
Bring your wisdom upon leaders of nations
to work for peace among all peoples.
May your Spirit open conversion
for those who contradict your will,
that we may live in harmony.
Give us the grace to be united in truth and freedom,
And to always seek your will in our lives.
Through Christ our Lord. Amen.
Our Lady, Queen of Peace, pray for us!

—Archbishop William E. Lori, archbishop of Baltimore and supreme chaplain of the Knights of Columbus

CHAPTER REVIEW

Chapter 2: The Church Grows in the Midst of Persecution

3

THE DEVELOPMENT OF DOCTRINE

AND THE DECLINE OF THE EMPIRE

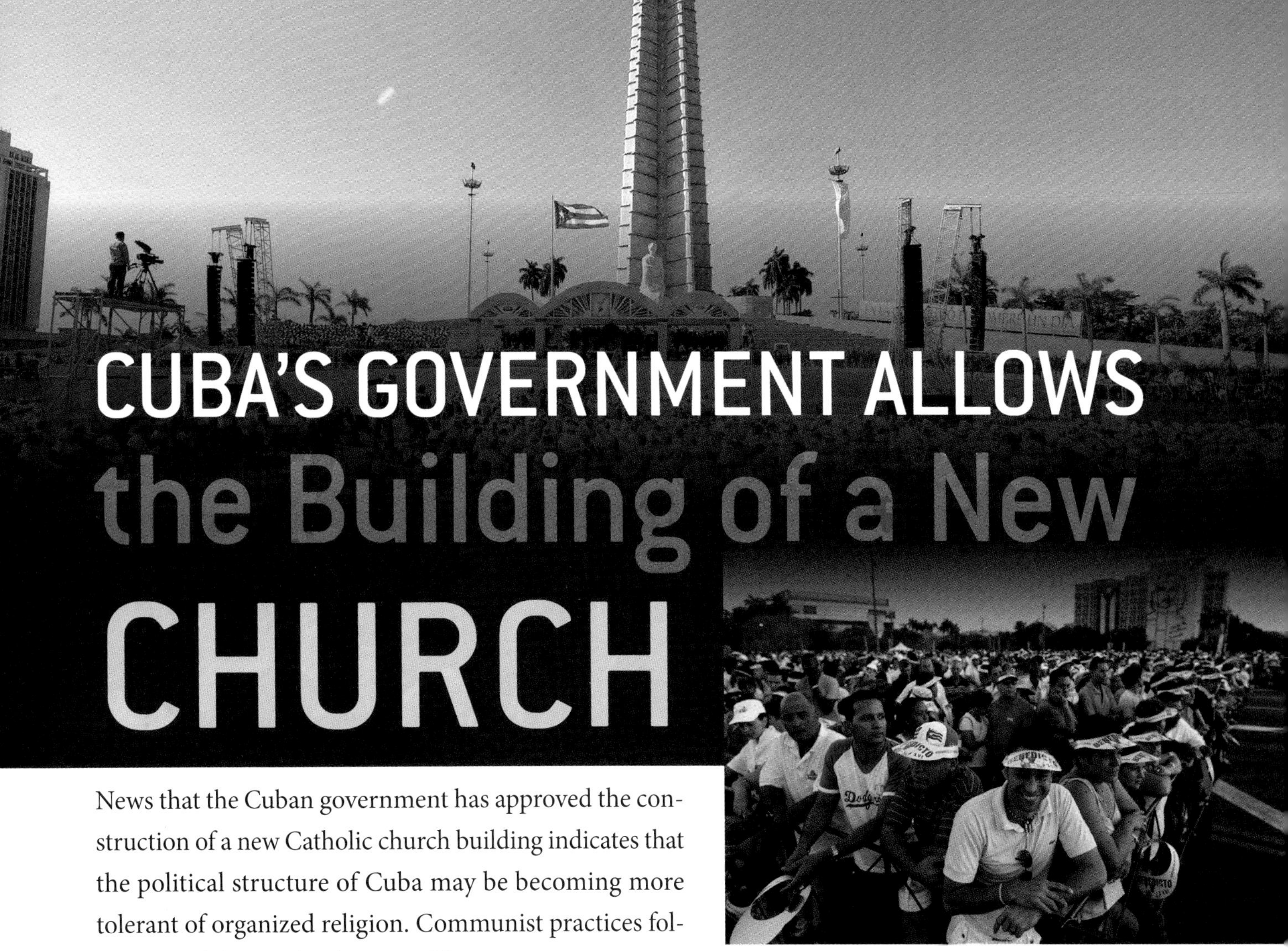

CUBA'S GOVERNMENT ALLOWS the Building of a New CHURCH

News that the Cuban government has approved the construction of a new Catholic church building indicates that the political structure of Cuba may be becoming more tolerant of organized religion. Communist practices following Fidel Castro's takeover of the government in 1959 led to decades of political and religious persecutions in Cuba. Cuban citizens have sought refuge in other nations, especially the United States.

The construction of the new church was planned for the small Cuban town of Sandino. Before the project could begin, local bishop Jorge Enrique Serpa Pérez had to not only receive the necessary permission from the Cuban government but also secure all of the building materials and funds. The Catholic Diocese of St. Petersburg, Florida, contributed a significant sum to fund the construction. When the church was completed, it proved to be a rather small structure, with seating for barely two hundred. Still, the building of a new church in Cuba was noteworthy.

The thaw in the Cuban government's war against religion and the Church began in 1998 with the historic visit of Pope John Paul II. Pope Benedict XVI (2012) and Pope Francis (2015) later took missionary trips to Cuba. The government of Cuba no longer forbids its Communist Party members from having membership in a church, and certain Christian holidays are now recognized. The building of this new church in Sandino could signal an increasingly hopeful future for Cuban citizens in terms of religious freedom.

FOCUS QUESTION

How do the CREED AND DOCTRINE defined in the era of the Church Fathers IMPACT CATHOLICS TODAY?

Chapter Overview

INTRODUCTION

The Era of the Church Fathers

MAIN IDEA
The era of the Fathers of the Church spanned the first century through the eighth. Following the tumultuous times of suppression by the Roman Empire, the Church was able to flourish amid open theological discourse.

The era of the Church Fathers spanned the first century through the eighth century (from the time of Christ until AD 700). Much of this era was turbulent for Christianity (not unlike other eras in history, through today, in which the Church must coexist with oppressive governments) because it included the period of the mid-60s through the early fourth century, when Christians had to live under the frequently oppressive reign of the Roman Empire. The writings of the Church Fathers during this time helped combat heresy, explain the collapse of the Roman Empire to their contemporaries, and formulate doctrine for all time. The great intellects and holiness of these theologians were major influences on their times and the future direction of the Church. They helped develop a range of ways to teach the faith that preserve the immensity of the gift of Christ's love.

The Three Divisions of the Era of the Fathers of the Church

The Fathers of the Church are frequently divided by time period into three distinct groups: the Apostolic Fathers, the Ante-Nicene Fathers, and the Post-Nicene Fathers. Occasionally, the Post-Nicene Fathers are referred to as the "Nicene Fathers" as well.

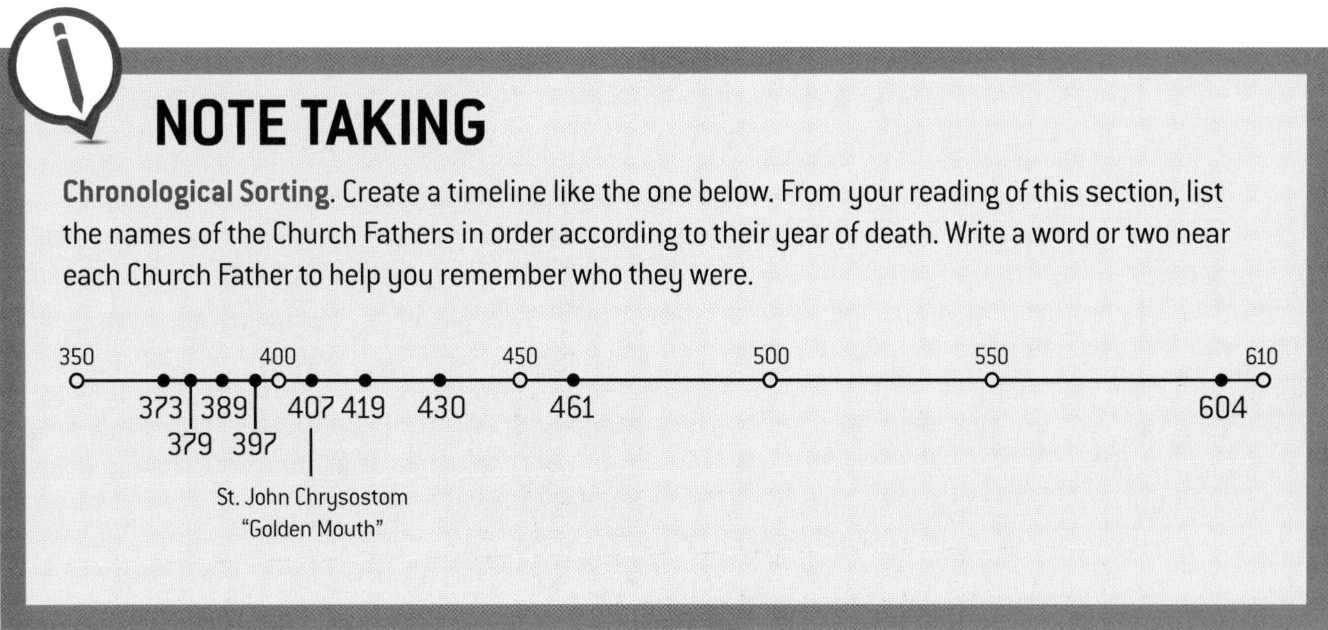

NOTE TAKING

Chronological Sorting. Create a timeline like the one below. From your reading of this section, list the names of the Church Fathers in order according to their year of death. Write a word or two near each Church Father to help you remember who they were.

THE APOSTOLIC FATHERS

were those whose lifetimes overlapped with that of the Apostles. Some of the Apostolic Fathers were most likely taught by the Apostles themselves. Three Apostolic Fathers were St. Clement of Rome (d. ca. 99), St. Polycarp of Smyrna (d. ca. 156), and St. Ignatius of Antioch (d. ca. 108).

THE ANTE-NICENE FATHERS

lived in the period after the Apostolic Fathers but before the **First Council of Nicaea** took place in 325. St. Justin Martyr (d. ca. 165) and St. Irenaeus of Lyons (d. ca. 200) were Fathers of this period. They lived during the Roman Empire's brutal persecution of Christians.

THE POST-NICENE FATHERS

lived after the First Council of Nicaea. During this period, since Christianity had been legalized, they had the ability not only to practice their faith publicly but also to hold public discourses regarding important matters of faith. Post-Nicene Fathers include St. John Chrysostom (d. 407) and St. Augustine of Hippo (d. 430).

All of the Church Fathers were highly esteemed in their day, both in their local communities and throughout the universal Church. They were likewise recognized in succeeding generations due to their writings, which significantly guided the trajectory of biblical scholarship. The wealth of wisdom that they provided to the Church is incalculable.

You learned about some of the Apostolic Fathers and Ante-Nicene Fathers in Chapter 2. The next section profiles several Church Fathers from the post-Nicene era.

First Council of Nicaea The first ecumenical council; a meeting of three hundred bishops that took place in 325, most importantly to provide a response to the Arian heresy and a common profession of faith.

Arianism A heresy of the fourth century that took its name from Arius, a priest from Alexandria. The heresy denied the divinity of Jesus, claiming that he was like the Father except that he was created by the Father.

Key Post-Nicene Fathers of the Church

Here are descriptions of some important Fathers of the Church from the post-Nicene era, featuring some basic biographical information and some of their contributions. This chapter will provide historical context and refer to many of these Church Fathers.

St. Athanasius

(ca. 296–373)

St. Athanasius, bishop of Alexandria, reiterated the teachings of the First Council of Nicaea (325) regarding the divinity of Jesus Christ. Athanasius spoke out against **Arianism** before the Council. Athanasius firmly taught that Christ "was made man that we may be made divine." He asserted that if Christ were only a man, it would be impossible for him to be Savior. St. Athanasius is also well known for his support of monasticism. While in exile in Trier (in present-day southwest Germany), he spread the ideal of desert monasticism to Western Christianity.

St. Ephrem

(ca. 306–373)

St. Ephrem was born into a Christian family in Syria but was not baptized until he was an adult. He was a teacher who may also have been a deacon. He wrote numerous extensive works, including popular hymns and poems, all of which served to inspire and encourage Christians to live holy lives. In fact, Ephrem wrote his hymns as a response to heretical ideas he had heard in the lyrics of other hymns of the day. In one hymn, he responded to a Syrian heretic who had denied the truth of the Resurrection of Christ: "How he blasphemes justice, and grace, her fellow worker. For if the body is not raised, this a great insult against grace." Eventually, Ephrem took on the life of an ascetic, living by himself in Edessa, about one hundred miles from his home. When a famine struck the area, St. Ephrem was instrumental in organizing relief. He died shortly after the famine abated.

St. Basil the Great

(ca. 330–379)

St. Basil the Great was a bishop and prolific writer. His most lasting contribution is his theology of the Holy Spirit, which led to the expansion of the Nicene Creed to the form we have today. He also designed a form of community that emphasized austerity, poverty, and obedience. Basil fostered a spirit of intellectualism within monastic life. The main work of his monks was to be in prayerful union with God; however, they were also to engage in works of charity for poor and sick people. His ascetic writings helped Christians put into practice their spiritual beliefs. *Asceticism* comes from the Greek *askesis*, which means "practice" or "bold exercise," and formed the foundation of Byzantine monasticism. *Byzantine* was the name used to designate the Eastern Roman Empire during the empire's later stages.

St. Gregory of Nazianzus

(ca. 329–389)

St. Gregory of Nazianzus was a celebrated theologian of the Eastern Church who studied theology extensively in Athens, Greece. His beautiful and profound writings on the Trinity, specifically how God can be a unity among Persons, were part of texts called his "Theological Orations." He was the bishop of Constantinople, which is now Istanbul (capital of Turkey). St. Gregory defended the Nicene Creed's teaching on Christ's divinity, supporting St. Athanasius. In 2004, in an effort to promote Christian unity, Pope John Paul II returned to Istanbul the relics of St. Gregory of Nazianzus, which had been taken to Rome in the eighth century. The pope also returned the relics of St. John Chrysostom, which Crusaders had taken in 1204.

St. Ambrose

(ca. 339–397)

St. Ambrose was born into nobility and became the governor of Milan. Later he became bishop of Milan in an unusual way: he was elevated into the role of bishop based on the strong support of his fellow citizens of Milan. When a riot broke out in the city over who was to succeed the late Arian bishop, Ambrose led the military guard to the cathedral to settle the affair. It was there that the people shouted for Ambrose to be made bishop. He explained to them that he was not even baptized, but even after he went into hiding, they sought him out. The Roman emperor encouraged him to accept the position of bishop, and in short order he received the Sacraments of Initiation, was ordained a priest, and was consecrated a bishop. He immediately donated all of his personal wealth to the poor of the city. He was known for his beautiful rhetoric and homilies, and he effectively argued against the Arians. St. Ambrose is also known for his influence on St. Augustine of Hippo. His words finally penetrated the heart of Augustine, who had previously ignored his mother St. Monica's pleadings to convert and be baptized.

St. John Chrysostom

(ca. 347–407)

Born and raised in Antioch, St. John was nicknamed Chrysostom ("Golden Mouth") because of his skills as a preacher. After his ordination as a priest in 386, his preaching in Antioch won him high acclaim, leading to his consecration as bishop of Constantinople in 398. There, his fiery rhetoric against moral laxity in high places earned him the enmity of the empress Eudoxia, the hatred of local clergy whom he tried to reform, and the displeasure of other influential people, including the patriarch of Alexandria, who was jealous of him. St. John was driven into exile, reinstated to his post as bishop, and then exiled a second time. He died during this second exile.

St. Jerome

(ca. 347–419)

Born in northeastern Italy, St. Jerome was sent to Rome to study Latin and Greek literature when he was still young. He continued studying throughout his life, later learning Hebrew, and became one of the most formally educated Church Fathers. Jerome was baptized at age eighteen. While continuing his studies in Antioch, Jerome had a vision in which he was criticized for his devotion to secular learning, for being "a follower of Cicero and not of Christ." Ordained a priest in Antioch, Jerome traveled to Constantinople and studied under St. Gregory of Nazianzus in 380. He eventually became the secretary to Pope Damasus I, who recognized beneath the irascibility of Jerome a holy demeanor. Pope Damasus commissioned Jerome to translate the Bible from the original Hebrew and Greek into Latin, a task that eventually took him to Bethlehem, where he founded a monastery. Laboring relentlessly in a cave with the help of his disciples, he completed the translation, with commentary, a task that took twenty-three years. Known as the Latin Vulgate, Jerome's translation was used in the Catholic Church up to modern times.

ST. AUGUSTINE OF HIPPO

(ca. 354–430)

The greatest of the Western Church Fathers was St. Augustine, the most influential theologian in the West after St. Paul. He was born in northern Africa and raised a Christian, though he was not baptized. His mother was St. Monica. A brilliant student, Augustine studied Latin classics and mastered law and rhetoric in Carthage, where he ended up teaching. During his adolescence, Augustine entered into a decades-long period of depravity, effectively abandoning his Christian faith. He fathered an illegitimate son by the name of Adeodatus; he joined the Manichaeans, a heretical group that rejected the Old Testament. Eventually he made his way to Milan, where he accepted a teaching position. It was there that he came under the influence of St. Ambrose. In his famous spiritual autobiography, *Confessions*, Augustine wrote about how he converted to Jesus Christ and accepted Baptism in 387:

> I was . . . weeping . . . when all at once I heard the singsong voice of a child in a nearby house. . . . "Take and read, take and read." At this I looked up, thinking hard whether there was any kind of game in which children used to chant words like these, but I could not remember ever hearing them before. I stemmed my flood of tears and stood up, telling myself that this could only be a divine command to open my book of scripture and read the first passage on which my eyes should fall. . . .
>
> So I hurried back to the place where Alypius [bishop of Tasgate] was sitting, for when I stood up to move away I had put down the book containing Paul's epistles. I seized it and opened it, and in silence I read the first passage on which my eyes fell: "Not in carousing and drunkenness, not in sexual excess and lust, not in quarrelling and jealousy. Rather, put on the Lord Jesus Christ, and make no provision for the desires of the flesh" (Rom 13:13–14). I had no wish to read more and no need to do so. For in an instant, as I came to the end of the sentence, it was as though the light of confidence flooded into my heart and all the darkness of doubt was dispelled. (*Confessions*, VIII, 12)

After his conversion, Augustine returned to Africa. His mother, St. Monica, died along the journey home. When Augustine arrived in Africa, his beloved son also died. Augustine then gave away his fortune and founded a monastery; he became so popular with the people that he was named bishop of Hippo in 396. From that post, Augustine became an eminent preacher and a sensitive pastor who lived simply among his people. He organized works of charity, administered the sacraments, and served as judge in the bishop's court. Furthermore, he tirelessly defended the Catholic faith against heresies such as Manichaeism, Donatism, Arianism, and Pelagianism. In addition, Augustine authored some of Christianity's most influential theological works.

Augustine's final years saw the dissolution of the Roman Empire. He lived to see the Vandals' invasion of North Africa and grieved at the destruction of many churches and the persecution of many Christians. He opened Hippo to refugees and comforted them in their sorrow. Augustine died on August 28, 430, before his own diocese was sacked by the Vandals.

Among St. Augustine's most famous writings are his *Confessions* and *On the Trinity*, a brilliant theological treatise on the Blessed Trinity still studied today. Another famous work is *The City of God*, which he wrote in the wake of the Visigoth Alaric's sack of Rome in 410. *The City of God* takes a sweeping view of human history. It divides history into a massive struggle between the sinful inhabitants of the City of Man, exemplified by the dying Roman Empire, and the pilgrims or believers in God who live in the City of God. Citizenship in these cities depends on one's love. Augustine points out, however, that the Church is not automatically the City of God. Because the Church includes sinners, it must always cooperate with God's grace and work diligently to be a sign of God's active love in the world.

St. Leo the Great

(ca. 401–461)

St. Leo the Great was pope near the end of the Roman Empire. In addition to his formal role as bishop, Leo also took care of civic affairs within Rome, including feeding the poor and taking care of governmental affairs. He is best known for convincing Attila the Hun to spare Rome from attack in 452. His most significant contribution to the Church was his ability to use biblical, historical, and legal arguments to assert the primacy of the pope among all bishops, taking the title *Pontifex Maximus* ("Highest Bridge Builder"), used formerly by the emperor to describe his role as high priest in the religion of Rome. St. Leo the Great was also influential at the Council of Chalcedon in 451. He taught the doctrine of the **hypostatic union**: the teaching that in Jesus Christ one Divine Person subsists in two natures, the divine and the human. He wrote:

> Accordingly while the distinctness of both natures and substances was preserved, and both met in one Person, lowliness was assumed by majesty, weakness by power, mortality by eternity. (*The Tome of St. Leo the Great*)

After Pope Leo I provided his teaching on the hypostatic union, the Council of Chalcedon fathers proclaimed that "Peter has spoken through Leo."

hypostatic union From a Greek term (*hypostasis*) employed to describe the union of the human and divine natures of Jesus Christ, the Son of God, in one Divine Person. The First Council of Ephesus (431) used this term and it was expanded and affirmed at the Council of Chalcedon (451).

Adding to a Prayer to the Holy Spirit

St. Augustine of Hippo is credited with writing the following "Prayer to the Holy Spirit":

> *Breathe* in me, O Holy Spirit, that my thoughts may all be holy.
> *Act* in me, O Holy Spirit, that my work, too, may be holy.
> *Draw* my heart, O Holy Spirit, that I love but what is holy.
> *Strengthen* me, O Holy Spirit, to defend all that is holy.
> *Guard* me, then, O Holy Spirit, that I always may be holy.
> Amen.

ASSIGNMENT

Note the italicized verbs in the prayer. Add your own stanza in the style of St. Augustine to the prayer to the Holy Spirit using the following verbs:

- *Inspire*
- *Share*
- *Motivate*
- *Counsel*

Also add two more verbs of your own choosing to complete your "Prayer to the Holy Spirit."

MONASTICISM HAD MANY BENEFITS

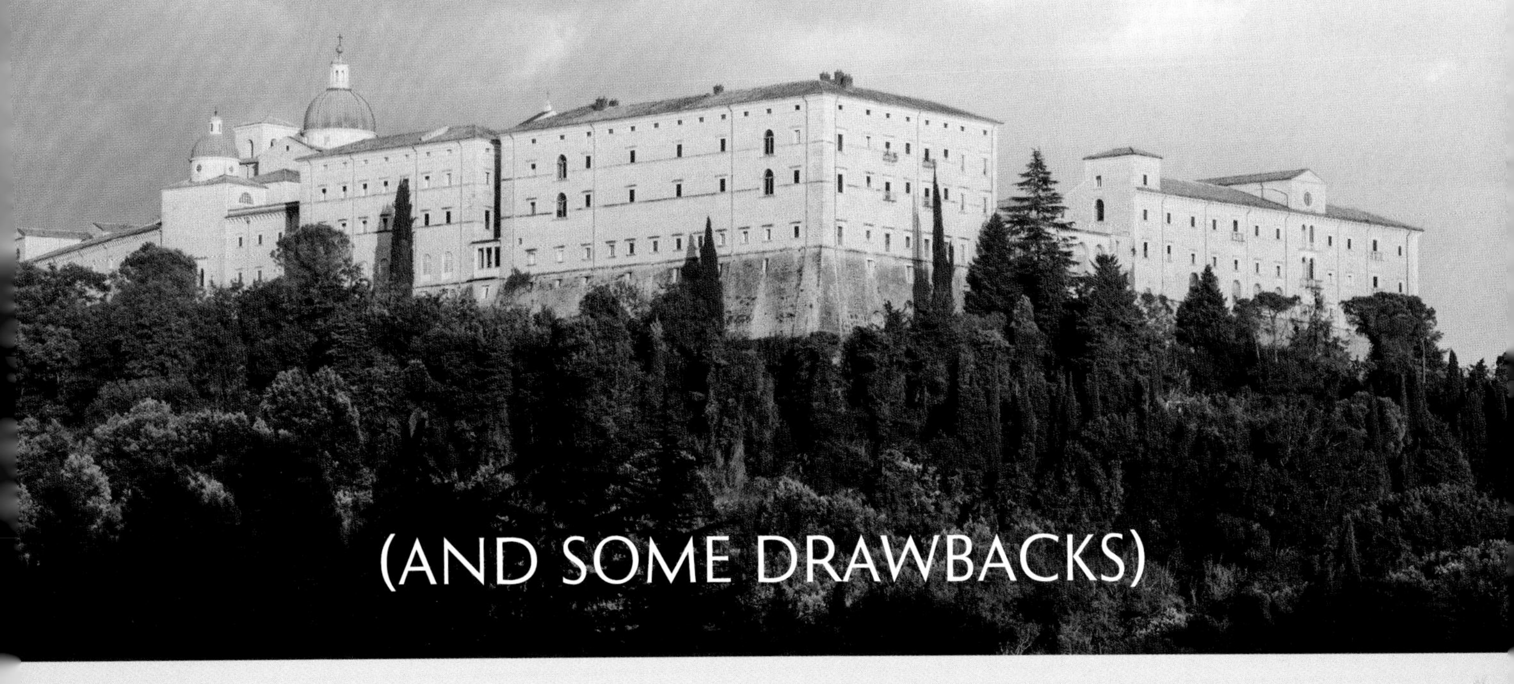

(AND SOME DRAWBACKS)

St. Benedict of Nursia (480–547), the patron saint of Europe, founded the most influential form of **monasticism**. In 529, he built his famous, self-sustaining monastery on Monte Cassino, a hill south of Rome. Not far from there, Benedict's twin sister St. Scholastica (480–543) founded a monastery for women. The monks and nuns, who came from ordinary lives, were taught to read so they could study the Bible and read their daily prayers. They lived a simple, practical form of monasticism, one marked by prayer and work (*ora et labora* in Latin).

Around the same time, St. Columban (559–615) began his missionary endeavors, starting from the island of Ireland. St. Columban spent much of his youth in prayerful solitude. He later traveled to what is now France with a small group of fellow Celtic missionaries. The Columbans gained a solid reputation among the people of the European mainland based on the quality of their preaching, their self-discipline, and their charitable endeavors. Just like his contemporary St. Benedict, St. Columban established monastic communities throughout Europe, and they became faithful hubs of culture and education.

Building on the experience of monks such as St. Pachomius, St. Basil, St. Jerome, and others, the Rule of St. Benedict is a lasting testament to the period and a practical approach to religious life based on moderation—two meals a day, a little wine, adequate clothing, sufficient sleep. Benedictines took the vows of poverty,

monasticism Religious life in which men or women leave the world and enter a monastery or convent to devote themselves to solitary prayer, contemplation, and self-denial. After martyrdom became rare, monasticism became the most demanding way to live out a Christian vocation.

chastity, and obedience to the abbot (for men) or abbess (for women), who held the office for life. These vows and the Rule of St. Benedict became the model for Western monasticism and characterize religious community life in the Catholic Church to this day.

There were many benefits to monasticism for the Church and society, including the following:

- Economically self-sufficient monasteries provided the rural countryside a good example of land management and helped reestablish agriculture after the Barbarian invasions.
- The monks taught respect for the liturgy and the value of prayer in daily life. Monasteries were spiritual beacons. They provided a countercultural response to a Christianity that had grown tepid.
- Monasteries were islands of stability in unsettled times. They gave refuge to travelers. And as centers of learning, they educated many future Church leaders who often administered secular affairs as well.
- As missionary centers, monasteries Christianized Europe. They kept Christianity alive and spread it.
- The monks fostered a life of contemplating the divine mysteries and of praying for the salvation of the world.

The following were some of the drawbacks of monasticism:

- Monastic asceticism sometimes went overboard. For example, some monks engaged in self-mutilation to tame their weak human nature. Also, St. Jerome praised celibacy excessively, so much that he ended up teaching that marriage is not a means to holiness but a necessary evil.
- Monasticism sometimes indirectly encouraged a limited view regarding the diversity of modes and spiritualties in the pursuit of holiness. The educated people in the Church were often monks who considered the religious life to be the only true model of holiness. As a result, a healthy lay spirituality, in which the holiness of every believer was encouraged, was underemphasized for centuries.

The monastery on Monte Cassino has had to be rebuilt a number of times since it was first built in 529, most recently after it was bombed by Allied forces who had discovered German soldiers hiding in the monastery in the Battle of Monte Cassino in 1944.

Pope Gregory the Great

(ca. 540–604)

Pope Gregory the Great helped to promote the role of the pope in the century following the collapse of the Roman Empire. He was the first pope to assume the title "Servant of the Servants of God." Through his many sermons, letters, books, and commentaries and through his reform of the liturgy (he introduced a type of singing that came to be called *Gregorian chant*), Pope Gregory the Great secured the authority of the pope and stabilized the Church throughout Europe.

The period of the Church Fathers is generally held to have ended near the start of the sixth century. The lives of all of the Church Fathers were characterized by holiness of life, orthodoxy of doctrine, and approval of the Church. The Church Fathers all had a significant impact on the development of Christian theology and doctrine.

SECTION ASSESSMENT

NOTE TAKING

Use the timeline you created to complete the following matching exercise.

1. St. John Chrysostom	A. Bishop of Constantinople
2. St. Ephrem	B. "Golden Mouth"
3. St. Augustine of Hippo	C. Wrote popular hymns to combat heresies
4. St. Jerome	D. Fostered spirit of intellectualism
5. St. Gregory of Nazianzus	E. The Vulgate
6. Pope Gregory the Great	F. Greatest theologian after St. Paul
7. St. Basil	G. Made bishop in short order
8. St. Ambrose	H. Taught the doctrine of the hypostatic union
9. St. Athanasius	I. Reformed liturgy after collapse of Rome
10. St. Leo the Great	J. Argued against Arianism

COMPREHENSION

11. Explain the distinction between the three eras of Church Fathers: Apostolic, Ante-Nicene, and Post-Nicene.
12. How did the passage from Romans 13:13–14 figure into the conversion of St. Augustine?
13. Who were the Church Fathers, and how did they influence the Church?

ANALYSIS

14. Why do you think it is important for scholars today to continue to study the contributions of the Church Fathers?

positive

SECTION 1

The Legalization of Christianity

MAIN IDEA

Through his Edict of Milan in 313, the emperor Constantine permanently established the practice of Christianity throughout the Roman Empire, ushering in an era in which Christians were free to worship publicly while the Church increasingly enjoyed support and patronage.

In 313, the **Edict of Milan**, a political agreement between the Roman emperor, Constantine, and his counterpart in the East, Licinius, allowed free exercise of all religions in the empire. Christianity became officially tolerated in the divided Roman Empire, and special favors were even granted to the Church. In 324, Constantine defeated Licinius and became the sole emperor, an absolute monarch who united the divided Roman Empire. He moved the capital from Rome to Byzantium (modern-day Istanbul, Turkey), which he renamed Constantinople.

The legalization of Christianity impacted Christians in many ways. On the positive side, Christians no longer had to practice their faith privately out of fear of government harassment, imprisonment, or death. Church leaders and Christian values became more embedded in the public consciousness, and there were

Edict of Milan A joint declaration by the Roman emperor Constantine and Licinius in the East in 313 that legalized the practice of Christianity and other religions throughout the Roman Empire.

NOTE TAKING

Venn Diagram. Create a Venn diagram like the one below. From your reading, note what you perceive to be positive, negative, and neutral results of the legalization of Christianity.

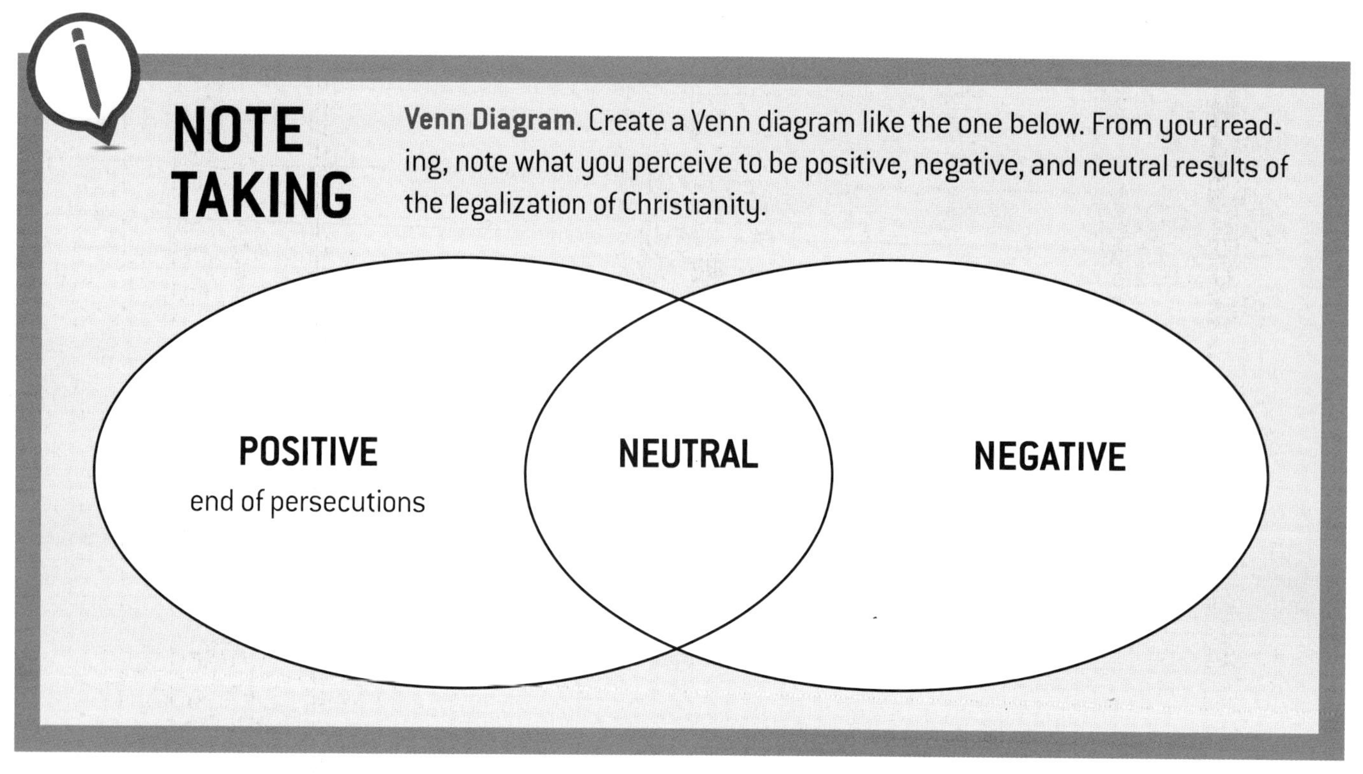

Constantine and the Final Days of Christian Persecution

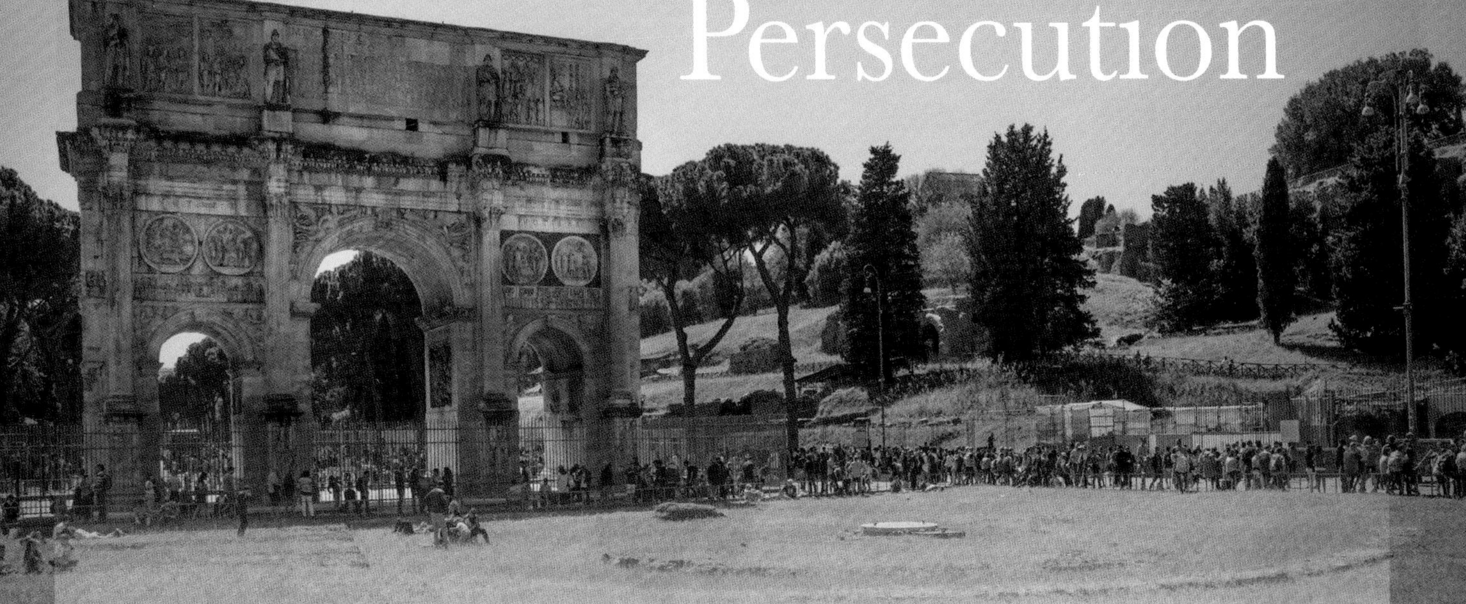

The Edict of Toleration, issued by Emperor Galerius, officially ended the persecution of Christians in the Roman Empire.

The final and worst persecution of Christians occurred during the reign of the emperor Galerius (305–311). Galerius himself was the driving force behind the persecutions. He blamed Christians for all the problems in the Roman Empire. Then in 311 Galerius was stricken with a very painful disease. Apparently he became convinced that his illness was a punishment from the Christian God, for in April 311, he issued an edict stating that Christians would be allowed to practice their faith. A second edict demanded that in return for this tolerance Christians must pray to their God for the well-being of the emperor and empire.

The persecution of Christians ended, but Galerius died five days later. The Christian historian Lactantius voiced the belief of many Christians when he said that Galerius's repentance came too late.

continued on next page

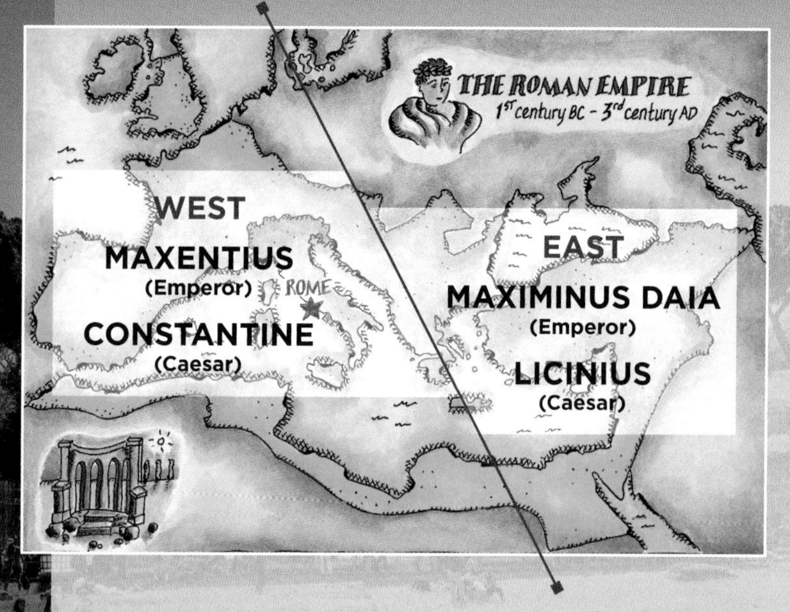

Following Galerius's death, the Roman Empire was divided among Licinius, Maximinus Daia, Constantine, and Maxentius. Constantine began a campaign to take control of the empire. In a surprise attack, he marched on Rome, Maxentius's capital city. Although Constantine's forces were inferior, Maxentius was unable to defend his strongholds and was forced to fall back to Rome with his troops. Then, rather than fight from within the well-fortified city, Maxentius chose to go out and fight.

With the prospect of a new battle looming, Constantine ordered his soldiers to place a Chi-Rho symbol on their standards. In Greek, *chi* and *rho* are the first two letters of the name *Christ*. According to two Christian historians who knew Constantine, this order was prompted by a vision from God. Eusebius wrote that Constantine saw a vision of the Chi-Rho symbol in the sky along with the words "in this sign you shall conquer." Lactantius wrote that Constantine was told in a dream to place a Christian symbol on his soldiers' shields. At any rate, Constantine did so, his army defeated that of Maxentius, and Constantine became the ruler of the entire western half of the empire. After this victory, Constantine formed a new alliance with Licinius in the East. Part of their agreement was that all persecution of Christians would stop and all confiscated properties would be returned to Christians.

negative

more opportunities for devotion to catechesis, theology, and charitable works.

However, a social stratification began to develop in the Church paralleling that of society; the gap between rich and poor became more pronounced. Clerical positions became important political positions, and a clerical aristocracy with less connection to the poor began to develop. These developments caused many Christians to flee to the desert to take up a hermit's life and embrace poverty. This phenomenon was viewed as the most extreme and austere way to witness to the Faith now that opportunities for martyrdom were rare. These austere Christians who withdrew from society were known as the **Desert Fathers**.

Consequences of Legalized Christianity

A great benefit to the legalization of Christianity was that the work of evangelization to nonbelievers and Barbarians (people migrating into the Roman Empire of Germanicor Hunnic origin) became easier. The emperors supported the Church's convocation of **ecumenical councils** to settle disputes and combat divisive heresies. The rapidly growing Church adopted a Roman style of administration. For example, parishes and dioceses modeled themselves on Roman political divisions. Church provinces imitated their civic counterparts. Bishops in provincial capitals acquired more prestige and authority than their civic colleagues in the province. Rome, Constantinople, Alexandria, Antioch, and Jerusalem emerged as the five great patriarchates, with Rome preeminent because Peter had been the first bishop there and had died there. Pope Damasus I, St. Leo the Great, and Pope Gelasius I asserted their primacy as bishops of Rome, especially in the power vacuum that resulted after the empire's capital moved to Constantinople.

In spite of all the benefits of legalized Christianity, the Church faced new challenges. Forceful emperors saw themselves as defenders of the Church, but their interference in Church affairs also led to abuses, the most severe of which was known as **caesaropapism**, the combining of the power of the secular government with the authority of the Church. The Eastern Churches were especially subject to the whims of political rulers. The Western Church was more independent due to the authority and proximity of the pope, the relative weakness of the Western emperors, and the distance from the Eastern capital.

Another negative aspect of legalization was that many people became Christians simply to keep their Roman citizenship; their commitment to the Gospel was lukewarm. Many superstitions lingered; for example, some Christians believed relics had magical powers. And whereas before Constantine's conversion, Christians witnessed to peace, by the fifth century, a soldier with Roman citizenship had to be baptized a Christian. Some ordained men became powerful secular rulers. They gathered wealth, waged war, and often put civil affairs before spiritual matters.

Desert Fathers Christians of about the fourth century who withdrew into the desert to live an ascetic life of prayer, fasting, and abstinence. Their teachings had a profound impact on the theology and spirituality of the Church and the development of monasticism.

caesaropapism The political theory often practiced when Christianity was legalized that held that a secular ruler could also have authority over the Church, including in matters of doctrine.

ecumenical councils Meetings of Catholic bishops from around the world, typically convened in order to discuss and resolve pressing theological topics.

Public Worship and the Proclamation of God in Society

With the opening of the Roman Empire to the practice of Christianity, visible signs of the Christian faith were increasingly evident. Citizens were allowed not only to live openly as Christians but to worship publicly as well. This meant that the Roman ecclesial and governmental authorities saw to the construction of churches throughout the empire. Foremost among these churches was the Archbasilica of St. John Lateran, which was in use as of 324. The construction of church buildings meant that liturgical celebrations could include many people, sometimes in the thousands, without fear of persecution.

Within the churches, those attending liturgies could contemplate—through artwork, architecture, and other religious representations—God's transcendent qualities within structures. An even more public example would be a large cross displayed above a church building.

The legalization of Christianity allowed for the building of churches, such as the Archbasilica of St. John Lateran.

In the Spirit of Hermits

The Church encourages modern hermits who devote themselves to lives of silence, solitude, and penance. In that spirit, do all of the following:

- Choose one day to be absent from social media.
- Spend one hour in a place devoid of people and sound.
- Spend thirty minutes in prayerful Adoration before the Blessed Sacrament.
- Offer a donation of goods or money to an agency that supports people in need.

ASSIGNMENT

Write a one-page reflection on these actions, explaining what you did, what the experience was like, which part you found most difficult, and which part you found most rewarding.

SECTION ASSESSMENT

NOTE TAKING

Use the Venn diagram you completed to help you answer the following questions.

1. What do you deem the most positive aspect of the legalization of Christianity in the Roman Empire? The most negative?
2. How would you label "the loss of opportunity for martyrdom" on your Venn diagram? Explain.

COMPREHENSION

3. Name the five great patriarchates.

VOCABULARY

4. What was the purpose of *ecumenical councils*?
5. Who were the *Desert Fathers*?
6. Why was the Western Church less subject to *caesaropapism* than the Eastern Churches?

ANALYSIS

7. Compare Constantine's conversion with Jesus' words in Matthew 7:24–27.

SECTION 2

The Church and the Collapse of the Empire

MAIN IDEA

The move of the capital of the Roman Empire to Constantinople and the westward migrations of Barbarians increased the civic responsibilities of popes in the last years of the empire.

Following the legalization of Christianity and as the era of the Church Fathers continued, the Church grew within an empire that was increasingly divided between East and West. After Constantine's death, Roman rule was passed on to his sons. Constantius ruled in the East (337–361) and was the sole emperor from 350 to 361. He favored Arianism, a heretical misunderstanding of Christianity that is discussed in greater depth in Section 4. Constantine's other son, Constans, who ruled in the West from 337 to 350, promoted orthodox teachings from the First Council of Nicaea. Julian the Apostate (361–363) was emperor next. He tried unsuccessfully to stamp out Christianity and revive paganism. However, Christianity was so favored that even emperors who were disposed to Arianism did not want a return to paganism.

The move of the capital of the empire to Constantinople had a deep impact on the Church. Without an emperor present in the West, the Church took over the political divisions and structures of the empire. The pope and other bishops were consulted on many civic matters. The pope was responsible for providing for many of the material needs of the citizens and for protecting the West from attacks from invaders from the north. The **patriarchs** of the East did not face as many civic responsibilities. Other differences arose between the Eastern and Western Churches; for example, the

NOTE TAKING

Connecting People and Events. In your notebook, write phrases summarizing key events using dark ink. Then lightly write the name of the person connected with the event over the phrases as in the examples below.

Ruler who favored Arianism CONSTANTIUS	Negotiated peace with Attila the Hun ST. LEO THE GREAT

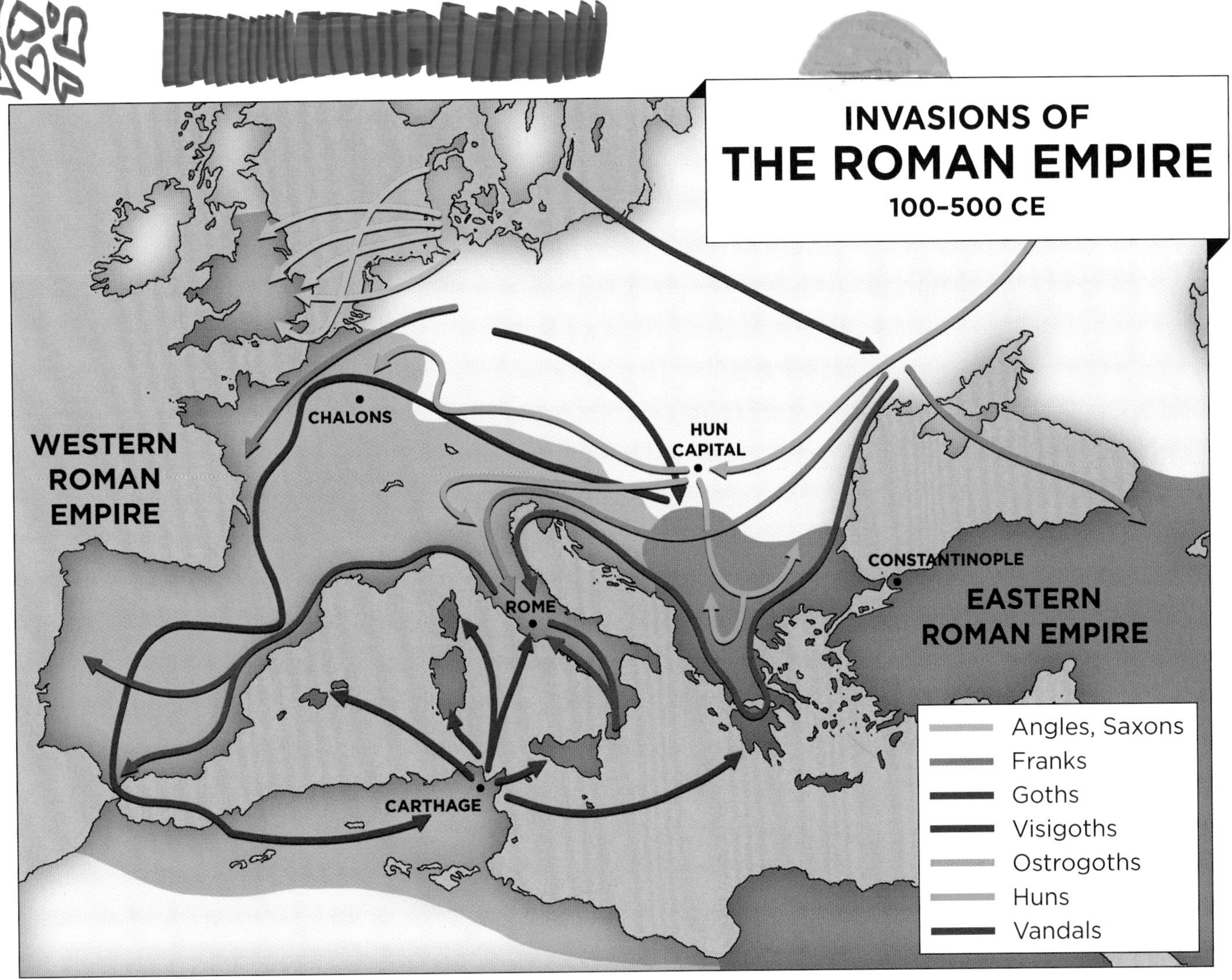

Map of the Barbarian invasions of the Roman Empire from 100 to 500

Western Church used Latin as its official language, while the Eastern Church increasingly used Greek, leading to strained communication between the two.

By 350, there were approximately thirty to forty million Christians in the empire, roughly 57 percent of the total population of the Roman Empire. Christianity increased further when Emperor Theodosius I, the last emperor of both the East and West, promulgated an edict that ordered everyone in the empire to become Christian. Christianity hence became the official religion of the empire. Unfortunately, while Christianity was prospering, the empire was lurching toward collapse.

patriarchs Bishops of one of the five episcopal sees, the name for the places of residence of bishops: the Eastern patriarchates of Jerusalem, Antioch, Constantinople, and Alexandria; and the Latin patriarchate of Rome. In the early Church, the bishop of Rome (the pope) was acknowledged the principal patriarch.

The Barbarian Invasion

Even before the birth of Christ, there was a large migration of people from the east to the west. In the fourth century, this east-to-west migration was more pronounced than ever. The Asiatic Huns migrated west to benefit from fertile lands and economic opportunities and to gain protection from other warring tribes. Members of Germanic tribes had served for years in the Roman army as mercenaries; these tribes too began a progression toward Rome. From the fifth to the eighth centuries, the Visigoths invaded Gaul and

Spain, the Vandals moved into North Africa, and the Ostrogoths and Lombards headed into Italy.

By and large, the Barbarian invaders were taught the Faith and converted due to the quiet and persistent witness of the Christians whom they had conquered. Some of the conversions of Barbarians had to do with a legitimate faith experience, but other conversions were primarily a means of establishing political stability as the Roman Empire teetered toward its end.

An example of conversion based on faith were the Franks, a Germanic tribe that eventually took control of Roman lands. The majority of the Franks accepted Baptism shortly after their leader converted to Christianity. The Visigoths who conquered the Roman lands prior to the Franks, however, accepted Christianity in an effort to stabilize the region.

The papacy of this era continued to grow into the role of protecting hope and order. For example, Attila the Hun invaded Italy. There was no army to stop him on the way to Rome, for the Roman emperor was too weak and too poor to do anything. Pope Leo I left Rome and went to meet with Attila. After the meeting, Attila turned north and spared Rome. In a similar incident three years later, Pope Leo I negotiated with the Vandals and kept their army from burning the city.

In the sixth century, after the fall of the Western empire, it was the Lombards who were poised to conquer all of Rome. At the time, floods had destroyed much of the Roman food supply and an epidemic had broken out in the city itself. Pope Gregory the Great, who was a monk at the time, worked with Pope Pelagius II to organize sanitation and food for those in need. Later, reluctantly named pope, Pope Gregory the Great organized food distribution within the city of Rome and oversaw the rebuilding of the city's aqueducts and defenses. He also negotiated peace with the Lombards. Although he still thought of himself as a religious leader, by default he was the social, economic, and political leader of Rome as well.

The Fall of Rome and the Fate of the Byzantine Empire

Rome was attacked by the Visigoths in 410. This attack was the impetus leading to the final collapse of the Roman Empire. To make sense of the overwhelming change taking place, St. Augustine wrote his brilliant *City of God* (see the Introduction to Chapter 3 under the heading "St. Augustine of Hippo"). The year 476 traditionally marks the definitive demise of the Roman Empire in the West, the origin of which can be traced back to 27 BC.

The collapse of the Western empire was a cataclysmic event for pagans and Christians alike. Pagans blamed Christians and their God for the collapse of Rome. Christians questioned how God could permit the deaths of innocents and the destruction of the center of civilization.

The empire continued to exist in the East as the Byzantine Empire. The Byzantine emperor Justinian I, who ruled from 527 to 565, married a popular actress, Theodora, who as empress had a strong influence on her husband. Justinian's general Belisarius defeated the Vandals in North Africa, the Goths in Italy, and the Visigoths in Spain. These victories gave Justinian control of Rome. But he was often at odds with the popes, even imprisoning some of them because of Theodora's sympathies with a dissenting group called the Monophysites, who taught that there is only one nature in the Person of Christ, in contrast to the Council of Chalcedon's teaching that Christ has two natures. His ineffective leadership led to local schisms in Italy and ill-fated military campaigns. On the positive side, Justinian supervised the rebuilding of the magnificent church Hagia Sophia (Holy Wisdom) in Constantinople that still stands today as a museum. He also

The Hagia Sophia is a former Greek Orthodox church. When the Ottomans conquered the Byzantine Empire, Hagia Sophia was converted to a Muslim mosque.

instituted a major reform of civil law (the **Justinian Code of Law**).

Justinian's successors were weak. They tried to play the patriarch of Constantinople against the pope. Neither the Byzantine emperors nor the patriarchs of Constantinople wanted to take direction from the pope in Rome. This unwillingness perhaps indirectly contributed to the tragic **schism** between Eastern and Western Christianity in 1054. But Eastern Christianity made many positive contributions to the Faith: a vibrant liturgical life, exquisite art and music, and a spiritual depth that inspired the foundation of hundreds of monasteries. The Byzantine Empire survived, though greatly weakened, until its ultimate capitulation in 1453 to the Ottoman Turks. The Ottomans were Muslims, followers of the Islamic faith. Islam would eventually shake the very foundations of Eastern Christianity.

Justinian Code of Law A collection of laws written in Latin that were instituted by the Byzantine emperor Justinian (527–565) and became the basis of European law. Its Christian orientation gave women and children more protection than earlier law, but it still reflected the customs of its times, such as bodily mutilation as punishment for some crimes and repressive measures against non-Christians, including Jews.

schism A break in Christian unity that takes place when a group of Christians separates itself from the Church. This happens historically when the group breaks union with the pope.

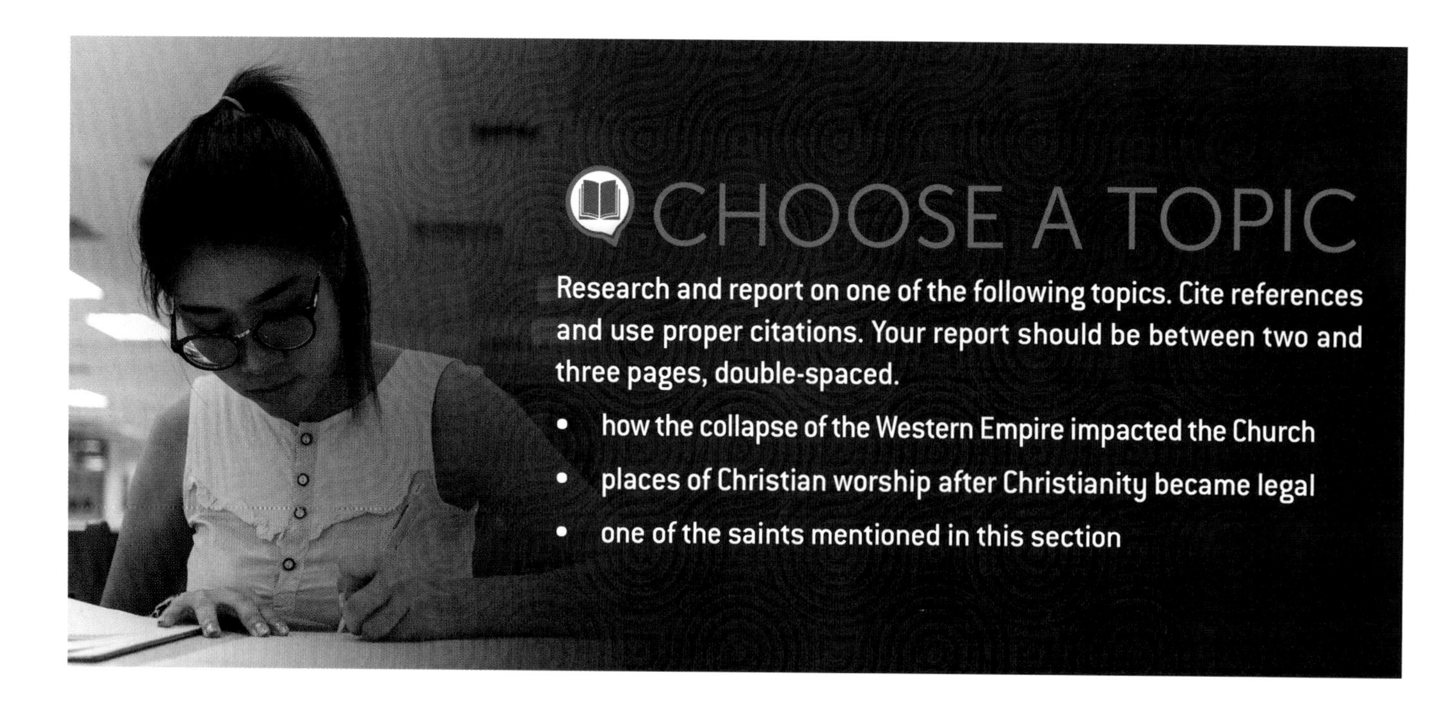

CHOOSE A TOPIC

Research and report on one of the following topics. Cite references and use proper citations. Your report should be between two and three pages, double-spaced.

- how the collapse of the Western Empire impacted the Church
- places of Christian worship after Christianity became legal
- one of the saints mentioned in this section

SECTION ASSESSMENT

NOTE TAKING

Use the phrases and people you connected to help you answer the following questions.

1. Which of Constantine's sons promoted the teachings of the First Council of Nicaea?
2. Which pope organized food distribution and rebuilt the aqueducts and defenses of the city of Rome?

COMPREHENSION

3. Name some positive contributions to Christianity that came about in the Byzantine Empire.

VOCABULARY

4. Define *patriarchs*.

CRITICAL THINKING

5. Why did the pope become a social, economic, and political leader after the capital of the Roman Empire was moved to Constantinople?

SECTION 3

The Development of Sacred Scripture and the Liturgy of the Eucharist

MAIN IDEA

The first centuries of the Church witnessed the development and approval of the canon of Sacred Scripture and the development of the Liturgy of the Holy Eucharist.

Even prior to the legalization of Christianity, written records of Church history, doctrines, and faith began to be collected. Following a brief apostolic period of oral history, the Sacred Scriptures, other witness statements, and liturgical guides emerged to partner with catechetical documents such as the *Didache*. The development of Sacred Scripture and the liturgy is detailed in this section.

canon The official list of inspired books in the Bible. The Catholic canon lists forty-six Old Testament books and twenty-seven New Testament books.

Sacred Scripture

Within the Church, the collection and organization of Sacred Scripture lasted from when the writings were compiled through when they were accepted into the scriptural **canon**. This process extended roughly from the first century AD to the fourth century. The books of the Old Testament, most of which were inherited directly from Judaism, were already in place, so the task of the early Church was to determine which writings were to be considered sacred.

Preeminent among the early Church writings are the books of the New Testament, composed from around AD 50 (1 Thessalonians) to perhaps as late as 130 (2 Peter). The four Gospels recount the life, teachings, Death, and Resurrection of Jesus Christ. Acts of the Apostles tells the story of the early Church, focusing on the ministries of Peter and Paul. The thirteen epistles either written by or ascribed to St. Paul, the Letter to the Hebrews, and the seven Catholic epistles of 1 and 2 Peter; 1, 2, and 3 John; James; and Jude are filled with

NOTE TAKING

Identifying Main Ideas. As you read, create an outline like the one started below that traces the formation of Sacred Scripture and the development of the Liturgy of the Eucharist.

I. Formation of the canon of the Christian Bible
  A. Acceptance of Old Testament books
    1.
    2.
  B. Acceptance of New Testament books
II. Development of the Liturgy of the Eucharist
  A.

theological reflections on Christ and instructions on how to live a Christian life. The Book of Revelation is an apocalyptic book with profound symbolism meant to interpret the achievement of Jesus' self-sacrificing love, seen on a cosmic, worldwide, and even divine scale. These twenty-seven books are divinely inspired, foundational, and normative for the Church.

In agreeing on the canon of the New Testament, Church leaders used three main criteria to determine the sacredness of a book:

- *Apostolic origin.* A book had to have come from the Apostles, either directly or through those who had known them.
- *Orthodox content.* A book had to portray Jesus in a way that was compatible with the Faith as they themselves received it from the Apostles and as articulated in creeds.
- *Universality.* A book had to enjoy widespread and frequent use in the worship and teaching of the Church; in other words, it had to be genuinely universal.

By the late second century, many bishops recognized the four canonical Gospels and the Pauline letters as part of the "memoirs of the Apostles" and used them in liturgical worship. However, it took longer to determine the authenticity of some of the other New Testament books. Church Fathers such as St. Clement of Alexandria, St. Ignatius of Antioch, and St. Polycarp of Smyrna made regular reference to these Sacred Scriptures. Clement's theology applied Platonic philosophy to explain Christian teaching, and he used the allegorical method adeptly to study the meaning of the Scriptures.

Codex Vaticanus From the early fourth century, the oldest complete copy of the Bible in existence; it features the forty-six books of the Old Testament and the twenty-seven books of the New Testament.

Also during this time, a theologian named Marcion rose to prominence in Rome. Marcion led a group into schism in 144 by claiming that the Old Testament God was a different God from the loving and merciful Father of Jesus. In order to refute Marcion, the Church Fathers—especially St. Justin Martyr—emphasized the importance of the Old Testament as it relates to the New Testament, pointing to the complementary nature of these two components of Sacred Scripture.

St. Irenaeus of Lyons was the first Church Father to quote nearly every book (twenty-one of the twenty-seven) that is now within the New Testament canon. Even so, there was still an ongoing process of discernment in the formation of the specific books that, when placed together, would reflect the faith of the whole Church as received from the Apostles. Eusebius of Caesarea (ca. 270–340), a bishop and prominent Church historian, made collective reference to multiple New Testament books. In 367, Church Father St. Athanasius was the first to definitively affirm the twenty-seven books of the New Testament in the order in which they are arranged today. Thus, the unity of the Old Testament and what comes to be the New Testament is also a profession about who God is and, therefore, who Jesus is. Athanasius's listing of the books of the New Testament is reinforced by the ***Codex Vaticanus***. In 382, St. Jerome (see "St. Jerome" in the Introduction to Chapter 3) completed the Vulgate, the translation of the Sacred Scriptures from their original languages to Latin. The ecumenical councils during these early centuries did not take up the matter of which books should be considered part of the canon; rather, a consensus gradually developed over time.

Liturgy of the Eucharist

The Eucharist is the "source and summit of the Christian life" (*Lumen Gentium*, 11). An instruction by the Sacred Congregation of Rites written shortly after the Second Vatican Council teaches that the Eucharist is

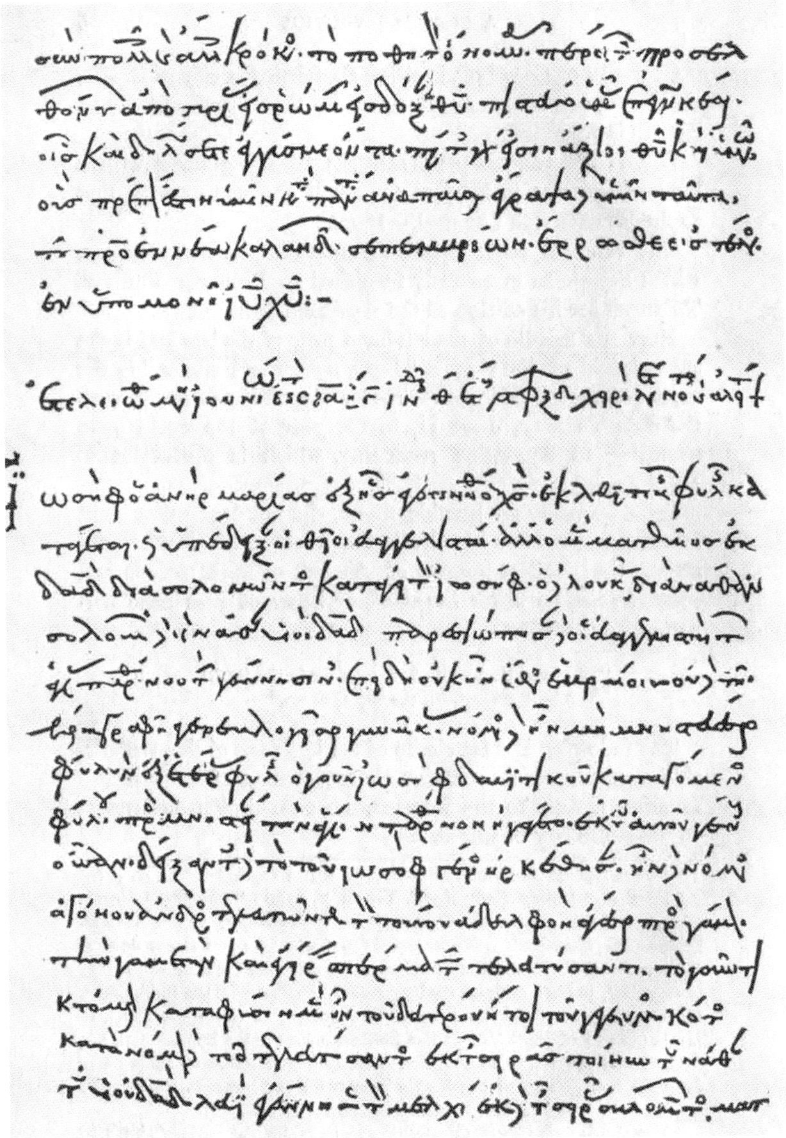

The Didache *provided early Christians instruction on the faith, including teaching on Baptism and the Eucharist.*

"the culmination both of God's action sanctifying the world in Christ and of the worship [we] offer to Christ and through him to the Father in the Holy Spirit" (*Eucharisticum mysterium,* 6). In addition, every celebration of the Eucharist anticipates Christ's return.

In the early Church, the Eucharist kept Christians from being too rooted in the present. The Paschal Mystery of Christ was a historical event, but it also transcends all time. The Eucharist "makes present the one sacrifice of Christ the Savior" (*CCC,* 1330). At Eucharist, the Christians united themselves with the heavenly liturgy and anticipated eternal life, "when God will be all in all" (*CCC,* 1326).

The first-century *Didache* highlights the early Church's understanding that the Eucharist forms Christians into a new people: "Even as this broken bread was scattered over the hills, and was gathered together becoming one, so let your Church be gathered together from the ends of the earth into your kingdom" (9). No one was to come to the Eucharist without having resolved any disagreements that might prevent the community from being truly united in the Lord (see Matthew 5:23–24). The *Didache* teaches:

> But every Lord's day gather yourselves together, and break bread, and give thanksgiving after having confessed your transgressions, that your sacrifice may be pure. But let no one who is at odds with his fellow [neighbor] come together with you, until they may be reconciled, that your sacrifice may not be profaned. (14)

Preaching and the breaking of bread were essential elements of the Eucharist from the very beginning. The early format of the Eucharist is outlined in the Gospel story of Jesus' appearance on the road to Emmaus (see Luke 24:13–35). The earliest liturgies follow the pattern of the Emmaus story: Jesus traces salvation history from the saving action of the Father in the Old Testament through the saving action of the Paschal Mystery. He then offers a prayer of thanksgiving and breaks the bread. At the breaking of the bread, the presence of Jesus is revealed.

By the middle of the second century, there was an identifiable, fixed pattern for the Eucharist. The basic form of liturgy was standardized, but the prayers of the liturgy varied from region to region. No serious effort was made to regularize liturgical prayers and form, although the liturgy of Rome was sometimes used as a model for churches in other regions.

In approximately 155, St. Justin Martyr wrote the first surviving outline of the Rite of Eucharist. It began with a **Liturgy of the Word**, in which the memoirs of the Apostles or the writings of the prophets were read. These readings, which at times were quite lengthy, were followed by a sermon. After the sermon, everyone stood and offered their prayers and then greeted one another with a kiss of peace. The bread and wine (and water on the occasion of Baptism) were brought in, and the presider (bishop or priest) offered prayers of thanksgiving; these prayers were not fixed but dependent on the ability of the presider. The congregation gave their assent by saying *Amen,* Hebrew for "so be it." Then the consecrated elements were received. In his *First Apology*, St. Justin Martyr made it clear that the bread and wine were no longer "common" bread and wine: "We have been taught [that they are] the flesh and blood of the incarnate Jesus."

Liturgy of the Word The part of the Mass that includes the "writings of the prophets" (the Old Testament readings and psalms) and the "memoirs of the Apostles" (the Gospels and the New Testament epistles), the homily, the profession of faith (Creed), and the intercessions for the world.

SECTION ASSESSMENT

NOTE TAKING

Using the outline you created, complete the following items.

1. How did the Church respond to the Marcion heresy?
2. What are the three criteria the Church used to evaluate books for the New Testament canon?
3. Which New Testament books were first accepted by the Church?
4. Name the main parts of the Liturgy of the Eucharist as outlined by St. Justin Martyr.

COMPREHENSION

5. What did the *Didache* say that Christians should do before celebrating Eucharist?
6. Which Gospel story forms the pattern for the Liturgy of the Eucharist?
7. What were the essential elements of Eucharist from the very earliest times?

REFLECTION

8. Write a brief prayer addressed to the Holy Spirit that you could say prior to reading, studying, and praying with Sacred Scripture.

SECTION 4

The Church Defines Doctrine at the Early Councils

MAIN IDEA

In the first seven ecumenical councils, the Church clarified and proclaimed matters of doctrine and faith and responded to several heresies of the first eight centuries. However, the councils were not enough to reverse the widening rift between the Church in the East and the Church in the West.

In order to clarify important Christian beliefs, deepen the Church's understanding of the faith, and respond to misunderstandings and heresies that were brewing in the first centuries, Church leaders met in ecumenical councils, "aided by the theological work of the Church Fathers and sustained by the Christian people's sense of the faith" (*CCC*, 250). Seven councils were held between the fourth and eighth centuries. All the councils took place in the East, with the greatest participation by the Eastern bishops, although the decrees of the councils had to be confirmed by the canons and decrees of the popes or one of his representatives. Throughout Church history, ecumenical councils have contributed to "the ministry of catechesis" (*CCC*, 9), and the councils have taken place over the course of centuries (see *CCC*, 192). From the First Council of Nicaea (325) to the Second Vatican Council (1962–1965) there have been twenty-one ecumenical councils.

The First Seven Ecumenical Councils

This section offers a brief overview of some of the topics and decisions of the first seven ecumenical councils.

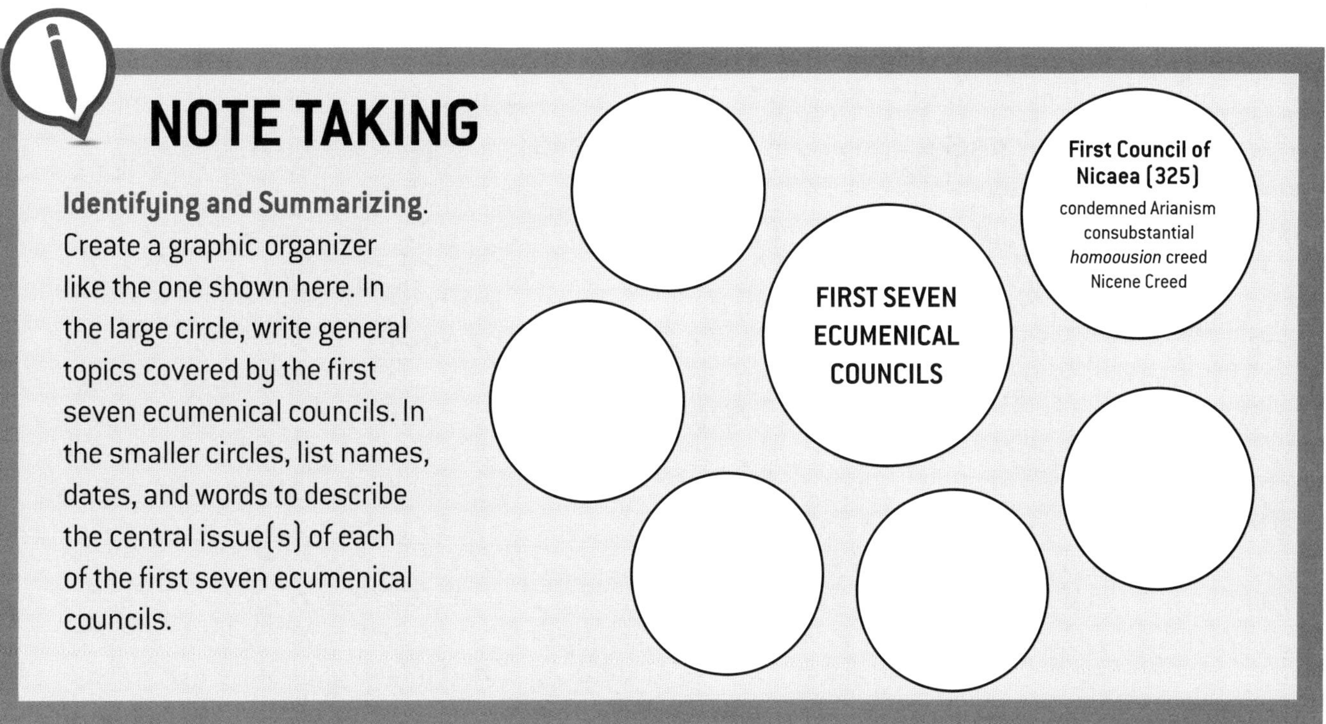

These are councils recognized by both Eastern and Western Christians that delineated important topics, including an understanding of the Trinitarian nature of God and beliefs about the Incarnation, the event in which the eternal Son of God took on flesh and entered human history. Many councils of this period dealt with heresies and challenges related to the Church's understanding of the Divine Person of Christ and the Triune God that were being spread throughout segments of the Church ever since the fourth century. In this way, you can see how later councils built on the teachings of those that came before.

First Council of Nicaea (325)

The First Council of Nicaea was called by the emperor Constantine in conjunction with Pope Sylvester I in response to *Arianism* (named for an Alexandrian priest), which denied Jesus' divinity by claiming that Jesus was not of the same substance as God the Father. Constantine's main objective was to preserve unity in the Church and thereby peace in the empire.

Three hundred bishops, all but six from the East, came to Nicaea, a small town near Constantinople, at the government's expense. They were accompanied by priest assistants who were not allowed to vote. With only six votes against, the bishops quickly condemned Arius's teaching and offered a creed that spelled out clearly that Jesus is *consubstantial* or "of the same substance" (Greek *homoousion*) with the Father. The **Nicene Creed**, proclaiming Jesus' divinity and equality to the Father, is recited by Catholics at Mass to this day.

In addition to addressing the topic of *homoousion*, the Nicene Creed also affirmed that Christ was "true God from true God, begotten not made." These two affirmations opened the door to a more substantial understanding of the Blessed Trinity, but they were not acceptable to Arians, who did not believe in the divinity of Christ, or to some others in the East. Over the next years, the Nicene Creed was defended tirelessly by St. Athanasius (ca. 297–373), the bishop of Alexandria, who reiterated the council's teaching on the divinity of Christ. Recall that he firmly taught that Christ "was made man that we may be made divine." He correctly held that if Christ were not God, then he could not be Savior, for only God could restore people to communion with him. Three Eastern Church Fathers—St. Basil the Great of Caesarea (ca. 330–379), his younger brother St. Gregory of Nyssa (ca. 330–395), and St. Gregory of Nazianzus (329–389)—supported Athanasius and continued to appeal to the moderate Arians, who incorrectly held that the Son was "like to" the Father or "substantially like" the Father.

The First Council of Nicaea took other actions besides formulating the Nicene Creed. One of these was establishing a uniform date for the celebration of Easter.

> **Nicene Creed** The foundational statement of Christian belief that was produced by the Church leaders gathered at the First Council of Nicaea in 325.

First Council of Constantinople (381)

The First Council of Constantinople was called by Pope Damasus I and Emperor Theodosius I. This council further solidified the doctrinal matters that had been decided by the First Council of Nicaea by refuting the heresy of *Macedonianism*, named for a fourth-century bishop of Macedonia, which held that the Son created the Holy Spirit, who was in turn subordinate to the Father and the Son. The council firmly taught the divinity of the Holy Spirit. However, the council did not address the relationship between the Son and the Holy Spirit. This unaddressed issue would be a major factor in the 1054 schism within the Church between East and West, known as the Great Schism.

The First Council of Constantinople

Council of Ephesus (431)

After the First Council of Constantinople, a theological debate developed around how Christ was both divine and human. Several incorrect teachings on **Christology** were circulating at the time. For example, theologians from Alexandria maintained that Christ's perfect divinity so penetrated his human nature that an internal unity resulted, like a blending or mixture of his human and divine natures. Theologians in Antioch stressed Christ's perfect humanity as unmixed and distinct from his divinity, as if his divinity indwelled in the man Jesus just as a person might dwell in a tent.

Nestorius, the patriarch of Constantinople, heightened the debate when he refused to acknowledge Mother of God as a title for Mary. He held that there were two *persons* in Christ—one divine, the other only human—and that Mary was only *Christotokos*, mother of the human Jesus. The issue is about who Mary gave birth to: Was Christ truly God or was he someone else? St. Cyril of Alexandria (376–444) corrected this erroneous teaching and defended the title *Theotokos* (that is, "God-bearer"), or Mother of God, for Mary. He also taught that Jesus was one Divine Person, the Second Person of the Trinity. Emperor Theodosius II called the Council of Ephesus in 431. The council endorsed the position of St. Cyril, condemning **Nestorianism** and the other heresies regarding the nature of Jesus.

Council of Chalcedon (451)

The Council of Ephesus did not end the Christological debates that raged during the fifth century. After the death of St. Cyril, Eutyches, the chief abbot of the monks at Constantinople, with the support of Dioscorus, the successor to St. Cyril, and other Alexandrian theologians, voiced disagreement with the Ephesus formula and preached that Christ's human nature was absorbed into his divine nature "like a drop of honey into the water of the sea."

The Emperor Marcian convoked the Council of Chalcedon. He had asked St. Leo the Great (ca. 400–461) to attend, but the pope sent his representatives instead. The Council of Chalcedon brought to an end the Church's long era of Christological debate about who and what Jesus is. An important result of the Council of Chalcedon was the statement known as the *Chalcedonian Creed* or *Chalcedonian Definition*. Opponents of the Creed held that Christ possessed only one nature—a divine nature. They were termed

Christology The systematic contemplation within the Church on the Divine Person and work of Jesus Christ. In short: Who is Jesus? What salvific work did he do and why does this matter?

Nestorianism The heresy spread by Nestorius, a fifth-century patriarch of Constantinople, that asserted that some of Christ's traits were purely human and others were purely divine.

"Monophysites." In effect, **Monophysitism** denied that Christ was really a human being. Another outcome of the Council of Chalcedon was a repudiation of Monophysitism and a further delineation of Christ's two natures: fully divine and fully human.

Second Council of Constantinople (553)

The Second Council of Constantinople was called by the emperor Justinian I in an attempt to reunite Christians who supported the decisions of the Council of Chalcedon, including the Chalcedonian Creed, and those, mainly from the Eastern provinces of the empire, who persisted in upholding Monophysitism. This council condemned those who opposed the Chalcedonian Creed, corrected some theological errors taught in the past, and offered several clarifications of Christology to expand on the teachings of the Council of Chalcedon. The Second Council of Constantinople also had the important role of confirming the orthodoxy of the first four councils.

Third Council of Constantinople (680–681)

The Third Council of Constantinople was convened to restate prior teachings: Jesus Christ is one Divine Person with two distinct natures—one human, the other divine. It also condemned **Monothelitism** by asserting that because Jesus has two natures, he also has two wills—one a divine will, the other a human will. The council's teaching declared that Christ has "two natural wills or willings . . . not contrary one to the other . . . but his human will follows, not as resisting or reluctant, but rather subject to his divine and omnipotent will."

Monophysitism The heresy taught in the fifth century that asserted that there is only one nature in the Person of Christ—his divine nature.

Monothelitism The heresy taught in the seventh century that claimed that Jesus has two natures but only one will—his divine will.

Second Council of Nicaea (787)

By the eighth century, several conflicts were brewing between the Eastern and Western branches of the Church over the authority of the pope. In one ongoing conflict, St. Leo the Great condemned Canon 28 of the Council of Chalcedon shortly after the conclusion of the council in the fifth century. Canon 28 had given the patriarchate of Constantinople jurisdiction over all the territories of the Byzantine Empire on the grounds that Constantinople was the "new Rome." Pope Leo reaffirmed that he was, as successor to St. Peter, the legitimate source of authority.

A second dispute involved the use of icons or sacred images in liturgy. The Church's position was that the veneration of icons was an important means of educating the largely illiterate laity in the sacred mysteries of the faith. Eventually the Second Council of Nicaea supported the pope's view of this emotion-laden issue by permitting the use of icons in liturgy or for personal devotion.

The Second Council of Nicaea was the last of the seven councils recognized by both the Western Church and the Eastern Church. Beyond the first seven ecumenical councils, the Roman Catholic Church has had fourteen further councils, which have exercised the authority of the Magisterium within the Church (see *CCC*, 891). This is in keeping with the role that the bishops, and the pope in particular, play in leading the faithful to better understand Church doctrine (see *CCC*, 884).

Patriarch Bartholomew I, head of the Eastern Orthodox Church, kisses Pope Francis's head in blessing during Pope Francis's 2014 visit to Turkey. The two leaders are working together to lessen the differences between the Roman Church and the Eastern Orthodox Church.

Rifts Leading to Separation between the Roman Church and Eastern Orthodox Church

It is evident that the original seven ecumenical councils were successful at facilitating dialogue on matters of doctrine. Unfortunately, they did not prevent the rupture between the Roman Church and some churches of the East between the fifth and eleventh centuries, culminating in a full break in 1054 between the Roman Church and what became known as the Eastern Orthodox Church. The Eastern Orthodox Church should not be confused with Eastern Catholic Churches that continued to remain united with the Church of Rome under the pope's leadership after the Great Schism of 1054.

The Great Schism unfolded over centuries. Ever since Emperor Constantine transferred the capital of the Roman Empire from Rome to Constantinople in the fourth century, theological and liturgical disputes, not to mention cultural and political differences (see the opening of Chapter 3, Section 2), had divided some segments of the Church in the East. Disagreement regarding papal authority over the eastern patriarchs further led to schism. Three years in particular along the path to schism are historically significant: 431, 451, and 1054.

Recall that in 431 the Council of Ephesus condemned Nestorianism (see "Council of Ephesus" earlier in this section). However, despite the council's condemnation, some Christians continued to profess Nestorian beliefs. This eventually led to a rift known as the Nestorian Schism, during which the Assyrian Church in the East broke with the Byzantine Church. In turn, this episode led to friction between the Roman Church and some Eastern Churches.

The next period of discord between the Roman Church and Eastern Churches came in 451 during the

Patriarch Athenagoras I greets Pope Paul VI in 1967, two years after they undid their respective excommunications.

Council of Chalcedon when St. Leo the Great condemned the council's ruling that gave the Church of Constantinople the authority to make decisions for all the territories in the Byzantine Empire. The pope could not accept surrendering Church authority that was properly his as bishop of Rome.

The final point of disagreement involved the Roman Church's addition of the phrase ***Filioque*** ("and from the Son") to the Nicene Creed (first appearing in the sixth century) without the approval of an ecumenical council. Some Eastern Churches wanted the Creed to say that the Holy Spirit descended *through* the Son, not *from* the Son. In the 860s, Photius, the patriarch of Constantinople, condemned the Roman Church, accusing her of heresy—a serious charge that went way beyond any other discord that had surfaced previously between East and West.

The ultimate severing of relations between the Roman and some Eastern Churches is known as the Great Schism of 1054. Opposed to the Western practice of clerical celibacy, the Western use of unleavened bread for the Eucharist, and the *Filioque* clause in the Nicene Creed, Patriarch of Constantinople Michael Cerularius closed all churches in his city that were loyal to the pope and excommunicated priests who said the Mass in Latin. In response, Cardinal Humbert of Silva Candida (serving on behalf of Pope Leo IX) excommunicated the patriarch; in turn, the patriarch convoked a council and excommunicated the pope. Most Eastern Churches sided with the patriarch and refused to recognize the primacy of the pope. These Churches eventually took the name *Orthodox*, meaning "correct or right opinion."

This mutual excommunication was not lifted until 1965, when Pope Paul VI and Patriarch Athenagoras I of Constantinople undid their Churches' respective excommunications. In modern times, there have been many and ongoing efforts at dialogue between the Catholic Church and the Orthodox Churches, and leaders of both remain "in a position to contribute in many and fruitful ways" (*CCC*, 887) to this reconciliation.

Eastern Churches that remained in union with Rome after the Great Schism are called Eastern Catholic Churches, or often the Eastern Church. Remember: If the name Eastern Church has "Orthodox" in its title, it is not in union with Rome. Eastern Churches (without Orthodox in the title) are fully Catholic and accept the pope as leader of the Church.

Filioque Latin for "and from the Son"; a phrase added to the Nicene Creed by the Western Church without the agreement of the Eastern Church to specify that the Holy Spirit proceeds from both the Father *and the Son*; it became a point of contention within Eastern Orthodoxy.

SECTION ASSESSMENT

NOTE TAKING

Use the graphic organizer you completed to help you complete the following items.

1. How did the First Council of Nicaea respond to Arianism?
2. Differentiate between *Christotokos* and *Theotokos* in regard to Mary.
3. Match the definition of the heresy with its name.

i. Monothelitism	a. The Son of God has only one nature as result of the Incarnation
ii. Macedonianism	b. Jesus has two natures but only one will
iii. Monophysitism	c. The Holy Spirit is not God

COMPREHENSION

4. How many ecumenical councils have taken place in Church history? Which is the most recent?
5. Name the series of events that led to the Great Schism.

REFLECTION

6. How do you understand St. Athanasius's teaching that Christ "was made man that we may be made divine"?

Section Assignments

Focus Question

How do the creed and doctrine defined in the era of the Church Fathers impact Catholics today?

Complete one of the following:

→ Research the life of one of the Church Fathers. Report on ways in which he contributed to the life of the early Church and what his enduring legacy is in the Church today.

→ Research and write a follow-up report on the progress of religious freedom in Cuba since the government allowed a new Catholic church to be built in Sandino. For example, cite information from the Archdiocese of San Cristóbal de la Habana. Alternatively, report on another place in the world today where the Church is facing persecution or an increase in acceptance by the national government.

→ While celebrants at liturgy had considerable freedom to compose their own Eucharistic prayers for Mass in the early centuries of the Church, standardization developed as communities began to adopt the prayers of the more eloquent celebrants. Read the "Anaphora of Hippolytus" from the third-century treatise *Apostolic Tradition*, which is credited to St. Hippolytus. Compare it with Eucharistic Prayer II from today's liturgical rites.

INTRODUCTION

The Era of the Church Fathers

Why do you think that the term *Church Fathers* is an appropriate title? In what ways did the Church Fathers serve the needs of the growing Church?

SECTION 1

The Legalization of Christianity

Write about any three consequences for Christianity in the aftermath of the conversion of Constantine.

SECTION 2

The Church and the Collapse of the Empire

Research and write a one-page report on two reasons for the collapse of the Roman Empire that were not presented in this section.

SECTION 3

The Development of Sacred Scripture and the Liturgy of the Eucharist

Read and summarize the following *Catechism of the Catholic Church* paragraphs on the history of the Eucharist: 1094, 1342–1346, 2176, and 2178.

SECTION 4

The Church Defines Doctrine at the Early Councils

Examine each of the statements of the Nicene Creed. Choose one statement you would like more clarification about, and write down your essential question about this statement. Research the answer and write your findings in two to three well-developed paragraphs.

Chapter Assignments

Choose and complete at least one of the three assignments to assess your understanding of the material in this chapter.

1. Symbols of Christianity in the Early Church

During the time of Christian persecutions in the first three centuries, two prominent signs other than the cross were used to identify Christians.

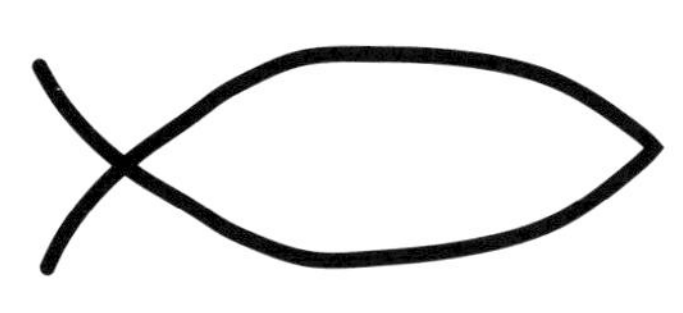

The fish was a secret sign known as the *ichthys* (pronounced "ick this"). It was used frequently when Christianity was illegal to identify Christian homes or to mark the graves of Christians. The letters for the Greek word for fish were also the first letters of the words in the phrase "Jesus Christ, God's Son, Savior" in Greek.

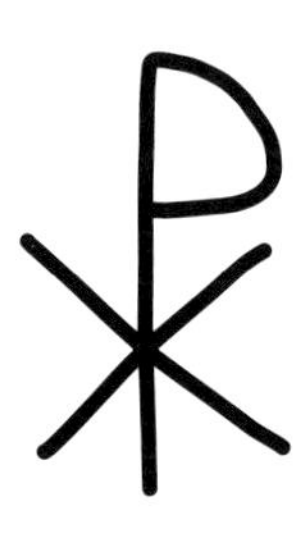

The other sign is known as the Chi-Rho (pronounced "ki ro"); these are the first two letters in Greek of "Christ." The Chi-Rho became a very public sign of Christianity, especially after the emperor Constantine replaced the Roman eagle on the shields of his soldiers with the Chi-Rho and subsequently won the battle for Rome; this victory directly led to the legalization of Christianity (see Section 1, "The Legalization of Christianity").

Using an art medium of your choice (watercolors, stencils, embroidery, tiles, etc.), create a replica of either the *ichthys* or the Chi-Rho. Make sure your finished project is able to be displayed in your classroom.

2. Tracing the History of Items Used at Eucharist

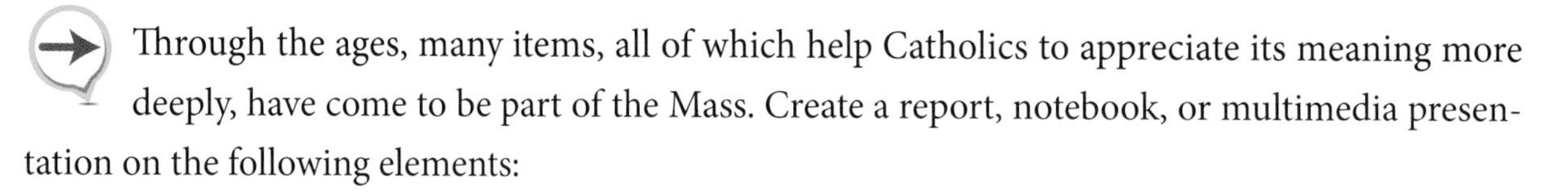

Through the ages, many items, all of which help Catholics to appreciate its meaning more deeply, have come to be part of the Mass. Create a report, notebook, or multimedia presentation on the following elements:

- vestments (e.g., stole, alb, cincture, chasuble)
- altar
- tabernacle
- sacred vessels (e.g., chalice, paten, ciborium, cruets)
- liturgical books (e.g., sacramentary and lectionary)
- crucifix
- incense

For each item, include the following: (1) its name and definition; (2) its purpose in the liturgy; (3) its origins (when, where, and why it came into use); and (4) one or more images.

3. The *Filioque*

A 2003 United States Conference of Catholic Bishops document "The Filioque: A Church Dividing Issue?: An Agreed Statement" concludes with some theological reflections on this topic that was central to the division between Eastern and Western Christians in 1054. Look up the report online at www.usccb.org, and do the following:

- Write ten sentences that summarize the "Historical Considerations" section of the document.
- Write two paragraphs summarizing the agreements between the Western and Eastern traditions on the *Filioque* (see "Theological Reflections").
- Write two paragraphs summarizing the recommendations made in this article (see "Recommendations").

Prayer

Prayer of Origen

Jesus, my feet are dirty. Come even as a slave to me, pour water into your bowl, come and wash my feet. In asking such a thing I know I am overbold, but I dread what was threatened when you said to me, "If I do not wash your feet, I have no fellowship with you." Wash my feet, then, because I long for your companionship.

CAUTION
CAUTION
CAUTION
I SUPPORT
HB113
DO YOU?
I SUPPORT
HB113
DO YOU?

4

THE CHURCH IN THE MIDDLE AGES

CATHOLIC UNIVERSITY HOSTS A SYMPOSIUM on the Second Vatican Council's Document *Nostra Aetate*

Representatives of the world's major religions came together at The Catholic University of America (CUA) in 2015 both to celebrate interreligious dialogue and to mark the fiftieth anniversary of the Second Vatican Council document *Nostra Aetate* (*In Our Times*): *The Relation of the Church to Non-Christian Religions. Nostra Aetate* is the shortest of the sixteen documents that were produced at the Council, but one of its most important.

Nostra Aetate makes a particular call for an end to anti-Semitism as well as any other type of unjust religious discord. It is in this document that the Church acknowledges that Jesus is the link between Judaism and Christianity.

The first day of the symposium focused on Catholic–Muslim relations. Sayyid M. Syeed, the national director of the Islamic Society of North America, praised the document as a "major leap" in Catholic relations with Muslims. Seyyed Hossein Nasr, a professor of Islamic studies at George Washington University, explained that Catholics and Muslims have much in common in today's world, especially in confronting modernism and secularism. "There is a great battle going on in the world between dark and light, and on almost every issue we are on the same page," Nasr said.

The second day of the symposium was devoted to Catholic-Jewish dialogue. Rabbi Noam E. Marans referred to *Nostra Aetate* as a "life-saving document" and added that its "power is not limited to the past, but is ongoing." Later in the event, Rabbi Irving Greenberg, former president of the Jewish Life Network/Steinhardt Foundation, told the symposium that Christians and Jews "need to show that in humility we can work together and be an extraordinary witness."

CUA president John Garvey also addressed the symposium, drawing on the Gospel story of travelers walking on the road to Emmaus as an illustration of modern interreligious dialogue. "Interreligious dialogue is also an act of friendship," Garvey said. "We engage in dialogue to share with one another what we have found to be the greatest source of joy."

(From the article "Catholic, Muslim and Jewish Scholars Gather for Nostra Aetate Conference" http://publicaffairs.cua.edu/releases/2015/nostra-preview.cfm.)

FOCUS QUESTION

How does the Church **PERSIST IN PROCLAIMING THE GOSPEL** during evolving political, religious, and social upheaval?

Chapter Overview

INTRODUCTION

The Church Offers Spiritual Recourse

MAIN IDEA
The Middle Ages is commonly recognized as the period from the fall of the Roman Empire in 476 through the dawn of the Renaissance in the fifteenth century. The Church provided security in the midst of the political and religious upheaval of the period.

The Middle Ages forms the middle period in the classical division of European history into three ages from the time of the Roman Empire to modern times. The Middle Ages—known also as the *medieval period*—commonly dates from the fifth-century fall of the Western Roman Empire and the Barbarian invasions to the start of the Renaissance in the fifteenth century. The Middle Ages itself is further divided into three periods.

1 Early Middle Ages (476–1000)

This period began with the fall of the Roman Empire in the West. Several events of this period were discussed in Chapter 3. During this period, Europe faced an authority vacuum, weakened civil rulers, and the absence of services to meet the needs of its citizens. The Church stepped in to fill the void and frequently brought order to the chaos. Christianization of the Germanic tribes occurred in this period, which also eventually led to a Christian Europe, also called *Christendom.* This period is also known for the rise of Islam and the establishment of the Papal States.

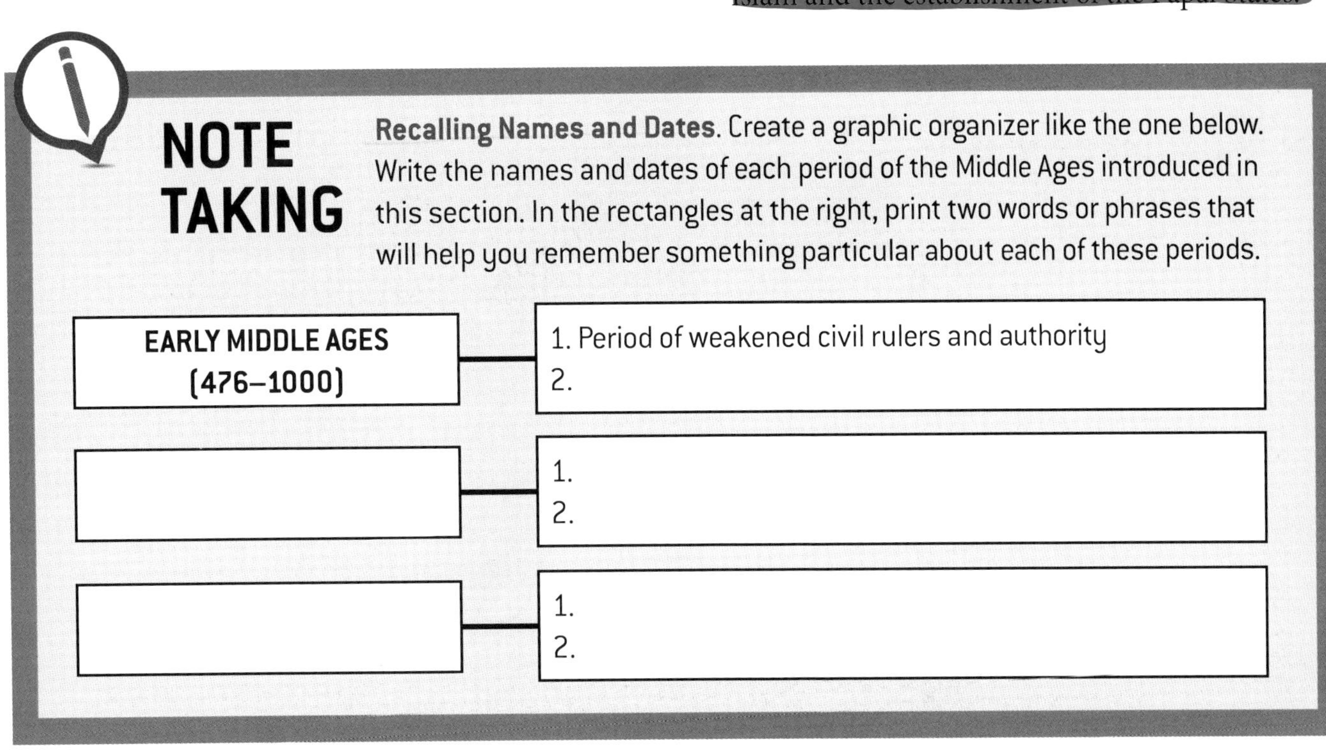

NOTE TAKING

Recalling Names and Dates. Create a graphic organizer like the one below. Write the names and dates of each period of the Middle Ages introduced in this section. In the rectangles at the right, print two words or phrases that will help you remember something particular about each of these periods.

EARLY MIDDLE AGES (476–1000)	1. Period of weakened civil rulers and authority 2.
	1. 2.
	1. 2.

2 High Middle Ages (1000–1300)

Several key developments in the Church marked this period. The Great Schism of 1054 was the climax of several centuries of growing religious and political differences between the Eastern and Western Churches. After a long period of corruption in the Roman Church, reforms were brought about by Pope Gregory VII and promulgated at the Fourth Lateran Council in 1215. This period also included the founding of the university system, the development of Gothic architecture, and the birth of new religious orders. St. Thomas Aquinas, one of the Church's greatest theologians, wrote the *Summa Theologiae* in the thirteenth century. The Crusades and the Cluniac reforms also took place during this period.

Doctors wore distinctive clothing when treating patients afflicted with the plague. The mask held spices and perfumes thought to combat the spread of the disease.

3 Late Middle Ages (1300–1450)

This period, leading to the Protestant Reformation, was marked by strife and suffering, some caused by the epidemic of the bubonic plague, called the Black Death, which killed more than a third of Europe's population.

Characteristics of the Period

Historians have typically characterized the Middle Ages as a time dominated by political chaos and disease and have sometimes characterized the period as the "Dark Ages." This term is a misnomer for this period in many ways. There were many positive developments in society, science, and theology throughout the era. As Roman civilization crumbled and Europe seemed to be slipping into anarchy, protection and security of the population took precedence but did not necessitate the complete abandonment of overall learning. Monasteries became beacons for the preservation of Western learning. The Church played an important role in providing security and fostering education but more importantly in offering spiritual recourse amid the difficulties of the time.

The Church as a Sheepfold

Because of the turmoil of the period, the Church was increasingly valued for her ability to provide protection and security, not only from the dangers of this world, but from the uncertainty of the next world. An image of the Church as a *sheepfold* (a pen or shelter for sheep) developed in the Middle Ages. The Church was known as a place in which her people were protected from the "wolves" of earthly evil and eternal damnation.

For example, in the early Middle Ages, during the time of Pope Gregory the Great, the belief in purgatory

solidified in Church teaching. Pope Gregory was particularly concerned with how people could make amends for their sins. He reaffirmed the necessity of priestly absolution and also encouraged the practice of offering Masses to assist those who were in Purgatory into heaven. In a world where danger and punishment seemed to be everywhere, the Church offered her faithful protection from eternal suffering.

The image of the Church as sheepfold remained prominent throughout all three periods of the Middle Ages because fear was a constant presence, especially as the bubonic plague struck Europe in the fourteenth century. In many ways, the Church offered a lasting sense of comfort, peace, and security to those who were afraid, as Jesus intended when he said:

> "Amen, amen, I say to you, whoever does not enter a sheepfold through the gate but climbs over elsewhere is a thief and a robber. But whoever enters through the gate is the shepherd of the sheep. The gatekeeper opens it for him, and the sheep hear his voice, as he calls his own sheep by name and leads them out. When he has driven out all his own, he walks ahead of them, and the sheep follow him, because they recognize his voice." (Jn 10:1–4)

The Church's role as a sheepfold that gathered in and cared for people facing suffering and death was a product of the events of the times. The Church also faced several external and internal threats in the Middle Ages, including the rise of a new religion, Islam, and corruption within. In her ongoing renewal, the Church in the Middle Ages was also known for her great reformers, including St. Dominic de Guzmán and St. Francis of Assisi, the founders of the Dominican and Franciscan religious orders.

This chapter examines the role of the Church in several key events and trends of the Middle Ages and introduces key figures of the era.

SECTION ASSESSMENT

NOTE TAKING

Use the information in the graphic organizer you created to help you to answer the following questions.

1. What years did the entire Middle Ages encompass?
2. Name one key development of the High Middle Ages.
3. What was a main cause of strife and suffering in the Late Middle Ages?

COMPREHENSION

4. Why might the term "Dark Ages" really be a misnomer?

SECTION 1

Early Middle Ages (476–1000): The Rise of Islam and the Founding of the Papal States

MAIN IDEA

In the Early Middle Ages, the Church forged alliances with European leaders and tribes, leading to the conversion of many to Christianity. These alliances helped to defend the West and Christianity itself from Islamic invasions.

It was a generally accepted principle prior to the Middle Ages that if a king converted, the people would follow his lead. This principle held true in the Early Middle Ages: the Magyars became Catholic because of the conversion of their king, St. Stephen; the Bohemians because of the Baptism of their duke, St. Wenceslaus; the Poles because of the conversion of their leader, Mieszko.

Another factor that hastened evangelization was the establishment of monasteries and the work of legendary missionaries:

ST. PATRICK

(389–461)

St. Patrick (389–461) was born a Roman citizen in Britain. At the age of sixteen, he was captured by Irish pirates and enslaved in Ireland. He learned Celtic customs and the difficult Celtic language while there. After six years of captivity, he returned to Britain and entered a monastery. Made a bishop in 432, he returned to Ireland and traveled throughout the island, converting most local Celtic kings while establishing monasteries that continued his work of evangelization.

NOTE TAKING

Identifying Main Ideas. Create an outline like the one started below to help you identify the main ideas in this section. Include mention of how various indigenous peoples came to Christianity. Add as many subpoints as necessary.

The Early Middle Ages

I. Christianity Spreads in the West
- A. Conversion of Kings
  1. Magyars (St. Stephen)
  2.
  3.

II. The Rise of Islam
- A. Foundations
  1. Muhammad
- B. Islamic invasions

III. Alliances with the Franks
- A. Pepin the Short
- B. Charlemagne

ST. AUGUSTINE OF CANTERBURY
(d. 605)

St. Augustine of Canterbury (d. 605) and Benedictine missionaries were instrumental in the conversion of the Anglo-Saxon king Ethelbert in England. King Ethelbert, however, did not force Christianity on his people, instead following the instructions of Pope Gregory the Great (ca. 540–604) to "destroy as few pagan temples as possible" but rather fill the temples with holy water and relics "so that, if the temples have been well built, you are simply changing their purpose" ("Letter to Mellitus," XI, 56).

ST. BONIFACE
(675–755)

It wasn't until a century later that St. Boniface, a British monk, evangelized on the European continent. After being named a bishop, he set up monasteries and was a wandering preacher in direct contact with converts in Germany. A famous story tells of how he chopped down a sacred oak tree dedicated to Thor, a Frankish god. When pagan witnesses saw that Boniface was not killed by Thor, many converted.

Muhammad The founder of Islam, regarded as a prophet by Muslims.

The Church's alliances with these formerly pagan tribes proved to be a great help in the security and defense of Christians and Western Europe itself during the Early Middle Ages, as several new external threats loomed. For example, St. Boniface developed an effective relationship with the Frankish leaders—first Charles Martel and then his son, Pepin the Short. As the pope's representative, St. Boniface crowned Pepin the Frankish king in 751. This helped cement an alliance between the Franks and the papacy that would bear great fruit under Pepin's son, Charlemagne.

The Rise of Islam and the Weakening of the Byzantine Empire

According to Islam, "There is no God but Allah, and **Muhammad** is his prophet." In 610, an Arabian merchant, Muhammad (570–632), had a conversion experience. Muhammad claimed that the angel Gabriel visited him and gave him a series of revelations that his followers recorded in writing in a sacred text called the Qur'an. Muhammad lived in Mecca in what is now Saudi Arabia for ten years after his conversion, teaching and developing his faith, but in 622, he and his followers, known as *Muslims*, met persecution. Their flight to Medina, called the *Hegira*, is the event that

Al Aqsa Mosque, the third holiest site in Islam, sits in the forefront with the Mount of Olives in the background in Jerusalem, Israel.

marks the first year of the Muslim era. Muhammad raised an army in Medina and returned to Mecca as a triumphant warrior. Their new faith, called *Islam* (Arabic for "submission"), spread like wildfire across the Arabian deserts.

After Muhammad's death in 632, his early successors spread the Islamic faith through previously Christian areas such as Damascus and Antioch in Syria, Jerusalem in Palestine, Alexandria and Carthage in northern Africa, Cyprus, southern Italy, and even parts of Spain. A war-weary, collapsing Byzantine Empire was virtually defenseless against the onslaughts of the Muslims. Although Muslims in general did not force their vanquished peoples to convert, they did impose taxes on the *infidels* (nonbelievers). This was incentive enough for many Christians to embrace Islam, especially in the East.

Fortunately for Christian survival, divisions within Islam over leadership helped weaken its forward thrust. The Byzantine emperor Leo the Isaurian curtailed the eastward expansion of Islam in 717. And in the West, the Franks under Charles Martel ("the Hammer") finally stopped the Muslim advance at the Battle of Tours (or Poitiers) in what is now northern France in 732.

The Islamic invasion had enormous consequences for Christianity. The three ancient patriarchates of Jerusalem, Antioch, and Alexandria fell; as a result, their influence in the Church ceased. The Byzantine Empire was continually occupied with fending off the advancing Muslims. Before the founding of Islam, Christianity had embraced the Mediterranean Basin, with its axis running from west to east. Now in the West, the center of Christianity shifted from the pope's see in Rome to the northern kingdom of the Frankish dynasty—the Carolingians—who were the pope's strongest ally in these perilous times.

Papal States The territory in modern-day central Italy that was overseen by the pope from the eighth century until 1870.

Because the Muslims controlled the Mediterranean Basin, Europe became economically, socially, and culturally isolated. The disorder and strife of the age helped create the feudal system, in which feudal lords made their own law and often declared war on their neighbors. However, the cooperation between the Franks and the Church helped create the Christian Middle Ages and spread Christianity throughout Europe.

The Western Church Aligns with the Franks

Between the aggressive nature of Islam and the expansionist activities of the Lombards, who captured Ravenna, a prominent city in what is now northern Italy, the Byzantine emperor was becoming less able to help protect the West. This forced the pope to look to the Franks for protection. At first he turned to Frankish leader Charles Martel, who saw no personal benefit in entering into an alliance with the papacy against Lombard aggression. But Martel's successor, his son Pepin the Short, saw great advantage in allying himself with the pope.

By Pepin's way of thinking, aligning himself with the pope would gain him status as the legitimate Christian ruler of the Franks. Pepin had recently usurped the Frankish throne from the Merovingians, and he petitioned Pope Zachary to declare him the legitimate Frankish ruler due to his de facto power. Pope Zachary consented and had St. Boniface crown Pepin king of the Franks in 751. Pope Zachary's successor, Pope Stephen III (752–757), recognized Pepin as king and his sons' right to succeed him. Subsequently, when the Church appealed to Pepin and the Franks for protection against the Lombards, Pepin's forces not only defeated the Lombards but also returned to the pope several previously captured territories.

Pope Stephen III in Paris petitioned Pepin the Short for help against the Lombards.

Pepin recognized the pope as ruler of a large part of Italy, granting him control of a wide strip of land in the middle of the Italian peninsula, the foundation of the **Papal States**. This controversial grant to the papacy of both land and the right to rule it—called the Donation of Pepin (756)—was enormously important for the pope's secular power and provided a major source of revenue for the papacy.

The Crowning of Charlemagne

Pepin's son, Charlemagne ("Charles the Great"), was a devoted family man, a devout Christian, a visionary ruler, and a powerful knight. Charlemagne emerged in 771 as a powerful king who ruled for forty-three years until his death in 814. Charlemagne's goal was the Christianization of Europe.

Under Charlemagne, the Franks were relentless in combating the Lombards. After Charlemagne led a victory over the Lombards in 774, Pope Adrian I gave him the title "Protector of the Papacy." In gratitude to Charlemagne, the pope submitted to his directives on how to rule the Papal States. A vigorous military leader, Charlemagne believed in the forceful conversion of conquered peoples, such as the Saxons. Among his many military campaigns, Charlemagne suffered a few military setbacks, but by the year 800, Charlemagne had created the most powerful empire in the West since the Roman Empire.

The crowning of Charlemagne as Holy Roman Emperor helped cement the relationship between the Church and the empire but further strained the relationship between the Church in the West and the East.

CHURCH INVOLVEMENT IN Feudalism IN THE EARLY MIDDLE AGES

King

PROVIDES

Fief and Peasants

Loyalty and Military Aid

GIVES BACK

Lords (vassals to king)

PROVIDES

Food, Protection, and Shelter

Homage and Military Service

GIVES BACK

Knights (vassals to lords)

PROVIDES

Food, Protection, and Shelter

Farm the Land and Pay Rent

GIVES BACK

Peasants (Serfs)

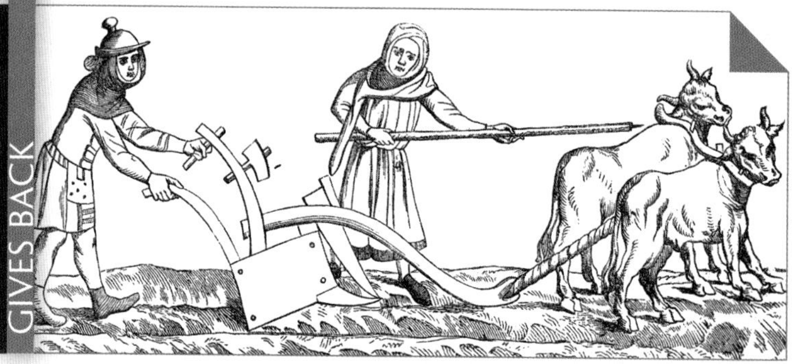

Because the Church was a landholder, she got caught up in the web of economic and political relationships that was feudalism. Some bishops and abbots became powerful barons involved in vassal relationships and endless warfare. Their spiritual responsibilities often fell by the wayside. Other bishops became vassals of strong lords and even kings. This made them subservient to secular leaders and led to the practice of **lay investiture**, by which secular lay leaders (such as the emperor of Germany, Otto I) selected the bishops throughout their domains.

Lay investiture and Church involvement in feudalism led to many abuses. One of these was **simony**, the buying and selling of Church offices, usually to a layperson, for financial gain. The feudal system handsomely rewarded holders of Church offices. Men who aspired to Church positions were often greedy and unspiritual. To secure power, they willingly took orders from the barons and kings.

lay investiture A practice in the Middle Ages whereby secular rulers chose the bishops for their territories, thus usurping the right of the pope to choose bishops.

simony The controversial practice of selling and buying positions or favor within the Church. The Church condemns this practice.

feudalism The governing system that prevailed in Europe in the Middle Ages in which a superior or lord granted land to a vassal in return for military services of that vassal.

Pope Leo III recognized Charlemagne's importance to Western Christianity by crowning him "Holy Roman emperor" at the Christmas Mass in Rome in 800. The Holy Roman Empire covered a territory that included present-day Europe but was centered in Aachen (Germany). The creation of the Holy Roman Empire alienated the Byzantine Empire. It clearly indicated the Church's break from the East. For the next four hundred years, the pope would crown each Holy Roman emperor, stressing that the Roman Catholic faith was the principle of unity holding together the various and often warring groups in the West.

For his part, Charlemagne had a genuine love of the Church, evidenced by his establishment of monasteries and schools for the training of clerics and others. He arranged for the copying of manuscripts. He appointed educated bishops and directed them to reform the clergy throughout the realm. He donated property and money to the Church and insisted on tithing to support the Church's work. He also adopted the *Roman Sacramentary*, a book for use in the liturgy, hoping that the common use of Latin would be a unifying force throughout the empire.

When Charlemagne died in 814, the Holy Roman Empire resembled what would become modern Europe. Unfortunately, the Holy Roman Empire itself would soon divide into East and West. Viking invasions from the north and the lack of strong imperial leaders led to **feudalism**, with its system of patrons and vassals. For both Europe and the Church, feudalism became the dominant political and economic system during the coming difficult centuries.

SECTION ASSESSMENT

NOTE TAKING

Use the outline you created for this section to help you answer the following questions.

1. Briefly describe how the following peoples came to Christianity: Bohemians, Irish, and Germans.
2. Trace the founding of Islam, and give the meaning of the name.

COMPREHENSION

3. What were Pope Gregory the Great's instructions regarding pagan temples after the people had converted to Christianity?
4. Identify Pepin the Short.
5. How was Islamic expansion slowed?
6. How did Charlemagne exhibit a genuine love for the Church?

VOCABULARY

7. What were the *Papal States*?
8. Define *simony*.

CRITICAL THINKING

9. How did the rise of Islam lead to a further split between the Eastern and Western Churches?

SECTION 2

High Middle Ages (1000–1300): Instability Leads to Reforms

MAIN IDEA

The Church in the High Middle Ages faced several internal and external challenges, beginning with the Great Schism of 1054 and including the damages that occurred in relation to the Crusades. However, reforms encouraged improvements, including a clarification of papal rule and doctrinal understandings of the Eucharist. There were many intellectual advances during this period (see Section 4).

In the High Middle Ages, political instability and the ongoing military and financial resources necessary for the Church to defend against Islam, especially in the East, were all factors that contributed to the Great Schism of 1054 (see the subsection "Rifts Leading to Separation between the Roman Church and Eastern Orthodox Church" in Chapter 3, Section 4), a truly wrenching event in the history of Christianity. This period and the time leading up to it were also marked by an influx of new invasions in the West, including the following:

- The Norsemen ravaged England and Ireland, demolishing most of the important monasteries that had served as centers of learning and missionary work.
- Danish Vikings penetrated deep into Europe, cruising up and down rivers and pillaging everything in their path. They destroyed Hamburg and sacked Paris. For fifty years they terrorized Europe.
- From the east came the ancestors of the Hungarians, the Magyars, who raided Germany, central France, and Italy until they were turned back by Otto the Great in 955.

Meanwhile, the Muslims renewed their attacks, even successfully raiding Rome and destroying several shrines there.

NOTE TAKING

Synthesizing Information. In your notebook, write one sentence that summarizes the internal and external challenges to the Church in the ninth to eleventh centuries. Then create a graphic organizer like the one on the right that summarizes the Church reforms that took place in the High Middle Ages. Add as many rectangles as necessary.

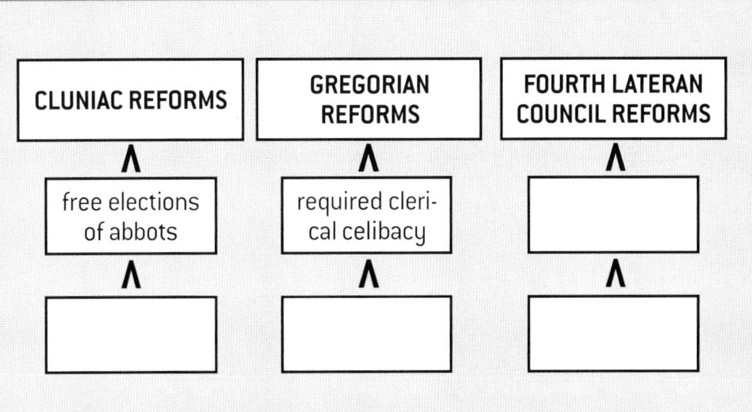

Finally, write one sentence that summarizes the three reasons Christians undertook the Crusades.

Cluny Abbey had a large effect on the Church. In addition to leading reform, the abbey produced four popes and its first six abbots were canonized.

Internally, the papacy of the ninth century through the first half of the eleventh was filled with corruption. Because the pope ruled the Papal States, his office became desirable for the dominant noble families who wanted to rule these lands. The fact that the Church survived this era of papal corruption and did not veer from the teaching of true doctrine or morals is proof that Christ is indeed faithful to his promise: "And behold, I am with you always, until the end of the age" (Mt 28:20).

Reforms from Cluny

In 910, the layman William of Aquitaine donated land for a new Benedictine monastery, Cluny, in France. From its founding, the monastery was to be free of the corrupt control of lords and bishops. It had free elections of abbots and was answerable only to the pope. Prayer was to be the primary activity, and a strict observance of the Rule of St. Benedict was the norm. Serious Christian discipleship, sacrifice, and generosity to the poor became the hallmarks of the Cluniac lifestyle.

As a result, Cluny became a fountainhead of reform activity. It founded many connected monasteries that were answerable only to Cluny. This helped unify Christian communities all over Europe and wrested some control of the Church from the secular authorities. Within two hundred years, more than twelve hundred monasteries adopted Cluniac reforms. Several able abbots from Cluny called for a general reform in the Church. Free from the clutches of feudalism, the reforms begun at Cluny eventually influenced some strong-minded reformers. One of these was St. Peter Damian.

Through the reforms of Cluny, a series of forceful popes sought to free the Church from secular control. A German, Pope Leo IX (1049–1054), was the first of these reformer popes. A relative of Holy Roman emperor Henry III, he traveled widely to fight against the abuses of clerical incontinence, lay investiture, and simony. A successor, Pope Nicholas II (1058–1061), is credited with creating the College of Cardinals, a body that would elect future popes. Hildebrand, a brilliant monk from Cluny who became Pope Gregory VII, was one of the most spiritually inspiring popes of the High Middle Ages.

THE WAY TO HAPPINESS IS LOVE

ST. BERNARD OF CLAIRVAUX (1090–1153), considered the last Church Father, was also a crusading reformer, brilliant organizer, and spiritual master of his day. In 1112, St. Bernard joined a new order of religious, the Cistercians, who lived a very strict form of the Benedictine Rule. Due to his magnetic personality, thirty of his friends and relatives followed St. Bernard, and he eventually built his own monastery in Clairvaux, France.

St. Bernard lived a life of strict fasting and penance. He wrote on many spiritual topics, especially on the love of God as the perfect way to happiness. Here are some of his lofty thoughts from his *Book on the Love of God*:

> Admit that God deserves to be loved very much, yea, boundlessly, because he loved us first, he infinite and we nothing, loved us, miserable sinners, with a love so great and so free. This is why I said at the beginning that the measure of our love to God is to love immeasurably. For since our love is toward God, who is infinite and immeasurable, how can we bound or limit the love we owe him? Besides, our love is not a gift but a debt. And since it is the Godhead who loves us, himself boundless, eternal, supreme love, of whose greatness there is no end, yea, and his wisdom is infinite, whose peace surpasses all understanding; since it is he who loves us, I say, can we think of repaying him grudgingly? "I will love you, my strength. The Lord is my rock and my fortress and my deliverer, my strength, in whom I will trust" (Ps. 18.1f). He is all that I need, all that I long for.

ASSIGNMENT

Write a short reflection, poem, journal entry, or prayer that tells of your commitment to love God with all of your heart.

St. Bernard of Clairvaux

The Fourth Lateran Council was the largest council to the date. The decisions reached at this council stood until the Council of Trent (1545–1563).

Reforms of Pope Gregory VII and His Successors

Pope Gregory VII's pontificate (1073–1085) was a milestone, the beginning of a reform that gained for the Church unparalleled status and power in Europe over the next two centuries. Baptized Hildebrand, Gregory VII gained the nickname "Hellbrand" for his fiery temperament, intellectual brilliance, and unflagging devotion to the Church's independence from secular government.

Gregory VII's reforms included an insistence on clerical celibacy throughout the Church, a move that led to revolts in some areas. He also moved staunchly to eradicate simony and stamp out lay investiture, the means used by secular rulers to control the Church. Pope Gregory VII firmly held that Christ founded the Church and commissioned her to welcome all humanity into a single society ruled by divine law. He believed that because the Church was founded by Christ, she is above all other human societies, including the state.

Pope Gregory VII's foundational beliefs were expressed in his controversial *Dictates of the Pope*, which, in twenty-seven propositions, spelled out the rights of the pope in relationship to secular rulers. Claiming absolute spiritual and temporal power, Pope Gregory VII decreed that only the pope could make new laws, depose emperors, wear imperial insignia, and convoke councils. The pope also claimed the power to release vassals from fealty (loyalty) to sinful rulers. The *Dictates* banned lay or imperial election of bishops or the pope.

The German emperor Henry IV crossed Pope Gregory VII on this matter and was excommunicated, a move supported by the German aristocracy and the peasants who were their serfs. Excommunication was a powerful weapon because medieval people believed that death outside the Church was a sentence to eternal damnation. A politically savvy Henry IV begged for the pope's forgiveness by standing barefoot in the snow outside a castle in Canossa, Italy, in 1077, where Pope Gregory VII was on his way to a council. Henry

IV received his pardon from Pope Gregory VII; however, he was quick to display his true colors when he returned to Germany and reestablished his power there. He marched on Rome with his armies, deposed Pope Gregory VII, and set up his own puppet pope. Rescued by some Normans, Pope Gregory VII died shortly afterward, proclaiming, "I have loved justice and hated iniquity; therefore, I die in exile."

Though it took several decades to sort out the mess Henry IV created by appointing an antipope (a false claimant of the Holy See), papal reform was well underway. The Concordat of Worms (1122) finally solved the question of lay investiture in a compromise that distinguished between the spiritual and temporal aspects of conferring power on a bishop. The emperor invested the bishop with the temporal sign of the office (the scepter), but only other churchmen could invest him with the spiritual signs (Book of Gospels, miter, ring, and pastoral staff).

Popes who succeeded Pope Gregory VII also instituted several reforms. The medieval papacy reached its zenith of worldly influence under Pope Innocent III, a brilliant canon lawyer who believed that Christ granted both spiritual and secular leadership to the pope. Pope Innocent III viewed Europe as one large monastery with himself as the abbot. People were to live as brothers and sisters and obey their father, the pope. If kings or others disagreed, they were disciplined. Pope Innocent III's greatest achievement was convoking the Fourth Lateran Council in Rome (1215). Attended by more than 1,200 leading churchmen, this council was a call to spiritual reform. Among its many teachings were the following:

- specification that instructions to the faithful were to be in vernacular, the language of the people
- reform of clerical life, including enforcement of clerical celibacy and the elimination of simony
- condemnation of heresies such as **Albigensianism**
- declaration of the secrecy of the confessional (betraying this would result in the loss of the priestly office and lifelong penance)
- requirement of annual Confessions and reception of Eucharist during the Easter season
- fixing of the number of sacraments at seven
- the clear definition of the doctrine of Jesus' Real Presence in the Eucharist (**transubstantiation**)
- an emphasis on increased devotion to the Eucharist, including Eucharistic Adoration, that coincided with widespread celebration of the Feast of Corpus Christi (Latin for "the Body of Christ"), first in a local diocese and then in the universal Church in the thirteenth century

The Middle Ages eventually saw, in large part due to the continuation of Gregorian reforms, an increase in personal piety on the part of the laity. The papacy united both spiritual and temporal power to help create a glimmer of **Christendom**, the Christian world envisioned by Pope Gregory VII. However, in later centuries, kings increasingly resented Church encroachments into the secular realm; the secular outreach of papal power was not to last.

Albigensianism A heresy that falsely taught that all matter is evil and the spirit is inherently good (with the two being therefore opposed to each other). Albigensianism spread throughout much of France in the thirteenth century.

transubstantiation Church teaching that holds that the substance of the bread and wine is changed into the substance of the Body and Blood of Christ at the consecration at Mass.

Christendom A time of great achievement in the Middle Ages when the Church and Western society were one. It refers to a group of nations in which Catholicism was the established religion of the state. In a wider sense, the term refers to a larger territory where most people are Christian.

The Crusades

In the centuries after the founding of Islam, there were some periods of peace between Christians and Muslims. However, there were also many instances of armed conflict. The **Crusades** began as a unified military response from Christians seeking to recover custody of holy sites in the Holy Land that had fallen under Muslim control centuries earlier. The Seljuk Turks conquered Palestine in 1073. Previously, Christian pilgrims had been allowed by the Muslim authorities to visit the Holy Land, but the Turks began to persecute Christians, preventing them from making pilgrimages to the holy sites.

A second religious motivation for the Crusades was defense of the Faith against heretics such as the Albigensians. The Albigensian Crusade took place from 1209 to 1229. The Albigensian heresy led to the creation of the **Papal Inquisition** by Pope Gregory IX in 1233 to confront future heretics. A third motivation was the objective of reuniting the Eastern and Western Churches as Christians from both sides would participate in the common effort of the Crusades. In exchange for their participation, crusaders were promised special graces (for example, the remission of suffering in **Purgatory**). There were other less noble objectives for the Crusades as well. Economic and political factors also stoked the crusading spirit, as landless peasants and lords hoped to gain territory from the Muslims. And the Crusades unfortunately resulted in the marginalization, and even brutal persecution, of both Muslims and Jews.

There were eight Crusades in total. A brief chronology provides a lens for examining both their positive and negative impact:

- The goal of the First Crusade (1095–1099) was to gain control of Jerusalem, and it was a military success. Called by Pope Urban III in 1095, the first Crusade set out from Constantinople. The crusaders captured Nicaea in June 1097 and Antioch in June 1098. Jerusalem fell on July 18, 1099. A massacre of Muslims and Jews ensued. When the battle ended, many knights went home, but others remained and ruled the Crusader states of Jerusalem and the surrounding areas until 1187.
- The Second Crusade (1147–1149), an effort to retake Edessa (in what is now Turkey), was a disaster. It was led by King Louis VII of France and King Conrad III of Germany. Conrad's forces were destroyed by the Turks. Louis led his crusaders to Damascus, only to be forced to withdraw. The defeat damaged the spirit of the crusaders.
- The Third Crusade (1189–1192) was a response to the fall of Jerusalem in 1187. Led by King Richard the Lionheart of England, King Philip II of France, and the Holy Roman emperor Frederick Barbarossa, it failed to recapture the holy city, which the brilliant Muslim leader Saladin had reconquered. However, Christian pilgrims did gain the right to visit Jerusalem.
- Even while the Third Crusade was being fought, Pope Innocent III was rounding up crusaders for the Fourth Crusade (1202–1204). The pope intended for the Crusade to reconquer the Muslim influence in the Holy Land. However, opponents of the Byzantine emperor offered the crusaders

Crusades A series of military expeditions made according to a solemn vow to return holy places to the possession of the Church from the Muslims.

Papal Inquisition A Church tribunal established in the thirteenth century that was first designed to curb the Albigensian heresy. In collaboration with secular authorities, papal representatives employed the Inquisition to judge the guilt of suspected heretics with the aim of getting them to repent. Unfortunately, before long, many abuses crept into the process.

Purgatory The final purification of all who die in God's grace and friendship but remain imperfectly purified. Purgatory is the final cleansing away of all sin and of all consequences of sin.

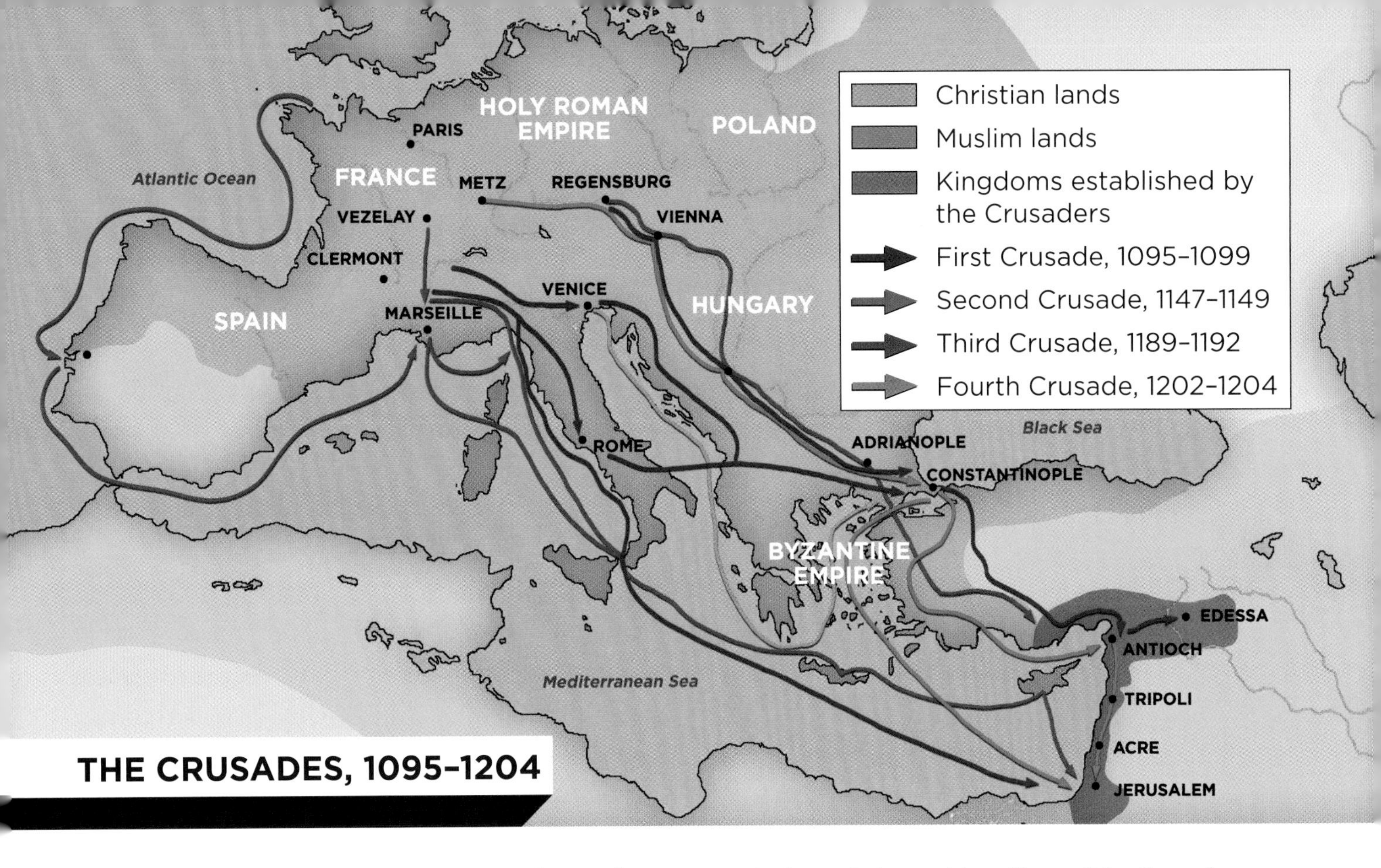

THE CRUSADES, 1095–1204

money to overthrow Constantinople on their behalf. The crusaders gave up on their original mission and took Constantinople on April 13, 1204, founding the Latin Empire of Constantinople. The Latin (Roman) liturgy was forced on the Byzantine population by the crusaders. The crusaders' behavior disgusted the pope, who now realized that many Catholic princes were more interested in their own power and enrichment than in winning nonbelievers over to the faith.

The other Crusades likewise were military failures. The so-called Children's Crusade (1212) was the most notable of the misguided efforts. Historians question how many children actually participated. It may have taken its name from a few well-known children crusaders. Most of the children who did participate and who didn't perish from starvation were sold into slavery to the Turks. The other Crusades also failed to achieve their intended goals. The last Christian stronghold in Muslim territory, Acre, fell in 1291, thus ending Christian control of the Holy Land.

In the end, the positive effects of the Crusades were mainly economic and intellectual. The Crusades stimulated trade and helped to weaken the feudal system, thus aiding the growth of cities and a new merchant class. They reopened Europe to the ideas, culture, and art of the East; importantly, they brought back the advances made by Muslim scientists, astronomers, mathematicians, and architects. The crusaders acquired Arabic commentaries on Aristotle, which significantly contributed to the revival of Christian philosophy and theology. In addition, the Crusades saw the rise of some notable semireligious orders of knights, such as the Knights Templar, loosely based on the Rule of St. Benedict. These orders promoted religious observances such as Mass attendance and prayer among their members and provided guards to protect Christian pilgrims. The Crusades also strengthened the idea of chivalry. Finally, the Crusades did open up the Holy Land to pilgrims. Like the Crusades themselves, pilgrimages were important for bringing people together and reinforcing the idea of a universal Church.

SECTION ASSESSMENT

NOTE TAKING

Using your sentence summary and the graphic organizer you created, answer the following questions.

1. Why did noble families seek to control the papacy in the ninth to eleventh centuries?
2. What was the benefit of monasteries founded in connection with the Benedictine monastery at Cluny?
3. What was one ruling Pope Gregory VII expressed in his *Dictates of the Pope*?
4. What were two teachings of the Fourth Lateran Council regarding the Eucharist?
5. In the end, what were the positive effects of the Crusades?

COMPREHENSION

6. How were the High Middle Ages proof that Christ is indeed faithful to his promise to always remain present in his Church?
7. How and why did Pope Gregory VII gain the nickname "Hellbrand"?
8. Why did Pope Gregory VII teach that the Church was above all other human societies, including the state?
9. What was the compromise on lay investiture that was decided by the Concordat of Worms?

VOCABULARY

10. What was *Albigensianism*?

ANALYSIS

11. From your lessons in past courses and further research, write an expanded definition of the term *transubstantiation*.

CRITICAL THINKING

12. How do you envision major religions sharing holy sites that have central importance to each?

SECTION 3

Late Middle Ages (1300–1450): Hope Persists through Disease and Division

MAIN IDEA

The Late Middle Ages was a period marked by the Black Death, wars, and the Western Schism. The period also gave rise to great saints, including St. Joan of Arc, St. Bridget of Sweden, and St. Catherine of Siena.

Pope Innocent III (1198–1216) believed that a strong papacy would be able to control the secular powers of Europe. But with the breakup of feudalism, the corruption of the kings, and the decline in the prestige of the papacy beginning with Pope Boniface VIII, any vestige of Christendom was disappearing. By the time of Pope Boniface VIII's pontificate (1294–1303), political factions were on the rise. Strong leaders opposed him at every turn. Two of his notable opponents were the politically astute kings Edward I of England and Philip the Fair (Philip IV) of France, both of whom wanted to reassert their control over the Church in their territories. One way they did it was to tax the clergy.

Pope Boniface VIII met the threat to his authority by issuing a papal bull, *Clericis Laicos* (1296). (A *papal bull* is an official papal document sealed with a red wax seal known as a *bulla.*) The document forbade taxation of the clergy and threatened excommunication for anyone who tried to collect or who paid tax without papal permission. King Edward I retaliated by removing police protection of the clergy and issuing economic and other penalties on the Church. Philip the Fair refused to recognize one of Boniface VIII's candidates for bishop. Outraged at the direct challenge to his authority, Pope Boniface VIII issued yet another

NOTE TAKING

Recognizing Connections. As you read through the section, match the people, terms, or descriptions in the right column with the event from the Late Middle Ages listed in the left column. In your notes, write one or two sentences for each event that include the corresponding people, terms, or events.

Unam Sanctam	St. Bridget of Sweden and St. Catherine of Siena
Avignon papacy	Pope Urban VI
The Western Schism	Pope Boniface VIII
	Conciliarism
	Centralization
	Papal supremacy

The Avignon papacy, *the period during which the pope resided in France rather than Rome, covered seven papacies and lasted from 1309 to 1377.*

bull, *Unam Sanctam* (1302). It asserted that the pope had authority over kings in both spiritual and temporal affairs. His claim to papal supremacy was the strongest of any medieval pope: "We declare, we proclaim, we define that it is absolutely necessary for salvation that every human creature be subject to the Roman Pontiff" (*Unam Sanctam*).

Philip the Fair responded by arresting Pope Boniface VIII at Anagni, an Italian diocese near Rome. The pope died shortly thereafter, a broken old man of eighty-six. Philip's action was a warning: strong kings would no longer take directions from a foreign pope. After the brief pontificate of Boniface's successor, Pope Benedict XI (1303–1304), Philip manipulated the next papal election to secure the papal throne for a French cardinal, who took the name Clement V (1305–1314). At Philip's insistence, Clement V withdrew the decrees of Boniface VIII and moved his residence to Avignon in southern France. Thus began a sixty-eight-year exile of the popes from Rome, which in turn led to the *Western Schism* (1378–1417), a period during which there were at times two or even three popes. These events of the fourteenth and fifteenth centuries were among the factors that contributed to later reform efforts within the Church, including what eventually became the Protestant Reformation in the sixteenth century.

The Avignon Papacy

Under the control of the French king, Pope Clement V was the first of seven popes to reside in Avignon from 1309 to 1377. All seven of these popes were French, as were 90 percent of the cardinals of this period. This period was also called the "Babylononian Captivity of the Papacy" or simply the "Babylonian Captivity," referring back to Jewish history of the Old Testament times when the Chosen People were carried off to exile in Babylon.

The Avignon popes lived an opulent lifestyle, exemplified by their building a magnificent palace for their residence and engaging in an expensive program of centralizing Church government, both of which added to the cost of supporting the Church. As a result, to the large outcry of most Europeans, the French popes imposed new and heavy taxes throughout the Christian world. They also returned to the old abuse of simony whereby they put friends and relatives on the Church payroll.

The Avignon papacy weakened the papacy in the eyes of most Europeans, especially those engaged in combat. For example, England and France were waging the Hundred Years' War (1337–1453), begun when the French king tried to confiscate English territories

THE BLACK DEATH

Renaissance poet Petrarch, who lived through the Black Death, or bubonic plague, that swept through Europe, believed the period so full of death and misery that those in later generations would not believe how bad it was: "O happy posterity, who will not experience such abysmal woe and will look upon our testimony as a fable," he wrote.

The plague was certainly real and very woeful to those who lived in that era. With a likely origin in China, the plague was caused by bacteria carried by fleas that lived on rats. Returning from the Crimea through the Black Sea (hence the name "Black Death"), a Genoese ship infested with flea-ridden rats carried this highly contagious disease to Europe. For those infected, it caused glandular swelling, fever, and death within a matter of hours. At the height of the plague (1347–1350), some cities were devastated. For example, Venice and Florence each lost one hundred thousand people; in Siena, four-fifths of the population died. Scholars estimate that from one-third to one-half of Europe's population perished. Not one country was spared. The clergy suffered huge losses, especially mendicants such as the Franciscans who ministered directly to the suffering masses. Whole monasteries were wiped out. The plague returned several times during the following decades. Note the approximate years and extent of the Black Death in the map:

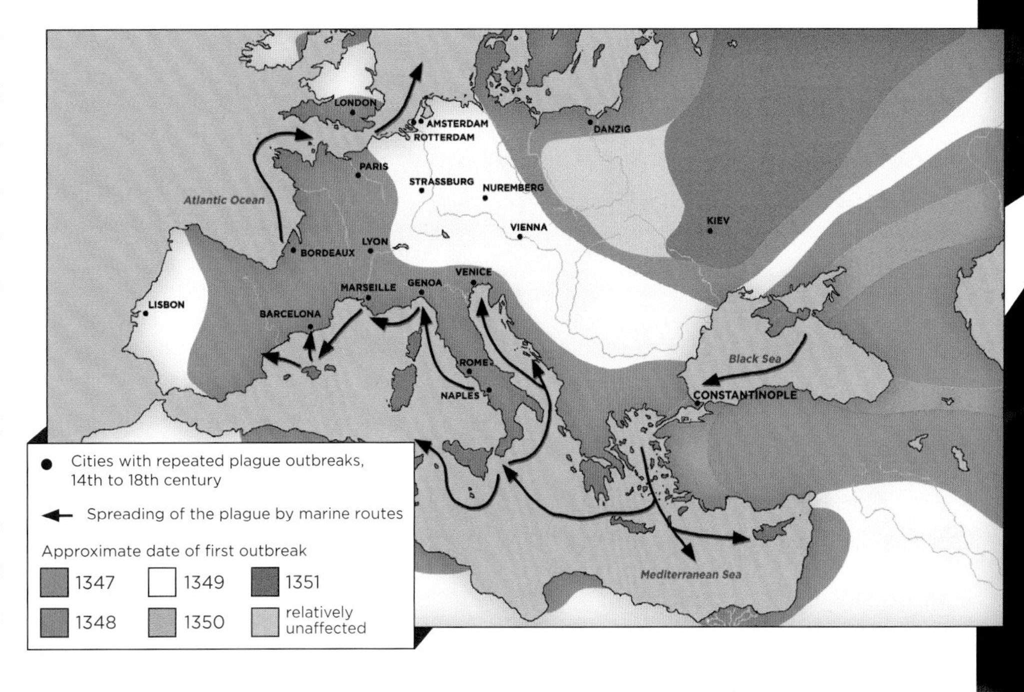

- The bubonic plague was spread along trade routes from Asia to Europe. Both cities and rural areas were affected. Only a few areas were spared.
- There was no medicine at that time that could cure the plague. Some doctors tried to drain sores on the skin of victims, but to little avail.
- Panic, despair, and lawlessness were rife. Worry over one's death became the central preoccupation. The primary occupation of the time was to bury the dead. When cities ran out of coffins, the dead were instead buried in huge pits.

ASSIGNMENT

One of the corporal works of mercy is "visit the sick." Put this work into practice in the next week. For example, visit an elderly neighbor or relative, bring schoolwork or social updates to a classmate who is ill, or volunteer at a local hospital or care facility. Write a journal entry with a reflection on your experience.

located in southwestern France. In the early years of this war, the English were especially incensed at the Avignon papacy, asserting that the pope was just another political agent of the French government. The infamous conflict—which consisted of raids and naval battles that were broken up by periods of uneasy peace—tilted toward the side of the English until the famous Battle of Orléans (1428–1429). It was during this battle that the young St. Joan of Arc, the Maid of Orléans, led a French force that defeated the English, thus turning the tide of the war in France's favor and leading to England's withdrawal from most French territory (except Calais). In addition to the English, the Germans and Italians were unhappy with the Avignon papacy as well.

Pious Christians were scandalized by the corrupt lifestyle of the Avignon papacy and unhappy that the pope was not living in Rome, the proper diocese of residence for the successor of St. Peter. The last of the Avignon popes, Pope Gregory XI, had considered returning to Rome but was reluctant to follow through. However, the pleadings of two remarkable and holy women, St. Bridget of Sweden (1303–1373) and St. Catherine of Siena (1347–1380), were instrumental in his overcoming his indecision. St. Bridget did not live long enough to see her dream of the pope's residing in Rome realized. A strong voice for reform, she wrote to Pope Gregory XI: "In your curia arrogant pride rules, insatiable cupidity and execrable luxury."

St. Catherine of Siena lived to see the pope's return to Rome. In 1376, she went to Avignon and pleaded with Gregory XI to return to Rome. She argued that from the See of Peter, he could better help Christians in the aftermath of the horrific Black Death, the scourge of bubonic plague that cost many lives. She also pointed out that he could be a more impartial broker for peace between warring England and France and the continually fighting Italian city-states if he lived in Rome. Historians debate how much the thirty-one-year-old saint influenced Pope Gregory XI's decision, but shortly after hearing Catherine's pleas, he did return to Rome.

Unfortunately, he lived only a short time longer. With the election of a new pope—the Italian pope Urban VI (1378–1389)—the Church faced one of the gravest crises in her history, one that would lead to a schism within the Church that would prove fatal to Christendom.

Though it looked as though society was disintegrating, all was not lost. During these despairing times, anonymous holy men and women endangered their lives to minister to the sick. Even at the opulent papal court in Avignon, the popes of the period organized aid for plague victims and offered sanctuary for Jews who were being scapegoated for causing the plague. Visionary and practical spiritual writers also emerged at this time to give the Church hope. For example, *The Imitation of Christ*, attributed to Thomas à Kempis (ca. 1380–1471), promoted a timeless path to personal holiness—following Christ—regardless of the vicissitudes confronting a Christian in the external world.

The Western Schism (1378–1417) and New Heresy

The return of the papacy to Rome was not a panacea for the corruption that had crept into the Church's hierarchy. During the Avignon papacy, Rome had become an impoverished city ruled in large part by mob violence. When Pope Gregory XI died in 1378, the cardinals, the majority of whom were French, wanted to leave Rome. However, due to a very strict law governing papal elections, the new pope had to be elected in the place where the previous pope had died.

As the cardinals met to elect a new pope, a mob broke into the palace where the election was being held and told the cardinals that they must elect a Roman pope or else their lives would be in danger. The cardinals did not elect a Roman, but they did choose an Italian, the bishop of Bari, who became Pope Urban VI. The cardinals attended Pope Urban's coronation ten days after the election and swore their loyalty to him. But three months later, the French cardinals, bothered by Pope Urban's obnoxious and abrasive behavior, claimed that they had been pressured into electing an Italian pope. They left Rome, announced to the world that they had made a mistake, deposed Urban, and elected a Frenchman as the new pope. He took the name Clement VII and, with his retinue of French cardinals and many Italian cardinals, headed to Avignon. He is known in history as an *antipope*—that is, a person who claims the papacy over a legitimately elected pope.

Neither man gave up his claim to the papal office. Upon their deaths, they were succeeded by other claimants to St. Peter's throne, each declaring his rival illegitimate. This was the Western Schism (also known as the Papal Schism); Western Europe was divided between two rival popes. Christians did not know who the true pope was. The French and Scots backed Clement VII; the English and Germans backed Urban VI. During the period of the Western Schism there were four popes, including Urban VI, in the Roman line; one other Avignon pope, Benedict XIII, succeeded Clement.

conciliarism An erroneous idea, popular in the Middle Ages, that an ecumenical council of the Church had more authority than the pope and could depose him if they so desired.

The Western Schism gave rise to **conciliarism**, the erroneous theory that Church reform and governance could best take place through a council rather than through direct papal rule. Conciliarism held that bishops gathered in a council had final governing authority in the Church. The first council convened to solve the crisis took place at Pisa in Italy in 1409. More than five hundred delegates attended, the majority of them priests or nobles. The major topic of discussion was conciliarism itself. But the Council of Pisa only worsened matters. It deposed both rival popes and named a third pope, Alexander V, as a compromise candidate. Neither the Roman pope nor the Avignon pope acknowledged the authority of the council, and neither stepped down.

Eventually, Sigismund of Bohemia, who would become the Bohemian king, convoked the Council of Constance (1414–1418) to resolve the scandal. At first, the decrees of the council were hostile to papal authority, claiming that councils' rulings were superior to rulings of the pope, who was bound to obey their decrees. After the council was in session for several months, the Avignon pope Gregory XII (recognized by the Church as the legitimate pope) sent legates to Constance to convoke the council formally and thus make it legitimate from that point on. He then abdicated the papal throne of his own free will. The council deposed the other two popes. Cardinals and representatives from five different nations elected Pope Martin V (1417–1431), effectively ending the scandal.

John Hus before the Council of Constance

While the Council of Constance ended the schism, not all questions were resolved. For one thing, Pope Martin V never signed the council's decree giving councils supreme governing authority. This omission left fertile ground for a future clash between the backers of conciliarism and the supporters of papal primacy. According to the agreements made at the Council of Constance, councils were to meet frequently to work on reforming the Church. However, a crisis took place during the reign of Pope Eugene IV (1431–1449).

Pope Martin V had convoked the Council of Basel shortly before his death. His successor, Eugene IV dissolved the council, but many of the participants refused to leave. After more discussion, mainly involving the question of a council's authority in relationship to the pope, Pope Eugene IV eventually moved the council to Florence to discuss reunion with Greek Christians. The rebellious holdouts, who refused to assemble at the pope's new location, deposed him and elected the last antipope, Felix V. But by that point very few people inside or outside of the Church supported these schismatics. The Council of Basel lingered on until 1449, when the antipope resigned. Triumphing over conciliarism, papal primacy was reestablished once and for all. Pope Pius II formally condemned the "deadly poison" of conciliarism in 1460 and threatened to excommunicate anyone who would appeal to an ecumenical council's rulings over the pope's.

But rising political factionalism and the decline of papal prestige had opened the Church to attacks from a new generation of critics of the Church whom some considered heretics. England's John Wyclif (ca. 1320–1384), for example, severely criticized the financial policies of the Avignon papacy and attacked papal authority. He also dismissed the validity of the hierarchy, the sacraments, and the priesthood. Jan Hus (1369–1415) echoed Wyclif's teachings in Bohemia. He stressed the authority of the Bible and the important role of preaching, and he denied the ultimate authority of the pope in doctrinal matters. On a promise that he would not be harmed, Hus attended the Council of Constance to defend his ideas. However, before Hus could adequately explain his views, the council had him burned at the stake as a dangerous heretic. This shameful betrayal backfired, as followers of Hus's teachings extolled him as a martyr-hero. A bitter twenty-year civil war followed, hurting the cause of the Church in Bohemia for decades.

Some who attempted to reform the Church as they saw it—including some considered heretics such as Wyclif and Hus—anticipated in small ways the revolution that would soon take place. The Middle Ages were slowly giving way to a different period that was characterized by its reaction to the Middle Ages. Commerce was growing, and some merchant families, such as the Medici family of Florence, became fabulously wealthy. They dominated local governments, became patrons of the arts, and tried to influence the Church. (The Medici family produced several popes.) The Black Death helped contribute to a major decline in monasticism. The Church was ready and open to reform. Unfortunately this reform (to be discussed in Chapter 6) was accompanied by a fragmentation of Christianity.

SECTION ASSESSMENT

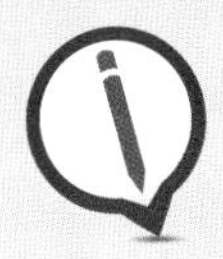

NOTE TAKING

Use the summary sentences you wrote in your notebook to help you answer the following questions.

1. What was the subject of the papal bull *Unam Sanctam*, written by Pope Boniface VIII?
2. What was another large expense to the Church during the Avignon papacy besides the centralization of the Church government?
3. What is the Church's teaching on *conciliarism*?

COMPREHENSION

4. Why was the period of the Avignon papacy referred to as the "Babylonian Captivity"?
5. What was St. Joan of Arc's role in the Hundred Years' War?
6. What were two arguments St. Catherine of Siena gave Pope Gregory XI for moving the papacy back to Rome?
7. How did the Church provide hope during the Black Death?
8. What was the decision of the Council of Constance?
9. Identify John Wyclif and Jan Hus.

REFLECTION

10. Imagine living during the time of the Black Death. How might the message of the Gospel have impacted your daily life during that time?

SECTION 4

Shedding Light on the "Dark" Ages

MAIN IDEA

To call the Middle Ages the "Dark Ages" is in many ways a misnomer as the period brought significant advancement in higher-level education, rational thought, and architecture. It was the time of St. Thomas Aquinas's seminal work, the *Summa Theologiae*, and the founding of mendicant religious communities, especially the Dominicans and Franciscans.

Though often called "dark," and in spite of its unstable politics and the bubonic plague, the period of the Middle Ages was not "dark" to the advancement of learning, philosophical thought, architecture and engineering, science, and religious devotion. And the Church played a crucial role in the development of all during the Middle Ages. Natural philosophy, or natural science, was a key subject and key overall framework of study at medieval universities founded by the Church.

Natural philosophy paralleled with **scholasticism**, an advanced form of reasoning that tried to reconcile the newly rediscovered philosophy of Aristotle with the truths of the Church. Aristotle, a brilliant Greek philosopher of pre-Christian times, had studied most fields of human knowledge. His detailed observations and conclusions cogently explained many natural phenomena in the world. However, from a Christian point

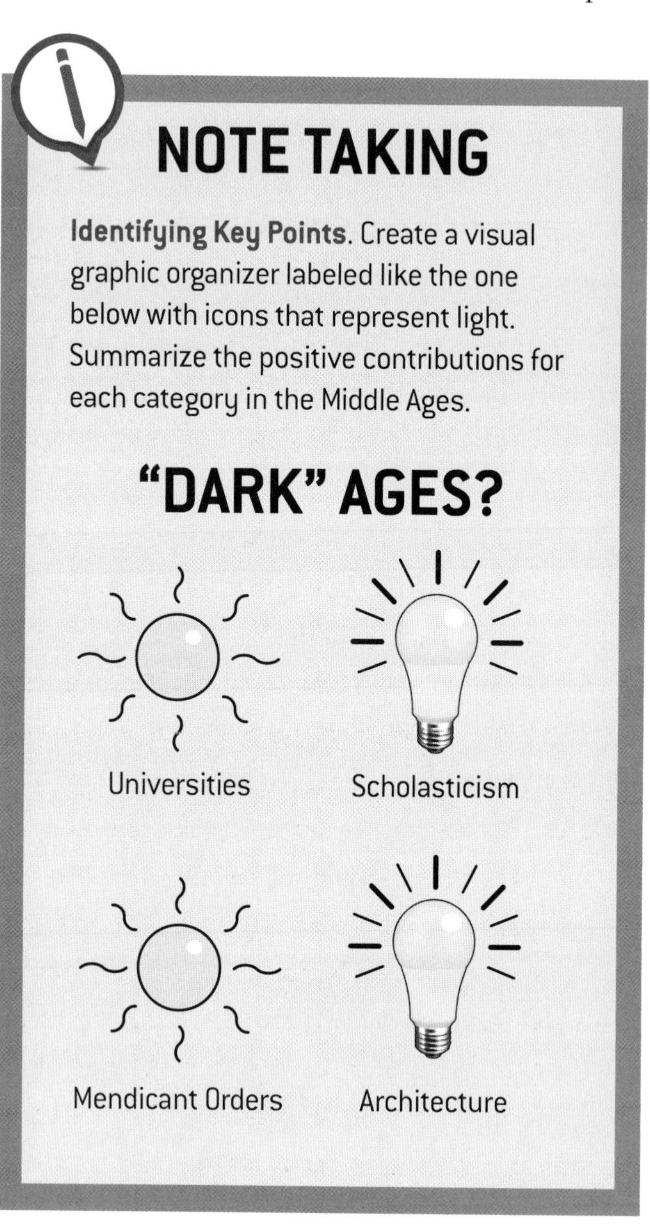

scholasticism The theological system that arose during the Middle Ages, developed notably by St. Thomas Aquinas, balancing faith and reason and relying heavily on classical philosophy and the Church Fathers.

The University of Paris, one of the oldest universities in Europe, continues to provide students with liberal arts education with an emphasis on theology.

of view, Aristotle could not explain everything, as he did not have the benefit of Divine Revelation to aid him in his quest for knowledge. A goal of the scholastics was to synthesize the knowledge of philosophy and theology and create one integral system of thought. This was a monumental task, but one of history's true geniuses—St. Thomas Aquinas—met it admirably.

The rise of medieval universities and the advanced reasoning in scholasticism leading to St. Thomas Aquinas's masterpiece of theological thought—the *Summa Theologiae*—alone dispel the supposed darkness of the Middle Ages. Other key accomplishments, including the development of the Gothic style of architecture and the founding of lasting mendicant religious communities such as the Dominicans, Franciscans, Carmelites, and Augustinians, further spread the light of faith and knowledge that was part of this era.

Rise of Universities

Well before the Early Middle Ages, cathedrals and monasteries often had schools attached to them so that not only the clergy but also others within society (typically the nobility) could achieve literacy and civil training. When the universities came into existence during the High Middle Ages, education became more accessible to more people.

More than eighty universities were founded before 1300. Imitating the guilds of craftsmen, universities came into existence when students and teachers grouped together for mutual protection, forming a *universitas*, a kind of corporation. As in guilds, the masters (teachers) had to earn a license while students earned degrees to mark off the progress of their studies. Students (males only) entered the university at age fourteen or fifteen and spent six years studying the *liberal arts*—arithmetic, geometry, astronomy, music theory, grammar, logic, and rhetoric—before earning a bachelor's degree. If students wanted to further their studies, they would take up to twelve more years to earn a master's and doctoral degree in one of three fields: medicine, law, or theology.

There were two major types of universities in the Middle Ages. The southern type, modeled on the University of Bologna in Italy (1088), stressed law and medicine. Students at these institutions controlled the corporation by hiring or firing teachers and determining the curriculum. If a teacher announced a series of classes, and students did not come, the teacher could not collect a fee and would lose his job. The northern universities such as Oxford (ca. 1200), Cambridge (1209), Padua (1222), Kraków (1364), and especially the University of Paris (late twelfth century) stressed theology, canon law, and the liberal arts. Professors had more authority in these institutions. For example, they made rules to govern student behavior such as swearing and gambling and fined students for breaking curfews or displaying bad table manners. The professors' salaries came from the Church, not from students.

Learning at the university consisted mainly of listening to lectures in Latin (since students came from many nations). Books, which were hand-transcribed, were expensive and limited, and notes were rarely taken. Students relied on their memories to learn and then proved their mastery of the subject by passing oral exams in which they gave reasons for or against the various propositions taught by the teachers.

St. Paul appears above St. Albert the Great and a young St. Thomas of Aquinas.

Scholasticism and St. Thomas Aquinas (1225–1274)

Scholasticism gradually developed at the universities as a way to advance learning. Peter Abelard's influential early twelfth-century work titled *Sic et Non* (*Yes and No*) helped develop the scholastic method of teaching, whereby various authorities and their contradictory positions were cited, analyzed, debated, disputed, and then reconciled. The scholastic method encouraged two or more masters (professors) and sometimes students to question, postulate, examine, and logically arrange details into a meaningful whole. Synthesis of the tradition and Church teaching was the driving force behind the method.

St. Thomas Aquinas's work of bridging the philosophy of Aristotle with theology and forming it into one integrated system of thought was the summit of the intellectual achievements of the Middle Ages. Born south of Rome around 1225, Thomas entered the Dominican Order against his family's wishes and eventually ended up at Cologne, where he became the student of St. Albert the Great, a brilliant scholastic thinker and teacher. Thomas's classmates called him "the Dumb Ox" because of his weight, seriousness, and slow movement. However, Albert defended his prize pupil by prophesying, "This dumb ox will fill the world with his bellowing." And St. Thomas Aquinas did just that. He lectured in many of the leading universities in Europe, including the top school of the day, the University of Paris. He also wrote prolifically, producing his masterpiece of theological thought, the *Summa Theologiae*.

In the *Summa*, St. Thomas Aquinas showed the rationality or intelligibility of faith. He also defended human intelligence as a prelude to faith. Thomas argued that human reason is supreme in its own domain but can't master everything, especially the mysteries of faith. However, Thomas showed that these revealed truths are not beyond rational explanation. With the gift of faith, believers can see the intrinsic intelligibility of the mysteries of Christianity—for example, the Incarnation, the Resurrection, and the Trinity.

St. Thomas Aquinas's masterful thought did not gain easy acceptance in his own lifetime. The archbishop of Paris believed his teachings were taboo because of his references to Aristotle. Others such as St. Bonaventure (1221–1274) emphasized the mystical approach to God through prayer, contemplation, and meditation. They stressed human will and downplayed the role of human reason.

In 1274, St. Thomas Aquinas had a mystical experience of God's presence. He said that all he had written was chaff compared to what he had experienced. He stopped writing, and three months later, he died.

Locate and read St. Thomas Aquinas's five proofs for the existence of God from the *Summa Theologiae*. Write a one-page report summarizing your findings.

Although **Thomism** had its opponents even after St. Thomas Aquinas's death, the Church eventually endorsed his thought: in his 1879 encyclical *Aeterni Patris* (*On the Restoration of Christian Philosophy*), Pope Leo XIII gave special theological prominence to Thomism. Thus, Thomas's writings—especially the *Summa*—have powerfully influenced Church teaching. St. Thomas Aquinas's clarity of thought, insistence on truth, respect for human reason, and defense of Christian Revelation have helped the Church explain and defend her teaching up to modern times.

The Influence of Mendicant Religious Communities

To respond to the ever-growing migration to cities, a new form of religious life developed in the Church during the High Middle Ages to serve the needs of the city people—the *mendicant* or "begging" orders. They served God's people by witnessing to simple Gospel values. Among the new religious orders founded at this time were the Carmelites, Augustinians, Dominicans, and the Franciscans. Unlike members of earlier orders who lived in monasteries, the early Dominican and Franciscan *friars* (brothers or priests) kept on the move. They lived a simple life of poverty, preaching in towns and begging for their food and shelter. In time, because hundreds of friars joined these orders, they had to settle for communal living arrangements and the ownership of property to help support their large numbers.

Thomism Teachings that follow the theology and philosophy of St. Thomas Aquinas, especially from the *Summa Theologiae*. St. Thomas presents five ways by which humans can infer the existence of God through reason. He also teaches that the highest truths are those which are freely revealed by God.

ARCHITECTURE OF THE MIDDLE AGES

The construction of magnificent cathedrals and abbey churches between 1000 and 1400 was another great accomplishment of the period. These churches symbolized the spirit and grandeur of the Church of the Middle Ages and testified to the influx of people to cities.

The older Romanesque style of cathedrals had very thick walls and small openings for light. Romanesque cathedrals' similarity to fortresses symbolized the strength of the Church against the forces of darkness in a turbulent society.

The construction of cathedrals required a tremendous investment of time and resources. As the largest buildings in each town, they also served as a meeting place for social activity and even trade. Pilgrims would sleep on their floors. Cathedrals also became a source of rivalry among towns, each trying to outdo the other constructing bigger and better cathedrals. The roof of the Romanesque Beauvais Cathedral in France collapsed several times as architects built the roof by trial-and-error using a new process.

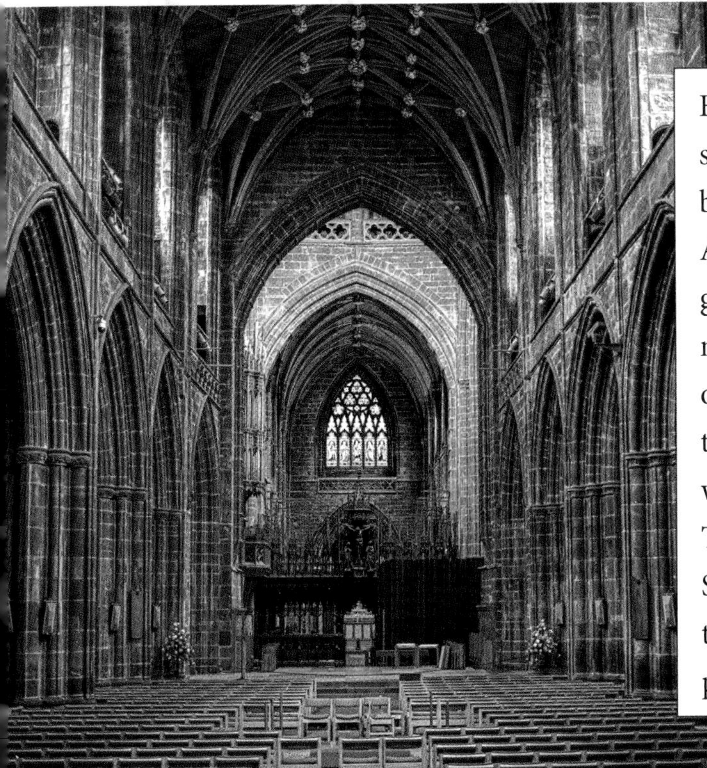

Each cathedral contained the bishop's *cathedra* (chair), symbolizing his teaching authority and power. Thus, the bishop's church, representing the successorship to the Apostles, serves as a symbol of unity for the people in a given diocese. The people would stand in the *nave*, the main body of the church, and witness the spectacle going on in front of them. The *chancel* (choir area) contained the high altar, the bishop's chair, and stalls for the priests who would chant the daily prayers of the Divine Office. The typical cathedral also had a high pulpit from which Sunday sermons would be preached to the faithful; a baptismal font; and along the nave, many side altars where priests would celebrate private or small-group Masses.

The Gothic style, appearing first in northern France in the twelfth century, featured high, thin walls, ribbed vaulting, and flying buttresses to distribute the weight of the ceilings. This style lent itself to the use of many stained glass windows, which allowed streams of colored light to filter in to the worshippers below. Stained glass windows often featured scenes from the life of Jesus and the Scriptures, performing a powerful visual catechesis to parishioners and visitors, who for the most part could not read. These cathedrals' high ceilings and soaring exteriors drew attention heavenward, leading parishioners to consider God and heavenly things; their central location within cities invited visits from neighboring townspeople and traveling pilgrims.

Europe's cathedrals stand as a living memorial to the countless anonymous ancestors in the Faith of today's Christians. Their hard work was part of an unprecedented institutional effort to praise God in stone.

The Franciscans (left) and the Dominicans (right) are mendicant orders founded in the early thirteenth century.

St. Dominic de Guzmán (1170–1221), a Spanish priest, founded his Order of Preachers (the Dominicans) to combat heresies, most notably the Albigensian heresy in southern France. The Dominicans modeled their rule on that of St. Augustine of Hippo and prized learning as an effective means to defend the Faith. Dominicans took the vow of poverty and became leaders in the emerging universities. In later years, they also assumed a prominent role on the court of the Papal Inquisition, the special Church tribunal set up to curb the spread of heresies. Pope Honorius III called the Dominicans "invincible athletes of Christ" whose main mission was to preach the Gospel. They are also known as the Black Friars because their religious habit is a white robe covered with a black cloak. St. Thomas Aquinas was a Dominican.

St. Francis of Assisi (1183–1226) founded the Order of Friars Minor, popularly known as the Franciscans. Like the Dominicans, the Franciscans took vows of poverty, chastity, and obedience and lived simply among the people, bringing Christ to the marketplace.

St. Francis never planned to found a religious order. But through following Christ in a literal way, preaching and living Gospel simplicity, Francis attracted followers. By 1208, when his number of followers grew to twelve, he traveled to Rome to ask for approval of his rule. Early Franciscans lived in Umbria, but members preached throughout Italy and were known for their life of poverty. Francis himself ministered to the sick and preached peace, even joining the Fifth Crusade in an attempt to share the Gospel with Muslims (1219). St. Clare of Assisi (1194–1253), a friend of Francis's, left her affluent family to found an order of religious women known as the Poor Clares.

The mendicant orders helped the Church at a critical time. Radical reforming groups such as the *Waldensians* (founded by Peter Waldo in the late twelfth century) had begun to emerge as a critical response to a Church grown rich and powerful. These heretical reformers attacked the hierarchical nature of the Church and her sacramental and priestly system and preached that the only true Christian was one who vowed total poverty. In contrast, the mendicants showed that Christians could live the Gospel within the hierarchical Church.

SECTION ASSESSMENT

NOTE TAKING

Use the graphic organizer you created to help you answer the following items.

1. Explain the importance of the scholastic method.
2. Why were primarily oral exams used in the universities of the Middle Ages?
3. What was the purpose of high ceilings in Gothic cathedrals?
4. What was the difference between mendicant orders and earlier religious communities that lived in monasteries?

COMPREHENSION

5. How did the *Summa Theologiae* show the rationality of faith?
6. What was the difference between the southern and northern universities?
7. What was the *cathedra*? What did it symbolize?

REFLECTION

8. What might attract you to a mendicant order?

CRITICAL THINKING

9. In your opinion, does the moniker "Dark Ages" fit the Middle Ages or not? Give several reasons to support your opinion.

Section Assignments

Focus Question

How does the Church persist in proclaiming the Gospel during evolving political, religious, and social upheaval?

Complete one of the following:

- Prepare a one- to two-page biographical synopsis on the life of one of the popes or secular leaders mentioned in this chapter.

- Read the short document *Nostra Aetate* (*In Our Times*): *The Relation of the Church to Non-Christian Religions* (www.vatican.va). In three to four well-constructed paragraphs, write three specific things the document teaches about the Church's relationship with Hinduism, Islam, and Judaism.

- Research one of the monasteries that were built during the Early Middle Ages in the centuries following the fall of the Roman Empire. Write three to four paragraphs on its history, its role within the society of the country where it was located, and other interesting features, such as whether it is still in operation to the present day.

INTRODUCTION

The Church Offers Spiritual Recourse

- Why did the Church's image of sheepfold gain prominence during the Middle Ages? Describe and explain an image you have for the Church that reflects events in the local and universal Church today.

SECTION 1

Early Middle Ages (476–1000): The Rise of Islam and the Founding of the Papal States

- Research and share an example not named in this section of how monasteries contributed to the preservation of formal scholarly knowledge and regional cultural elements in medieval Europe.

SECTION 2

High Middle Ages (1000–1300): Instability Leads to Reforms

State in one succinct sentence the overall goal of the Church in most of the Crusades. What was the overall outcome of the Crusades, and what is their legacy?

SECTION 3

Late Middle Ages (1300–1450): Hope Persists through Disease and Division

Research and write a three-paragraph report on the history and current status of Palais des Papes, the seat of antipopes during the Late Middle Ages.

SECTION 4

Shedding Light on the "Dark" Ages

How did the newly forming mendicant orders and Catholic universities throughout Europe work together, at least on a complementary basis, to support the work of the broader Church? Research your answer and write your response in three to four written paragraphs.

Chapter Assignments

Choose and complete at least one of the three assignments to assess your understanding of the material in this chapter.

1. Comparing and Contrasting Religious Order Ministries

You will recall from this chapter that the Benedictines, the Dominicans, and the Franciscans were three of the key religious orders founded during the Middle Ages. Briefly research the work that these three religious orders are involved in throughout the world today. How do their ministries continue to reflect the goals of their founders so many centuries ago? Write a two- to three-page essay comparing and contrasting the current primary ministries of these three religious orders. Your essay may be organized as follows:

I. Introduction

II. The Benedictines

A. Founding

B. Charism

C. Primary ministry

(Repeat this structure for the Dominicans and Franciscans.)

V. Conclusion

A. How are these religious orders alike?

B. How are these religious orders different?

Make sure to label all references, include citations, and write your essay using MLA style.

2. The Holy Characteristics of the Saints of the Middle Ages

Holiness is a mark of the Church. It is a grace that allows a person to become fully human. It is the mark of the Church that calls all people to saintliness. How did the saints and popes of the Middle Ages exhibit holiness? Do the following:

- Choose five figures from the following list, or wait for your teacher to assign you five people.

St. Albert the Great

St. Benedict of Nursia

St. Bernard of Clairvaux

St. Catherine of Siena

St. Clare of Assisi

St. Columban

St. Dominic de Guzmán
St. Francis of Assisi
St. Gertrude
Pope Gregory VII (Hildebrand)
St. Joan of Arc
Pope Leo IX
St. Margaret of Scotland
St. Patrick of Ireland
St. Thomas Aquinas

- For each individual,
  - prepare one visual slide (e.g., PowerPoint or Prezi) with the figure's name, a one-paragraph biography, and a photo;
  - prepare a second slide with an image that represents how the saint or pope lived his or her holiness; and
  - on a third slide, display a short quotation by or about the figure that represents his or her holiness.

Plan a five- to seven-minute live oral presentation of the slides. If you are not able to share this presentation during class, videorecord it.

3. Gothic Stained Glass Window Project

Replicate a stained glass window from a Gothic church or cathedral of the Middle Ages (e.g., Milan, Notre Dame de Paris, Cologne, Chartres). There are several ways to complete the project. One simple way is to (1) find a photo of a stained glass window; (2) tape a copy of the photo to a window; (3) place another blank piece of paper over the copy and lightly trace the outline with a pencil; and (4) use colored pencils to fill in the stained glass design while erasing the pencil lines and replacing them with color.

Include a one-page written report with your stained glass illustration. Your report should include the following information:

- background on the cathedral (e.g., years of construction, year of dedication)
- significant event that occurred at the cathedral during the Middle Ages
- information about the stained glass window you chose (e.g., its subject, artist)
- how the cathedral is being used today

Prayer

St. Thomas Aquinas's Prayer for Students before Study

Ineffable Creator,
who, from the treasures of your wisdom,
have established three hierarchies of angels,
have arrayed them in marvelous order
above the fiery heavens,
and have marshaled the regions
of the universe with such artful skill,
you are proclaimed
the true font of light and wisdom,
and the primal origin
raised high beyond all things.

Pour forth a ray of your brightness
into the darkened places of my mind;
disperse from my soul
the twofold darkness
into which I was born:
sin and ignorance.

You make eloquent the tongues of infants.
Refine my speech
and pour forth upon my lips
the goodness of your blessing.

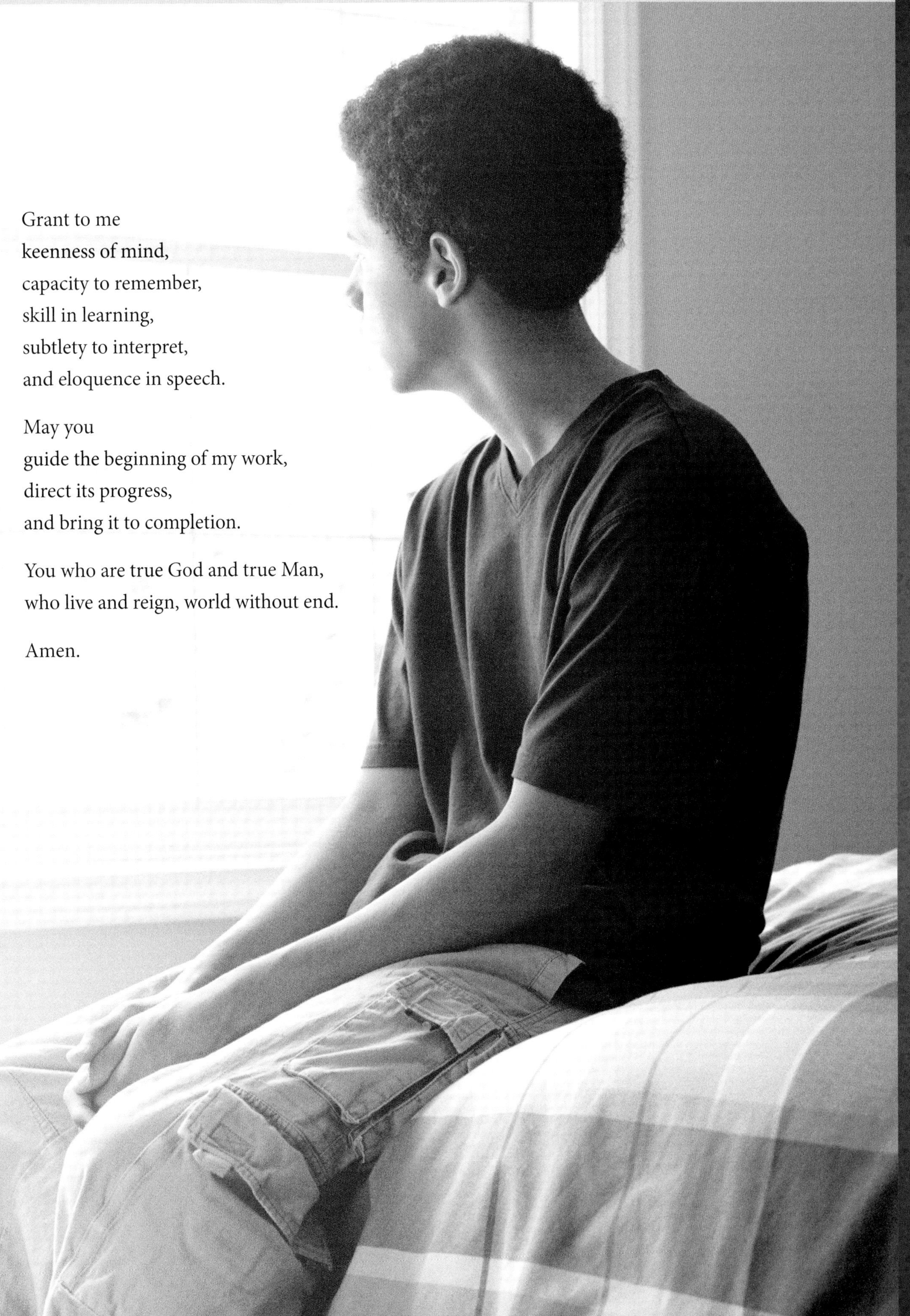

Grant to me
keenness of mind,
capacity to remember,
skill in learning,
subtlety to interpret,
and eloquence in speech.

May you
guide the beginning of my work,
direct its progress,
and bring it to completion.

You who are true God and true Man,
who live and reign, world without end.

Amen.

5

THE CHURCH IN THE RENAISSANCE AND THE AGE OF EXPLORATION

BRAZIL AND THE WORLD CELEBRATE THE *CHRIST THE REDEEMER* STATUE

The *Cristo Redentor*, or *Christ the Redeemer*, statue is a 125-foot-tall structure designed by Brazilian architect Heitor da Silva Costa and located on Corcovado Mountain, where it towers over the sprawling city of Rio de Janeiro, Brazil. The immense structure was officially inaugurated in October 1931, and it is a popular site due to its iconic status. You possibly became aware of it during coverage of the 2016 Summer Olympic Games in Rio.

Former Brazilian Olympic volleyball player Maria Isabel Barroso Salgado held the Olympic torch high aloft over the city while standing beneath the statue. From there the torch made its last leg toward Maracana Stadium and the Olympic opening ceremonies. Fr. Omar Raposo, rector at the Christ the Redeemer Sanctuary, located at the base of the statue, says the statue "has a lot of spiritual meaning" in the predominantly Catholic country.

Michelle Boorstein, a religion writer for the *Washington Post*, said that the statue means different things to Brazilians. "Some see it as a tribute to Catholicism while others consider it a salvo against secularism. Still others in the rapidly diversifying country consider it a general symbol of welcome, with arms open wide." Count Celso, one of the original masterminds of the statue, called it a "monument to science, art, and religion."

The *Christ the Redeemer* statue receives more than one million visitors annually (an average of more than 2,700 people per day). The mist from the surrounding tropical forest that often shrouds the statue adds even more of an aura of mystique to the already impressive construction. It is sometimes illuminated by colored lights in order to bring awareness to some particular movement. Ultimately, the *Christ the Redeemer* statue is so majestic that it is classified as one of the "New Seven Wonders of the World."

FOCUS QUESTION

What was the Church's impact on **THE RENAISSANCE** and the **AGE OF EXPLORATION** and vice versa?

Chapter Overview

INTRODUCTION

The Origins of the Renaissance and the Age of Exploration

MAIN IDEA

The rise of Christian humanism was associated with the Renaissance, an era during which art, music, and architecture featured classical themes. In the midst of this cultural rebirth, the Age of Exploration led to the Church's spreading the Gospel around the globe.

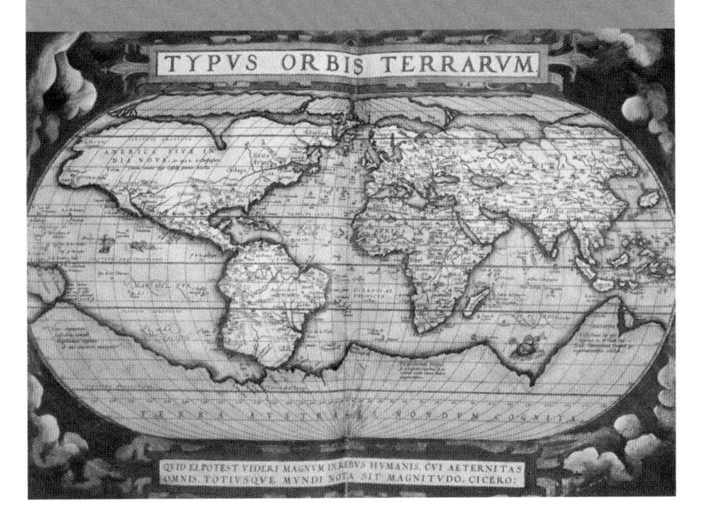

The period known as the **Renaissance** (French for "rebirth") began around the conclusion of the Late Middle Ages; it lasted from approximately the fourteenth century through the seventeenth century, partially overlapping the Late Middle Ages. As with most other historical epochs, historians commonly recognize that the Renaissance had no definitive beginning or end; rather, it was a steady and gradual shift within European society and a historical bridge between the Middle Ages and the Enlightenment, which you will learn more about in Chapter 7.

Renaissance A cultural rebirth begun in the Late Middle Ages that rediscovered the ancient civilizations of Rome and Egypt. The Renaissance stressed the natural and the human. It emphasized the pleasures of life, glorified the human body, and celebrated education.

The Beginnings of the Renaissance

The Renaissance had its origins around Florence and other northern Italian city-states such as Venice, Genoa, Milan, and Bologna. The period was characterized by extensive personal expression, particularly in visual art, music, and architecture.

The city-states that covered the Italian peninsula maintained relative economic and political prosperity at the time and therefore had the resources to support the arts. Those dedicated to producing paintings, literature, architecture, and other cultural expressions received ample support from both private and public patrons. For example, the Medici family was prominent in Florence and famously endorsed large-scale artistic projects as well as schools for the community. The Church was also a patron of the arts in the Renaissance as well. The cultural activity of the Renaissance, which was furthered by its association

NOTE TAKING

Focusing Ideas. Copy the following writing prompts in your notebook. Before you read the section, write two or three sentences under each prompt summarizing what you know about each topic.

- ***The Church's Role in the Renaissance***
- ***The Church's Role in the Exploration of the New World***

Christian HUMANISM

Since human beings in all their natural glory were at the center of the Renaissance, the new outlook took the name *humanism*. The idea of *Christian humanism* evolved to combine this revived interest in humanity with the Christian faith. The Renaissance humanists built on the Church's long-standing tradition regarding what it means to be a person—that is, to be created by God and redeemed by him.

Around Christian humanism, the Church came to recognize that evangelization does not mean replacing a people's language or cultural identity; rather, just as the early Church began in the midst of different cultures (Middle Eastern, North African, Roman, and Germanic, among various others), the Gospel is directed toward all of humanity. Thus, it is possible to remain faithful to the Gospel while honoring the use of different languages and unique cultural gifts

Among the Christian humanists of the Renaissance were scholar Erasmus of Rotterdam and artists Michelangelo, Raphael, and Leonardo da Vinci.

Image (above): Jesuit missionary preaching to Native Americans and fur traders in the wilderness

with **humanism**, made an impact on European society that endures to this day.

Partly due to the plague, the Middle Ages were characterized by a strong preoccupation with spiritual concerns such as death and eternal judgment. With the risks of the plague reduced, the Renaissance celebrated an increased appreciation for more human pursuits and emphasized the individual. Visual art highlighted human physiology in very much the same way that Greek art from around fifteen hundred years earlier emphasized the glory of the human body. Sculptures and other artistic renditions were more lifelike than they had been in previous eras. Characteristics of scholarship during the Renaissance included a continued reliance on Greek philosophy as well as a return to studies of classical civilizations, cultures, and languages.

It is important to note that the humanist scholars and artists of the Renaissance did not seek somehow to replace the spiritual dynamics of society; rather, in much the same way that the scholastics had relied on the rationales of classical Greek philosophers to better explain Christianity, so too did many humanists use artistic expression to emphasize Christian principles. (This is done in modern times as well, such as with the *Christ the Redeemer* statue in Rio de Janeiro.) For example, sculptors made busts of Jesus, Mary, and other biblical figures that attempted to capture their emotions, emphasizing that their humanity qualified them to lead others to seek that which is beyond earthly life—the eternal implications of the Gospel. Painters used vivid colors (rather than the darker and duller colors that were often used during the Middle

humanism A cultural and intellectual movement of the Renaissance that emphasized the rediscovery of the literature, art, and civilizations of ancient Greece and Rome.

Ages) to show that God is the source of all that is good, holy, and beautiful. Writers and musicians experimented with new styles to represent the joy that comes with being a disciple of Christ.

However, it is not inaccurate to say that the Renaissance stressed the human more than the divine. Whereas medieval society looked heavenward, the Renaissance period highlighted earthly, human creativity. As it brought about great advances in learning and unsurpassed achievements in art, the spirit of the Renaissance changed the way people thought about their world and about the Church. During the Renaissance, the Church was no longer seen as the *only* source of beauty and guidance.

In light of the humanism that was at the heart of the early Renaissance, it is important to note that the humanism being discussed here must be understood as *Christian* humanism rather than a materialistic view that saw human pursuits as the ultimate goal of one's existence (see "Christian Humanism" on the previous page). In fact, most humanists of the period were Christians.

Portuguese navigator and explorer Pedro Álvares Cabral (ca. 1467–1520) was the European discoverer of Brazil.

The Beginnings of the Age of Exploration

Just as the Renaissance did not have a definitive beginning or end, neither did the Age of Exploration, though it is commonly dated between the fifteenth and seventeenth centuries. Exploration of what came to be called the **New World** by Viking explorers began in the tenth century, but it was during the late fifteenth century that Catholicism became truly global, as missionaries introduced the faith to previously unknown lands.

The Age of Exploration did not begin with religious motives; rather, leaders of influential seafaring European nations—especially Spain, Portugal, the Netherlands, and England—viewed trade, commerce, and eventually **colonization** primarily as a source of financial benefit to the home nation. This was a controversial time in history, given the human rights abuses that followed from the greed and selfishness of many explorers and the settlers who came after them. In the middle of this quest for "gold and glory," the Church sought to bring the Gospel to people around the globe. In fact, those evangelizers who were faithful to the Church served the will of God by speaking out against the injustices suffered by native groups.

New World A term applied to the Americas, as compared to the "Old World" of Europe.

colonization The process by which a nation establishes a prominent presence by exerting an element of power or control in an area beyond their original borders.

As the Church undertook missionary efforts around the globe—particularly in the Americas, Asia, and somewhat in Africa—she sometimes met with openness and acceptance and other times with opposition, if not outright hostility. The response was typically mixed. The native populations from across many different lands in which the Gospel was eventually accepted have enriched the ethnic and cultural diversity of the Church, so that today the Church celebrates a rich treasure of faithful disciples of all different backgrounds, experiences, languages, and even liturgical practices that complement one another while participating in the Church's norms.

SECTION ASSESSMENT

NOTE TAKING

Use the summary statements you wrote to help you complete the following question.

1. Although the Renaissance and the Age of Exploration overlapped within history, which of the two do you think was most effective in allowing the Church to emphasize what it means to be a human, and why?

COMPREHENSION

2. In what ways was the Renaissance a "rebirth"?
3. How did the features of the Renaissance support the work of the Church?
4. What did *Christian* humanism in particular mean?
5. In what ways did missionaries within the Church speak out against worldly-minded leaders who were only interested in gold and glory?

VOCABULARY

6. Define *humanism*.

REFLECTION

7. If you were to meet a missionary from the Age of Exploration, what would you ask him? Provide three specific questions.

SECTION 1

The Rebirth of Classical Writing and Scholarship

MAIN IDEA

During the Renaissance, the rebirth within society of interest in classical works was led by various prominent Christian humanists, including Erasmus and St. Thomas More.

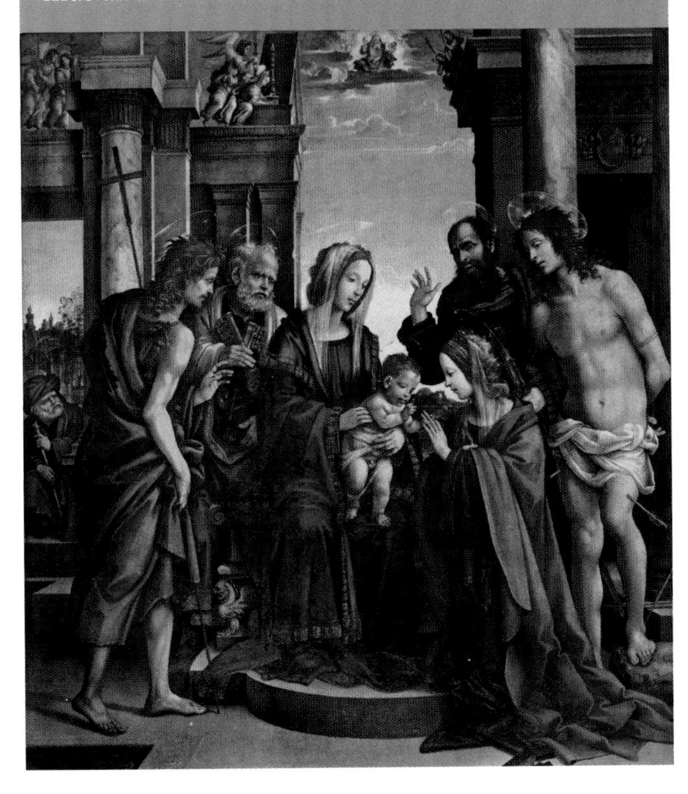

During the Renaissance, thinkers and artists advanced different expressions of Christian humanism, although many in the Church cautioned against a reduction of God to worldly terms. For the best and most faithful theologians in every age see that thinkers—especially in ages of great art and achievement—run the risk of confusing worldly beauty with the unfathomable and staggering beauty of God's glory.

Renaissance thinkers placed great emphasis on the Greek and Roman classics and on the study of the classical Greek and Latin languages. Greek and Roman poems and theatrical works were analyzed and studied, and certain facets of the Greco-Roman world seemed to pervade European society again. The Church was generally supportive of these efforts, encouraging the study of Greek and Latin within society. During this period, tutors educated the youth of the nobility in classical scholarship.

Experts in the classical languages were tasked with producing manuscripts of ancient writings of the

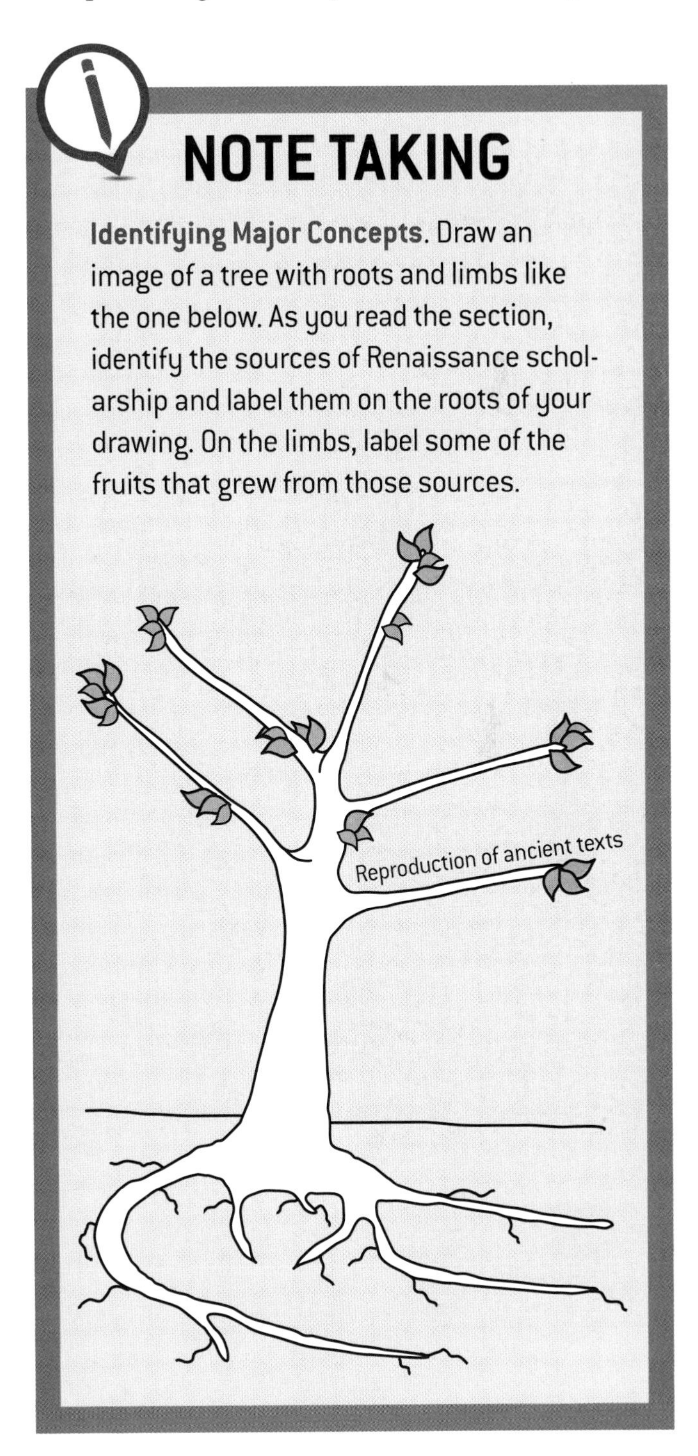

Greeks and Romans. Figures such as Poggio Bracciolini (1380–1459) went to libraries throughout Europe to find ancient texts and reproduce them. Much of this study was supported by and took place within monasteries run by different religious orders. Although the Church did support the task of copying and studying ancient texts, Church leaders had to remind the copyists that, while many ancient texts had clear merit, the emphasis should be on identifying and relying upon those texts that supported Christian theological principles.

Two important Renaissance thinkers featured in this section are Desiderius Erasmus of Rotterdam and St. Thomas More.

Two Christian Scholars of the Renaissance

Christian humanists produced lasting works of scholarship during the Renaissance. Desiderius Erasmus of Rotterdam (1466–1536) was, like many other humanists of the period, devoted to his faith in Christ. Destitution led Erasmus to monastic life, although he eventually left the monastery and pursued serious scholarly efforts while traveling throughout Europe.

During his travels, Erasmus began to exchange letters with civil leaders, nobility, Church leaders, and fellow Christian humanists. Erasmus circulated the works of ancient Christian writers and compiled a scholarly translation of the Greek New Testament. In his 1511 work *In Praise of Folly*, Erasmus offered critiques of corrupt leaders—both civil and ecclesial—and errant mindsets within society, such as superstition and a focus on worldly concerns. Erasmus urged both political and Church leaders to remain focused on Christ and the Gospel. To this end, Erasmus encouraged Catholics to ensure that their devotion to saints—while having its own merit—should not cloud their recognition of the prominence of Christ: "There are some

Desiderius Erasmus of Rotterdam

more Catholic saints petitioned to upon all occasions, as more especially the Virgin Mary, whose blind devotees think it manners now to place the mother before the Son" (*In Praise of Folly*).

St. Thomas More (1478–1535) was a contemporary humanist and friend to Erasmus. "In serious matters, no man's advice is more prized," Erasmus wrote of him. Thomas More was born into a well-to-do English family and from a young age interacted with civil and Church leaders. His studies were extensive; he attended Canterbury College at Oxford, where he studied Latin, Greek, theology, philosophy, the law, music, and literature. After considering but ultimately deciding against a religious vocation, More was, among other roles, a prominent lawyer, philosopher, statesman, and writer.

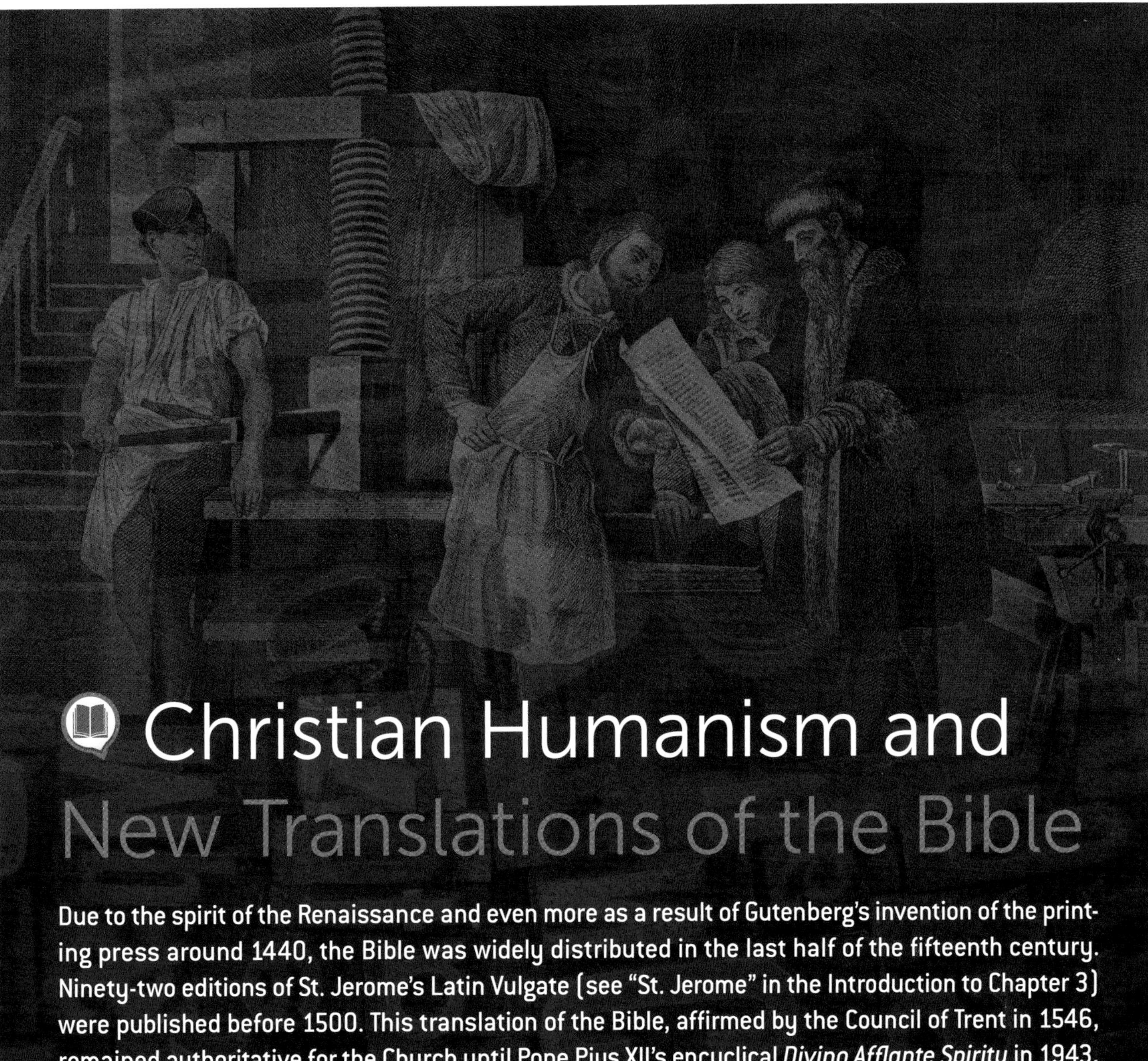

Christian Humanism and New Translations of the Bible

Due to the spirit of the Renaissance and even more as a result of Gutenberg's invention of the printing press around 1440, the Bible was widely distributed in the last half of the fifteenth century. Ninety-two editions of St. Jerome's Latin Vulgate (see "St. Jerome" in the Introduction to Chapter 3) were published before 1500. This translation of the Bible, affirmed by the Council of Trent in 1546, remained authoritative for the Church until Pope Pius XII's encyclical *Divino Afflante Spiritu* in 1943, which allowed modern translations of the Bible from the original languages.

After Gutenberg published his Bible, Christian humanist scholars produced and had printed many new translations of the Bible. Several of the new translations were developed from the original biblical languages (Hebrew and Greek) into the languages of the local people. For example, eighteen German translations of the Bible were printed before 1521. A full French translation was printed in 1487. Spanish, Italian, Dutch, and Bohemian translations all appeared in the fifteenth century. It is important to note that some translations were not authorized by the Church, such as those by John Wyclif (ca. 1320–1384), Myles Coverdale (1488–1569), and William Tyndale (1494–1536).

ASSIGNMENT

Read paragraphs 14 and 15 of *Divino Afflante Spiritu*, and answer the following question: Why might it have been more appropriate for the Church to consider new biblical translations in the mid-twentieth century than at the time of the Renaissance?

St. Thomas More

His most famous work described a world in which society was run by reason.

As Thomas More's career advanced, he was elected to the English Parliament, where he earned a good reputation for his honesty and industriousness. Meanwhile, he continued to study theology and write. As a lawyer and a statesman, More earned steadily higher positions in the court of the English king Henry VIII (see "King Henry VIII (1491–1547)" in Chapter 6, Section 2). However, he eventually fell out of favor with King Henry VIII for not supporting the divorce of Henry VIII and his wife Catherine and for not supporting Henry VIII's attempts to break with the pope and the Roman Church. Even after Thomas More resigned from his court position, Henry VIII invented charges against him that eventually led to his conviction for treason. More was sentenced to beheading, yet he proclaimed his loyalty to both the king and to God. His neck was severed while he was praying. His last words were directed to the executioner: "Pick up your spirits, man, and don't be afraid to do your office. My neck is very short, take heed therefore you strike not awry for having your honesty."

The goals of Erasmus, St. Thomas More, and other Christian humanists were cultural advancement and human flourishing. They championed sound scholarship, the preaching of the Bible, the reading of the Church Fathers, and the correction of administrative abuses in the Church. Their proposals were also an indispensable preparation for the reforms the Church would undertake during the Catholic Reformation and beyond.

SECTION ASSESSMENT

NOTE TAKING

Use the notes you made on the drawing of a tree with roots and branches to help you complete the following items.

1. What ancient sources did scholars and writers study during the Renaissance?
2. Name and describe two written contributions Erasmus made to the Church.
3. What goals did Erasmus, St. Thomas More, and other Christian humanists champion for the Church?

COMPREHENSION

4. Why were the Church leaders cautious about the mindset of the Renaissance?
5. What were some features of St. Thomas More's life that indicate his holiness?

CRITICAL THINKING

6. How did the study of ancient languages during the Renaissance influence the Church's approval of new translations of the Bible in the twentieth century?

SECTION 2

Religious Art of the Renaissance

MAIN IDEA
The Church and prominent Catholic families sponsored artists, musicians, and architects, whose work helped promote the Gospel and God's Kingdom.

During the Renaissance, certain prominent Catholic families and individuals contributed extensively to fueling and funding the achievements of the Renaissance, which in turn allowed the Church to better support religious art, music, and architecture. Various popes were patrons of Renaissance projects; Pope Nicholas V (1447–1455) was the first pope documented to have used Church funds to sponsor large-scale art projects.

Occasionally, unscrupulous measures were used to finance these artistic efforts. One of these ways was the Church's selling of **indulgences**, which promised remission of time in Purgatory for sins that were already forgiven. It is important to note that the selling

indulgences The remission before God of the temporal punishment still due to forgiven sins. Indulgences are, as the *Catechism of the Catholic Church* teaches, "closely linked to the effects of the sacrament of Penance" (*CCC*, 1471).

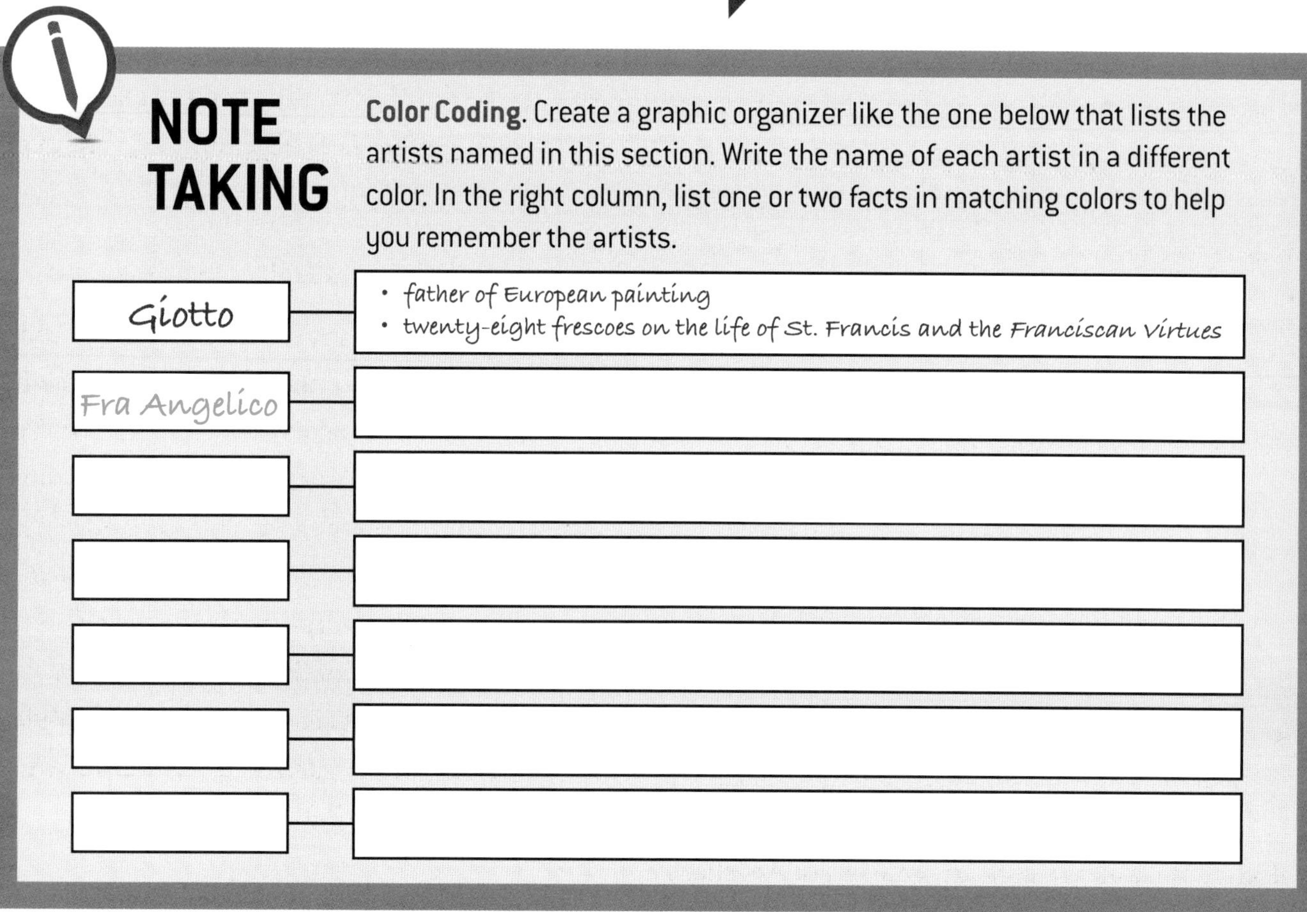

of indulgences was an abuse by certain churchmen and not an action of the Church herself.

Prominent Artists of the Renaissance

The Renaissance period is known for some of the most famous, lasting, and beautiful artistic work the world has ever seen, before or since. Perhaps most prominent of all the works are St. Peter's Basilica and the Sistine Chapel, both commissioned by Pope Julius II (1503–1513). This section briefly describes seven key Renaissance artists in the areas of visual art, music, and architecture.

Giotto (ca. 1266–1337)

Giotto di Bondone is one of the earliest Renaissance artists. Born in Vespignano, which is near Florence, Giotto is often called the "father of European painting." He is credited, for example, with painting the twenty-eight *frescoes* (mural paintings) of scenes in the life of St. Francis in the upper church of the Basilica of San Francesco in Assisi and the *Franciscan Virtues* frescoes in the lower church there. These scenes were groundbreaking for the humanity their figures exhibited. Giotto's most famous works are in Rome: the mosaic of *Christ Walking on Water* over the entrance to St. Peter's Basilica; the altarpiece painted for Cardinal Stefaneschi now housed at the Vatican Museum; and the fresco fragment of *Pope Boniface VIII Proclaiming the Jubilee* in St. John Lateran Church. According to Giotto, "Every painting is a voyage into a sacred harbor."

Fra Angelico (ca. 1395–1455)

The frescoes of Guido di Pietro, or Fra Angelico ("Angelic Brother"), who was born in Florence, were typical of the early Renaissance in particular. They were characterized by serene and somber imagery, reflective of classical Greek art. One of Fra Angelico's most famous pieces is *The Annunciation,* depicting the Archangel Gabriel's announcement to Mary that she would be the Mother of Jesus (see Luke 1:26–38). This fresco is located in the Convent of San Marco in Florence.

The Annunciation *by Fra Angelico*

Bramante (ca. 1444–1514)

Architect Donato Bramante developed the style known as "High Renaissance architecture." Bramante's first commissioned monument was for the tomb of Pope Julius, designed by Michelangelo. Bramante would be the first of twelve architects, including Michelangelo, to work on the new St. Peter's Basilica, a project that lasted through twenty-two popes. Bramante was named chief architect of the new basilica, and construction began in 1506. St. Peter's Basilica in Vatican City acts as the pope's church and the "headquarters" of the global Catholic Church.

In addition to the famous Creation of Adam *scene, the Sistine Chapel's ceiling also contains more scenes from the Book of Genesis and images of the ancestors of Christ.*

Michelangelo (1475–1564)

Michelangelo di Lodovico Buonarroti Simoni, or simply Michelangelo, is perhaps the best-known Renaissance artist. His contemporaries referred to him as *Il divino*, "the divine one." Born in Florence, Michelangelo received formal training at the Medici palace. He studied anatomy and immersed himself in analyzing the frescoes in the Brancacci chapel at the Church of Santa Maria del Carmine. Michelangelo had immediate success as a sculptor. In Rome, he sculpted the *Pietà*, now in St. Peter's Basilica, at the request of a French cardinal. Beginning in 1515, he and his successors were special patrons of the Church, working at first in Florence and Rome but later, after 1534, in Rome exclusively.

Pope Julius commissioned Michelangelo to paint the ceiling of the Sistine Chapel in 1508. It was a grueling four-year project. Michelangelo even designed his own scaffolding. When it was completed, Michelangelo sent his money home to his family. He never married but was devoted to his strict father. "I will send you what you demand," he wrote, "even if I have to sell myself as a slave." The ceiling painting—including the prominent *Creation of Adam* scene—and the *Last Judgment* on the end wall of the chapel (a project that took five years to complete) tell the story of creation, the fall of humanity, and the reconciliation of the world to God.

Raphael (1483–1520)

Raffaello Sanzio (Raphael in English) was an expert architect and painter from the High Renaissance period. Commissioned by Pope Leo X, he was one of the architects for St. Peter's Basilica. Raphael was also the painter in the papal courts of both Pope Julius II and Pope Leo X. Raphael painted various images of the Blessed Virgin Mary, including *Sistine Madonna*. His depiction of the human form was characteristic of the Renaissance's reliance on various elements of humanism, and some of his works had classical Greek references, such as his *School of Athens*, which depicts a conversation between Plato and Aristotle, who are flanked by prominent thinkers of the West who preceded them.

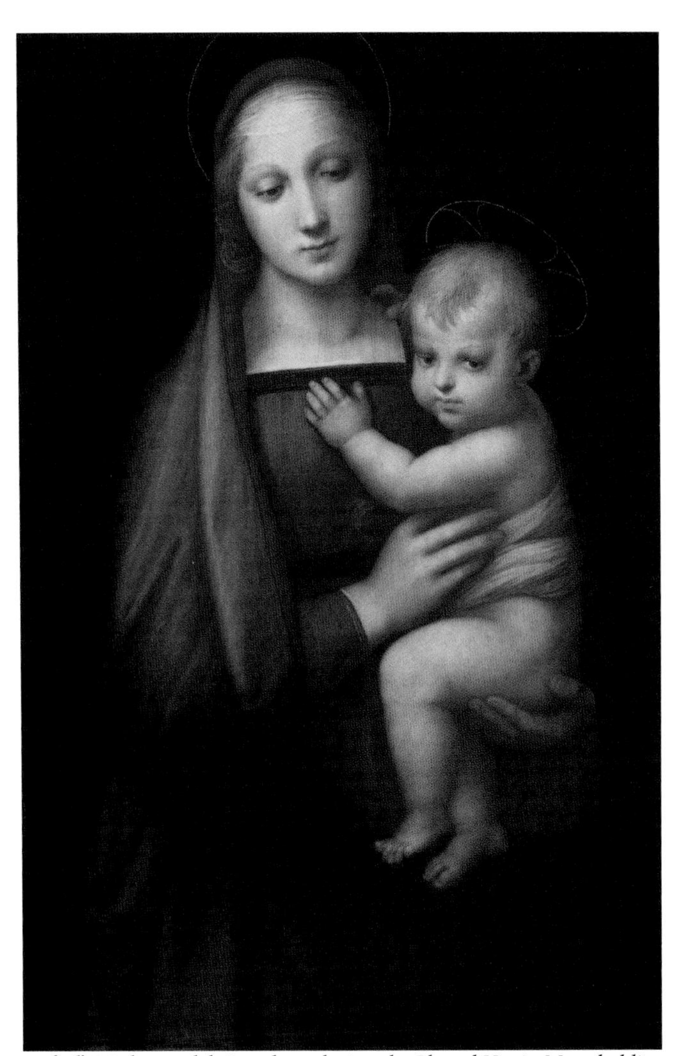

Rafael's Madonna del Granduca *depicts the Blessed Virgin Mary holding the infant Jesus and shows the influence of Leonardo da Vinci in the soft transitions between colors.*

St. Philip Neri (1515–1595), Palestrina (1525–1594), and Baronius (1538–1607)

Though not a musician or scholar himself, St. Philip Neri, a Florence-born priest of the High Renaissance period, had a profound impact on both of these disciplines during that period and beyond. In Rome, St. Philip Neri began the Congregation of the Oratory, also known as the "Oratorians" because they rang a little bell to call their priests to prayer and Mass. As a priest, St. Philip devoted much of his time to hearing Confessions. He was accessible to all and full of joy. He has been called "the humorous saint." St. Philip Neri would undertake charitable works throughout Rome for the rest of his life and is often referred to as the "Apostle of Rome."

Because of his deep friendships with artists, St. Philip had a great influence on the arts. For example, Giovanni Pierluigi da Palestrina, the greatest composer and reformer of liturgical music of all time, gained insight from St. Philip on the "spirit of the liturgy" that helped him set the Mass to polyphonic music in a way that had never before been accomplished.

When Cesare Baronius met St. Philip, Baronius was a student of civil and canon law. St. Philip and the good works of the priests and laymen at the Oratory inspired Baronius to a different life. He became a disciple of St. Philip Neri, burned his secular awards and diplomas, and was ordained to the priesthood. St. Philip encouraged Baronius to respond to the Protestant Reformation by writing a history of the Church. His twelve-volume *Annales Ecclesiastici* clearly demonstrates the foundation for Catholic beliefs and practices from apostolic tradition; because of it, Baronius is known as the "Father of Church History."

Bernini (1598–1680)

Gian Lorenzo Bernini is credited with developing the Baroque style of sculpture in the seventeenth century. *Baroque* is derived from a Portuguese word that means "rough or imperfect pearl." Baroque sculptures were meant to be displayed in open spaces rather than against walls. They were fluid, with many angles and many parts expressing movement. Bernini created several notable pieces, including *The Ecstasy of St. Teresa*, a sculpture of white marble set elevated at the Cornaro

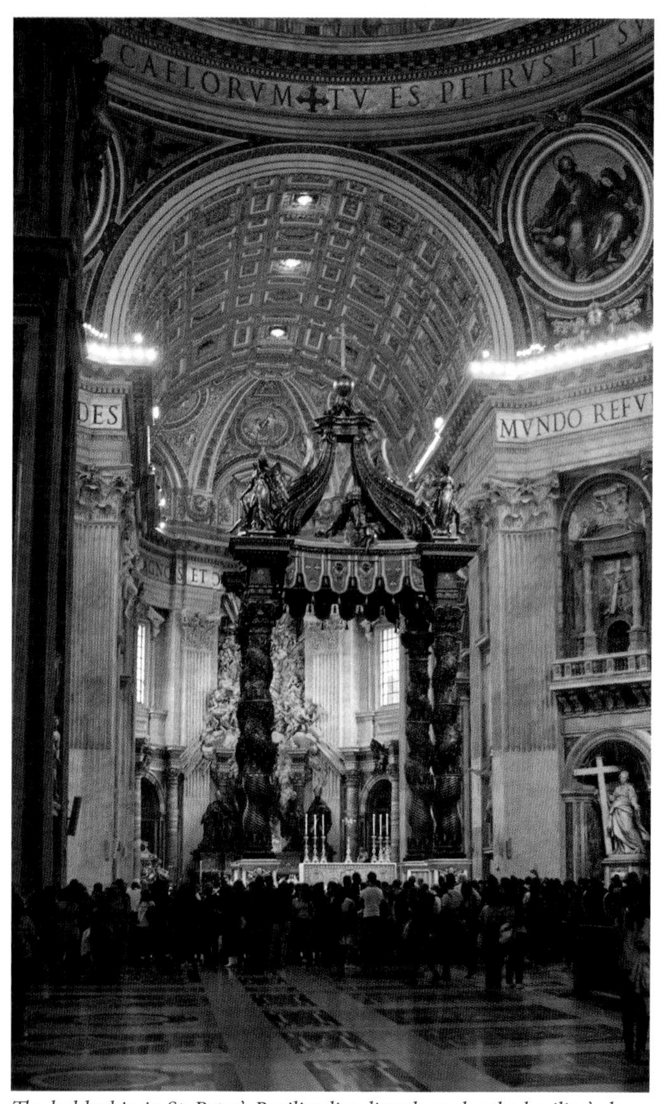

The baldachin in St. Peter's Basilica lies directly under the basilica's dome and marks St. Peter's tomb, which lies below it.

Using the Cathedral to TEACH OTHERS ABOUT CHRIST

There were differences in architectural style between cathedrals of the Middle Ages (see the feature "Architecture of the Middle Ages" in Chapter 4, Section 4) and those of the Renaissance. In keeping with the focus of the era, Renaissance cathedrals imitated ancient Greek and Roman architecture styles in their symmetry, proportions, and consistency in components. For example, several Renaissance cathedrals (and churches) incorporated exteriorly the classical Greek and Roman style façade with a variety of columns and domes.

One icon of Renaissance architecture is the Cathedral of Santa Maria del Fiore in Florence, Italy, which is one of the world's largest churches. The Cathedral of Santa Maria del Fiore was built between 1418 and 1434, and it is so well designed that it has withstood earthquakes, lightning strikes, and the ravages of the centuries. This and other Renaissance cathedrals remain symbols of Renaissance art and architecture that reflect the glory of the Church and the Kingdom of God by extension. Along with the sacraments that are celebrated there, such cathedrals themselves serve as opportunities to pray, learn, and share more about the Faith.

ASSIGNMENT

Visit the website of the Cathedral of Santa Maria del Fiore. Write a two-page report in travelogue style that details basic information about it: the dome, the baptistery, Giotto's bell tower, the crypt of Santa Reparata, and the cathedral museum. Include information about travel to and tours of the cathedral to benefit pilgrims who are planning a visit.

Chapel at the Santa Maria della Vittoria Church in Rome. His *Baldacchino*, which stands over the main altar of St. Peter's Basilica in Rome, remains his most iconic masterpiece.

The art, music, and architecture of the Renaissance were lasting testaments to the greatness of God's creation and his ongoing presence in human history. The movement of Christian humanism led the faithful to deeper acceptance of the beauty of the Gospel.

SECTION ASSESSMENT

NOTE TAKING

Use the color-coded chart you made to help you complete the matching exercise. Match the Renaissance artist (or supporter of the arts) in the left column with something he is associated with from the right column.

1. Giotto	A. Chief architect of St. Peter's Basilica
2. Fra Angelico	B. *Sistine Madonna* and *School of Athens*
3. Bramante	C. Developed Baroque style of sculpture
4. Michelangelo	D. Created frescoes with serene imagery
5. Raphael	E. "The divine one"
6. St. Philip Neri	F. "Father of European painting"
7. Bernini	G. Mentor to Palestrina and Baronius

COMPREHENSION

8. Explain the role that popes played in furthering the artistic achievements of the Renaissance.
9. How did the arts of the Renaissance reflect the overall spirit of the period?

VOCABULARY

10. Define *indulgences*, and explain their role in the Renaissance.

REFLECTION

11. Choose a piece of religious art captured in a photo in this section. Answer the following: Which photo did you choose? What is your initial reaction to the image? How does this photo expand your thinking about the Gospel and God's Kingdom?

SECTION 3

Evangelization and the Age of Exploration

MAIN IDEA

Church missionaries accompanied explorers as they set out to discover new opportunities for trade and commerce. The missionaries spread the Gospel to the New World, the Far East, and Africa. Their efforts at evangelization were sometimes accompanied by harsh treatment of native peoples.

Explorers had traveled the world well before the late fifteenth century, the time of Christopher Columbus. But from the time of Columbus's first voyage to the New World in 1492 through the seventeenth century, European explorers traveled not only to the Americas but to the Far East and Africa as well, seeking new trade routes and opportunities for earning new profits for European nations in these unknown lands.

Wherever explorers went in the New World, missionaries who were charged with the evangelization of the native people followed. In 1493, Pope Alexander VI, to avoid conflict between nations, sent Portuguese missionaries to Brazil and Spanish missionaries to the rest of the New World. Spanish missionaries were the first to arrive in what would become the United States—in what is now California, the Southwest, and the Southeast.

This section offers an overview of the Church's missionary outreach during this period.

NOTE TAKING

Labeling. Recreate a simple line drawing of a world map as shown below. As you read the section, label particular areas in the New World, Far East, and Africa with key people, dates, and events that mark the Church's efforts at evangelization of those areas.

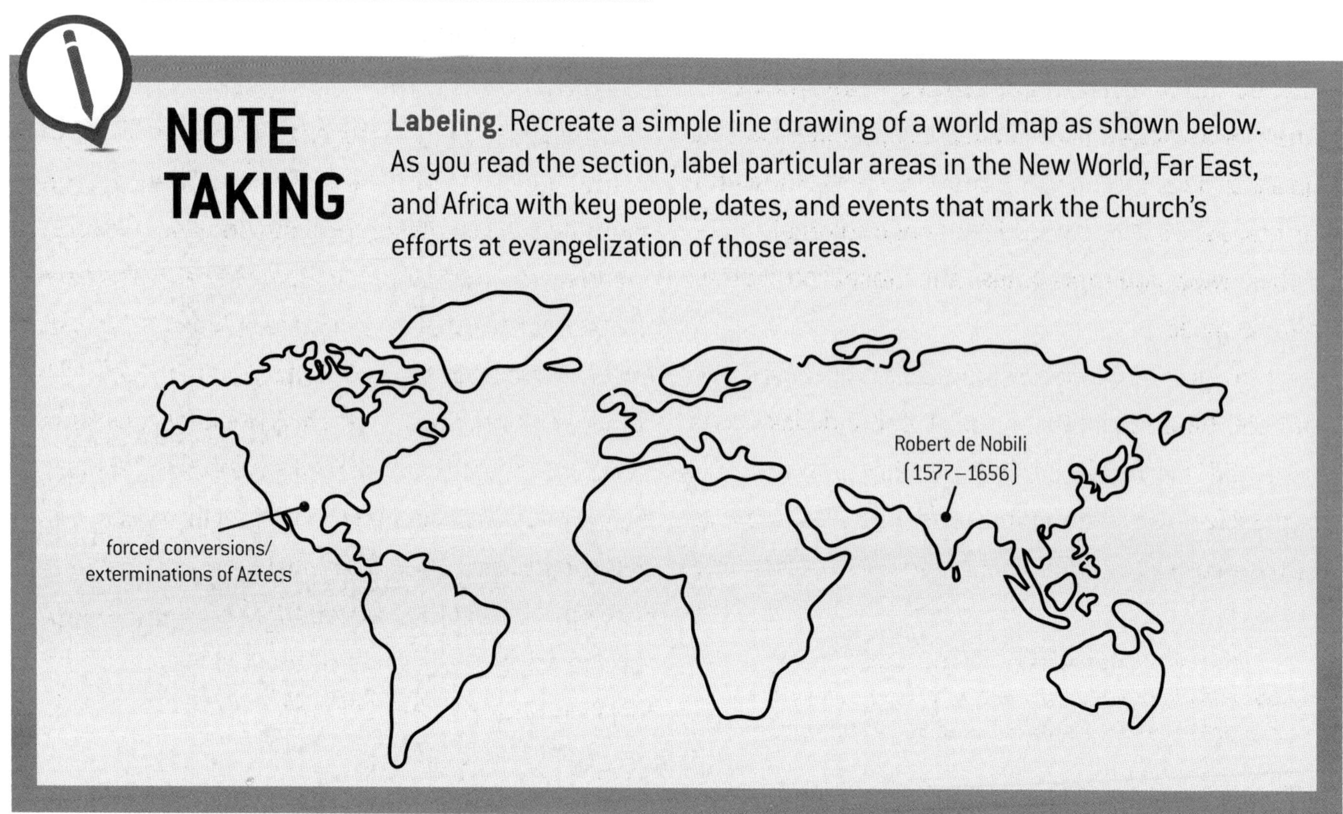

Missionaries in the New World

The saga of missionary activity in the New World includes the stories of many brave Franciscans, Jesuits, Dominicans, and others who risked their lives to evangelize the indigenous peoples. Many of the missionaries were saintly and good to the native peoples, learning their languages, teaching them the Faith, and instructing them in new trades.

Unfortunately, the story of these missionary efforts also has a dark side because they were so closely wedded to the practice of military conquest at any cost. The **conquistadors** who accompanied missionaries had a thirst for gold that seemed to override any other motive—as, for example, when they conquered the Aztecs in Mexico and the Incas in Peru. The colonizers often thought of the native populations as inferior. Some missionaries had a crusading attitude in their work. The missionaries often served as government officials who looked after birth and death records and the collection of taxes, so the natives saw them more as tools for Spain or Portugal than as Christians entrusted with the care of souls. Forced conversions, the extermination of thousands of natives, exploitation of the populace, refusal to ordain native men as priests for fear that native clergy would challenge colonial rule—all these were attempts to use the Gospel to further political goals.

Many good missionaries fought these abuses. For example, Dominican bishop Bartolomé de las Casas (1474–1566) worked vigorously for the rights of native people. He was instrumental in securing the passage of the so-called *New Laws,* which forbade slavery and

conquistadors Spanish for "conquerors"; those explorers who left Spain to conquer new faraway territories and claim them in the name of the Spanish crown.

Hernan Cortes honors Spanish missionaries

the forced labor of native populations and extended to them other rights as well (see also the opening of Chapter 5, Section 4). Jesuit St. Peter Claver (1581–1654) ministered to the slaves in Colombia and the West Indies. Dominican lay brother St. Martin de Porres (1579–1639) earned the nickname "The Wonder Worker of Peru" for his ceaseless devotion to lessening the evils of slavery. Jesuits also set up model communities in Paraguay and Brazil that tried to preserve native culture while providing education and the benefits of Western civilization. Unfortunately, complex political realities forced the Jesuits to abandon these missions.

French efforts at evangelization in the New World came later than the Spanish. Their activities were concentrated in North America and, in general, were less successful than Spanish efforts. Some of the French missionaries, such as Fr. Jacques Marquette (1637–1675), were great explorers. Marquette not only established missions in places such as Michigan but also was among the first Europeans to explore the Mississippi River. Jesuit missionaries in the northeastern United States and Canada lived among the native people in an attempt to win new Christians. Their success—punctuated with the witness of martyrdom—was often delayed until later generations.

Church history

Missionaries in the Far East

Missionary activity in the Far East differed from that in the West. Many missionaries followed the example of St. Francis Xavier, a Jesuit, who founded missions in India, Indonesia, and Japan. Many missionaries, including the Italian Jesuits Matteo Ricci (1552–1610) in China and Robert de Nobili (1577–1656) in India, tried to adapt Christianity to the cultures of these Eastern civilizations. Ricci, for example, won the Chinese over because of his knowledge of astronomy. He spoke their language, adopted their dress, and respected their traditions. He gradually began to share his religion, trying to show how Christianity could enhance the Chinese culture.

Missionaries in Africa

Christianity arrived in Africa very early, perhaps by the first and second centuries in North Africa specifically. Tertullian, Sts. Perpetua and Felicity, and St. Augustine of Hippo were all African, for example. However, the Muslim conquest of northern Africa from the late seventh through the early eighth centuries essentially eradicated the Christian presence from once-thriving communities on the Mediterranean.

In the Age of Exploration, areas of sub-Saharan Africa were evangelized during the fifteenth and sixteenth centuries by Portuguese explorers who brought the Gospel to coastal regions, including what are now Angola, Benin, Madagascar, Mozambique, and São Tomé and Príncipe. In the Congo (present-day Zaire), spirited evangelization began in 1490 due in great part to the efforts of the Franciscans. Christianity spread in these areas as more missionaries arrived from Portugal.

Also in the sixteenth century, evangelization took place on the east coast of Africa. St. Francis Xavier stopped in Mozambique on his way to Asia. In 1591, the mission in Mozambique boasted twenty thousand Catholics.

A service at St Peter's Catholic Church in the Mbare district in Harare, Zimbabwe

By the nineteenth century, Christianity had again waned in sub-Saharan Africa. One reason is that Portugal was unable to supply enough missionaries to the region. Another is that the Portuguese government was more committed to commercial interests than the spreading of the Faith. There was little effort to penetrate beyond the coastal regions of Africa for any reason. Language barriers also played a part in the stagnant nature of evangelization.

Note that recent evangelization of the African continent from the nineteenth century to the present has occurred as Catholic missionaries have eagerly brought the Good News of Jesus Christ to the hitherto isolated regions of central Africa. A recent study by the Center for Applied Research in the Apostolate at Georgetown University points out that while the Catholic population in the world has grown 57 percent since 1980, the African Catholic population has risen by 238 percent, compared to only a 6 percent growth rate in Europe.

SECTION ASSESSMENT

NOTE TAKING

Use the map with key words you recorded in your notebook to help you answer the following questions.

1. How did Bishop Bartolomé de las Casas advocate for the native people in the New World?
2. Who was "The Wonder Worker of Peru"?
3. Which priest was one of the first explorers of the Mississippi River?
4. What skill did Jesuit Matteo Ricci use to try to win the Chinese over to Christianity?
5. Explorers from which nations were significant in bringing the Gospel to the coastal regions of Africa in the fifteenth and sixteenth centuries?

COMPREHENSION

6. How did the natives in Mexico often view Christian missionaries?
7. Which area of the world has the highest rate of new Catholic converts since 1980?

VOCABULARY

8. What impact did the *conquistadors* have on evangelization in the New World?

CRITICAL THINKING

9. Imagine yourself as a Christian missionary in the New World during the Age of Exploration. How would you judge your work to be a success? Share in detail.

SECTION 4

Saints in the Age of Exploration

MAIN IDEA

The Holy Spirit provided the Church with humble and devoted servants to promote the Christian faith and care for those in need in new places throughout the world.

The success of evangelization in the Age of Exploration varied depending on the region of the world and the style used by the missionaries. The aim of Franciscan missionaries in Mexico and the southwestern United States was to establish native settlements with European organizational structures. These missionaries established schools, markets, and churches. They taught the Gospel of Christ along with European agricultural techniquesand domestic skills. Rather than adapt Catholicism to the culture of the native people, these missionaries tried to adapt the native people to European culture. For example, the Franciscans expected newly baptized Native Americans to speak only Spanish.

Especially in Mexico, abuse of natives took place in the *encomienda* system, a system in which a native person was "entrusted" to a settler from Spain to be "civilized" and taught the basics of Christian doctrine. In return for this instruction, the native was expected to work for the settler. The system of encomiendas was actually far worse than the system of slavery, for the Spanish settlers had no economic investment in those who had been entrusted to them and therefore no motivation to protect their health or well-being. Abuse ran rampant.

In 1515, four years after Bartolomé de las Casas, a Catholic priest, heard a sermon by Dominican friar Antonio de Montesinos in Santo Domingo (present-day Dominican Republic) condemning the exploitation of native peoples through encomiendas, las Casas travelled with Montesinos to Spain to convince the Spanish government to protect the native people with legislation. The *New Laws*, which

NOTE TAKING

Making Connections. Write one sentence to summarize the life and work of each of the saints and missionaries profiled in "Sharing the Gospel in New Places." Use one of the following words in each sentence.

- humility
- prayerfulness
- devotion
- courage
- creativity
- faithfulness

The Church's Apology FOR PAST WRONGS

In his "Day of Pardon" homily of March 12, 2000, Pope John Paul II specifically addressed the need of the Church to apologize for the culturally insensitive and often exploitive treatment of native peoples by some Church missionaries.

ASSIGNMENT

Read the entire homily (available on the Vatican's website at www.vatican.va). Write three sentences from the homily that offer instruction on what Catholics are to do in the spirit of seeking pardon and forgiveness.

prohibited encomiendas in the Spanish colonies, were eventually signed by Spain's ruler in 1542. When las Casas was named bishop of Chiapas in Mexico, he repeatedly battled with Catholics there who would not give up encomiendas. Eventually, las Casas grew frustrated and went back to Spain, where he spent the rest of his life writing books about the way the Spanish were treating the natives in Mexico.

Missionaries and Martyrs in the North American Northeast

Jesuit missionaries employed a different style of evangelization from Franciscan missionaries. While the Franciscans disallowed the traditional religious practices and cultures of the native peoples, the French Jesuits in the northeastern region of North America quickly realized that the only way to have any influence on the Huron tribes was to live with them and learn their languages and customs. One of the first and most respected Jesuit missionaries was St. Jean de Brébeuf. In his first three years among the Hurons, he baptized only one person, but he demonstrated a remarkable physical endurance that impressed many in the Huron tribe, who had come to view Europeans as weak.

In fact Brébeuf himself died much like a Huron warrior. On March 16, 1649, Brébeuf and his fellow Jesuit Gabriel Lalemant were captured by the Iroquois as they ministered to Huron villagers who were suffering from war injuries. Rather than kill them outright, their Iroquois captors stripped Brébeuf and Lalemant, tore out their fingernails, and led them to a nearby village for ritual slaughter. No matter how much he was tortured, Brébeuf refused to flinch or cry out. His only words were those of concern for his fellow captives and calls for his captors to repent. The Iroquois did all they could to break his spirit and make him beg for mercy, but their efforts were unsuccessful. When Brébeuf died, his tormentors were so impressed by his bravery that they ate his heart, as they would the heart of an enemy warrior, in order to acquire his courage. Brébeuf died as he lived, doing all that he could to earn the respect of those he hoped to convert.

SHARING *the* GOSPEL IN NEW PLACES

The Christian call to holiness is extended to all people. Holiness is a share in God's own life and is a grace that has transformed people and dark events in every era of the Church's history. The Holy Spirit has always provided exemplars of true Christian holiness—like those described on these pages—when they are most needed.

ST. JUAN DIEGO CUAUHTLATOATZIN

St. Juan Diego Cuauhtlatoatzin was born in 1474, near what is now Mexico City, Mexico. He was a member of the Chichimeca, a seminomadic people who lived in Mexico and the southwestern United States. Around the age of fifty, Juan chose to be baptized by Franciscan missionaries. His life was about to take a turn.

On the morning of December 9, 1531, while he was on the way to Mass, the Blessed Virgin Mary appeared to Juan and told him that she wanted a shrine built on nearby Tepeyac Hill and that he should make this request of the local bishop. Juan took Mary's request to his local bishop, Juan de Zumárraga, but the bishop refused.

On December 12, Mary appeared to Juan again and told him to pick roses from Tepeyac (which were in bloom even though it was winter). Mary rearranged the flowers in Juan's outer garment, called a *tilma*. Juan then returned to Bishop Zumárraga, and when he opened his tilma and the roses spilled out, a miraculous image featuring a depiction of Mary had become part of the tilma. It was a miracle, and the bishop was convinced; he directed the construction of a shrine on Tepeyac in honor of Our Lady of Guadalupe. The town of Guadalupe, now incorporated into Mexico City, is the site of the shrine.

St. Juan Diego Cuauhtlatoatzin died in 1548. Under the patronage of Our Lady of Guadalupe, the evangelization of Mexico continued. Today, the miraculous image of Our Lady of Guadalupe on Juan's tilma is on public display at the Basilica of Our Lady of Guadalupe in Mexico City.

ST. PETER CLAVER

St. Peter Claver was born in 1581 in Verdú, Spain. His family was prosperous, though that fact did not ever prohibit Peter from keeping an eye out for those in need. In 1601, Peter was ordained a Jesuit priest. During his studies, he was inspired to serve in the Jesuit missions in South America.

In 1610, Peter arrived in Cartagena, a port city in what is now Colombia where African slaves were received into the country, about ten thousand per day. Peter remained there for more than three decades serving the slaves, particularly by finding them food and shelter as they came off the ships. Peter also used the short time he had with them to share the Gospel and baptize as many as were willing. Before the slaves were taken away by their masters, he would also pray for the masters and implore them to treat slaves humanely. It is estimated that St. Peter Claver baptized more than three hundred thousand slaves before he was stricken with the plague in 1651.

ST. MARTIN *de* PORRES

St. Martin de Porres was born in 1579 in Lima, Peru. His father was a Spanish conquistador, and his mother was a freed slave from Panama. When his father saw that Martin had dark features, he abandoned the family. Martin, his mother, and his younger sister were plunged into dire poverty.

From a young age, Martin exhibited extraordinary holiness and kindness. When he was twelve, Martin's mother helped him attain an apprenticeship, from which Martin learned to dress wounds, draw blood, and care for the sick in many ways. At age fifteen, Martin applied to join the Dominican Convent of the Rosary. He was admitted, but to the lower position of *tertiary* (lay helper) due to his mixed race. Martin happily accepted.

After eight years of Martin's humble service, the prior of the convent chose to defy Peruvian law and allowed Martin to become a full member of the Third Order of St. Dominic. Martin spent the remainder of his life caring for the poor, sick, and injured of his local community until his death in 1639. Given his humility in performing any task, St. Martin de Porres became regarded as the "Saint of the Broom."

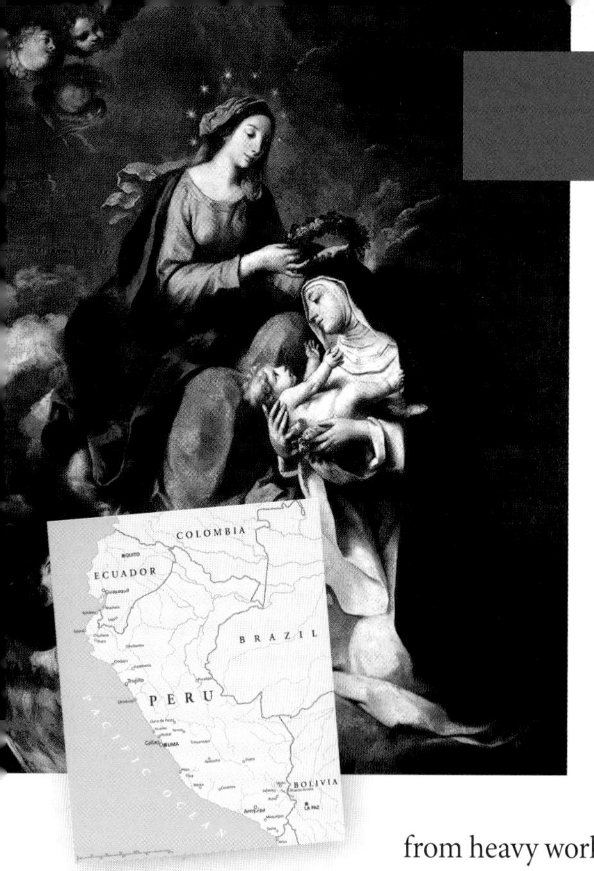

ST. ROSE *of* LIMA

St. Rose of Lima was born Isabel Flores de Olivain 1586 to Spanish colonists in Lima, Peru, who wanted an advantageous marriage and motherhood for their daughter. She took on the name Rose when she was confirmed.

From a young age, Rose had a strong devotion to the infant Jesus and to the Blessed Mother. After reading about the life of St. Catherine of Siena, Rose began to emulate Catherine's life. She was very strict on herself and practiced many penances. Rose also had a great devotion to the Holy Eucharist; she spent hours before the Blessed Sacrament each day.

Throughout her life, Rose—who was known for her beauty—practiced virtuous humility and chastity. She cut off her hair, in part to keep suitors away, wore coarse clothes, and kept her hands rough from heavy work. Rose's parents eventually resigned themselves to the life their daughter had chosen and allowed her to stay in seclusion in her room, praying for hours on end. Her brother also helped to construct a makeshift grotto in their yard, where Rose spent many nights in prayer.

At age twenty, Rose joined the Third Order of St. Dominic, and in addition to continuing to practice harsh penances, she began take in homeless children and care for the elderly and sick. Upon her death in 1617 at only thirty-one years old, Rose was so beloved by her community for her holiness that her funeral was a large-scale event, drawing the faithful from all levels of society. The first saint of the Americas, St. Rose of Lima was canonized in 1671 by Pope Clement X.

ST. FRANCIS XAVIER

St. Francis Xavier (1506–1552) was born in Navarre, which is now part of Spain. He helped St. Ignatius of Loyola found the Society of Jesus, the Jesuits. After studying in Paris, he felt called to the missions. He arrived in Goa in India in 1542 and spent a few months preaching, caring for the sick, and directing people to a local church where he taught the Faith. In around October 1542, Francis Xavier made his way to the southern coast of India, where he hoped to restore a Christian community that dated back to the first century, when the Apostle Thomas was purported to have ministered there.

St. Francis Xavier's travels were not finished. While in a Portuguese settlement in Malaysia, Francis Xavier met a Japanese man named Anger, who gave him quite a bit of information about Japan. Anger, whom Francis baptized a Catholic, led Francis Xavier to Kagoshima in Japan in 1549. He spent the first year learning the language, and by 1551, though he had faced much resistance, Francis Xavier had established the nucleus of the Catholic Church that survives to this day in Japan. Francis Xavier also planned an evangelization trip to China. He reached a small island, Shangchuan, off the Chinese coast, but became ill before he could reach the mainland. He died on December 2, 1552, on Shangchuan. Because of his extensive travels over a very short, ten-year span, St. Francis Xavier is known as the greatest Church missionary since St. Paul the Apostle.

Depiction of the death of St. Francis Xavier

MATTEO RICCI

Matteo Ricci was born in 1552 in Macerata, a town in present-day Italy. He entered the Society of Jesus in 1571, and in 1577, he requested to be transferred to Asia. He was sent to China, where Christianity had been brought as early as 635 by some Persian Christians. However, whatever communities they established had not endured.

Ricci learned the Chinese language and familiarized himself with Chinese history and culture. When he arrived in China in 1583 with his Jesuit companion Michele Ruggieri, Ricci dressed as a Buddhist monk; later he dressed as a Confucian mandarin. He immediately attracted attention among the Chinese ruling class. In 1601, Ricci became the first Western missionary to be invited to meet with the Chinese emperor. Ricci accommodated Chinese culture and religion in other ways: he allowed converts to Catholicism to continue to embrace Chinese ancestor worship. At the time of his death in 1610, Ricci left behind 2,500 Catholics in China, mostly in the educated classes.

In 1705, nearly a century after Ricci's death, Pope Clement XI declared that Ricci and other Jesuits' techniques of cultural **accommodation** were not advisable, setting in motion an era of persecution of Christians in China and Japan.

accommodation The method by which religious missionaries, such as the Jesuits, adjust their evangelization methods to match the cultural and linguistic elements of the group whom they are evangelizing.

The North American Martyrs, also known as the Canadian Martyrs, were all killed between 1642 and 1649 during warfare between the Huron, to whom they were ministering, and the Iroquois.

In total, five French missionaries were martyred during this period in Canada and another three in New York—the North American Jesuit Martyrs. Those who were killed in New York were St. Isaac Jogues, St. René Goupil, and St. Jean Lalande.

In recent years, the Church has been criticized, sometimes fairly, for how some of those representing the Church treated native peoples. However, it is also important to recognize the contributions of Catholics such as Bartolomé de las Casas, St. Jean de Brébeuf, and others in the work of evangelization in the New World, Far East, and Africa.

The Church is always a missionary Church. From the time Jesus first sent his Apostles out to the ends of the earth, the Church has continuously reached out to people who have not heard the Gospel. This mission was very pronounced in the Age of Exploration, as explorers went out to seek new avenues to wealth and to discover new routes of transit around the world. As the Church entered new lands steeped in ancient traditions, cultures, and religions, the initial results were typically painful; accepting Christ and the Catholic faith is an "either/or" proposition. Catholicism requires that new members cut several ties to old ways of living. The missionary efforts in the New World, Asia, and Africa planted the roots of a vital Church in each of these places—roots that have needed the centuries since to produce blossoms.

SECTION ASSESSMENT

NOTE TAKING

Use the summary sentences you wrote on the saints and missionaries to help you answer the following items.

1. What qualities did most of the saints and missionaries of this period share?
2. Name two instances of a saint or missionary exhibiting humility.
3. Besides the words listed for your Note Taking sentences, share two other characteristics that most of these saints and missionaries have in common. Explain why you chose the words that you did.

COMPREHENSION

4. What was particularly abusive about the encomienda system?
5. Who was Bartolomé de las Casas, and what did he do to combat the encomienda system?
6. Explain the difference in styles of missionary work employed by the Franciscans and the Jesuits.
7. Why were the Huron natives impressed with St. Jean de Brébeuf?
8. Why is St. Martin de Porres often referred to as the "Saint of the Broom"?

CRITICAL THINKING

9. Why do you think the Blessed Mother asked St. Juan Diego Cuauhtlatoatzin to take her request to the local bishop?

ANALYSIS

10. Compare and contrast the missionary approaches of St. Francis Xavier and Matteo Ricci.

REFLECTION

11. St. Martin de Porres experienced a fair amount of mistreatment, especially during his youth, because he was of mixed ethnicity. Describe how he looked beyond his circumstances in order to serve the Lord first and foremost.

APPLICATION

12. Explain the importance of following the Gospel even when you are surrounded by pressures to oppose it, such as those experienced by many of the first saints of the Americas during their lifetimes.

Section Assignments

Focus Question

What was the Church's impact on the Renaissance and the Age of Exploration and vice versa?

Complete one of the following:

- Is it more accurate to say that the Renaissance and the Age of Exploration affected the Church or that the Church affected the Renaissance and the Age of Exploration? Or was there a combination of the two realities? Defend your response in three to four paragraphs, reinforcing your argument with historical evidence.

- Write a brief synopsis of the life of a Renaissance artist, detailing how this figure was able to provide religious imagery to the period, whether by painting or sculpting (or both) or by designing and building religious structures (churches or parts thereof).

- Research the life of a saint who was either born in or ministered in a European colony during the Renaissance. What attributes of this man or woman's life contributed to his or her canonization? If the saint came from within the ruling class of the colonized area, make sure to pay close attention to how this saint served and otherwise interacted with those who belonged to the less powerful social classes or who were otherwise marginalized by the ruling powers in society.

INTRODUCTION

The Origins of the Renaissance and the Age of Exploration

Explain the difference between humanism and Christian humanism.

SECTION 1

The Rebirth of Classical Writing and Scholarship

- Research the lives of Erasmus and St. Thomas More. Do the following: (1) Write one fact you discovered in your research about each person that was not mentioned in this section; and (2) share evidence of the friendship between Erasmus and St. Thomas More.

SECTION 2

Religious Art of the Renaissance

Tour the Vatican Museums online at www.museivaticani.va. Write a brief report on one of the great Renaissance artworks represented on the tour.

SECTION 3

Evangelization and the Age of Exploration

Compare and contrast the way the Church evangelized the Roman Empire in the first three centuries with how she undertook evangelization in the Age of Exploration.

SECTION 4

Saints in the Age of Exploration

Name two examples of how Catholic missionaries strove to further the cause of human rights for the native peoples in colonized areas.

Chapter Assignments

Choose and complete at least one of the three assignments to assess your understanding of the material in this chapter.

1. Ongoing Human Solidarity

As was sometimes the case during the Age of Exploration, human rights violations take place today by governments around the globe. Compare the words of Antonio de Montesinos, a Dominican friar who delivered the homily that inspired Bartolomé de las Casas to seek out legislation to protect the natives, with Pope Paul VI's words in the encyclical *Populorum Progressio* (*On the Development of Peoples*).

Antonio de Montesinos

Why do you keep them so oppressed and weary, not giving them enough to eat nor taking care of them in their illness? For with the excessive work you demand of them they fall ill and die, or rather you kill them with your desire to extract gold every day. And what care do you take that they should be instructed in religion? . . . Are these not men? Have they not rational souls? Are you not bound to love them as you love yourselves? (*The Spanish Struggle for Justice in the Conquest of America,* 17)

Pope Paul VI

Each person is a member of society. Each is part of the whole of humankind. It is not just certain individuals, but all persons who are called to the fullness of development. Civilizations are born, develop and die. But humanity is advancing along the path of history like the waves of a rising tide encroaching gradually on the shore. We have inherited from past generations and have benefited from the work of our contemporaries; for this reason we have obligations toward all, and we cannot refuse to interest ourselves in those who will come after us to enlarge the human family. The reality of human solidarity, which is a benefit for us, also imposes a duty. (*Populorum Progressio*, 17)

Do all of the following:

- Write *one complete paragraph* naming and explaining a common theme in the words of Antonio de Montesinos and Pope Paul VI.
- Write *two complete paragraphs* naming and describing—by people, place, and history—a situation from the current news that qualifies as a human rights violation.
- Write *three complete paragraphs* describing how the national government, the Church, and you personally can respond effectively to end the human rights violation you named.

2. Film Review: *The Mission*

The 1986 British film *The Mission* is one of the fifteen films recognized in the "religion" category on the Vatican film list. The film is set in the late eighteenth century in Argentina and Paraguay and focuses on a Spanish Jesuit priest, Fr. Gabriel, who attempts to set up a mission for the native people. The film depicts tensions between Fr. Gabriel and his mission and Spanish mercenary slave traders who are attempting to capture and sell natives.

Your assignment is to watch the entire movie (available free online) and write a two-page, double-spaced review. You are encouraged to use outside sources, which should be cited in MLA style. Include the following in your review:

- Film title
- Summary of the plot. This section should be concise and to the point. Offer some brief background or context on the plot. You can also include whether you like or dislike certain parts of the film as long as you give concrete reasons why. Avoid writing things such as "it is boring" or "I loved the acting" unless you have reasons to support these kinds of statements.
- The filmmaker. Research some information about the filmmaker: Why did he choose this topic? What point was he trying to get across? What sort of feedback did he get from reviewers and the public after the film was released?
- Creative elements. Review elements of the cinematography, casting, costumes, and setting. How did these elements enhance the film?
- How the film relates to your course. In your conclusion, make connections between the film and the material you have learned in this chapter and course. This is also the place to comment on the historical accuracy of the film.

3. Reflection on the Life of St. Kateri Tekakwitha

St. Kateri Tekakwitha (1656–1680) is the first Native American canonized a saint. She is often called the "Lily of the Mohawks." Her father was a Mohawk chief; her mother was an Algonquin who was captured by the Mohawks. She took the name Kateri, which means Catherine, as her Christian name when she was baptized at age nineteen. Pope Benedict XVI canonized St. Kateri Tekakwitha in 2012.

Conduct light research on the life of St. Kateri Tekakwitha. Then write a two-page reflective essay in which you answer, among other details, the following questions:

- What effect might the life and martyrdom of St. Isaac Jogues, one of the North American Jesuit Martyrs (see the subsection "Missionaries and Martyrs in the North American Northeast" in Section 4 of this chapter), have had on St. Kateri? He was martyred in her village in 1646, just ten years before her birth.
- How did St. Kateri's conversion and Baptism affect how many of her fellow villagers viewed her?

- What occurred toward the end of St. Kateri's relatively short life that provided those close to her with evidence of her saintliness?
- St. Kateri died at the young age of twenty-four. How can her life serve as an example to teenagers and young adults who are trying to live as disciples of Christ?

Prayer

Prayer for Missionaries

Lord, our God, help us to walk with you
on the pathway to the Beatitudes and
to live out your mission in today's world.
Bind us to all men and women of our time
so that together we may bring the
Good News to the ends of the earth.
Open our hearts and our Christian communities
to the needy, the afflicted, the oppressed.
May we radiate the Living Christ
and transform our lives in the hope of the Resurrection.
This prayer we make to you
who is the living God, now and forever.
Amen.
—Courtesy of the Archdiocese of Vancouver, Canada

6

THE CALL FOR CHURCH REFORM

Pope Francis Holds Meeting with AMERICAN TELEVANGELISTS AT THE VATICAN

While a high five between Protestant televangelists and a pope won't solve all the divisions between Protestants and Catholics, it can't hurt. In June 2014, Pope Francis met with a delegation of various prominent televangelists at the Vatican. The delegation included such well-known Protestant figures as Kenneth Copeland and James Robison. In the middle of the meeting, Robison mentioned that Pope Francis's preaching of the Gospel had had an emotional impact on him. It was at that point that he asked for and received a high five from Pope Francis!

Pope Francis meets often with Protestant leaders in the spirit of ecumenical dialogue. In July 2016, for example, he discussed points of agreement with evangelical leaders in Rome. Later, in the fall of 2016, the pope visited Sweden to participate in ecumenical events marking the five hundredth anniversary of the Protestant Reformation. The events were structured around the themes of thanksgiving, repentance, and commitment to common witness.

FOCUS QUESTION

What issues led to **PROTESTANTISM**, and how did the Church **RESPOND WITH A COUNTERREFORM**?

Chapter Overview

Introduction: Martin Luther and the Roots of Protestantism

Section 1: The Church's Response and a Division in Christianity

Section 2: Protestantism Spreads to New State Churches

Section 3: The Council of Trent and Clarification of Church Doctrine

Section 4: The Church Enacts Reforms

INTRODUCTION

Martin Luther and the Roots of Protestantism

MAIN IDEA

A Catholic priest, Martin Luther, led a protest against the Catholic Church that initiated a break from the Church and several divisions within the Church.

The Protestant Reformation occurred in sixteenth-century Europe, beginning in Germany. Its consequences, however, extended beyond that place and time; in fact, they persist today. Prior to the sixteenth century, the Church herself had initiated many reforms designed to enhance her ministry and administration. But the Protestant Reformation was different; it went beyond mere reform. The Protestant Reformation ultimately led to a division of the Church and a shift in the religious and political structure of Western Europe. From the mid-sixteenth century on, Europe became very divided, both religiously and politically.

The Beginning of the Reformation

Martin Luther was a German priest, a friar in the Augustinian Order. Born in 1483, the son of strict merchant-class parents, Luther began his adult life as a law student; however, after he narrowly escaped a frightful lightning storm, he vowed to enter the monastery. Living a strict monastic life once he became a friar, he eventually earned a doctorate in theology. The Augustinians sent him to teach moral theology and Scripture at the University of Wittenberg.

Luther had many religious scruples. He had an overwhelming sense of unworthiness, a dread of sin, and a fear of death and judgment. He imagined God as

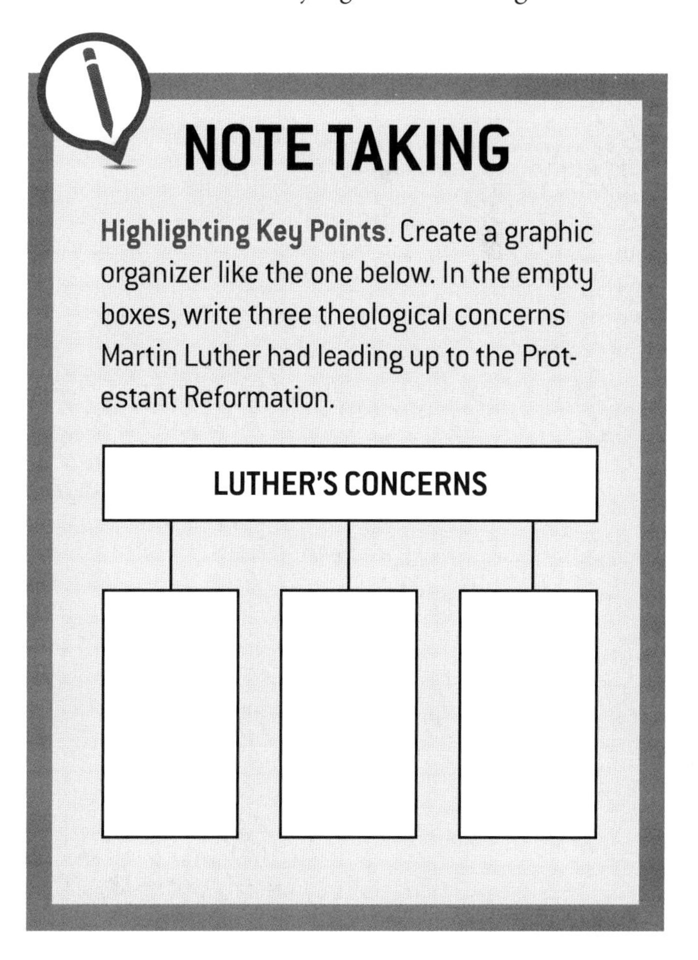

On October 31, 1517, Martin Luther nailed his Ninety-Five Theses *to the door of the church in Wittenberg, Germany. This document was also known as the "Disputation on the Power and Efficacy of Indulgences."*

a stern judge. No matter what penances he performed, he could not get a sense of God's love and his offer of salvation. One day, while studying Romans 3:21–28, Luther concluded that only faith in God's mercy *justifies* sinners (reunites sinners with God). Luther's insight brought him joy and peace. He began to teach it to others. The issue of the selling of indulgences gave Luther the opportunity to contrast his views with an almost superstitious piety that had arisen in the Church. *Indulgences*, the remission of temporal punishment in Purgatory due for sins already forgiven, were a spiritual benefit that some churchmen abused in Luther's day. The Church teaches that she can dispense indulgences from the richness of graces won by Jesus' sacrifice on the Cross to remove the temporal punishment for sin. However, it was a scandal in Luther's day that the Church was selling these spiritual benefits to finance building projects (such as St. Peter's Basilica in Rome) and to pay off debts incurred by absentee bishops.

When the Dominican Johann Tetzel traveled throughout Germany to sell indulgences using slogans such as "Another soul to heaven springs when in the box a shilling rings," Luther acted. On October 31, 1517, Luther posted his *Ninety-Five Theses* on the door of the church in Wittenberg, Germany, to protest Tetzel's preaching and challenge other theologians to debate his ideas. The *Ninety-Five Theses* also expressed Luther's concern regarding the corrupt practices of some members of the clergy and the widespread ignorance of the laity in matters of faith.

This chapter addresses some of the other concerns Luther detailed that contributed to the Protestant Reformation as well as questions such as the following:

- Why did the call for reform go beyond a mere debate between Martin Luther, a Catholic priest, and Church authorities?
- What were the results of the Protestant Reformation, and what were its effects on the political and religious landscape?

This chapter also addresses how the Church responded with her own **Catholic Reformation**. The impact of both the original protests and the Church's response is still felt well into the twenty-first century.

Catholic Reformation Also known as the Counter-Reformation, the response of the Catholic Church to the protests of Martin Luther and others who had separated from the Church. It consisted of an effort to clarify and re-present the teachings and pastoral practices inherent to Catholicism.

SECTION ASSESSMENT

NOTE TAKING

Use the graphic organizer you created to help you answer the following items.

1. What were Luther's three main concerns expressed in his *Ninety-Five Theses*? How would you rank them in order of importance, from least important to most important? Explain your reasoning.

COMPREHENSION

2. Who was Johann Tetzel?
3. What action did Luther take to set the Protestant Reformation into motion?

VOCABULARY

4. Define the *Catholic Reformation.*

CRITICAL THINKING

5. What role might the Renaissance and the Age of Exploration have had in the start of the Protestant Reformation?

SECTION 1

The Church's Response and a Division in Christianity

MAIN IDEA

The Church responded to Martin Luther with edicts that resulted in his excommunication. Luther broke from the Church, the beginning of Lutheranism. Eventually, the Peace of Augsburg established the principle of *Cuius Regio, Eius Religio*, which meant that subjects had to adopt the faith of the ruler in the lands where they lived.

Martin Luther sent copies of his *Ninety-Five Theses* to bishops throughout Germany, with the goal of initiating debate and discussion of the issues. This dramatic event marked the beginning of the Protestant Reformation. At the time, Luther neither foresaw nor desired that his actions would cause such a rift in Christianity. He had no intention of leading a revolution or a break within the Church. The call to reform had begun, however, and there was no going back.

Pope Leo X and local bishops took the initial step of condemning many of the ideas that Martin Luther had presented in his *Ninety-Five Theses*. However, Luther continued to preach and spread his teachings, leading to an increase in their acceptance. Although Church officials had first viewed the issues brought up by Luther as an internal dispute within the Church, it soon became evident that what Luther was professing went far beyond an internal disagreement. Eventually, since Luther consistently refused to recant his misdirected teachings, and since he ultimately admitted he did not recognize the authority of the pope, Pope Leo X was left with no choice but to excommunicate him.

In June 1520, Pope Leo X issued *Exsurge Domine (Arise, O Lord): Against the Errors of Martin Luther and His Followers*, a papal bull condemning many of Luther's theses. The pope's personal envoy tried to deliver the bull to Luther and many of his followers

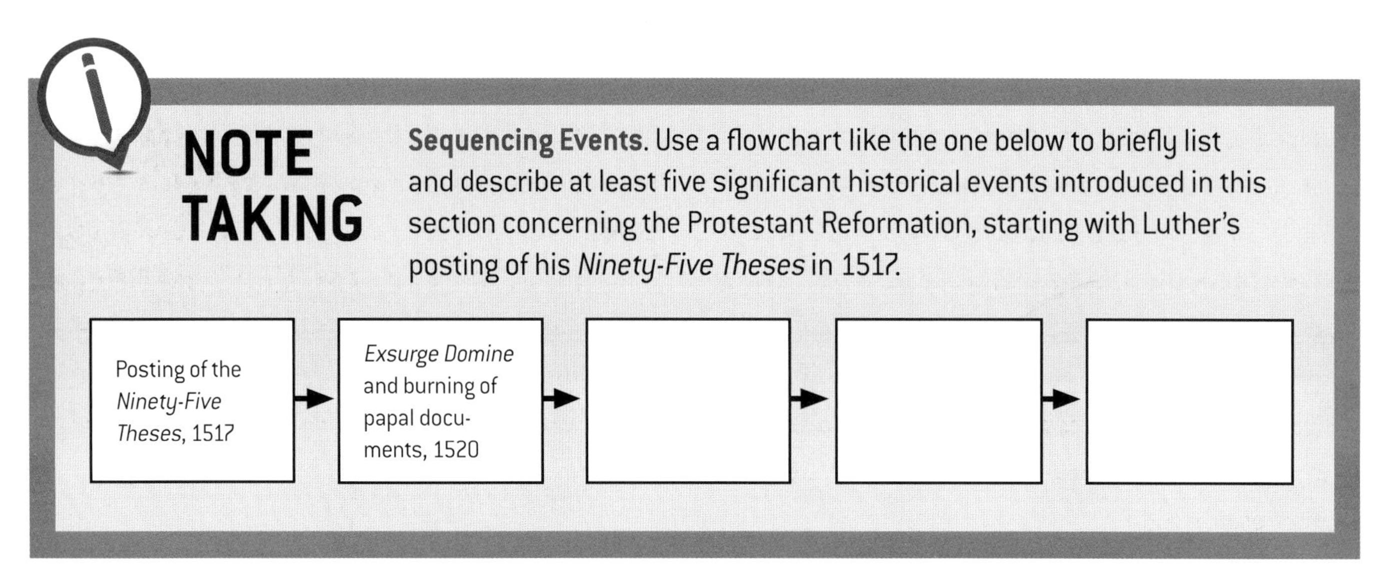

Martin Luther at the Diet of Worms in 1521

(including some of his students who attended the University of Wittenberg), only to have them collect the papal documents and burn them in December 1520. Pope Leo X's formal decree of Luther's excommunication, titled *Decet Romanum Pontificem*, was put in place on January 3, 1521, more than three years after Luther had first posted his *Ninety-Five Theses*.

Afterward, the Holy Roman emperor Charles V ordered Luther to appear before him and papal representatives for questioning at an event that came to be referred to as the *Diet of Worms*. Luther thought that he was being called to discuss some of the issues he had raised. Rather, he was being given one last opportunity to reverse his heretical teachings. He did not, instead responding, "Here I stand. I cannot do otherwise. God help me. Amen." In May 1521, as a result of Luther's ongoing refusal to recant his teachings, Charles V issued the *Edict of Worms*, which officially identified Luther as a heretic.

Luther had powerful allies among the German princes, especially Frederick of Saxony, who guaranteed him safe passage from the meeting at Worms and agreed to hide him. *Nationalism*, the movement for a united, independent German nation, helped to explain the strong support Luther received. The Germans had grown tired of the corrupt Italian papacy's extracting money from their country.

While in exile, Luther translated the Bible into German and wrote many pamphlets explaining his ideas. The recently invented printing press (ca. 1440–1450) helped him to reach many people. Eventually, Luther came out of exile, married, fathered children, preached widely, wrote catechisms, and composed many religious hymns. In 1530, his disciple Philip Melanchthon drafted the basic creed of the new religion, Lutheranism, under the title *Augsburg Confession*.

In addition to the deaths caused by the German Peasants' Revolt, fires and looting destroyed property.

The German Peasants' Revolt

The nationalistic agenda of the German princes was not the only political exploitation of the dispute between Luther and the Church. Other social classes were involved as well. For example, in 1524, many German peasants decided to associate their request for more opportunity and better treatment with the differences between Luther and the Church.

Although Luther first provided support for the German peasants, he withdrew his backing of them when violence broke out—first violence from the German princes against the peasants and subsequently violence among the peasants. Once the German princes perceived that they had the full support of Luther to use any means necessary to restore order against the peasant uprising, the outcome was staggering: soldiers sponsored by the German princes killed well more than one hundred thousand peasants. This tragic episode became known as the *German Peasants' Revolt* (1524–1525). In its aftermath, large segments of the German lower social classes felt betrayed by Luther. Many members of the peasantry either returned to the Catholic Church or joined another newly formed Protestant church. Many German princes increasingly viewed Luther as a supporter of their political agendas.

Turmoil Leading to the Peace of Augsburg

In 1526, Archduke Ferdinand I of Austria convened an imperial meeting in Speyer, a city in what is now Germany, at which the decision was made to suspend the Edict of Worms that had declared Luther a heretic. This first Diet of Speyer also permitted every prince within the Holy Roman Empire to establish the religion of his domain. Some princes chose Lutheranism, while some chose Catholicism. However, in 1529, the second Diet of Speyer reinstated the charge of heresy against Luther. Some prominent Catholic figures renewed their call for Luther to be brought to justice due to his heretical teachings. Those German princes who had the greatest allegiance to Luther initiated a protest of the concessions that the Catholics had requested; this led to their eventual acquisition of the name *Protestants*. Other terms for the new religions, such as *reformed churches*, also arose.

Throughout the decades that followed, there were various attempts to reunify Catholics and Protestants. While progress was made in some regards, the efforts were ultimately unsuccessful. Therefore, in 1555, the imperial assembly of the Holy Roman Empire within Germany made a decision known as the *Peace of Augsburg*, which decreed that the leader (whether a prince or a king) of each region could choose either the Catholic faith or the Lutheran faith as the official one for his area of political control. This policy was known as *Cuius Regio, Eius Religio*, Latin for "Whose Realm, His Religion."

The goals of the Peace of Augsburg were similar to those of the first Diet of Speyer. However, a key

The Peace of Augsburg (September 25, 1555) was signed by Charles V and the forces of the Schmalkaldic League during the Diet of Augsburg.

difference was that under the Peace of Augsburg, the only Protestant church that was allowed was Lutheranism. Furthermore, the treaty specified that if a Catholic bishop became Lutheran, he had to part with all of his property. Those who did not want to convert to the official religion of their region were expected to migrate to an area where their faith was permitted under the principle of *Cuius Regio, Eius Religio*. In less than four decades, between 1517 and 1555, the Protestant Reformation had changed the religious outlook and political fabric of Europe.

SECTION ASSESSMENT

NOTE TAKING

Use the flowchart on which you briefly listed five significant events in the Protestant Reformation to help you answer the following questions.

1. What was the subject of the Edict of Worms?
2. Why were some peasants disillusioned with Lutheranism after the German Peasants' Revolt?
3. What decision did the second Diet of Speyer overturn?
4. What is the *Augsburg Confession*?
5. What was decided by the Peace of Augsburg?

COMPREHENSION

6. What was Luther's response to the Catholic Church officials who called on him to recant statements that they had determined were heretical?
7. When did the term *Protestant* first come to be used?
8. Explain the meaning of the Latin phrase *Cuius Regio, Eius Religio*.

CRITICAL THINKING

9. Of the factors that led to the Protestant Reformation, which one do you think is the most significant, and why?

SECTION 2

Protestantism Spreads to New State Churches

MAIN IDEA

After Martin Luther unleashed a division in Christianity, other Protestant reform movements spread throughout most of Europe.

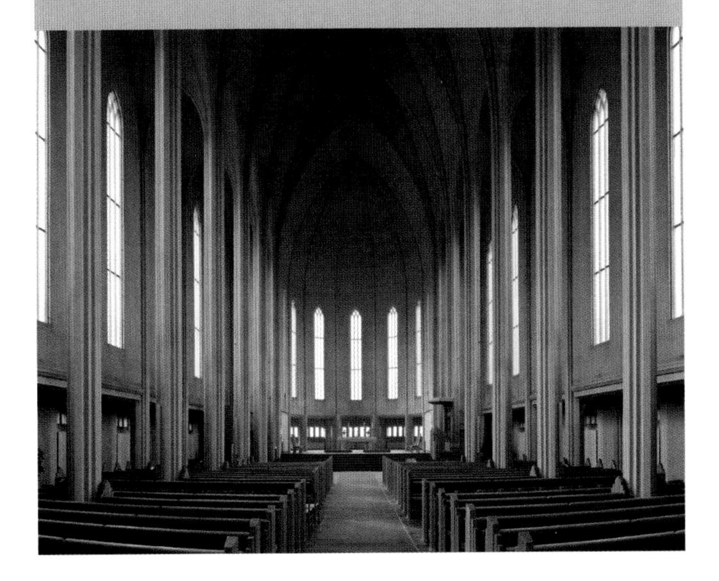

Lutheranism and the rise of nationalism were catalysts for more division within the Church in the sixteenth and seventeenth centuries as new state churches arose in Europe. In addition to Martin Luther in Germany, four prominent figures in particular played a considerable role in forming state churches in their respective countries: Ulrich Zwingli and John Calvin in Switzerland, John Knox in Scotland, and King Henry VIII in England.

Ulrich Zwingli (1484–1531)

Ulrich Zwingli led Protestant reform in Zurich, Switzerland, beginning in 1522, when he encouraged a democratic rule for his Swiss Reformed Church. More anticlerical and anti-institutional than Luther, Zwingli removed images from churches, banned religious music, and abolished fast days. He taught that the Eucharist only symbolizes Jesus' presence. Zwingli's reform influenced the religious practice of all Switzerland even to modern times.

Interestingly, Luther did not consider Zwingli to be a Christian. Zwingli, himself, claimed to have started the Reformation before he even heard of Luther.

John Calvin (1509–1564)

John Calvin was a Frenchman who gained a master's degree in theology and a doctorate in law. He left Paris for Switzerland, where he wrote his famous *Institutes of the Christian Religion* (1536), the most important

NOTE TAKING

Identifying Main Ideas. Create a flowchart like the one on the right. As you read this section, record main ideas chronologically about the spread of Protestantism throughout Europe and the world. Add more boxes as necessary.

Ulrich Zwingli institutes reform in Switzerland; encourages democratic rule.

systematic theology of the Reformation. Calvin taught the primacy of Scripture and the absolute sovereignty of God. He denied Catholic teaching on the sacraments and condemned the papacy, monasticism, and clerical celibacy. Calvin's best-known doctrine is **predestination**. According to this teaching, God selects people for salvation or damnation before they are born.

Calvin was strict and harsh, and his personality affected the type of church that he set up in Geneva, Switzerland. He created a *theocracy*, a civil government controlled by his church. He and his followers regulated all aspects of people's lives, even punishing children for laughing while playing. His council outlawed dancing, card playing, and many other forms of entertainment.

Calvin's influence throughout Europe grew because of his university at Geneva. Especially attractive was Calvin's brand of church governance, which included pastors, doctors (teachers), and deacons. Calvinism spread much farther than Lutheranism, which was mostly limited to Germany and the Scandinavian countries. Holland adopted Calvin's reforms, as did parts of France and Hungary.

John Knox (1505–1572)

Eventually, Calvin's reforms made their way to England. John Knox, a former Catholic priest, brought Presbyterianism, an offshoot of Calvinism, to Scotland. Knox stressed the equality of all believers, teaching that everyone is a priest (presbyter), thus rendering separate clergy unnecessary. Reformed, Congregationalist, and Presbyterian churches today all look to John Calvin as their spiritual father. Calvin's emphasis on clean living, a harsh and judgmental God, thrift in business dealings, and strictness in religious observance came to America with the Puritans.

King Henry VIII (1491–1547)

King Henry VIII cannot technically be called a reformer, because the Protestant Reformation came to England not due to a doctrinal dispute but because the pope would not allow Henry VIII (king from 1509 to 1547) to divorce his wife, Catherine of Aragon. Catherine had not borne him a male heir, so Henry VIII wished to marry Anne Boleyn in order to have a son. Henry VIII's solution to the conflict was to make himself head of the Church in England.

For the most part, Henry VIII accepted Catholic doctrine. In 1521, in fact, he had won the title "Defender of the Faith" for his eloquent rebuttal of Luther's teaching that Jesus intended only two sacraments. He later issued his *Six Articles* (1539), which insisted on Catholic teachings and imposed penalties on anyone who denied the Eucharist, Confession, or clerical celibacy.

His most controversial action, however, involved the Act of Supremacy of 1534, which required an oath of allegiance to himself as head of the English church. A few brave Catholics refused to take this *Oath of Supremacy*, most notably St. John Fisher and St. Thomas More (see the subsection "Two Christian Scholars of the Renaissance" in Chapter 5, Section 1). St. John Fisher was a cardinal, and St. Thomas More was Henry VIII's close friend and the Lord High

predestination A belief that one's actions are not only preknown by God but also predetermined, thus denying God's gift of free will. The Catholic position is that God does have knowledge of who will be saved and who will be lost, yet it is God's desire that all will be saved. To this end, he provides graces and helps, which people are free to accept or reject. This means that while God knows certain people will be lost, this is not the choice of God but of those individuals.

MAJOR EVENTS, TEACHINGS, AND BELIEFS OF THE PROTESTANT REFORMATION

Today, Protestantism refers to a large movement that encompasses hundreds of different denominations. The accompanying chart presents some of the major teachings of groups that arose in the sixteenth century.

LUTHERAN	CALVINIST	ANGLICAN
Key event: publication of *Ninety-Five Theses* in 1517	**Key event:** publication of *Institutes of the Christian Religion* in 1536	**Key event:** King Henry VIII declares himself head of the Church in England in 1534 (Act of Supremacy)
1. Human beings have a fallen nature. Only faith brings salvation.	1. Human nature is utterly depraved.	1. Accepts most Catholic teachings about faith and good works. Does not recognize papal primacy.
2. Primacy of the Bible. Encourages individual interpretation of Scripture.	2. The doctrine of predestination. Christ died only for the elect. The elect cannot resist God's grace nor can they backslide.	2. The monarch is head of the church in England. The monarch establishes what is allowable religious practice in the realm.
3. Accepts only the sacraments of Baptism and the Eucharist. Believes in *consubstantiation*—body and blood of Christ coexist with the bread and wine, which do not change.	3. Accepts only Baptism and Communion. Believes that Christ's presence in the Eucharist is spiritual only. Encourages Bible reading, sobriety, capitalism, and a strict Sabbath observance. Stresses the priesthood of all believers and democracy in the church.	3. Accepts the Seven Sacraments. Liturgy very similar to Catholic liturgy. Bishops head dioceses, and priests serve in parishes. Priests can marry.
4. **Rejects:** Holy days, fast days, honoring saints, indulgences, the Rosary, monasticism, the other five sacraments.	4. **Rejects:** Whatever is not in the Bible—for example, vestments, organs, hymns.	4. **Rejects:** The *Roman Missal* and many Roman Catholic beliefs and practices, though the acceptance varies among Anglicans; for example, some who hold a more evangelical theology might only accept that two sacraments—Baptism and Eucharist—are instituted by Christ.

Chancellor of England. Nevertheless, More refused to violate his conscience, which forbade him to deny the primacy of the pope. Henry had both Fisher and More beheaded in 1535.

Henry confiscated the monasteries, claiming for himself vast Church holdings and sapping the strength of the Catholic Church in England. This prepared the way for Calvinists. After Henry died, the archbishop of Canterbury, Thomas Cranmer, exerted considerable influence through his *Book of Common Prayer* (1549) and the *Forty-Two Articles of Religion*. Half of these articles contained Catholic doctrine, while the other half espoused Calvinist and Lutheran teachings.

Mary Tudor (1553–1558), daughter of Henry and Catherine of Aragon, tried to restore Catholicism during her reign, but she did it through violent means. She executed almost three hundred people, earning the name "Bloody Mary" from her Protestant opponents. Her attempts at a Catholic restoration failed. When she died, the Catholic restoration in England ended. The long reign of Elizabeth I (daughter of Henry VIII and Anne Boleyn) from 1558 to 1603 established the state religion in England; Elizabeth I synthesized Calvinist, Lutheran, and Catholic elements into what became known as the *Anglican* faith. Anglicanism upheld traditional forms such as the episcopate and elaborate liturgical worship, but it also fostered doctrines that were Calvinist at heart. Like her father, Elizabeth I required the Oath of Supremacy and persecuted Catholics and radical Protestants who refused to take it. Priests were executed if they were caught celebrating the Catholic Mass.

Due to these persecutions, more than twenty thousand Puritans, followers of a branch of Calvinism, left England in the 1620s and 1630s and sailed to the New World. They were the new land's pilgrims, who came to set up holy commonwealths. However, they mirrored the religious prejudice of their day and passed laws against other religious groups (for example, Catholics and Quakers). Some Catholics also left England for America in the 1630s, as much for financial opportunity as for religious freedom. They largely settled in Maryland, which was founded by a Catholic family, the Calverts. Maryland was the first colony to allow freedom of worship.

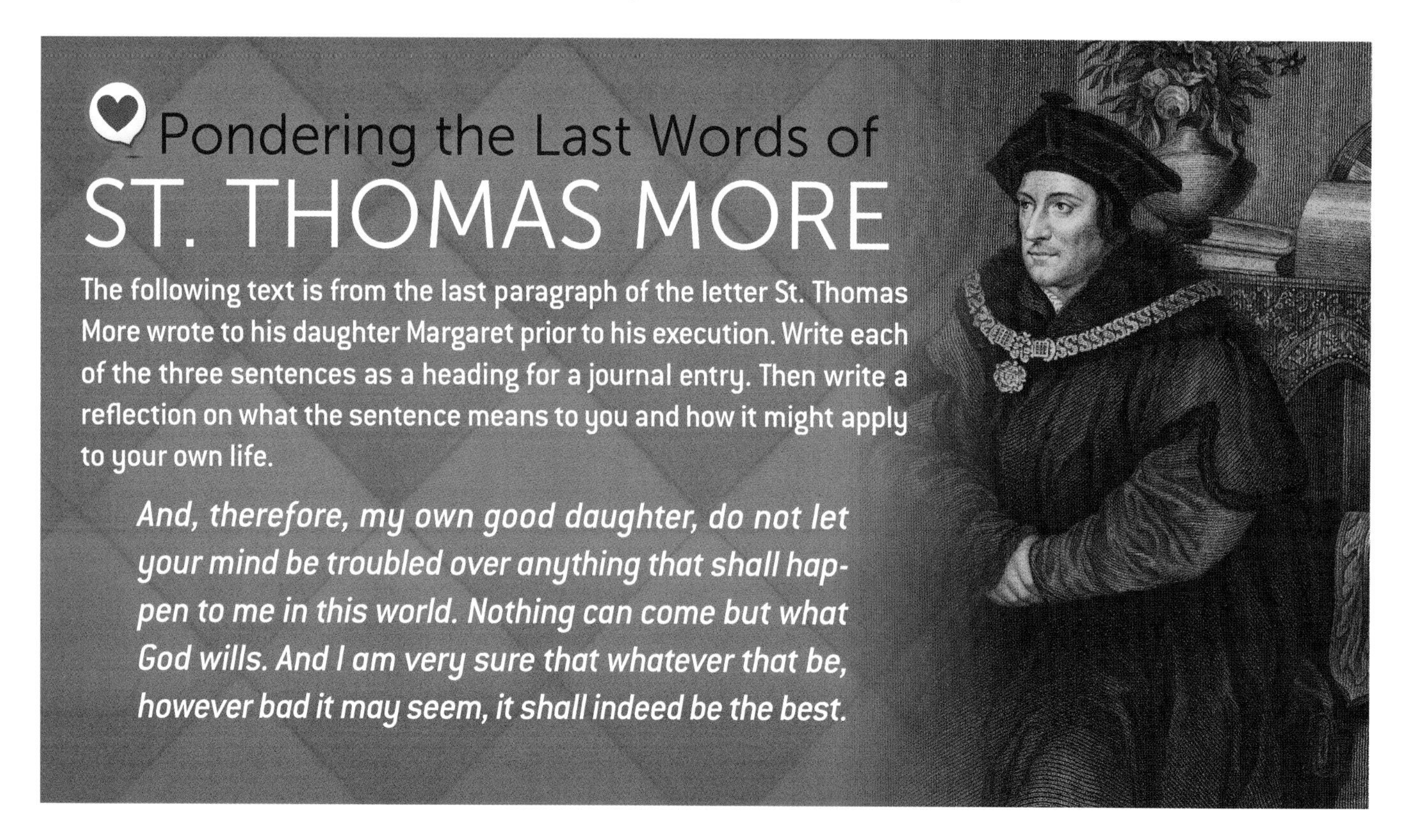

Pondering the Last Words of ST. THOMAS MORE

The following text is from the last paragraph of the letter St. Thomas More wrote to his daughter Margaret prior to his execution. Write each of the three sentences as a heading for a journal entry. Then write a reflection on what the sentence means to you and how it might apply to your own life.

> *And, therefore, my own good daughter, do not let your mind be troubled over anything that shall happen to me in this world. Nothing can come but what God wills. And I am very sure that whatever that be, however bad it may seem, it shall indeed be the best.*

SECTION ASSESSMENT

NOTE TAKING

Use the notes from your flowchart to help you complete the matching exercise below.

1. John Knox	A. Predestination
2. John Calvin	B. Democratic rule
3. King Henry VIII	C. Presbyterians
4. Ulrich Zwingli	D. *Act of Supremacy*

COMPREHENSION

5. What are two reasons that Calvinism was able to spread to a larger geographic region than Lutheranism?
6. Why can't King Henry VIII technically be considered a reformer?
7. Explain why Catholicism was unable to be restored in England after the reign of King Henry VIII.

ANALYSIS

8. Add a fourth column with the heading "Roman Catholicism" to the chart "Major Events, Teachings, and Beliefs of the Protestant Reformation." Summarize Catholic beliefs for each row.

SECTION 3

The Council of Trent and Clarification of Church Doctrine

MAIN IDEA

In order to confront doctrinal errors put forward by Martin Luther and other Protestant reformers, the Catholic Church clarified her teachings at the Council of Trent and initiated a major reform within Catholicism.

The Protestant reformers introduced doctrinal and sacramental teachings and practices that demanded an official response from the Church's Magisterium. For example, Protestant reformers began to allow public worship in the *vernacular*, or language of the local population, instead of Latin, the universal language of the Church. They also called for editions of the Bible to be published in the vernacular. The most popular translation from the period, the Anglican-inspired *King James Bible*, published in 1611 in England, remains widely used in many Protestant churches today.

Protestant reformers also held several contradictory beliefs about the sacraments. Most of the reformers declared that there were just two valid sacraments—Baptism and the Eucharist—as compared to the Seven Sacraments of the Catholic Church. In particular, Luther claimed that confessing sins to a priest was unnecessary; he maintained that the Sacrament of Penance placed too much emphasis on human behavior. Luther and other reformers were also opposed to the Sacrament of Holy Orders, the sacrament required to ordain ministers whose task is to administer the other sacraments. Luther and other reformers advocated for a married clergy rather than the Church's

NOTE TAKING

Summarizing Information. Draw a concept web like the one shown here. As you read the section, fill in the blank circles with the teachings offered by the Council of Trent in response to Martin Luther and other reformers. Add more circles as needed.

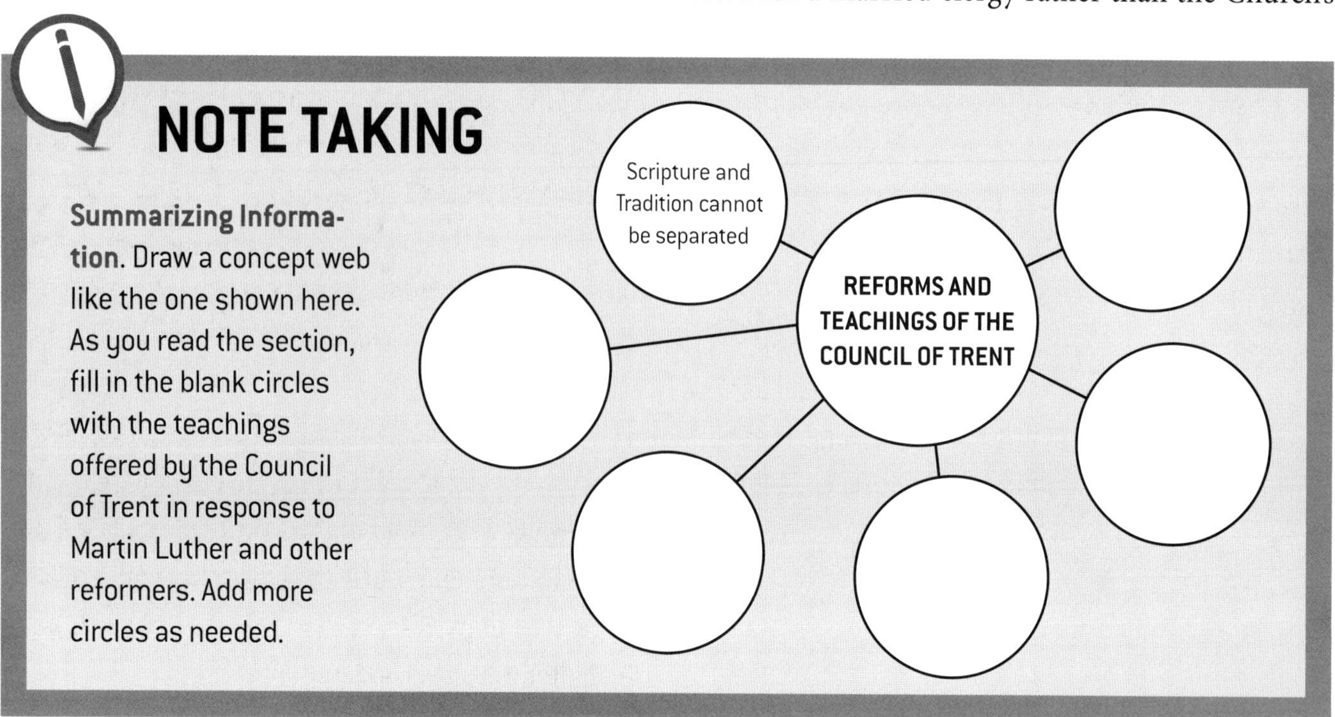

Council of Trent *by Bartolomeo Bossi*

requirement for a celibate priesthood. Recall that Luther himself married after he was excommunicated from the Catholic Church.

The ongoing political chaos of the time stalled the Church's efforts at clarifying her teaching and offering her own reform. The thought of calling a Church-wide council brought up fears of conciliarism, which might have further threatened the papacy. Also, continuous warfare between the Holy Roman emperor and the king of France made finding a suitable place to meet, free from political control of monarchs and other secular leaders, almost impossible. Pope Paul III first attempted to call a council in 1536 in Mantua, Italy, but the Holy Roman emperor Charles V reportedly did not like the location, so the start of the council was delayed.

The Convocation of the Council of Trent

Eventually, Pope Paul III convoked the nineteenth ecumenical council of the Church in Trent, a town in what is now northern Italy. The Council of Trent had more than twenty-five meetings in three sessions (1545–1547, 1551–1552, and 1561–1563) that were interrupted by various wars. In the beginning as few as thirty-four bishops participated, but in the later meetings, more than 230 bishops attended.

The Council of Trent had two primary goals: (1) acknowledging and reforming problems related to the clergy and religious life, and (2) clearly stating Church doctrine, especially on matters that had been distorted by the reformers. Some of the major decisions and doctrinal teachings of the Council of Trent are explained in the following subsections.

Renewal of Clergy and Religious Life

Priestly training was given top priority. Because the quality of priests had been dreadfully low, the council mandated the establishment of seminaries. St. Charles Borromeo created a model seminary in Milan, Italy. Later, Pope Gregory XIII would create many colleges for priests. The most famous of these still operating today is the Pontifical Gregorian University in Rome. Other clerical abuses were corrected. Priestly celibacy was reaffirmed. Bishops were ordered to live in their own dioceses. Priests were to reside in their own parishes, monks in their monasteries, and nuns in their convents. Additionally, priests were required to wear clerical clothing that allowed them to be easily distinguishable from the laity. The council also reaffirmed the supremacy of the pope.

Correcting the Reformers on Doctrinal Issues

The Council of Trent sought to clarify the Church's position on some erroneous doctrines that originated with Luther. One of the central errors was Luther's insistence that only Scripture was necessary for a complete understanding of theology. This claim was known as *sola scriptura* (Latin for "Scripture alone"). The Council of Trent taught that Sacred Scripture and Sacred Tradition must be considered together for a proper understanding of theology. Recall that Sacred Tradition refers to the faith that was handed on by Christ to his Apostles and by those Apostles to their successors, the pope and bishops.

The Council of Trent also made it clear that Sacred Scripture cannot be separated from Sacred Tradition, because Scripture was part of the Tradition of the Church before it was Scripture; furthermore, it was the Church that decided what writings would be considered Sacred Scripture. Scripture is the written account of the earliest understanding of the Faith, and it is the core on which all subsequent understandings are built. Nonetheless, Sacred Tradition cannot be reduced to only what is in Scripture. The council taught that, as it was in the beginning, so it continued to be: the Word of God must be interpreted by the Church, and more explicitly by the Magisterium, in order that it might be properly understood and applied in each generation.

Related to this decision, the council further declared that the Latin translation of the Bible (the Vulgate) was to be considered the authoritative version of the Bible because it was the version of the Bible that had been used by the Church for one thousand years and was therefore part of Sacred Tradition. The council fathers were also concerned that the numerous new translations of the Bible were filled with errors, misinformation, and inaccurate notes.

Luther also argued for *sola gratia* ("[God's] grace alone"). He said that no person could possibly keep all of God's commandments and that everyone would be condemned if salvation hinged upon human behavior rather than God's grace. He and other Protestant reformers believed that the key to salvation was found in a person's faith alone (*sola fide*) and not his or her actions. The Council of Trent agreed in part with the Protestant reformers: people are saved because of the grace of God and the sacrifice of Jesus Christ, not through their own merit. The council reemphasized that a person receives this saving grace first and foremost in the Sacrament of Baptism. The council agreed that a person cannot be justified (reunited with God) without faith.

However, the council also pointed out that Baptism, not personal faith, is the first step toward salvation. Baptism is the "sacrament of faith." Baptism is not only the sign but also the instrument of the faithful relationship a person has with God. In other words, people do not approach the Church because their faith in God is so strong that they have special

The Mass of Saint Martin of Tours *by La Sueur Eustache*

knowledge that they belong to the People of God. Rather, they come to the Church because they *want* the faith that the Church can offer them. When they receive that faith, they also receive the gifts of hope and charity (love). The council taught that unless hope and charity are added to faith, a person is neither united with Christ nor a living member of Christ's Body, the Church.

Related to this response, the council reaffirmed all Seven Sacraments. All the sacraments are efficacious, meaning God works through them. Your behavior does not determine the power of the sacrament, but it does determine the degree to which the sacrament is able to take root your life. No one is saved by his or her good works; rather, a person is saved only by the grace of God. Nonetheless, without good works the grace of God will not take root in your life, because even in offering you grace God does not take away your free will.

Likewise, the Council of Trent disagreed with Luther about the impossibility of keeping God's commandments, declaring that it is possible for a person united with Christ to keep the commandments. A Christian who breaks the commandments deliberately rejects God and loses the grace he or she has already received in Baptism. This grace can be regained only if it is given again by God. The council thus reminded Catholics of the necessity of the Sacrament of Penance.

Additional Doctrinal, Pastoral, and Disciplinary Matters

The Council of Trent also took up several other essential doctrinal and pastoral matters, including the following:

- At the consecration of the Mass, the reality (substance) of the bread and wine changes into the reality of Jesus—his risen, glorified Body and Blood (the council reaffirmed the doctrine of transubstantiation). The Lord is present whole and entire for as long as both **Eucharistic species** subsist.
- The Mass is a true sacrifice, an extension of Calvary through which Christ's sacrifice is made present. Jesus empowered the Apostles to offer this new sacrifice; the Sacrament of Holy Orders passes this power to priests.
- The Sacrament of Penance is the only ordinary means to obtain forgiveness of mortal sins committed after Baptism. Although confession of

Eucharistic species The Real Presence of Jesus' Precious Body (under the mere appearance of the bread) and Jesus' Precious Blood (under the mere appearance of grape wine), accompanied by the fullness of his soul and divinity, after the bread and wine have been consecrated by the priest at Mass.

The Thirty Years' War (1618-1648)

Nowhere was the hatred spawned by unwavering religious conviction more in evidence than in Germany of the seventeenth century. After the reforms of the Council of Trent were put into practice, Catholics were successful in winning back to the Church many areas of central Europe. St. Francis de Sales converted parts of Switzerland, and similar gains were made in Bavaria, Austria, Bohemia, and Poland. Supporting these gains was the House of the Habsburg, a royal family that controlled Germany and which had the support of the emperor of Austria and the king of Spain.

For his decisive victory over the Spanish during the Thirty Years' War, Louis de Bourbon became famous as le Grande Condé.

But the Habsburgs had many political enemies, especially in France. These enemies joined forces with various Protestant groups who feared a Catholic takeover of Germany. The two sides engaged in a series of wars that lasted between 1618 and 1648, the infamous Thirty Years' War. These conflicts involved elements of civil war, with various German princes at times supporting the Habsburgs and at other times trying to overthrow them. The politically and religiously complex Thirty Years' War devastated Germany, causing the death of half its population. Historians rate the Thirty Years' War as the most barbaric in Europe's history up to that time, a war tragically fueled by the religious intolerance of Lutherans, Calvinists, and Catholics.

Attack of the German Imperial Lancers on the Swedish infantry

Looting and destruction of a village during the Thirty Years' War

At one point in the conflict, the Catholic rulers seemed on the point of victory until France came to the aid of the Protestant princes. Ironically, two famous cardinals were in charge of French policy at the time—Cardinal Richelieu (1585–1642) and Cardinal Mazarin (1602–1661). In this battle, the cardinals put the national interests of their mother country over the Catholic identity of Europe.

The ultimate outcome of the war was devastating for Germany. Survivors in Germany were reduced to severe poverty. The Habsburg Empire was devastated, and Spain was no longer Europe's most powerful nation. France emerged as the strongest nation on the continent.

Religiously, the Peace of Westphalia (1648), a series of treaties that ended the Thirty Years' War, legalized Calvinism in Germany and gave Protestantism equal status with Catholicism. The treaty reaffirmed the principle of citizens' following the religion of the prince (*Cuius Regio, Eius Religio*). It drove the last nail in the coffin of the ideal of a united Christendom in Europe.

Historical satirical image about the lack of soldiers during the Thirty Years' War

venial sin is not necessary, it is a good way to grow in virtue.

- There are Seven Sacraments. Matrimony, for example, is a true sacrament, and marriage is indissoluble. Marriages must be performed before a priest and two witnesses.
- Purgatory exists, and the souls in Purgatory benefit from the prayers of people on earth, especially the Mass. True indulgences have spiritual value, as does veneration of the saints. The Council of Trent condemned those who "assert that indulgences are useless or who deny that the Church has the power to grant them." However, the council rejected superstitious abuses concerning relics, statues, and indulgences.

The Council of Trent also addressed some additional matters of *discipline* in the Church, authoring Church laws that affected the daily lives of Catholics. For example, the council clarified laws about the Lenten fast, fasting before receiving Communion, and abstaining from eating meat on Fridays. It also enacted marriage laws. Additionally, the council created an *Index of Forbidden Books* to keep Catholics from reading radical and heretical ideas. Unfortunately, the *Index* grew over the years to include some important intellectual works by such figures as René Descartes, John Milton, Jean-Jacques Rousseau, Immanuel Kant, Victor Hugo, and Gustave Flaubert.

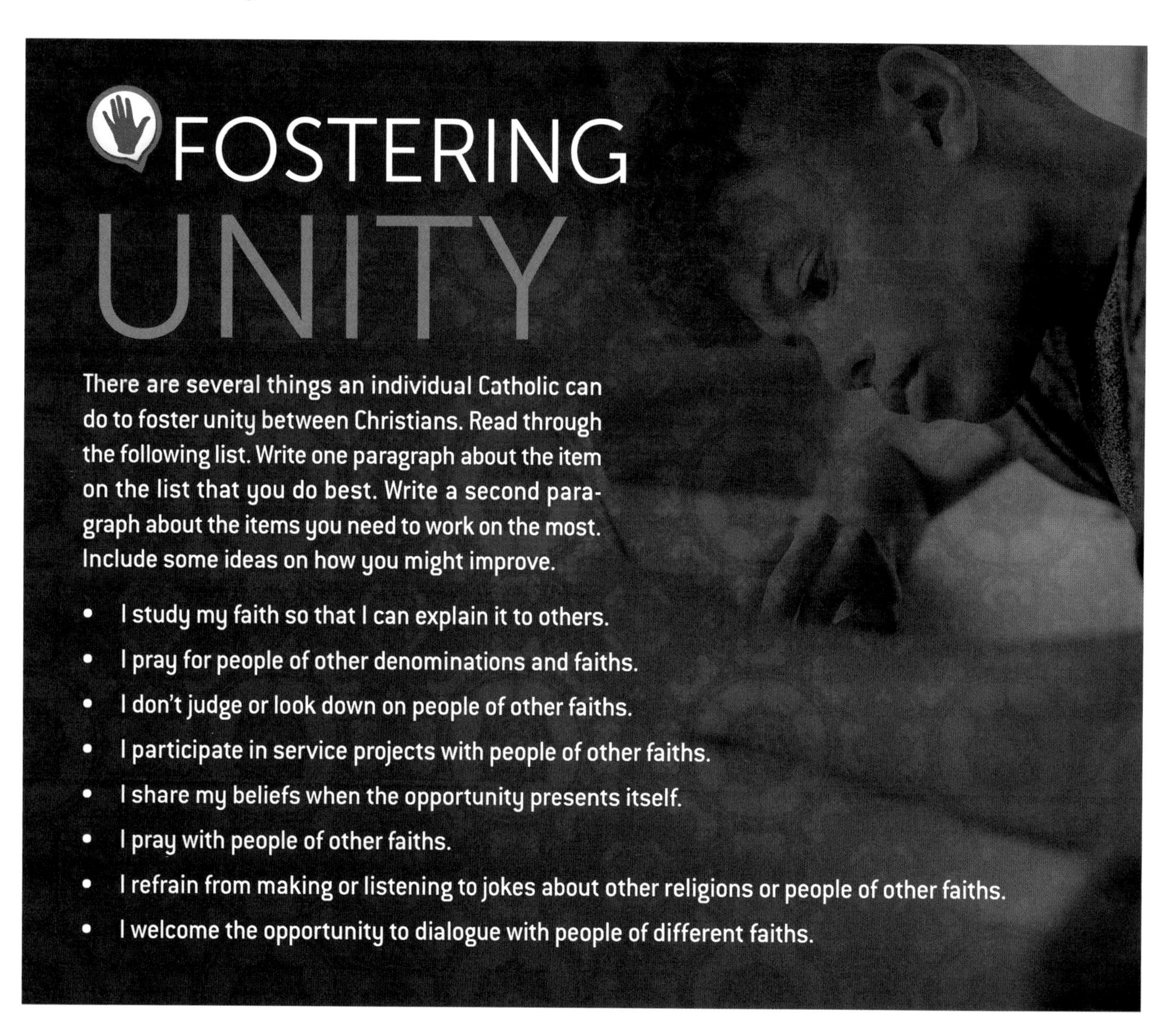

FOSTERING UNITY

There are several things an individual Catholic can do to foster unity between Christians. Read through the following list. Write one paragraph about the item on the list that you do best. Write a second paragraph about the items you need to work on the most. Include some ideas on how you might improve.

- I study my faith so that I can explain it to others.
- I pray for people of other denominations and faiths.
- I don't judge or look down on people of other faiths.
- I participate in service projects with people of other faiths.
- I share my beliefs when the opportunity presents itself.
- I pray with people of other faiths.
- I refrain from making or listening to jokes about other religions or people of other faiths.
- I welcome the opportunity to dialogue with people of different faiths.

SECTION ASSESSMENT

NOTE TAKING

Use the concept web you completed to help you answer the following questions.

1. What were the two primary goals of the Council of Trent?
2. Name three decisions of the Council of Trent that addressed the renewal of the clergy and religious life.
3. How did the council respond to Luther's insistence on *sola scriptura*?
4. Why did the Church insist on the use of the Vulgate?
5. The council agreed with Luther that a person cannot be justified without faith. How did the council part with Luther on the application of this teaching?
6. What are two of the Council of Trent's teachings on the sacraments?

COMPREHENSION

7. Why was there a delay in calling a council to address the protests of Luther and the other reformers?
8. What does it mean to say that the sacraments are efficacious?
9. Name three matters of Church discipline addressed by the Council of Trent.
10. What was the result of the Thirty Years' War according to the Peace of Westphalia?

REFLECTION

11. What do you find positive about being a member of a Church that encompasses both a "teaching Church" and a "learning Church"?

SECTION 4

The Church Enacts Reforms

MAIN IDEA

In the aftermath of the Reformation, as Protestant congregations gained prominence in various areas of Western Europe, the Catholic Church enacted the decisions of the Council of Trent in a period known as the *Catholic Reformation*.

The era beginning with the Council of Trent (1545–1563) and extending for approximately eighty-five years afterward (through the close of the Thirty Years' War in 1648) is sometimes called the *Counter-Reformation* or Catholic Reformation. The period is associated with the **Baroque** period of art, architecture, sculpture, music, and literature. In fact, the Church encouraged a Baroque perspective—in which God and heaven could be depicted vividly and with emotion—on all of life. The Church intended for people to see the connection between this world and the world to come. Ornate, colorful expression was highlighted in churches of the period; the Church of the Gesù in Rome, the mother church of the Society of Jesus, represents this style.

The Baroque style also manifested an interest in the humanity of Jesus. Several devotions arose during this period, including devotion to the **Sacred Heart of Jesus** following the visions of St. Margaret Mary Alacoque. The *Spiritual Exercises* of St. Ignatius of Loyola encouraged people to truly experience and feel the reality of God in their lives. The attention to humanity also characterizes another practice of the time: the preaching about and care for the poor and neglected,

NOTE TAKING

Connecting People with Main Ideas. Create a graphic organizer like the one below. As you read the text, list the names of people who contributed positively to the Catholic Reformation. In the right column, briefly note their contribution. Add rows as needed.

PERSON	CONTRIBUTION TO THE CATHOLIC REFORMATION
St. Margaret Mary Alacoque	Devotion to the Sacred Heart of Jesus
Pope Pius V	
St. Francis de Sales	

A Catholic church in Baroque style (left) and a more simply designed Protestant church (right)

as through the charitable efforts of St. Vincent de Paul and other saints of the period, some of whom are introduced in this section. Other hallmarks of this time were a revitalization of the Eucharistic liturgy, the creation of a *Roman Catechism*, and the holistic approach of Jesuit education.

Baroque Influence on Church Design and Liturgy

Protestant congregations, in order to emphasize the reading of Scripture and the proclaiming of a sermon by the minister, built churches mostly devoid of religious architectural features and art. Religious statues and paintings were absent. There was a scaling down of the decor in the sanctuary. The altar was replaced by a simple, more ordinary table, a reminder that the high point of the service was not the sacrifice on the altar, commemorating the Last Supper, but the preaching of God's Word by a minister. A particular goal of the Catholic Reformation was to contrast the ornate decoration of Catholic churches with this barren and plain design of Protestant churches.

Regarding the liturgy itself, the Catholic Mass in the Baroque period sought to appeal to the senses of the faithful. A far cry from the more solemn and perhaps pessimistic outlook of medieval times, the Baroque liturgy emphasized that the celebration of the Catholic faith was not intended to be dark and gloomy but bright and joyous. This was represented, for example, through the inclusion of instrumental music in more varied tones. In 1570, under Pope Pius V (1566–1572), the Church published the *Roman Missal*, which set up a uniform liturgy throughout the Church. These

Baroque An artistic movement or dramatic style in art, architecture, and music originating around 1600 that, among other goals, sought to emphasize the truth of Catholic doctrine through direct emotional connection. The word *baroque* has origins in a Portuguese term that means "rough or imperfect pearl." The French etymology of the word is also associated with "odd."

Sacred Heart of Jesus A devotion that recognizes that Jesus, both fully divine and fully human, deeply loves his people with an outpouring of love from his human heart.

are some features of the *Tridentine Mass*, also known as the Mass of St. Pius V:

- use of Latin throughout the Mass
- the requirement for the priest to face east during the Liturgy of the Eucharist, with his back to the congregation
- a firm adherence to the *rubrics*, or instructions regarding the priest's movements within the structure of the Mass
- more silent prayer, and less interaction (a more passive role) on the part of the lay congregation

Previously, as many as three texts had been used to celebrate Mass: a *Sacramentary* with prayers, a book for the Scripture readings, and another book for the antiphons. The ritual prayers of this *Roman Missal*, revised by Pope Clement VIII (1604) and Pope Urban VIII (1634), remain the unchanging standard of Catholic worship through today. The *Roman Catechism*, a clear summary of Catholic beliefs that also served the Church until modern times, was also published under Pope Pius V's direction. Various liturgical reforms have taken place over the years, including some that followed the Second Vatican Council (1962–1965). These will be covered in Chapter 9, Section 4, under "Liturgical Changes Following the Second Vatican Council."

Saints from the Era of the Catholic Reformation

The seventeenth century was a violent one due to religious hatred and intolerance. Various groups of Christians fought constantly among themselves for political and religious domination. Thankfully, as in every era of Church history, there were examples of gentleness and kindness, Christians who believed more in the power of love to attract than in the games of rivalry and hate that lead to meaningless death.

St. Francis de Sales

One such Christian was St. Francis de Sales (1567–1622), who was bishop of Geneva, Switzerland, a Calvinist stronghold that had been captured by the Catholic Duke of Savoy.

As a young man Francis suffered a religious crisis over Calvin's notion of predestination, despairing of his own salvation. He fervently prayed before a statue of the Blessed Mother, asking for deliverance from his despair, and one day his temptation fell away from him "like the scales of leprosy." He came away completely convinced of God's unconditional love for everyone, a theme that would be at the heart of his apostolic work. His own spiritual struggles made him a sympathetic counselor to the hundreds of people who would come to him for advice.

After his ordination to the priesthood in 1593, Francis embarked on a mission of preaching to reconquer Calvinists by love and thus restore peace to the Christian family. His preaching was charismatic yet simple and supported by the philosophy that one who preaches with love preaches effectively. One of Francis's famous sayings is widely quoted even today: "A teaspoon of honey attracts more flies than a barrel of vinegar."

At first, Francis's travel in Calvinist territory was fraught with danger and almost insurmountable difficulties. One time, wolves attacked Francis; on other occasions, crowds beat him and assassins tried to take his life. Undaunted, Francis began to produce small pamphlets to explain points of Catholic doctrine. These gentle tracts caught the interest of Protestants, who would then come to hear Francis preach. They listened not to some fiery condemner of Calvinist views but to a loving father concerned for his children. In time, Francis's sermons—characterized by love, understanding, and patience—became very popular. They led to the return of most of the inhabitants of the region surrounding Geneva (by some estimates, forty thousand Calvinists) to the Church.

Named bishop of Geneva in 1602, Francis put into action the decrees of the Council of Trent and was exemplary in fulfilling his duties. He administered the sacraments and taught catechism. His voluminous writings instructed, edified, and reformed the Christian community. Because of his writings, St. Francis de Sales, Doctor of the Church, is the patron saint of journalists.

Francis was also an excellent spiritual director. He taught that every Christian has a vocation to holiness. He counseled many laypeople and wrote for them the classic *Introduction to the Devout Life* and the treatise *On the Love of God*. The most famous person under Francis's spiritual direction was a widow, St. Jane Frances de Chantal. With her he founded the Order of the Visitation of Holy Mary, a community of sisters who became "daughters of prayer." Their motto remains "Live Jesus!"

St. Jane Frances de Chantal

St. Jane Frances de Chantal (1572–1641) was born into French nobility. She and her husband had six children, although three died as infants. Despite her wealth, Jane was very humble and generous, attending daily Mass and engaging in many personal acts of self-denial and charity. After her husband died in an accident when she was twenty-eight, Jane's great concern was for the well-being of her surviving children. For a time, she and her children lived in the home of her father-in-law, where they had to endure the servant in charge, who was difficult and evil.

In 1604, Jane heard St. Francis de Sales preach at a church near her own father's home at Dijon. She placed herself under his spiritual guidance. St. Francis encouraged her to found the Order of the Visitation of Holy Mary. One of the goals of this religious order was to provide a place for widows and young girls who desired religious life but were not suited to the very austere life of a cloistered convent. The order expanded rapidly; there were eighty-six convents by the time St. Jane Frances died in 1641. St. Jane Frances was often visited by influential aristocratic women, who would come from far away in order to seek her advice on how to live closer to Christ. Whenever she left to speak to groups outside of the convent, she was received warmly. St. Jane Frances said of the attention, "These people do not know me; they are mistaken."

St. Peter Canisius

St. Peter Canisius (1521–1597) was born in the Netherlands, but his work as a Jesuit in the Catholic Reformation to reintroduce the Catholic faith was mainly in Germany. After the Peace of Augsburg, he was appointed by St. Ignatius of Loyola to be the first superior of the German province of the Jesuits. Canisius realized that sermons, hymns,

St. Ignatius of Loyola and the Jesuits

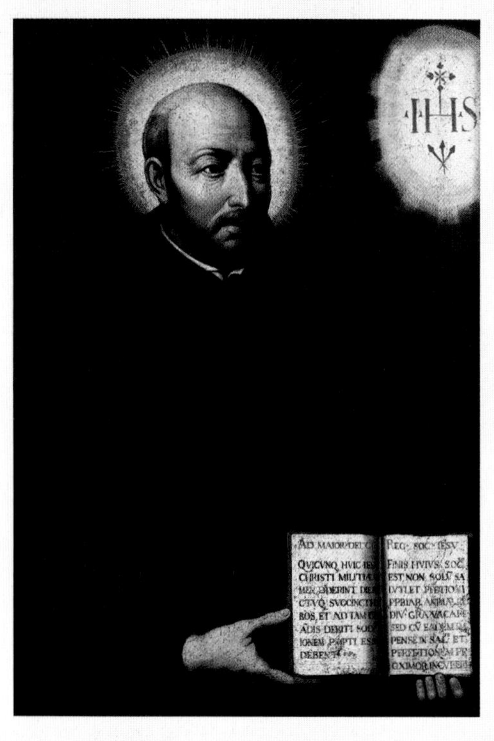

The most important religious order established to help the Catholic Reformation was the Society of Jesus—popularly known as the Jesuits. Its founder, St. Ignatius of Loyola (1491–1556), was a Basque from the Pyrenees in Spain whose career as a knight was ended by a leg wound. During his lengthy recovery, Ignatius read about the lives of Jesus and the saints and decided to serve the Kingdom of God as his new life's work. Ignatius spent a year in prayer and meditation. From this experience, he composed the *Spiritual Exercises* (1523), now a classical work on the spiritual life for both Jesuits and laypeople.

During a ten-year period of schooling, largely spent at the University of Paris, Ignatius gathered around him six companions, including St. Peter Faber and St. Francis Xavier, and they all took the traditional vows of poverty, chastity, and obedience. This company of zealous apostles also took a fourth vow—obedience to the pope as a sign of their commitment to fight against Protestantism. This vow distinguished the Jesuits from all other religious orders, making them so-called "shock troops" in the service of the pope. Pope Paul III approved the society in 1540; until his death in 1556, Ignatius served as general of the order, a term he chose as a carryover from his days as a soldier. From his offices in Rome, he wrote more than seven thousand letters, directing many important ministries around the world.

The Jesuits engaged in preaching, teaching, writing, and the founding of schools and colleges. They directed retreats, advised leaders, and served as confessors. They were also a vigorous missionary order that brought the Faith to the New World and to the East (see St. Francis Xavier, under "Sharing the Gospel in New Places" in Chapter 5, Section 4).

Jesuit accomplishments in the history of the Church are many. By the time of Ignatius's death, the Society of Jesus had more than one thousand members. Vigorous men such as St. Peter Canisius helped the Jesuits win back many Germans, Hungarians, and Bohemians as well as all of Poland to Catholicism. By 1749, the Jesuits had founded more than eight hundred schools. These schools swayed many to return to Catholicism and exerted a strong influence on the learned and the rich. Their success made the Jesuits a significant force in the politics of the day.

Assignments

- Write a more extensive biographical sketch of St. Ignatius of Loyola or one of the other Jesuit saints mentioned in this section.
- Research the impact of Jesuit universities on American higher education.

and catechisms written in the German language were a powerful tool in the spread of Lutheranism. He recommended the founding in Germany of universities dedicated to writing: "In Germany a writer was accounted more worth than ten professors." While he was Jesuit superior, nineteen schools opened in Germany. In 1555, he published a text, *Summary of Christian Doctrine*, and two other catechisms that helped to counter the spread of Lutheranism. These texts were translated into fifteen languages and reprinted over two hundred times during his life.

In the last thirty years of his life, it is estimated that he traveled more than twenty thousand miles by foot and horseback to preach and teach in parishes and on retreats. He generally opposed debating with Protestants, as he felt it only highlighted bitterness and division. Instead, he wrote in a letter to his Jesuit superiors: "We ought to instruct with meekness those whom heresy has made bitter and suspicious, and has estranged from orthodox Catholics, especially from our fellow Jesuits. Thus, by whole-hearted charity and good will we may win them over to us in the Lord."

St. Charles Borromeo

St. Charles Borromeo (1538–1584) was a priest and member of the influential Medici family of Italy. His uncle became Pope Pius IV. Charles is credited with encouraging Pope Pius to reconvene the council, and he contributed extensively to its productive last few years. As archbishop of Milan, Charles adopted a life of self-denial. He sacrificed much in order to bring about positive reforms to serve the clergy, the laity, and the Church hierarchy. Milan was the largest diocese in Italy at that time, with more than eight hundred thousand people and three thousand priests. The diocese had been riddled with corruption, and no bishop had resided there for some time. There was quite a bit of selling of indulgences, and many of the priests did not even know how to administer the sacraments. Charles immediately reduced the staff of the bishop, refused to accept gifts, and sold some of the Church's property to feed the poor. He made frequent visits to the parishes of his diocese in an effort to instruct and encourage his priests to celebrate the Mass and other sacraments in a proper and dignified manner. He founded the Confraternity of Christian Doctrine to teach the Faith to children, a model that remains in the Church today.

St. Robert Bellarmine

St. Robert Bellarmine (1542–1621) was an Italian Jesuit who would later be elevated to the role of cardinal. Despite Bellarmine's position in the upper ranks of the Catholic hierarchy, he chose to live a rather austere lifestyle, giving most of his material belongings to those living in poverty. St. Robert Bellarmine was a key figure in speaking out against the anti-Catholic sentiments of King James I of England. Bellarmine also wrote on the relationship between science and faith, even defending

Galileo against those who wanted to sanction him more severely. Bellarmine argued for democratic theory, showing that all authority comes from God and is invested in people who entrust it to rulers. This principle, greatly admired today, troubled the monarchs of both England and France. Finally, his catechisms for teachers and children were instrumental in handing on the Faith to future generations. He is the patron saint of catechists and is a Doctor of the Church.

St. John of the Cross

St. John of the Cross (1542–1591) was a Spanish priest in the Carmelite Order. John of the Cross collaborated with St. Teresa of Avila, another great Spanish Carmelite saint of the Catholic Reformation era, to inspire Church-approved reforms for the Carmelites. However, some members of the Carmelite Order who disapproved of his reforms kidnapped him and placed him in a six-by-ten-foot cell, where he stayed for nine months before escaping. It was during that time that St. John of the Cross composed some of his most profound poetry. One of his most enduring maxims is that "the soul must empty itself of self and of the things of this earth to be filled with God." In fact, St. John of the Cross's poetry was so rich in its treatment of matters related to the soul that St. John is considered both a **mystic** and a Doctor of the Church.

St. Vincent de Paul

St. Vincent de Paul (1581–1660) was a French priest who devoted his ministry to serving the needy and sick of France. He was one of the Church's greatest representatives of Baroque spirituality. He traveled far and wide, preaching, instructing the laity, and giving retreats throughout rural France. In 1625 he founded the Congregation of the Mission, also known as the Vincentians; one of its main purposes was the education of future priests. Vincentian seminaries prospered worldwide from that time on; during the time of the French Revolution, more than one-third of the seminaries in France were Vincentian seminaries. St. Vincent de Paul also established a congregation for women, the Daughters of Charity, at almost the same time. The women, many of them very affluent, began to care for orphans. Several houses were set up for this ministry. They also collected clothing and numerous other supplies for the poor. St. Vincent de Paul once stated, "Extend mercy toward others, so that there is no one in need whom we meet without helping." The work that began with the Daughters of Charity continues today under St. Vincent de Paul's name.

mystic A morally upright figure who strives to be open to God's direct and transformative presence oftentimes through contemplation, meditation, and prayer.

St. Louise de Marillac

St. Louise de Marillac (1591–1660) was a French contemporary of St. Vincent de Paul, and she was instrumental in assisting him in his efforts to serve the lower classes throughout French society through the Daughters of Charity. St. Louise headed the Daughters and helped to establish hospitals, educational systems, and various other charitable endeavors involving entire communities. At first, under St. Vincent de Paul's guidance, she drew from the affluent to help in the ministry, but she later found that practical work with the poor was better achieved by those of similar social status. She began to seek out humble women from the country who had a more conforming attitude and energy to work with the most downtrodden. "Be diligent in serving the poor. Love the poor. Honor them, as you would Christ himself," she said. In 1960, Pope John XXIII named St. Louise de Marillac the patroness of Christian social workers.

Evaluating the Catholic Reformation

In general, the Council of Trent and the subsequent Catholic Reformation were successful in correcting abuses and putting the Church on the right course. A series of good popes who ascended the papal throne after the council adjourned aided these efforts.

Pope Pius V was a noteworthy leader. He was strict in his remedies; for example, he imposed severe sanctions for swearing and violating Sundays and holy days. He also outlawed begging and had public whippings for adulterers. Pope Pius V helped promote a Holy League, chiefly made up of Spanish and Venetian forces, to support the fight against the Ottomans at the famous naval Battle of Lepanto (1571). In this historic victory, the Christian fleets inflicted a massive defeat to the Turkish navy, freeing the Mediterranean from Ottoman control. (Miguel de Cervantes, the author of *Don Quixote*, was wounded in this battle.) The pope believed that the Christians were victorious because of the intervention of the Blessed Mother and his call for Catholics to recite the Rosary before the battle began. He therefore established the Feast of Our Lady of Victory on October 7, the day of the battle. Pope Gregory XIII later moved this feast to the first Sunday of October, designating it the Feast of Our Lady of the Rosary.

Notwithstanding his publication of the *Roman Catechism* and his reform of the Mass through the *Roman Missal*, Pope Pius V's most significant contribution was eliminating corruption from the Roman Curia. He abolished the opulent papal court and insisted that cardinals live in Rome and live a simple and exemplary life.

Pope Gregory XIII (1572–1585) established the papal diplomatic office and reorganized the calendar, which is still known today as the Gregorian calendar. His successor, Pope Sixtus V (1585–1590), appointed reforming cardinals, fixing their number at seventy. Sixtus centralized Church government into fifteen Roman congregations, ministerial offices that helped govern the Church. Pope Paul V (1605–1621) published the *Roman Ritual*, which set up rules for the proper celebration of the sacraments.

Thankfully for the Church, a number of good popes assisted by able bishops (such as St. Charles Borromeo and St. Robert Bellarmine) brought mostly successful outcomes to the Catholic Reformation.

SECTION ASSESSMENT

NOTE TAKING

Use the chart you completed for this section to help you complete the following items. Each statement below is false. Rewrite each statement to make it true.

1. Catholic churches were devoid of artwork after the Council of Trent, and altars were redesigned as simple tables to emphasize the preaching of God's Word over the Sacrifice of the Mass.
2. St. Francis de Sales subscribed to the idea of *predestination*, which means that people are able to control their own salvation through their use of free will.
3. St. Jane Frances de Chantal placed herself under the spiritual guidance of St. Charles Borromeo.
4. The fourth vow taken by Jesuits is a vow of silence.
5. St. Robert Bellarmine founded the Confraternity of Christian Doctrine, a model for religious education that exists in the Church through today.
6. St. John of the Cross and St. Teresa of Avila are both known for aiding the reform of the Jesuit Order.
7. St. Louise de Marillac founded the Congregation of the Mission to help ensure seminarians were given proper training.

VOCABULARY

8. Define the *Baroque* era as it relates in several ways to Church life after the Council of Trent.

ANALYSIS

9. Discuss at least two of the means the popes used to put the decrees of the Council of Trent into effect.

CRITICAL THINKING

10. How were the Jesuits at the vanguard of the Church's response to the Protestant Reformation?

Section Assignments

Focus Question

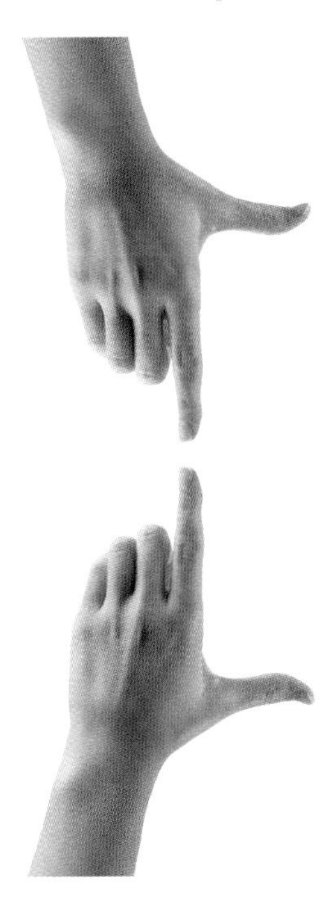

What issues led to Protestantism, and how did the Church respond with a counterreform?

Complete one of the following:

Find and list five passages from the New Testament that promote unity among believers in Christ (e.g., Jn 17:20–23). Write two or three sentences of commentary on each passage explaining what it teaches about unity in Christ.

Review some of the factors that contributed to the Protestant Reformation (see Chapter 6, Section 1). Write a one-page letter to the bishops attending the Council of Trent. In the letter, explain what you consider to be the three most important problems they must address. Include your proposals for counteracting the problems and improving Church unity.

The *Declaration on the Way* is a joint statement, released in 2015, of the United States Conference of Catholic Bishops' Committee on Ecumenical and Interreligious Affairs and the Chicago-based Evangelical Lutheran Church in America. Briefly summarize the background on the creation of the document and what it hoped to accomplish. Also, list three of its thirty-two points of agreement between Catholics and Lutherans today. See "USCCB > Beliefs and Teachings > Ecumenical and Interreligious > Ecumenical > Lutheran" from the USCCB website (www.usccb.org).

INTRODUCTION

Martin Luther and the Roots of Protestantism

Read what the Church teaches on indulgences in paragraphs 1471–1479 of the *Catechism of the Catholic Church*. Write a two-paragraph summary of this teaching.

SECTION 1

The Church's Response and a Division in Christianity

Review the causes of the Reformation as they are listed within this section. In your estimation, was the Protestant Reformation caused more by religious differences or by political differences? Write three paragraphs to support your stance. Include at least one outside source.

SECTION 2

Protestantism Spreads to New State Churches

Name a Christian denomination that has a church within five miles of your school. Write three to five paragraphs tracing its history back to one of the churches that formed at the time of the Protestant Reformation. Also include information about the history and mission of the local congregation.

SECTION 3

The Council of Trent and Clarification of Church Doctrine

There are more than one hundred references to teachings of the Council of Trent in the *Catechism of the Catholic Church*. Choose three references to Trent from the *Catechism's* Index of Citations. Explain how writings of the council enhanced or gave context to Church teaching on these particular topics.

SECTION 4

The Church Enacts Reforms

Search out and copy an inspiring quotation from one of the saints mentioned in this section. Write one to two paragraphs explaining why it is meaningful to you.

Chapter Assignments

Choose and complete at least one of the three assignments to assess your understanding of the material in this chapter.

1. Responding to a Decree on Ecumenism

Read the Second Vatican Council document *Unitatis Redintegratio* (*Decree on Ecumenism*), found on www.vatican.va. Provide a paragraph-long response for each of the following prompts.

After reading the Introduction, answer:

- What makes you hopeful about the future of ecumenism when it comes to the ongoing process of unitive dialogue between Catholics and Protestants?

After reading Chapter 1, answer:

- What are some of the methods of ecumenism that the Catholic Church has used throughout the centuries in order to foster enduring unity between Catholics and Protestants?

After reading Chapter 2, answer:

- How is ecumenism a practice that must be continually used and shaped in order to ensure that efforts at unity between Catholics and Protestants become a reality in the modern world?

After reading Chapter 3, do the following:

- Report on which of the two groups mentioned (Eastern Churches and separated ecclesial communities in the global West) you believe would be more likely to achieve reunification with the Catholic Church, and why.

2. Catholic Doctrine on Major Events, Teachings, and Beliefs

Review the chart in Section 2, "Major Events, Teachings, and Beliefs of the Protestant Reformation," comparing tenets of Lutheranism, Calvinism, and Anglicanism. For each of the tenets, succinctly summarize Catholic belief. Reference your summary from Church documents, especially the *Catechism of the Catholic Church*. Then turn the chart into a narrative form of your choice—for example, an oral presentation, a slide show, an essay, an article, or another format.

3. Timeline of the Five-Hundredth Anniversary of the *Ninety-Five Theses*

The Lutheran World Federation and the Pontifical Council for Promoting Christian Unity jointly created a document in preparation for commemoration of the five-hundredth anniversary of the Protestant Reformation in 2017. The document, *From Conflict to Communion: Lutheran-Catholic Common Commemoration of the Reformation in 2017*, is available on the Vatican website (www.vatican.va). Using material from the document, create an interactive timeline that you can share with your teacher and class. There are several online sites that provide free formatting for interactive timelines. Here are additional instructions:

- The information from the timeline should be taken from the document cited above.
- The timeline should extend from 1517 to 2017, beginning with Luther's posting of the *Ninety-Five Theses* and ending with the joint celebration between Catholics and Lutherans of the event in 2017.
- There should be ten slides broken down as follows: Luther's Protest (slides 1 to 4), the Church's Response at Trent (slides 5–8), the Second Vatican Council on Ecumenism (slide 9), the joint commemoration of the five-hundredth anniversary of Lutheranism in 2017 (slide 10).
- Each of these elements should be included in the timeline: (1) at least six different photos, (2) at least one quotation from Luther, (3) at least one quotation from the Council of Trent, (4) at least one quotation from the Second Vatican Council, (5) at least one video link, and (6) at least one news article link regarding Catholic and Lutheran unity during the 2017 anniversary commemoration.

Prayer

Prayer of St. Charles Borromeo

Almighty God, you have generously made known to human beings the mysteries of your life through Jesus Christ your Son in the Holy Spirit.

Enlighten my mind to know these mysteries which your Church treasures and teaches.

Move my heart to love them and my will to live in accord with them.

Give me the ability to teach this Faith to others without pride, without ostentation, and without personal gain.

Let me realize that I am simply your instrument for bringing others to the knowledge of the wonderful things you have done for all your creatures.

Help me to be faithful to this task that you have entrusted to me.

Amen.

7

THE CHURCH AND THE ENLIGHTENMENT

AN ATHEIST INTERVIEWS A CATHOLIC PRIEST

ON SCIENCE, FAITH, AND REASON

Is it possible for people of different beliefs to dialogue? What if one person has no faith at all and the other has devoted his entire life to his faith? In 2008, famed British biologist and professor Richard Dawkins, who identifies as an atheist, interviewed Fr. George Coyne, a scientist and priest who is the former director of the Vatican Observatory.

During the interview, which lasted approximately an hour, Professor Dawkins asked Fr. Coyne a multitude of questions regarding the intersection of science, faith, and reason. They discussed many points, including biology, evolution, and astronomy. Although the two men come from very different belief systems, the discussion remained civil and respectful, and each of the two listened intently to what the other had to say.

This interview was a momentous occasion for an atheist and a Catholic to discuss matters of faith. It is important to note that it was an interview rather than a debate per se. The interview did not conclude with either Fr. Coyne or Professor Dawkins necessarily becoming convinced of the other's claims, but it was a good example of the dialogue that can take place between science, faith, and reason. At one point, Fr. Coyne told Professor Dawkins, "God is not a God of explanation. If I was seeking for a God of explanation for evolution, I'd probably be an atheist. If all I'm looking for is explanation, I'd be driven to atheism."

The video of the full interview is available online.

FOCUS QUESTION

How have **QUESTIONS ABOUT FAITH** stimulated **DURING THE ENLIGHTENMENT** had an impact on the Church, faith, and religion ever since?

Chapter Overview

INTRODUCTION

What Was the Enlightenment?

MAIN IDEA

The Enlightenment, including the rise of rationalism and the scientific revolution, required the Church to address the balance of science, faith, and reason while confronting some new philosophical errors.

The Protestant Reformation, the Catholic Reformation, the religious wars that followed, the rise of nationalism, and the era of absolute monarchies all fed the development of philosophies that proved to be hostile both to the traditional divine rights of the monarchy and to religion itself. Thus began a period in the seventeenth and eighteenth centuries known as the *Enlightenment*, or the Age of Reason.

The term *enlightenment* implies that religious medieval people were in the dark. Most Enlightenment philosophers taught that only human reason, separated from religious belief, can bring people into the light. Their philosophy, known as **rationalism**, stressed the power of human reason alone to explain reality, with no help from Divine Revelation and religious authority. Also during this time a scientific model came to prominence as the preferred means to engage questions about the physical world. Episodes such as the Galileo controversy (see "The Scientific Revolution" later in this section) forced the Church to emphasize her support of science—provided that

rationalism A philosophy of the Enlightenment that taught that only human reason, separated from religious belief, can bring people into the light of knowledge.

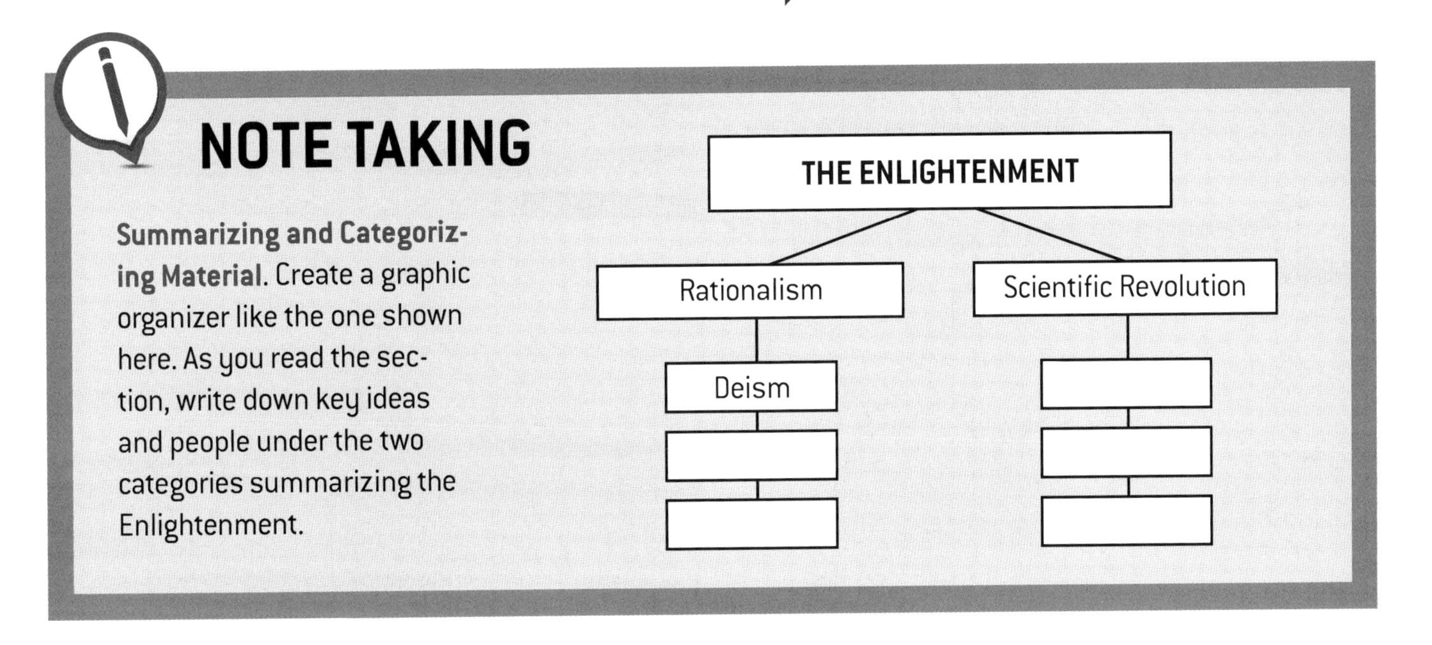

any consideration of the natural world referenced the supernatural world, the world governed by the eternal truths of God and faith.

Although the Enlightenment did lead many Europeans to dismiss faith and the practice of religion, the rationalist philosophy of the Enlightenment thinkers did not always inherently question the existence of a higher power. For example, **Deism** was a philosophical position adopted by many. Deism does not deny God's existence, but it does marginalize God's involvement in creation. The typical Deist imagines God as a "watchmaker": just as the watchmaker has nothing to do with his watch after he makes it, so God allows the laws of creation to govern without any involvement on his part.

As in other generations, great saints arose in the Church to counteract errors that developed during the period and to defend an accurate Christian understanding of God. Details follow on some of the beliefs and developments that the Church confronted during this period.

Rationalism

Reason refers to the power of the mind to think and form understandings based on its own logic. Rationalism led philosophers and others in society to rely more on human reason than on tenets of faith to explain essential truths. Figures such as the French philosopher and mathematician René Descartes (1596–1650) began to question principles that were once taken for granted, rejecting anything that could not be made absolutely clear to human reason. Descartes attempted to further the view that no fact or reality should be taken at face value; rather, everything had to be questioned. It was Descartes who first proclaimed the now-famous "I think; therefore, I am."

Deism A philosophical position that developed in the Enlightenment, it is the belief that while God does exist and did create the world, he refrains from any kind of interference or direct participation in his creation.

René Descartes

Descartes and other influential thinkers of the era throughout Europe, such as British scientist and philosopher Francis Bacon (1561–1626) and German philosopher Immanuel Kant (1724–1804), were suspicious of authority and tradition in general. There was an increasing belief that humanity could only evaluate that which can be observed by the senses within the natural world.

Leading up to the French Revolution, which began on July 14, 1789, prominent French philosophers, including Jean-Jacques Rousseau (1721–1778) and Voltaire (1694–1778), created an atmosphere in which religion was often attacked with ridicule. They readily criticized the Church within their writings, which were mostly political satire, including Voltaire's *Candide* (1759) and Rousseau's *The Social Contract*

(1762). It was a period of anti-intellectualism in which personal feelings of truth took precedence over traditional understandings of objective truth.

It is important to note that many Enlightenment thinkers did not necessarily oppose Christianity altogether; rather, many of them wanted Christianity to alter its scope and submit to the primacy of rational thought in matters of faith. Descartes himself was a practicing Catholic. Voltaire was a Deist who believed in the existence of God and of a primitive natural religion that housed a simple morality, yet he also rejected outright the authority of Scripture and the Church. It was in this atmosphere that the Church had to strive to show that neither reason nor faith alone could address all of humanity's questions. Instead, there had to be a balance of faith and reason, which scholasticism had sought to reinforce.

The Scientific Revolution

The Enlightenment began shortly after the start of a revolution in science that stressed a scientific model of independent knowledge derived from observable data. Nicolaus Copernicus (1473–1543) and Galileo Galilei (1564–1642) both taught that the earth travels around the sun and therefore is not the center of the universe. This view scandalized many Christians, and the Church rejected the discovery. According to the thinking of the time, if the earth were not the physical center of the universe, then neither the earth nor those who live on it could be central to God's plan for creation.

In response, certain theologians and philosophers taught that one could not affirm the centrality of Christ to the universe without also affirming the centrality of Christ's home, the earth, within the universe. Galileo, a faithful Catholic, was arrested and held "in the suspicion of heresy." Note that he was never charged as a heretic, nor were his teachings declared heretical. In a

In 1633, Galileo Galilei was brought before the Roman Inquisition to defend his writings. The Inquisition found Galileo suspect of heresy, banned one of his books, and sentenced him to a lifetime of house arrest.

private letter of January 20, 1610, Galileo wrote, "I am infinitely grateful to God who has deigned to choose me alone to be the first to observe such marvelous things which have lain hidden for all ages past." Galileo had two daughters, and both became religious sisters.

The seeming opposition between faith and science in the seventeenth and eighteenth centuries was more of an illusion than reality, a propaganda promoted by Enlightenment thinkers to bolster their own position and identity. This was unfortunate because the Church had consistently taught that faith and science are not opposed and, interestingly, a good many of the scientists of the time were Catholic priests. What the Church oftentimes opposed were the latest philosophies within various scientific theories that denied the existence of God.

As categories of human thought changed and the understanding of the differences between scientific and religious truth developed, it became clear that one could accept Galileo's teachings without rejecting Christianity. Although the essence of the teaching of various theologians regarding the centrality of Christ and the importance of the earth and its human inhabitance to God's plan has not changed, the way the teachings are expressed has changed completely. In 1992, 350 years after Galileo's death, Pope John Paul II expressed regret for the misunderstanding that held that faith and science are irreconcilable and for the Church's treatment of Galileo.

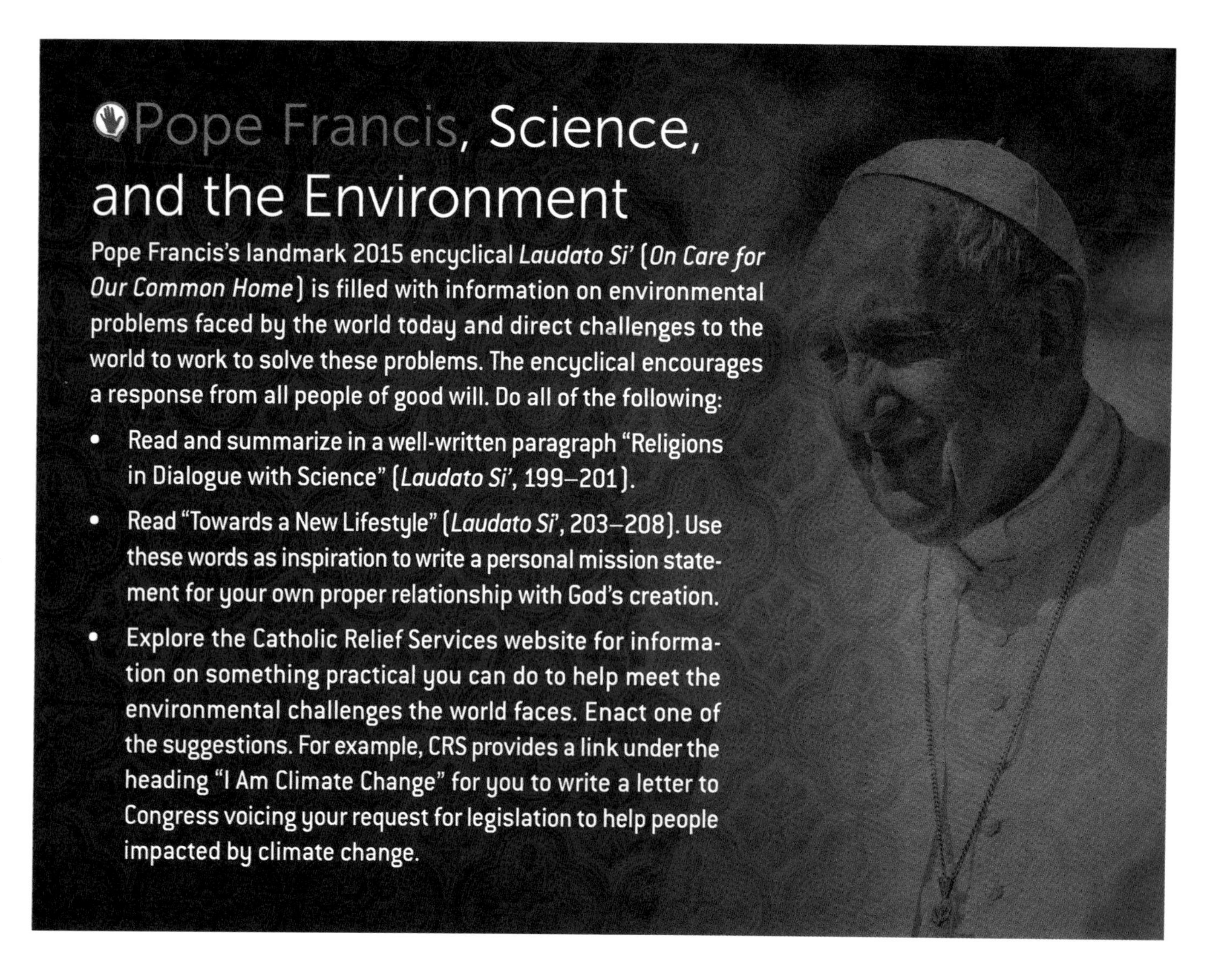

Pope Francis, Science, and the Environment

Pope Francis's landmark 2015 encyclical *Laudato Si'* (*On Care for Our Common Home*) is filled with information on environmental problems faced by the world today and direct challenges to the world to work to solve these problems. The encyclical encourages a response from all people of good will. Do all of the following:

- Read and summarize in a well-written paragraph "Religions in Dialogue with Science" (*Laudato Si'*, 199–201).
- Read "Towards a New Lifestyle" (*Laudato Si'*, 203–208). Use these words as inspiration to write a personal mission statement for your own proper relationship with God's creation.
- Explore the Catholic Relief Services website for information on something practical you can do to help meet the environmental challenges the world faces. Enact one of the suggestions. For example, CRS provides a link under the heading "I Am Climate Change" for you to write a letter to Congress voicing your request for legislation to help people impacted by climate change.

SECTION ASSESSMENT

NOTE TAKING

Use the graphic organizer you completed to help you complete the following items.

1. In general, what were the rationalist philosophers' attitudes toward religion?
2. What was the general attitude of rationalist thinkers to the Church's authority during the Enlightenment?
3. What did Copernicus and Galileo have in common?
4. Why did the Church originally reject Galileo's discovery that the earth revolved around the sun?

COMPREHENSION

5. Explain the Deists' understanding of God as "watchmaker."
6. What was Pope John Paul II's response to the Galileo controversy?

VOCABULARY

7. Define *rationalism*.

CRITICAL THINKING

8. What did Descartes mean by his famous statement "I think; therefore, I am"?

SECTION 1

The Tumultuous Period of the French Revolution

MAIN IDEA

The French Revolution brought societal upheaval that led to prejudice and persecution against the Church and her members.

The Enlightenment gave birth to political revolutions. Fed up with the autocratic rule of monarchs, people believed that human reason would enable them to rule themselves. The eighteenth century ended with successful revolutions against autocracy in both America and France.

Most of the Founding Fathers of the United States were Deists. Men such as Thomas Jefferson and Benjamin Franklin strongly feared any close alliance of Church and state, but they were not hostile to religion. The United States Constitution instituted separation of Church and state and extended religious toleration to all. The French Revolution that began in 1789 ushered in, by contrast, a time of terrible persecution for the Church.

Revolution was set in motion when King Louis XVI called representatives of the Third Estate (commoners) to come to his palace at Versailles to help settle a financial crisis. Once there, the Third Estate pressed the king for sweeping reforms of the absolute monarchy, the economic policies that oppressed the poor and the middle class, and the privileges that the noble class thought their right by birth. At first, the king seemed to compromise with the Third Estate, but he also commissioned mercenary soldiers to protect his absolute power. In response to this power play, Parisians stormed the infamous prison known as the Bastille on July 14, 1789, and set up their own army, the National Guard. The Revolution was on, and there was no turning back.

Before long, the Revolution turned bloody, and the Catholic Church was one of its major victims. The Church had long been associated with the monarchy in France, and the clergy (the First Estate) were deeply involved in many activities of civic life. The higher clergy, including bishops, were named by the king and came exclusively from the nobility (the Second Estate).

NOTE TAKING

Identifying Main Ideas. As you read this section, create an outline like the one started below that traces the events of the French Revolution and its aftermath.

I. Before the Revolution
- A. King Louis XVI and the Third Estate
  - 1. Reforms requested at Versailles meeting
    - a. Reform of the monarchy
    - b. New economic benefits to aid the poor
- B. Issues with the Church

II. The Revolution begins

That said, a majority of the clergy sided with the major premises of the Third Estate's revolt. The Church also owned about 10 percent of the land in France and, with the feudal system still partially in place, retained a good deal of power. As a result, when fiercely anticlerical and antireligious elements got control of the Revolution, the Church suffered many losses of land and property. Church property was confiscated, and monks and nuns were forced to leave their monasteries and convents. Church land was sold to underwrite the cost of the Revolution. Universities, shrines, and charitable institutions were destroyed.

When Maximilien Robespierre (1758–1794) came to power, clergy were required to take an oath in support of the Revolution's anti-Christian and anti-Catholic manifesto, promising to obey the revolutionary government rather than take direction from the pope. The pope at the time, Pius VI (1775–1799), condemned the manifesto and forbade the clergy to take the oath, under pain of excommunication. About half of the priests and all of the bishops refused to take the oath. Many priests—upward of thirty thousand—fled the country. Some were killed. This began an approximately ten-year period when the clergy in France were divided into two hostile groups: those clergy who had taken the oath were called the *constitutional clergy* and those who refused to take the oath were called the *réfractaires*, the "stubborn ones."

The Reign of Terror

The horrific Reign of Terror (so named because of the proliferation of persecutions) began in September 1793. Before it ended the following July, the king and queen had been beheaded, and thousands of nobles, priests, nuns, and brothers had been executed. Not content with merely suppressing the clergy who would not sign an oath pledging allegiance to their radical government, French revolutionaries, including a political alliance known as the *Jacobins*, soon entered into

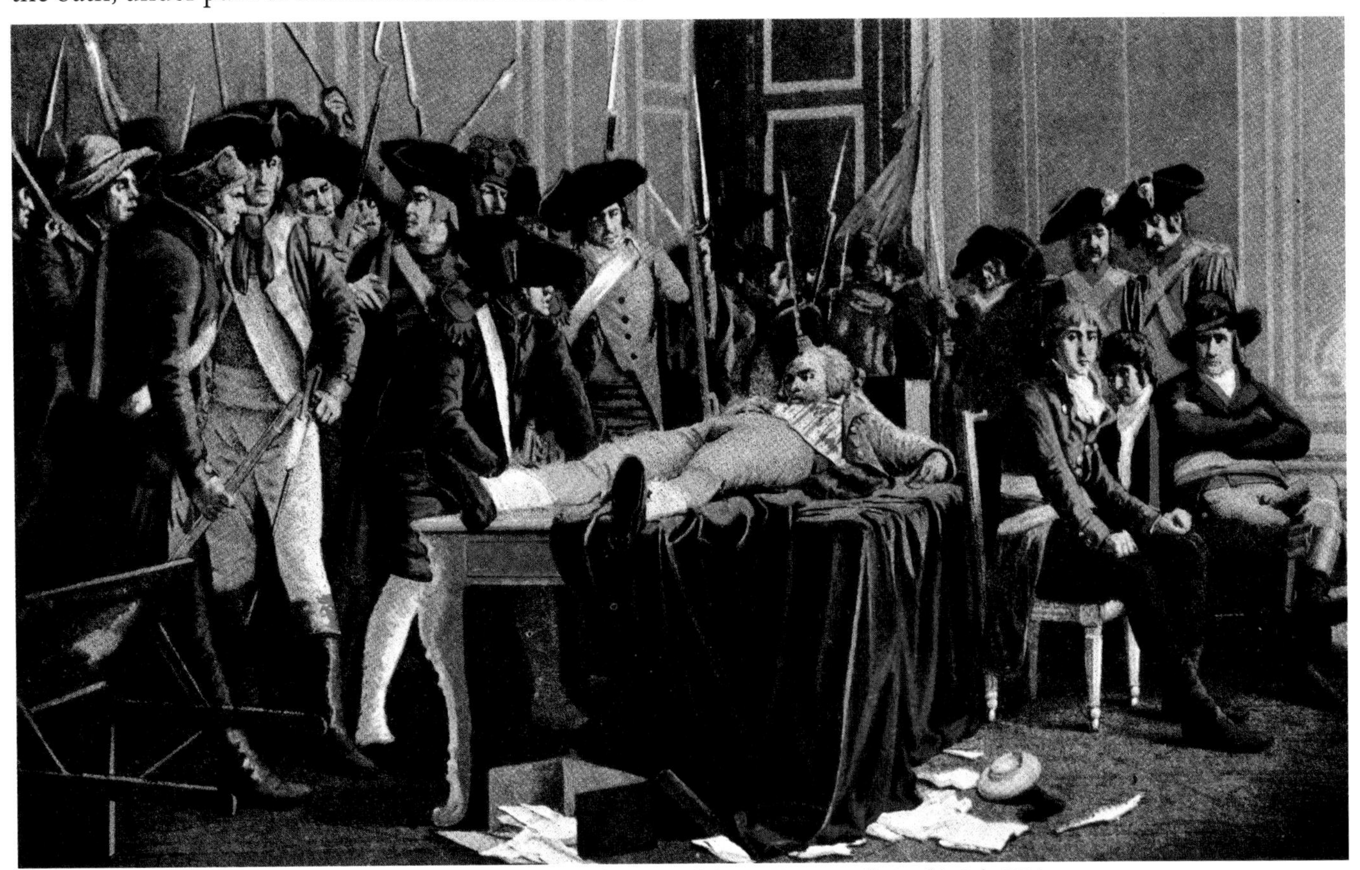

A wounded Maximilien Robespierre awaits his execution during the Reign of Terror. He was guillotined in July 1794.

outright persecution of the Catholic Church throughout France. Several things occurred:

In an effort to remove any signs of Christianity from within France, the revolutionary government attempted to set up a new state religion.

The Christian calendar was replaced with a secular calendar. The celebration of all Christian holidays, including the recognition of Sunday as the Lord's Day, ceased.

Catholic churches were seized and converted into "Temples of Reason," and statues of biblical figures and saints were replaced with statues of revolutionary philosophers. In acknowledgment of the human need to worship, a "Goddess of Reason" was placed in Paris's Notre Dame Cathedral and other churches.

Before long, the absurdity of the radical elements of rationalism lost some of their power in political and government circles. Christianity was allowed again in 1795, and the churches were reopened. Many of the *réfractaires* remained in exile, and the ones who remained wanted little to do with the clergy who had signed the oath. Beginning in 1797, though relations between the Church and the government remained poor, the Church in France began to recover. The shortage of priests led the laity to form groups that would eventually become religious orders. But another set of French revolutionary leaders was about to strike at the heart of the Church herself.

Napoleon's Treatment of the Church

Pope Pius VI had difficulty sorting between the antireligious and anti-Church rhetoric of the Jacobin political party and the legitimate desire of the revolutionaries for greater freedoms and human rights. He routinely condemned both groups. This proved to be a poor response because there was large sympathy for the revolutionaries in the Papal States. In 1799, a young general, Napoleon Bonaparte, assumed power over the revolutionary army in a coup d'état. Under Napoleon, the French armies occupied Rome. They captured Pope Pius VI and took him to France, where he died in prison.

However, Napoleon did come to realize how important the Catholic faith was to the French people. In turn, the new pope, Pius VII, wanted some semblance of order returned to the Church in France. In 1801, representatives of each leader negotiated a *concordat* (a treaty) between the French government and the Church that regulated the Church's rights in France, especially regarding the pope's role as head of the clergy. Among the provisions of the concordat was that the pope would be able to install new bishops in return for not pressing claims to Church property that had been seized during the Revolution. The French bishops would look to the pope for leadership, though Napoleon craftily attached seventy-seven articles to the concordat that made it difficult for the French bishops to communicate with the pope and with each other.

But Pope Pius VII was not Napoleon Bonaparte's puppet. He refused to grant Napoleon an annulment from his marriage to his wife Josephine or to join in his schemes against England. When Napoleon seized the Papal States in 1809, the pope bravely excommunicated him. To retaliate, Napoleon took Pope Pius VII captive, first at Savona, Italy, and then at Fontainebleau near Paris, and kept him isolated from the outside world for six years. Pope Pius VII's brave stand against Napoleon greatly enhanced the prestige of the papacy.

Eventually, after Napoleon was threatened by the other European powers, including England, Austria, and Prussia, he allowed Pope Pius VII to return to Rome, where he was welcomed as a hero. One of Pope

Signing of the concordat between France and the Holy See

Pius VII's first acts was to restore the Jesuit Order (see the feature "The Suppression of the Jesuits") so they could help revive the Church, which had suffered under Napoleon's policies and the wars that had inflamed Europe for years.

Aftermath of the Revolution

Following Napoleon's final defeat at Waterloo, the Congress of Vienna (1814–1815) brought peace to Europe. The congress turned its back on the Revolution and restored the Bourbon monarchs to the throne in France. Ultimately, though, the forces of history could not be reversed. Europe was changed forever because the revolutionary spirit had infected all countries. A secular and anticlerical mentality prevailed in France. In Germany, princely bishops lost their privileges. Catholics were put under Protestant rulers, and the Church was reduced to a state agency, with schools and clergy supported by the state. Spanish colonies in the New World underwent a number of revolutions that threw off Spanish colonial rule. Unfortunately, some of the new governments were openly hostile to the Church, which they saw as too aligned with the old order. In Mexico, for example, Church property was confiscated and priests were killed.

The Suppression of the Jesuits

It was of little surprise, when the European monarchies of the eighteenth century began to disavow themselves of papal influence in their territories, that the Society of Jesus came under fire as the Jesuits took a special vow of obedience to the pope. By 1750 there were twenty-two thousand Jesuits worldwide, and primarily because of the success of their educational system in Europe, they attracted much attention.

The Jesuits also came under scrutiny for their missionary work in South America. For example, they had set up model villages in Paraguay where the Native American converts could live in peace and prosperity and avoid the oppressive European colonizers. The Jesuits painstakingly developed an alphabet in the native languages and translated the Bible so that the Native Americans could better understand God's Word. These efforts disturbed some colonizers, who started rumors that the Jesuits were setting up a state within a state and might even rise up against the colonizing nations.

Meanwhile, in France, a Jesuit provincial superior was implicated in a corrupt financial deal involving West Indian trade. This incident led to the suppression of the Jesuits in France in 1764. Over the course of the next nine years, Portugal, Spain, and the Kingdom of Naples threatened to attack the Papal States unless the Jesuits were suppressed. In 1773, Pope Clement XI capitulated and suppressed the Jesuit Order worldwide. The suppression lasted until 1814, when Pope Pius VII reinstated the order. The Jesuits quickly regained their former influence as counsel to and supporters of the pope and rededicated themselves to a spirit of piety that survives today.

ASSIGNMENTS

Do one of the following:

- Research and write a one-page paper on the life of St. Ignatius of Loyola.
- Research and write a one-page paper about the suppression of the Society of Jesus and its removal from France in the eighteenth century.
- Research and write a one-page paper on the formation process for full membership in the Society of Jesus.
- Research and write a one-page paper about two Jesuit ministries other than education in the United States today.

During the nineteenth century, the Church naturally viewed revolutions negatively because they inevitably attacked the Church, a symbol of order and tradition. Socialist-inspired revolutions in 1848 and 1870 led to persecutions and legal restrictions on the Church. By 1870 the papacy had lost all secular rule in Italy, with the exception of Vatican City in Rome.

SECTION ASSESSMENT

NOTE TAKING

Use the outline you created for this section to help you complete the following items.

1. What were the requests of the Third Estate to King Louis XVI?
2. What are some ways the French Revolution impacted the Church?
3. How was the Church persecuted in France after the French Revolution?
4. What was the result of the concordat between Napoleon and the Church? How did Napoleon skirt his obligations to the concordat?
5. Why did the Church view the revolutions of the nineteenth century with skepticism?

COMPREHENSION

6. Write one sentence for each person listed below that describes his part in the French Revolution or its aftermath.

- King Louis XVI
- Maximilien Robespierre
- Pope Pius VI
- Pope Pius VII
- Napoleon

ANALYSIS

7. How did the French Revolution differ from the American Revolution?

CRITICAL THINKING

8. Imagine and describe a situation today in which Catholic clergy and laity would be asked to sign an oath in support of a government that oppresses the Church. Detail how you think both a majority and minority of Catholics would respond.

SECTION 2

Religious Revival in France following the French Revolution

MAIN IDEA

In the decades following the French Revolution, the Church in France was in crisis. However, new religious congregations were formed, and many prominent saints took seriously the call to proclaim the Word of God and revitalize the Church.

Following the French Revolution, the Church was not in an ideal situation. Many of those in the upper classes and growing **bourgeoisie** were reluctant to accept matters of faith since their mindset remained dominated by the rationalism of the Enlightenment. However, the lower classes had typically held on to their faith.

Seventeenth-century Catholic philosopher Blaise Pascal (see image at left) once argued that the Catholic Church's claim to divine origin had to be true because the Church established herself in a hostile world and spread throughout the world despite persecution. While the political revolutions spawned by Enlightenment ideals effectively ended the Church as a political power in Europe, these revolutions purified the Church. The Church finds power not in political or territorial control but from the Gospel of Jesus Christ, who desires the unity of all people to be based on love and justice, not on political power. Pascal would not have been surprised to see the Church weather the

bourgeoisie A term for the middle class, often used to denote the rising French middle class particularly in the centuries following the Middle Ages.

NOTE TAKING

Concept Web. Create a concept web like the one here. Add the names of the French saints discussed in this section to the smaller circles and words or phrases next to each circle to help you remember important and distinctive information about each.

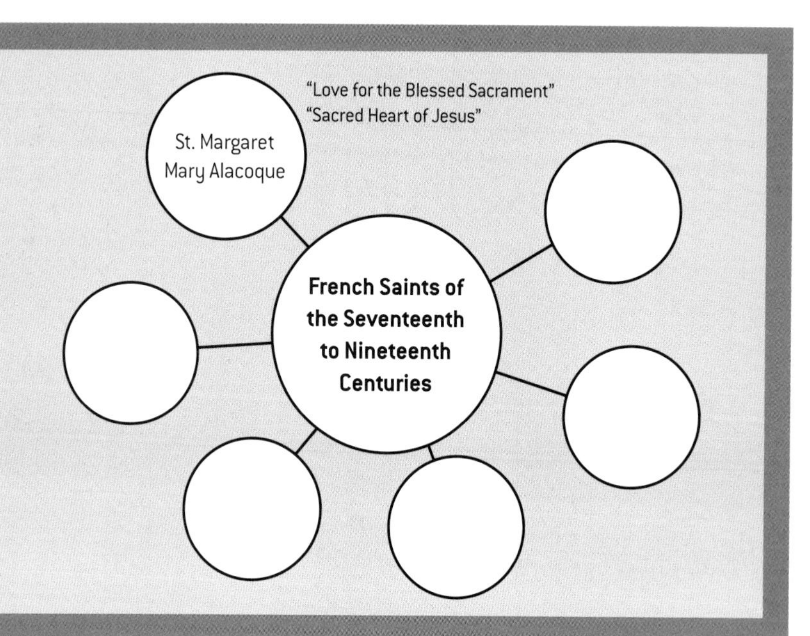

storms of the revolutionary era since he, like all true believers, held that the Church exists because the Lord remains with her. Holy women and men kept the Faith during times of persecution and witnessed to the strength of the Gospel. And although the secular power of the papacy weakened, Catholics still relied on the pope for spiritual leadership.

French Saints of the Seventeenth to Nineteenth Centuries

Among the holy men and women who kept and modeled the Faith during the eras surrounding the French Revolution, several French saints helped preserve the Church amid the turmoil and allow it to emerge even stronger. Two qualities the saints described here have in common are holiness and humility. Often living in obscure places and unnoticed by those in power, these saints aided the Church in her recovery in France and spurred a missionary outreach that spread worldwide and into the present.

St. Margaret Mary Alacoque

(1647–1690)

St. Margaret Mary Alacoque lived in the in the century prior to the tumultuous era of the French Revolution. She was born in Burgundy, a region in central France. From a young age, she had a deep love for the Blessed Sacrament. She preferred quiet time in prayer more than anything else. After she made her First Communion, Margaret prayed so intensely and practiced such severe penances that she was bedridden for four years. After she made a vow to the Blessed Mother to consecrate herself to religious life, her illness left her.

In 1671, Margaret entered religious life at the Visitation Convent. She was very devoted to the Eucharist, and she also received visions of Christ. In collaboration with another French saint, St. John Eudes (1601–1680), Margaret was instrumental in establishing a feast dedicated to the Sacred Heart of Jesus. It is a movable feast that falls nineteen days after Pentecost. Pope Clement XIII approved this devotion in 1765.

St. John Vianney

(1786–1859)

St. John Vianney (whose full name was Jean-Baptiste-Marie Vianney) was known as the *Curé d'Ars*, or the "Priest of Ars." Ars was the small town about two hundred miles east of Paris where St. John Vianney was assigned.

John was still a very young boy when the Reign of Terror swept through France in the early 1790s. During this time, he learned to have a high opinion of the clergy and religious who continued to spread the Faith and celebrate the sacraments. In 1809, John was drafted into Napoleon's army, but he was able to avoid actively participating in military service. After he was ordained in 1815, John—although he had struggled in school himself—began working to provide the youth of his region with an education in the Faith.

It was as a parish priest in the town of Ars that St. John Vianney achieved his greatest repute. During Mass, John would forcefully—but patiently and lovingly—deliver homilies to encourage his parishioners to turn away from their sin, pray, and receive the sacraments. Likewise, John was very dedicated to drawing the faithful back to God through the Sacrament of Penance, and he would often spend up to sixteen hours per day hearing Confessions without ever taking a break. People of all different levels of society, and from as far away as Paris, came to have the Curé d'Ars hear their Confessions and share his wisdom, which he always offered with much humility. By 1855, an estimated twenty thousand pilgrims per year came to Ars to meet with St. John Vianney.

St. Catherine Labouré

(1806–1876)

St. Catherine Labouré was born in Fain-lès-Moutiers, France. Catherine entered the Daughters of Charity in Paris as a young woman. When Catherine was a novice in the community in her midtwenties, the Blessed Virgin Mary came to her in an **apparition** on three separate occasions. Among other messages from the Blessed Virgin Mary, Catherine was told that she should persevere during times of suffering and seek the Lord in the Eucharist and that her life's mission would lead to great trials.

In 1830, during one of Mary's appearances, Catherine was allowed to see an image that is now referred to as the Miraculous Medal. Catherine was instructed to replicate the image as well as to spread word of the importance of wearing a Miraculous Medal. The image on the medal is of Mary standing on a globe with dazzling rays of light coming from her fingers to represent the graces intended for all those who ask for them. Around the figure are the words "O Mary, conceived without sin, pray for us who have recourse to thee." On the back of the medal is the letter *M* beneath a cross with a crossbar below it, and under that is the Sacred Heart of Jesus and the Immaculate Heart of Mary. Today, there is a worldwide devotion to the Miraculous Medal. Of course, this devotion is not to the object itself but rather to its symbolism of Mary as the Immaculate Conception and how she thus draws us closer to her Son, the Lord Jesus Christ.

apparition A supernatural appearance. A Marian apparition is an appearance of the Blessed Virgin Mary to a person, typically to deliver an important message. In order for an apparition to be considered authentic, it must be verified by the Vatican.

St. Bernadette Soubirous

(1844–1879)

St. Bernadette Soubirous was born in Lourdes in southwestern France, close to the border with Spain. Bernadette's family was very poor, and Bernadette suffered from physical ailments throughout her life.

On February 11, 1858, fourteen-year-old Bernadette and her sister were out collecting firewood when the Virgin Mary appeared to her in a grotto (cave) near her home. Bernadette immediately fell to her knees in prayer. Over the course of the following weeks, Mary repeatedly appeared to Bernadette in the grotto, and a spring of water erupted in the ground where there had not been one before. Bernadette's family, local townspeople, and Church authorities originally did not believe that Bernadette was seeing these visions. At first they wanted her to be placed in an asylum for those with mental illness. However, Bernadette defied them by continuing to visit the grotto. Mary eventually told Bernadette that a chapel should be built on the site.

It was on March 25 (the Feast of the Annunciation) that one of the most prominent of Marian apparitions occurred, during which Mary announced to Bernadette, "I am the Immaculate Conception,"

People gathered by the grotto at Lourdes

a title that had been approved for the Blessed Mother just four years earlier as a dogma of faith by Pope Pius IX. As a young girl from rural France with little formal education, Bernadette probably would not have been aware of this proclamation. Following multiple interviews by Church and governmental authorities, Bernadette's claims were eventually believed, and a large church, the Sanctuary of Our Lady of Lourdes, was built. It remains a major site visited by pilgrims from around the world. Over the course of a century and a half, hundreds of miracles—which scientific experts have been unable to explain—have taken place for some of those who have visited the miraculously healing waters at the Sanctuary of Our Lady of Lourdes.

St. Thérèse of Lisieux

(1873–1897)

Thérèse Martin was born in Alençon in the Normandy region of northwest France. Thérèse was raised in a very faithful Catholic family. In fact, her parents, St. Louis and St. Zélie Martin, were canonized by Pope Francis in 2016, the first husband and wife to be canonized together. When she was four, Thérèse's family moved to Lisieux, also in Normandy.

At the age of fifteen, Thérèse entered the Carmelite Order, after having been turned away a year before. Two of her sisters were already Carmelite nuns. She took the name Thérèse of the Child Jesus.

During her short life, Thérèse was plagued with many physical sufferings, but she remained faithful to the Lord, following her now-well-known "little way" of seeking holiness by sharing Christ's love in every circumstance. Thus, in all of her interactions with others, Thérèse showed a lovingly Christian demeanor, even when she was looked down upon and otherwise treated poorly by her peers. Thérèse remained humble throughout her short life, which was ended by a painful bout of tuberculosis when she was only twenty-four. Even in her tribulations, Thérèse never gave in to bitterness or despair.

When she was sick, and at the insistence of two mother superiors, Thérèse wrote her life story, *The Story of a Soul*. She completed it shortly before she died. It has become one of the most widely read classics on the spiritual life. In it, she described what most Christians strive to be: people totally dedicated to the love of Jesus Christ. Thérèse also showed that to be a saint, one doesn't have to be famous or do something dramatic. This, in essence, was the "little way."

In July 1887, Thérèse was brought to the convent infirmary. She was hemorrhaging continually. At the end of the month she was anointed, and in the middle of August she received Holy Communion for the last time. Her last agony was frightening. She said, "I feel especially that my mission is about to begin, my mission of making God loved as I love him, to give my little way to souls. If God answers my request, my heaven will be spent on earth up until the end of the world. Yes, I want to spend my heaven in doing good upon earth."

St. Thérèse of Lisieux was named a Doctor of the Church by Pope John Paul II in 1997.

St Thérèse of Lisieux was noted as a child for her acts of charity.

St. Thérèse's father gave her his blessing when, in 1888, she took the habit as a Carmelite novice.

French Influence on Catholic Education in the United States

St. Rose Philippine Duchesne

It would not be possible to survey the heroically faithful figures in postrevolutionary France without appreciating the contributions of St. Rose Philippine Duchesne, St. Anne-Thérèse Guérin, and Bl. Basil Moreau. These faithful religious were missionaries to the United States who made dramatic contributions to the foundations of Catholic education.

St. Rose Philippine Duchesne (1769–1852) lived through the French Revolution and the Reign of Terror. The French Revolution delayed her plans for religious life, though she continued to live by the rule of the Visitation of Holy Mary order at home while the convents were closed. In 1804, Sr. Philippine partnered with Mother Madeleine Sophie Barat, who had founded the Society of the Sacred Heart in 1800. After years of pleading, Mother Sophie gave Sr. Philippine permission to travel to the United States. After a short stay in New Orleans, Louisiana, she and four other sisters who accompanied her settled in St. Charles, Missouri, near St. Louis. On September 8, 1818, they opened the Academy of the Sacred Heart, the first free school west of the Mississippi and the first Catholic school in the Archdiocese of St. Louis. Later in her life, though frail, Sr. Philippine established a school for Potawatomi girls in Sugar Creek, Kansas. She was canonized by Pope John Paul II on July 3, 1988.

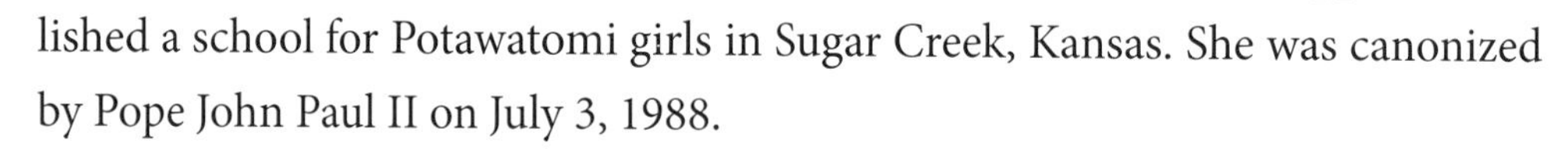

St. Anne-Thérèse Guérin

St. Anne-Thérèse Guérin (1798–1856), known as **Mother Théodore**, grew up in hardship in the small coastal village of Étables-sur-Mer, France. Her father was murdered by bandits when she was fifteen. Anne-Thérèse was responsible for caring for her mother and her young sister thereafter. These events delayed her entrance into the Sisters of Providence until she was twenty-five.

Mother Théodore was eventually asked to lead a group of Sisters of Providence to America, to the Diocese of Vincennes in southern Indiana. The bishop assigned the group a parcel of land in the wilderness north of Terre Haute. It was on this densely forested land that Mother Théodore opened a mission, Saint

Mary-of-the-Woods, that grew to include a motherhouse and a college in 1842. By the time of her death, Mother Théodore had established several schools throughout Indiana.

Bl. Basil Moreau (1799–1873) was born in the town of Laigné-en-Belinnearly ten years after the start of the French Revolution. He was ordained as a priest for the Diocese of Le Mans in 1821, and soon thereafter began teaching philosophy and theology at the seminary while undertaking many other ministerial duties.

Since Moreau had grown up in the aftermath of the Reign of Terror that had devastated the Catholic Church, he discerned a call from the Lord to address the severe lack of priests available to teach and spread the Gospel, especially in rural areas of France. He gathered together a group of priests to assist parish priests by preaching missions. The Congregation of Holy Cross, named for the town (Sainte-Croix) where it was headquartered, was formed when Moreau joined his priests with the Brothers of St. Joseph, founded by Fr. Jacques Dujarié. By 1837, Pope Gregory XVI had approved the congregation.

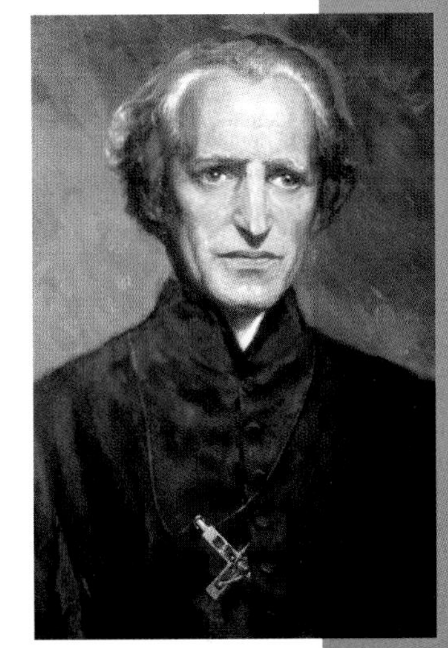

Bl. Basil Moreau

The union of priests and brothers was dedicated to rebuilding the schools destroyed by the French Revolution. Fr. Moreau called for his congregation to have a strong devotion to the Holy Family of Jesus, St. Mary, and St. Joseph. Later, Moreau would add a group of sisters, the Marianites of Holy Cross. A religious community comprising priests, brothers, and sisters was revolutionary for the time. Mary, Our Lady of Sorrows, was named the special patroness for the Congregation.

Moreau encouraged an apostolic model for the Congregation, sending missionaries to Algeria and eastern Bengal. (The Canadian saint André Bessette was a later member of the Congregation of Holy Cross.) Moreau also sent six brothers and Fr. Edward Sorin to the United States, where, in 1842, they founded the University of Notre Dame as well as six other parishes in northern Indiana.

Today, the Congregation of Holy Cross remains dedicated to education, with a continued presence in schools, parishes, and missions. In *Christian Education*, a document outlining the educational mission of the Congregation, Moreau wrote,

> With the eyes of faith, consider the greatness of the mission and the wonderful amount of good that one can accomplish. And also consider the great reward promised to those who have taught the truth to others and have helped form them into justice: "They will shine eternally in the skies like the stars of the heavens." With the hope of this glory, we must generously complete the Lord's work. (*Christian Education*, 9)

In light of Basil Moreau's important role in contributing to the restoration of the Catholic faith in France and later around the world, he was beatified by Pope Benedict XVI in Le Mans on September 15, 2007, the Feast of Our Lady of Sorrows.

Each of these French Catholics—St. Rose Philippine Duchesne, St. Anne-Thérèse Guérin, and Bl. Basil Moreau—born near the time of the French Revolution, was instrumental in bringing Catholic education to the United States, and their legacies remain today in the institutions they founded.

The impact of saintly men and women was not limited to the Church in France. Rather, there were other movements within the Church in the aftermath of the French Revolution and the centuries beyond. There were also other situations associated with the Enlightenment that altered the life of the Church in Europe.

SECTION ASSESSMENT

NOTE TAKING

Use the concept web you created to help you complete the following items.

1. Choose one saint and tell how he or she exhibited the quality of humility.
2. Choose a second saint and tell how he or she exhibited the quality of holiness.

COMPREHENSION

3. What did philosopher Blaise Pascal say about the resilience of the Church?
4. What happened to St. Margaret Mary Alacoque after she made a vow to the Blessed Mother?
5. Which of the sacraments is St. John Vianney particularly known for? Why?
6. What is the meaning of the rays of light coming from Mary's fingers on the Miraculous Medal?
7. What title did Mary announce to St. Bernadette Soubirous?
8. Explain the meaning of the "little way."
9. What was unique in the founding membership of the Congregation of Holy Cross?

VOCABULARY

10. Which saints described in this section received an *apparition*? Describe the subject and content of each apparition.
11. In general, what attitude did the *bourgeoisie* have about their faith after the French Revolution?

REFLECTION

12. In your opinion, which saint from this period did the most to repair the status of the Church in France and worldwide after the French Revolution? Explain the reason for your response.

SECTION 3

Liberalism and the Church of the Nineteenth Century

MAIN IDEA

The Enlightenment spawned the sociopolitical movement called *liberalism,* which called for the separation of Church and state and for the removal of clerical privileges. Into this milieu came the Church's longest-reigning pope, Pope Pius IX.

Out of the Enlightenment emerged another new set of ideas in the nineteenth century that came to be known as *liberalism*. In general, nineteenth-century liberals opposed rule by aristocrats. They called for constitutional government, the right to vote, complete religious liberty, freedom of speech and the press, and the equality of all citizens. They tried to abolish established churches and clerical privileges and supported the separation of Church and state. Liberals also wanted the state to secularize functions previously handled by the Catholic Church, including marriage, charitable efforts, and education.

Today's society and the Catholic Church embrace some of these liberal ideas. In fact, the Catholic Church is currently one of the most outspoken defenders of human rights and human freedom. For example, historians credit Pope John Paul II as a leading figure in the toppling of the former Soviet Union, one of history's most repressive totalitarian regimes.

However, in the nineteenth century many liberal programs were revolutionary and violently antireligious. Liberal thought was human-centered and often atheistic, holding that humans and societies are not bound by any divine law and that power and authority come from the people, not from God. Liberals saw the Church as part of the old order that was passing away.

NOTE TAKING

Highlighting Key Information. Summarize the text section by using the following phrases in sentences that explain their connection to Church life in Europe after the Enlightenment. You can use more than one word in a sentence.

Liberalism
Pope Pius IX
Kulturkampf
Papal States
Syllabus of Errors
Immaculate Conception of Mary
Bl. John Henry Newman

They did not distinguish between true religion (Christianity) and other ideologies such as social Darwinism (see "Two Flawed Economic Systems: Capitalism and Socialism" in Chapter 8, Introduction) that did not always promote true human freedom. Socialist reformers such as Karl Marx (1818–1883) went so far as to teach that religion is the "opiate of the people," a drug that keeps them content with their low station in life. Marx and his cohort Friedrich Engels (1820–1895) wished to abolish religion altogether. Socialist-inspired revolutions in 1848 and 1870 led to persecutions and legal restrictions on the Church.

Liberalism Leads to the Creation of New Nations

Nationalistic movements teamed up with liberalism to establish the modern states of Germany and Italy. Otto von Bismarck (1815–1898) helped create Germany by uniting many smaller German states into an empire under the king of Prussia. Part of his strategy for unification was the ***Kulturkampf***, a vigorous campaign to celebrate German identity. In tandem with the *Kulturkampf*, Otto von Bismarck saw the Church as an alien and intruding force in the new country. He wished to end papal influence in Germany and set up a national church. To this end, in the 1870s, he enacted laws that expelled the Jesuits, Redemptorists, and others; put the clergy and schools under state control; and fined, imprisoned, deposed, and exiled bishops and priests. Most Catholics remained loyal to their bishops and tried as best as they could to ignore the hostile legislation. Otto von Bismarck soon discovered that the Catholic Church was a force for stability. By 1878, with the election of Pope Leo XIII, the anti-Catholic laws were gradually moderated. The *Kulturkampf* was officially ended in 1887.

Kulturkampf A German term meaning "cultural struggle"; the steady attempts, between 1871 and 1887, of German chancellor Otto von Bismarck to control the Catholic Church in Germany through governmental officials.

There were similar trials for the Church in Italy. For centuries, Italy was divided into small *duchies* (territories controlled by dukes) under the control of rival families. A major barrier to a unified Italy was the Papal States, given to the Church by Pepin the Short in 755. Popes through the ages felt that they needed the income from these lands to help pay for the administrative costs of running the Church. But nineteenth-century nationalists saw the Church and the Papal States as a major stumbling block to Italian unity. Pope Pius IX worked against efforts for Italian unity because he feared the Church would become prisoner to the Italian government. An Italian revolution in the 1820s was suppressed by Austrian troops.

Another attempt at Italian unity came in 1848, this one more successful. Pope Pius IX was forced to flee Rome when Giuseppe Garibaldi, a nationalist general, declared an Italian republic. Spain and Austria rescued Pope Pius IX and temporarily suppressed the intentions of the 1848 rebellion. However, the days of the Papal States were numbered. In 1870, caught up in the Franco-Prussian War, France had to pull its troops from Rome, where they had been stationed in defense of the Holy Father. In that fateful year, the papacy lost the Papal States, including all secular rule in Italy, with the exception of Vatican City in Rome. From that location, Pope Pius IX would call himself the "prisoner of the Vatican." Until 1929, he and his successors would remain there without venturing out onto Italian soil.

Pope Pius IX Responds to Propositions Opposing the Church

While liberal thought was firing up revolutions and inspiring nations to unify and assault monarchies and

Kulturkampf caricature of Otto von Bismarck and Pope Pius IX playing chess

the clergy who supported them, Pope Pius IX, a pope of tremendous personal magnetism and strong beliefs, ascended Peter's throne.

Pope Pius IX (1846–1878) is the longest-reigning pope in history, with a pontificate of thirty-one years, seven months, and twenty-three days. (Pope John Paul II [1978–2005] had the second longest pontificate at twenty-six years, five months, and twenty-three days.) Pope Pius IX served as a point of continuity in a world transforming from one dominated by monarchies to one built on the ideals of liberalism. He has been called the "first modern pope."

In the first few months of his pontificate, many thought Pope Pius IX would himself be a strong advocate of liberalism. He did grant amnesty and exile to some political proponents of dismantling the Papal States, and he worked to improve civic administration in the Papal States. He also offered support for secular constitutional governments led by a prime minister. All of these reforms were very popular to proponents of liberalism. However, Pope Pius IX greatly opposed the overall dismantling of the Papal States. He saw the Papal States as part of a thousand-year legacy granted to the Church to maintain papal independence from foreign rulers and a source of income to provide for the governance of the Church. Also, Pope Pius IX's opinion of the liberal revolution was deeply affected by the violence that emerged from efforts to unify Italy, including his traumatic experience of being forced to flee Rome after a series of street riots in 1848. When the pope was able to return to Rome in 1850, he was decidedly against liberalism.

In his strongly worded December 8, 1864, encyclical, *Quanta Cura*, to which was attached the famous appendix *Syllabus of Errors*, Pope Pius IX clearly stated the Catholic position on liberalism. In a scathing attack on eighty propositions held by the liberals, the *Syllabus* condemned rationalism, socialism, liberal capitalism, **pantheism**, materialism, the defense of divorce, and attacks on the traditional family. The *Syllabus* also condemned many ideas those inside and outside the Church find quite acceptable today, including freedom of conscience and the separation of Church and state. Finally, the *Syllabus* condemned making accommodations to current modern ideologies, which outraged the pope's critics, who believed that the pope and the Church should come to terms with progress, liberalism, and modern civilization.

Allegorical apotheosis of Pope Pius IX on his throne, surrounded by angels and Jesus Christ

Other Aspects of the Papacy of Pope Pius IX

Though the reign of Pope Pius IX included the loss of the Papal States, it was a time of great religious renewal in the Church. Traditional religious orders grew and engaged in vigorous missionary activity. New religious orders, such as the Salesians of St. John Bosco (1815–1888), came into existence. Vocations to the priesthood and religious life increased. The diocesan clergy generally improved, inspired by humble and saintly priests such as the Curé d'Ars, St. John Vianney.

Catholic intellectual life was given a major boost when Bl. John Henry Newman (1801–1890) converted to the Catholic faith from Anglicanism. Made a cardinal thirty-four years after his conversion, Newman showed in his writings that the pursuit of a liberal arts education and a rigorous intellectual life were a fundamental part of the Catholic tradition. His series of lectures delivered in Dublin, Ireland, titled *The Idea of a University*, has profoundly influenced the development of Catholic liberal arts colleges since its publication in 1852.

Two other significant religious events during Pius IX's pontificate were the dogmatic definition of the **Immaculate Conception** in 1854 and the appearances of the Blessed Mother to St. Bernadette Soubirous (1844–1879) at Lourdes in 1858.

From a spiritual point of view, Pius IX's pontificate was a positive one. Developments in transportation made it possible for pilgrims to come to Rome to visit

Pantheism A false belief that identifies the universe as God or God as the universe.

Immaculate Conception The dogma that states that Mary, in view of the merits of Jesus Christ, was preserved free from the stain of Original Sin from the moment of her conception.

Pope Pius IX's coat of arms

him. He popularized huge papal audiences, which endeared him to Catholics from around the world, many of whom kept lithographs of him in their homes. The telegraph made communications to the world outside the Vatican easier, so the pope did not seem as distant as some of his predecessors.

Sympathy for the plight of the Holy Father, who did not leave Vatican City again after the dissolution of the Papal States, emotionally and spiritually bonded Catholics in many countries, themselves the victims of prejudice or oppression, to Pope Pius IX. Although his political power waned, his spiritual authority grew. Catholics fed up with repression in their own countries were *ultramontane*, meaning they advocated the supreme authority of the papacy in any matter of faith and morals. They looked to the pope as a beloved father and a symbol of faith in an era of rapid and troubling change that often ridiculed traditional ideas.

Against the background of the political controversies of the time and as Pope Pius IX refocused on the spiritual aspects of the papacy, he convoked the First Vatican Council in 1869. The subject of the council is addressed in Section 4.

At the time of Pope Pius IX's death, the Church was politically defensive and in retreat yet, at the same time, spiritually strong and vibrant. With the coming pontificate of Pope Leo XIII, the Church would take an increasingly active role in speaking out for human rights and against the evils of laissez-faire capitalism and the class warfare called for by Marxist communism (see "Two Flawed Economic Systems: Capitalism and Socialism" in the Introduction to Chapter 8).

SECTION ASSESSMENT

NOTE TAKING

Use the sentences that you completed, supplemented by what you read throughout the section, to answer these questions.

1. Why did Pope Pius IX eventually disassociate himself from liberalism?
2. As part of the *Kulturkampf*, what was the goal of Otto von Bismarck regarding the Catholic Church?
3. Why is Pope Pius IX sometimes referred to as the "first modern pope"?
4. Which point in the *Syllabus of Errors* outraged Pope Pius IX's critics?
5. What effect did the loss of the Papal States have on the pontificate of Pius IX and the pontificates since?
6. What was a lesson of Bl. John Henry Newman's writings that is still applicable today?

COMPREHENSION

7. What are some examples of Pope Pius IX's holiness that led to his beatification by Pope John Paul II?

VOCABULARY

8. Define *pantheism*.

APPLICATION

9. Write a short explanation of the *Immaculate Conception* you would offer to someone who has never before heard the term.

CRITICAL THINKING

10. Pope Pius IX had the longest pontificate in history, and his pontificate occurred following the Enlightenment. How did these two factors permit him to understand both how the world functions and the important role that the Church plays in the world?

SECTION 4

The Era of the First Vatican Council

MAIN IDEA

Pope Pius IX convoked the First Vatican Council in part to respond to the pastoral needs of the day, especially those around faith and reason.

As his political influence waned, Pope Pius IX wanted to assert and reaffirm the authority of the papacy in spiritual matters. He also wished to clarify Church teachings in response to attacks by Enlightenment thinkers. For these reasons, he convoked the First Vatican Council (1869–1870).

The worldwide council, attended by 714 bishops (including forty-six from the United States), reaffirmed the international reach of Catholicism. This was important in a revolutionary age that often stressed blind nationalism and hatred of anything foreign. Another benefit of the council was its emphasis on the spiritual authority of the Church. By 1870, the papacy had lost all secular power. However, Jesus endowed Peter and his successors with the power to proclaim and teach the Gospel authentically, promising that he would remain with his Church and her leaders to guide them in truth (see Matthew 16:18–19; 28:20).

The First Vatican Council discussed the key theological matters of the late nineteenth century, including how the Church was expected to engage with the world in the wake of the Enlightenment and among countries that were still mired in nationalism.

One of the most significant and lasting decisions of the council was the definition of papal infallibility

NOTE TAKING

Synthesizing Information. Use the headings below to summarize this section. In one sentence, write the main objective of the First Vatican Council. In a bulleted list, name the accomplishments of the council.

Objectives	Two main objectives of the First Vatican Council were . . .
Accomplishments	• More than seven hundred bishops from around the world attended the council, emphasizing the global nature of the Church.
	•
	•
	•

Altarpiece commemorating the proclamation of the dogma of the Immaculate Conception by Pope Pius IX in 1854

as dogma. When the council began, the issue of papal infallibility was not even officially on the agenda, though it had been widely discussed in the years prior. The ultramontane bishops did not believe it was necessary to define a belief that was already well understood, grounded in Scripture and Tradition, and upheld. But a faction of opposing bishops pushed for a formal declaration of papal infallibility, particularly as a response to the pope's recent loss of secular power.

The Council Fathers and *Dei Filius*

Major decisions of the First Vatican Council were developed and recorded in the dogmatic constitution *Dei Filius* (*Son of God*). *Dei Filius* was, of course, in line with Pope Pius IX's goal of proclaiming the role of the Church in the world. Principally, *Dei Filius* stressed the significance of the title "Holy Roman Catholic Church" and the need for reason and Divine Revelation to be considered together in order to arrive at a greater knowledge of God.

Dei Filius asserted that human reason leads a person to the knowledge that God exists; meanwhile, Divine Revelation indicates that God, in the Divine Person of Jesus Christ, the Son of God, came to earth in the flesh to share in our humanity. *Dei Filius* emphasized that neither reason nor Divine Revelation alone suffices and described the balance between faith and reason: Human reason is necessary for a person to be able to form rational beliefs. However, for a person to receive and enter into the mysteries of faith, Divine Revelation is necessary.

The council clearly condemned the teaching of the Enlightenment that the Faith can be understood by reason alone:

> If anyone says that in divine revelation there are contained no true mysteries properly so-called, but that all the dogmas of the faith can be understood and demonstrated by properly trained reason from natural principles: let him be anathema. (*Dei Filius*, 1)

One of the purposes of the First Vatican Council was to offer clear teaching in response to the Enlightenment, liberalism, modernism, and the other issues of the time, hence the clarity of *Dei Filius*'s statement on this subject of faith and reason.

Papal Infallibility

An important outcome of the First Vatican Council was Pope Pius IX's proclamation of *papal infallibility* as dogma. The doctrine of papal infallibility maintains that the pope does not err when he is teaching *ex cathedra,* "from the chair"—that is, when he teaches as pope, teacher, and shepherd of all Christians and as vicar of Christ and successor of St. Peter. *Ex cathedra* teaching is of a dogmatic scope when the pope "proclaims by a definitive act a doctrine pertaining to faith and morals" (*CCC*, 891). The doctrine of papal infallibility was actually widely held by Catholics throughout the history of the Church; the First Vatican Council simply solidified this teaching.

Occasionally, the Church's teaching on papal infallibility is misunderstood. Papal infallibility does *not* mean any of the following:

- That anything that the pope says is correct. For example, if the pope were to say, "I am in Australia," while he was on a boat in the Atlantic Ocean, he would not be speaking infallibly.
- That the pope is somehow divine or does not sin. The pope is a sinner like anyone else. Popes are known to confess their sins with frequent celebration of the Sacrament of Penance.
- That the Church's teachings do not need to be clarified. The Church's teachings are timeless, including her teaching on papal infallibility, but historical settings require them to be restated and explained, as popes have had to do on many occasions over the course of Church history.

There have only been two occasions in Church history when the pope spoke infallibly, *ex cathedra*: when Pope Pius IX declared the dogma of Mary's Immaculate Conception in 1854 and when Pope Pius XII declared the dogma of Mary's Assumption into heaven in 1950.

Abrupt End to the First Vatican Council

The revolutionary movement within Italy in 1870 unfortunately brought a quick end to the First Vatican Council. The council was never formally concluded, meaning that some important topics on the agenda were not discussed. However, some of these matters were eventually addressed during the Second Vatican Council, held from 1962 to 1965. In light of the seizure of the Papal States by the Italian forces, the First Vatican Council succeeded in underscoring the importance of the pope's pastoral role, a role that the popes following Pius IX have taken very seriously.

PRAYERS FOR THE CHURCH

In his opening words to convoke the First Vatican Council, Pope Pius IX offered petitions for the

- praise and glory of the holy and undivided Trinity—Father, Son, and Holy Spirit;
- increase and exaltation of the Catholic faith and religion;
- uprooting of current errors;
- reformation of the clergy and the Christian people; and
- common peace and concord of all.

ASSIGNMENT

Write your own prayer that includes five petitions for the current needs of the Church.

SECTION ASSESSMENT

NOTE TAKING

Review your notes on the objectives and accomplishments of the First Vatican Council and then answer the following questions.

1. Why was it important that the First Vatican Council occurred when it did?
2. What do you believe to be the greatest accomplishment of the First Vatican Council? Explain.

COMPREHENSION

3. Why does the Catholic Church profess that there is a necessary balance between reason and Divine Revelation?
4. Write a one-sentence definition of *papal infallibility*.

CRITICAL THINKING

5. Would you side with the ultramontane bishops at the First Vatican Council who believed that a formal declaration of papal infallibility was unnecessary or with the opposing bishops who believed the council should offer a formal declaration? Explain.

Section Assignments

Focus Question

How have questions about faith stimulated during the Enlightenment had an impact on the Church, faith, and religion ever since?

Complete one of the following:

Why was it important for the Catholic Church to hold the First Vatican Council when it did? How were the issues that the Church faced in society during the mid-nineteenth century similar to those she faced during the Protestant Reformation? How were the issues different? Write a one-page report that addresses these questions.

In a recent election year, it was revealed that political groups had sought to cause a division in the Church in the United States. Archbishop Joseph Kurtz responded with a statement titled "USCCB President Says the Gospel Serves the Common Good, Not Political Agendas." Read the statement, and summarize its message in your own words. What similarities do you see between this current situation and the situation around the time of the French Revolution?

Revolutionaries and statesmen of the nineteenth century wanted the state to secularize functions previously handled by the Catholic Church, including marriage, charitable efforts, and education. Write a two- to three-paragraph explanation of how the Church and the federal government both agree and disagree on these matters today.

INTRODUCTION

What Was the Enlightenment?

Research and provide a three- to five-paragraph explanation of the religious beliefs of one of the following philosophers of the Enlightenment: Francis Bacon, Immanuel Kant, Jean-Jacques Rousseau, or Voltaire.

SECTION 1

The Tumultuous Period of the French Revolution

Jansenism, a heretical belief of the seventeenth century that originated in France, taught that human nature is utterly depraved and that God's grace extends to only a few. Research and write a three-paragraph report on how the Church, and the Jesuits in particular, refuted Jansenism.

SECTION 2

Religious Revival in France following the French Revolution

St. John Vianney said, "The more we pray, the more we wish to pray. Like a fish which at first swims on the surface of the water, and afterwards plunges down, and is always going deeper; the soul plunges, dives, and loses itself in the sweetness of conversing with God." Write down five things you can do to improve your prayer life and form a deeper connection with God.

SECTION 3

Liberalism and the Church of the Nineteenth Century

Review the Church's teaching on the dogma of Mary's Immaculate Conception in paragraphs 490–493 of the *Catechism of the Catholic Church*. Note the quotation from Pope Pius IX. In two to three paragraphs, write your understanding of these words and phrases contained in the quote: "singular grace and privilege," "by virtue of the merits of Jesus Christ," and "preserved immune from all stain of original sin."

SECTION 4

The Era of the First Vatican Council

The doctrine of papal infallibility, defined at the First Vatican Council, has biblical roots. Read and explain in three to five paragraphs the roots of this doctrine as expressed in these Gospel passages: Matthew 16:17–19, Luke 22:32, and John 21:15–17.

Chapter Assignments

Choose and complete at least one of the three assignments to assess your understanding of the material in this chapter.

1. Essay: Considering the Value of Science at the Service of Faith

Read paragraph 2293 of the *Catechism of the Catholic Church*. Then, write a two-page essay titled "Christian Perspective on Scientific Research." In the essay, address the following questions in some detail. Cite other references to support the teaching found in the *Catechism*.

- What does it mean to say that man has "dominion over creation"?
- Why are science and technology considered "precious resources when placed at the service of man"?
- In what ways do science and technology "promote [man's] integral development for the benefit of all"?
- What are some limitations of science and technology in clarifying matters of faith and morality?

2. Recreating the Words of a Saint

Read and record quotations of a nineteenth-century saint (e.g., St. Thérèse of Lisieux, St. John Bosco, or Bl. John Henry Newman). These can be random quotations, quotations from written texts authored by the saints, or composed prayers or poems. A general theme of the quotations should be testimony to the Gospel of Jesus Christ and evangelization of the world. Prepare a witness statement on the Catholic faith using the saint's exact words. Perform the words in a dramatic reading on a video presentation, accompanied by a montage of images that represent the saint (e.g., contemporaries, native place, writings, the saint him- or herself). The recording should be three to five minutes in length.

3. Music of the Nineteenth Century

Trace the theme of freedom from lyrics of songs important in the eighteenth and nineteenth centuries. Compare the lyrics of at least four songs. Print and cite relevant lyrics that address freedom, liberty, victory, and faith, and design them on a poster board or a digital platform. Include author reference, year composed, and other background information about the composition. Also add one of the following: (1) your own short poem or song lyrics that address freedom and its related topics, or (2) an audio montage of the songs and lyrics you cited. Song suggestions:

- *Oh Freedom!* (Negro spiritual)
- *La Marseillaise* (French national anthem)

- *My Country, 'Tis of Thee* (American patriotic song)
- *Holy God, We Praise Thy Name* (German hymn; lyrics written in the late eighteenth century)
- *Veni, Creator Spiritus* (one of the hymns sung by the Compiègne nuns on their way to martyrdom)

Prayer

Prayer for the Intercession of St. John ("Don") Bosco (1815–1888)

St. John Bosco,
Friend of the young,
Teacher in the ways of God,
Your dedication to empowering the needy inspires us still.
Help me to work for a better world,
where the young are given the chance to flourish,
where the poor's dream for justice can come true,
and where God's compassion is shown to be real.
Intercede for me as I bring my needs to you and to
Our heavenly Mother, the Help of Christians. Amen.

—Courtesy of the Salesians of Don Bosco, Ireland

8

THE CHURCH IN THE MODERN WORLD

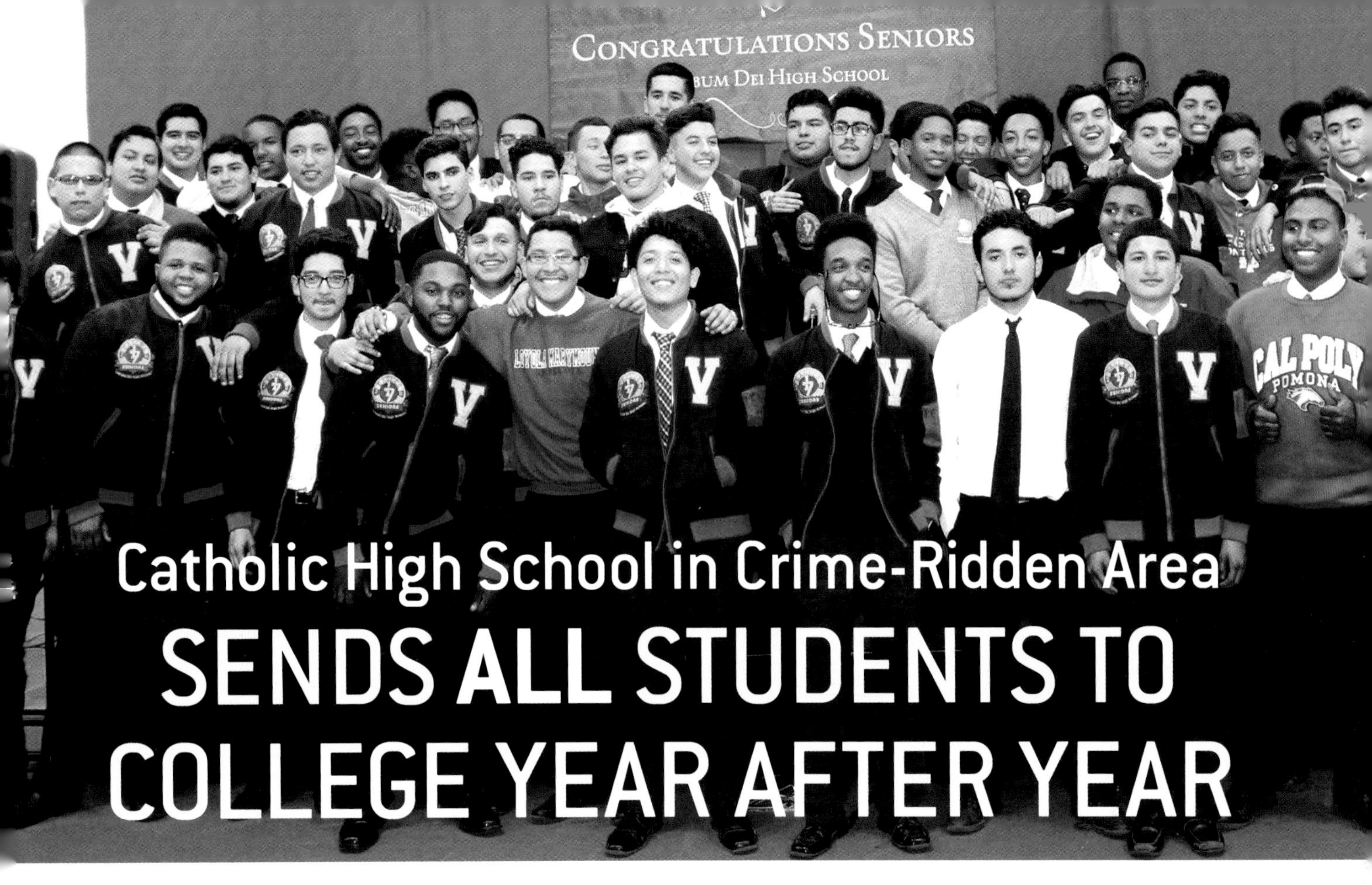

Catholic High School in Crime-Ridden Area SENDS ALL STUDENTS TO COLLEGE YEAR AFTER YEAR

In 2018, for the eleventh consecutive year, every senior in the all-male graduating class at Verbum Dei High School in the Watts area of South Los Angeles was accepted to college. The achievement is noteworthy because about 75 percent of the students would be first-generation college attendees and many of them faced a variety of personal struggles. To enroll in the school, whose student body is about 70 percent Latino and 30 percent African American, a boy's family must have an income equivalent to under forty thousand dollars a year for a family of four.

Since 2000, when Verbum Dei was in danger of closing, it has been staffed by the Jesuits, and it is also part of the Cristo Rey network of Catholic schools, which provides college preparatory education to disadvantaged urban teens. The teens' tuition is sponsored in great part by businesses that also employ students on work-study days away from school.

"The difference with our students is that they want it," said Antoinette Bowie, school counselor. "And if their parents want it—and they're committed to it—that commitment will lead them to where they are today." Throughout their four years at Verbum Dei, students spend class time reviewing college applications, learning what financial aid may be available, and looking into academic majors offered. The school sponsors a "college-ready" curriculum.

The students also take a regular theology curriculum at Verbum Dei. Mass attendance is required, as is a school uniform that includes a white shirt and tie. "I didn't wear a lot of ties before, but when we came here it was okay," said a recent Verbum Dei graduate, Miguel Morales. "It's kind of emotional, you know. My parents were always there for me. They were always supporting me and my friends. After a while, we started pushing each other to get to the finish line. Sometimes it was hard—a lot of stressful nights—but my mom would always say, 'It's going to pay off someday.'"

FOCUS QUESTION

What **WORLD EVENTS** of the nineteenth and early twentieth centuries led to the development and application of **MODERN CATHOLIC SOCIAL TEACHING**?

Chapter Overview

INTRODUCTION

The Industrial Revolution Brings New Challenges

MAIN IDEA
During the nineteenth century, while recovering from the effects of the Enlightenment, the Church was confronted with societal changes brought on by the Industrial Revolution.

Near the end of the nineteenth century and the beginning of the twentieth century, the Catholic Church and the rest of society came face-to-face with the modern world. In Chapter 7 you read about how Pope Pius IX addressed various dilemmas in the wake of the Enlightenment by emphasizing the irreplaceable contributions the Church made to the world. This chapter explores some of the ways in which the Church continued to serve humanity amid the challenges that came with **modernism** (not to be confused with modernity, which represents several distinct periods of time and in particular the rise of industrialism and capitalism), particularly in light of the Industrial Revolution, immigration around the globe, and other situations of the time.

modernism A movement of the late nineteenth and early twentieth centuries that attempted to reduce and/or limit Church teaching to modern advances in history, science, and biblical research.

NOTE TAKING

Naming and Labeling Results. Create a graphic organizer like the one shown here to help you chart the positive and negative results of the Industrial Revolution. Write results in the surrounding circles. Use colored pencils to lightly shade each circle, green to indicate a positive result and red to indicate a negative result.

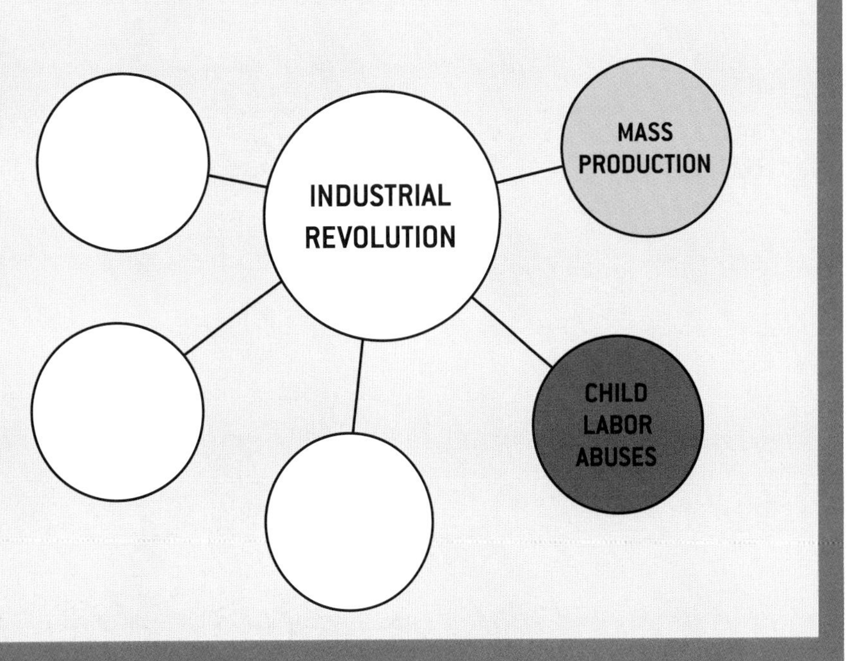

Societal Changes Accompanying the Industrial Revolution

Beginning in the late eighteenth century and continuing throughout the nineteenth century, an economic revolution took place in Europe that brought with it just as much societal upheaval as did the French Revolution. While the French Revolution led to the modification of the political realm within Europe, the Industrial Revolution noticeably changed the economic and social makeup of Europe. The advent of industrialization led to an increase in the production of goods, with large European nations such as Great Britain at the forefront. In prior generations, manufacturing took place at the local level, such as in shops and small farms within rural settings, but with the building of factories, production moved to cities. The production of goods was achieved more efficiently and on a much larger scale in these new settings.

Additionally, the invention of the steam engine at the end of the eighteenth century allowed for the creation of factories in new regions. Previous factories that operated on power produced by flowing water had to be located near a body of water. The steam engine also caused a boom in the railroad industry. For example, by the mid-nineteenth century, nine thousand miles of railroad track had been built in the United States. Food could be produced in a rural area and transported easily to an urban one. Inversely, goods and products manufactured in cities could easily be shipped to and sold in smaller, rural towns. People could move about the country more easily and were no longer as tied to the area in which they resided.

The Industrial Revolution changed societal roles of individuals and families. Working conditions were often inhumane. These changes led the Church to formally define her social teaching, beginning with these critical reminders:

- All are made in God's image and likeness.
- Material welfare is not the goal of a person's time on earth.
- Community is important to the functioning of society.
- Every person has human dignity and worth that cannot be violated.

The invention of the steam engine increased production in both rural and urban areas. For example, the steam threshing machine made it easier to separate the seeds of grain from their stalks.

These children worked as breaker boys. They removed impurities from coal by hand, and the dangerous work resulted in many losing fingers or limbs, developing lung problems, or dying.

Social Injustices during the Industrial Revolution

Human rights violations were rampant within the industrializing world. Powerful companies and organizations, frequently administered by owners concerned only with bottom-line profits, sought to control the means of production with little or no interest in the cares, concerns, and rights of workers. The Church opposed various offenses by speaking up for the poor and others who were voiceless, including children, who were part of the workforce in many of the urban factories.

One area of the Church's concern was the lack of a living wage that allowed an employee to support his or her family. Also, there was no employer contribution to a savings or pension program to help support older, retired workers. Children as young as six years old were made to work twelve to fourteen hours per day—and sometimes up to nineteen hours in one day—in cramped buildings known as *sweatshops*. Additionally, employees were forbidden from forming labor unions or opposing the abuses of their employers by creating a work stoppage or strike.

Two Flawed Economic Systems: Capitalism and Socialism

Two economic systems arose in response to the advent of industrialization: **capitalism** and **socialism**. It is important to understand each of these systems within their broader socioeconomic context.

Capitalism calls for a free market economy, wherein the government has at most a small degree of influence on how businesses are operated. If a business is not competing well against similar competitors, it is in danger of closing. Many capitalists embraced the concept of **social Darwinism**, based on theories introduced by Charles Darwin (1809–1882) in his *On the Origin of Species* (1859), a pioneering treatise on evolution. Darwin's theory of the "survival of the fittest" translated to the workplace, resulting in an image of the economic jungle and so-called *laissez-faire* ("hands-off") economics, or liberal capitalism. These ideas led to the type of human suffering Charles Dickens (1822–1870) described in his novels: sixteen-hour work days, six-year-old chimney sweeps, factory towns that enslaved workers, dangerous working conditions, and the lack of social security. Under capitalism, workers essentially had no rights, not even the right to collective bargaining.

SEEKING MIDDLE GROUND

between Socialism and Laissez-Faire Capitalism

Both laissez-faire capitalism and socialism have drawbacks that were identified by the Church. For example, the Church asserts that people, while having the right to own private property, do not have the right to do whatever they wish with their belongings. The Church does not support any government's right to confiscate an individual's private property, as in socialism. The Church also opposes strands of socialism that lead to atheism.

Some Catholic leaders understood the forces of economic change and were able to chart a middle course between socialism and unbridled capitalism in the nineteenth century. One such leader was Bishop Wilhelm Emmanuel von Ketteler of Mainz, Germany, who as early as 1848 insisted that workers could form their own associations. He also called for reasonable working hours, rest days, profit sharing, factory inspection, and regulation of child labor. England's Cardinal Henry Edward Manning also fought for workers' rights, while Cardinal James Gibbons of Baltimore, Maryland, in 1887 successfully defended the Knights of Labor after a similar organization had been condemned in Canada due primarily to holding secret meetings. The Knights of Labor was the most important American labor union of the time.

In other countries, Christian trade unions were formed to protect workers' rights. An example of such a union was Belgium's Young Christian Workers, founded by Fr. Joseph Cardijn (1882–1967). This union typified the Christian trade movement of the twentieth century. It stressed a spirit of collaboration in achieving workers' rights and championed the decentralization of industries in contrast to the socialist ideal of government control. Furthermore, as a Christian union, it underscored the value of the individual.

ASSIGNMENT

Read paragraphs 2426–2436 of the *Catechism of the Catholic Church*. Summarize the Church's teaching on economic activity and social justice in a one-page report.

Fr. John J. Curran, Cardinal Gibbons, President Theodore Roosevelt, and John Mitchell met together for Mine Workers Day. Gibbons spoke for the Catholic Total Abstinence Union and Mitchell for the United Mine Workers Union. Roosevelt praised the efforts of both organizations.

Meanwhile, socialism calls for a significant amount of governmental involvement in the operation of business organizations. German thinker Karl Marx (1818–1883) advocated for a form of socialism known as **communism** that sought to place most aspects of daily life under the control of the government. In his *Communist Manifesto* (1848) and *Das Kapital* (1867), Marx analyzed economics as a class struggle. The protagonists were the capitalists, who controlled the means of production, and the workers (or *proletariat*), whom the rich capitalists exploited. Marx believed that the revolution of the proletariat was inevitable and that the workers would eventually triumph and create a classless society. Marx was both an atheist and a *materialist* (one who holds that the only reality is what can be sensed). His brand of atheism was especially hostile to organized religion. He saw the Church as a negative force in society that taught people to be content with their lot in life.

Marx predicted that industrial nations such as Great Britain, Germany, and America would undergo violent revolutions. He did not live long enough to see these nations gradually curb the excesses of capitalism through law. Although the rich selfishly guarded their wealth, they began to see the wisdom of governments intervening to protect workers. Some nations, such as Russia and China, however, adopted Marx's philosophy and underwent communist revolutions in the twentieth century. In these countries, atheism became the official religion. Leaders such as Russia's Joseph Stalin tried to eradicate religion. Rule by the few—members of the communist party—became the official form of government. Marx's utopian dream of a classless society not only failed but wreaked havoc in the twentieth century.

The negative effect of both systems—unbridled capitalism and socialism that led to communism—on the rights of workers during the time of the Industrial Revolution demanded a response from the Church. Hence, the Church replied with an official formulation of her long standing social teaching.

capitalism An economic and sociopolitical system with limited governmental control, centered upon the free market and with an emphasis on private property, sometimes resulting in economic inequality.

socialism At its core, an economic and sociopolitical theory that advocates for the government or society as a whole to own and administer the production and distribution of goods.

social Darwinism The theories of Charles Darwin applied to the social realm. For example, the concept of "survival of the fittest" works in economics too, resulting in an image of the economic jungle and so-called laissez-faire economics, or liberal capitalism.

communism A socioeconomic and political system that aims to bring about a utopian society on earth as envisioned by Karl Marx. This theory includes the government's unrestrained control of citizens' property, the suppression of free speech and assembly, the oppression of religion in public life, and other denials of democratic values.

SECTION ASSESSMENT

NOTE TAKING

Use the graphic organizer you created to help you answer the following questions.

1. What were the effects on society of increased production, faster transportation, and reduced reliance on local economies during the Industrial Revolution?
2. What were some of the troubling details of children working in brutal factory conditions during much of the Industrial Revolution?
3. Why was there a need for a renewed understanding of human dignity in the midst of the commercial excesses of the Industrial Revolution?
4. What do you consider to be the most positive overall result of the Industrial Revolution? The most negative overall result?

VOCABULARY

5. What is *capitalism*, and why can it be problematic for society if not properly limited?
6. What is *socialism*, and why can it be problematic for society if not properly limited?
7. How does *communism* differ from socialism?

FURTHER RESEARCH

8. How is the technical revolution that occurred with the creation of the Internet similar to the Industrial Revolution? What are some concerns the Church has regarding the Internet age? How has the Church responded?

SECTION 1

Pope Leo XIII and Catholic Social Teaching

MAIN IDEA

Pope Leo XIII created the charter document of modern Catholic social teaching, the encyclical *Rerum Novarum* (*The Condition of Labor*), to address the concerns of workers at the time of the Industrial Revolution. Other popes have added to this body of social teaching.

Following the pontificate of Pope Pius IX, Pope Leo XIII (1878–1903) expanded on the Church's focus on social teaching. Pope Leo XIII authored *Rerum Novarum* (*The Condition of Labor*) in 1891. It steered a balanced course between liberal capitalism and communism. On the one hand, *Rerum Novarum* affirmed the right to private property and condemned a major tenet of communism: inevitable, violent revolution and class warfare. On the other hand, it defended the rights of workers to a living wage and to unionize and taught that the state can sometimes intervene in the economic sphere to defend workers.

Moreover, *Rerum Novarum* emphasized the principle of the **universal destination of goods**, meaning that the goods of the earth should be divided to ensure that all people have their basic human needs met. Primarily, this document made it clear that all people have basic rights that flow from natural law and that these rights should be respected.

Rerum Novarum was the first in a remarkable series of forward-looking encyclicals that popes since Pope Leo XIII have written to defend human rights in all areas of life, especially in relation to work. These

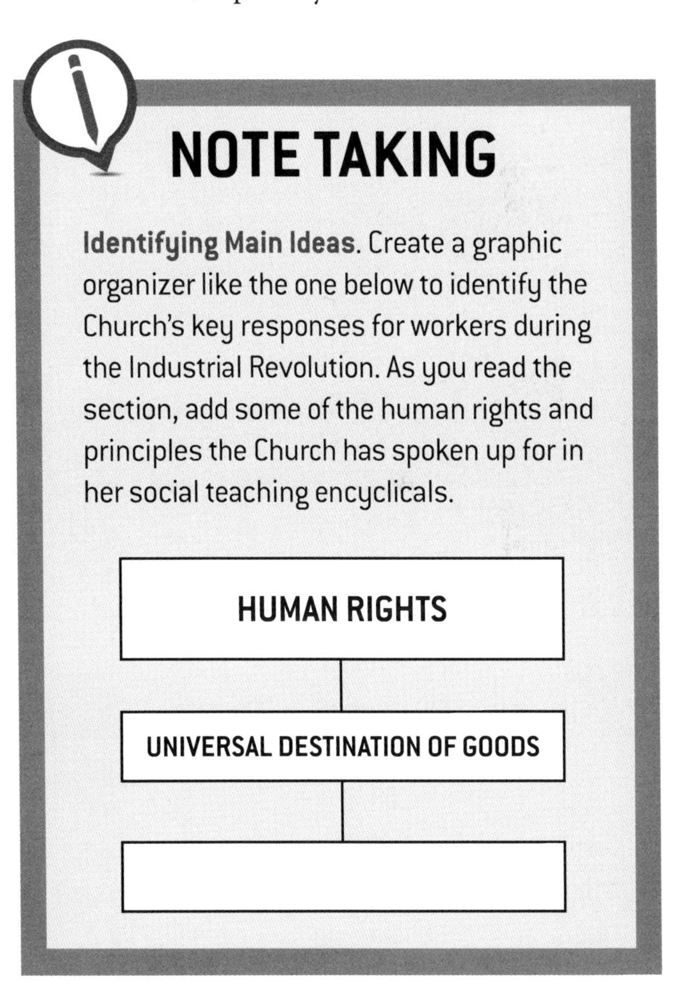

universal destination of goods The principle that resources and material goods within society should be accessible to humanity as a whole rather than restricted to the private realm.

Key Documents in Support of *Rerum Novarum*

Every pope since Pope Leo XIII has advocated for human rights, especially those threatened by economic and political changes. Several national Catholic conferences of bishops have also written on these issues, including the United States Conference of Catholic Bishops. Some of their key documents are listed and described here.

Quadragesimo Anno (On Reconstruction of the Social Order)

POPE PIUS XI, 1931

The document was written in commemoration of the fortieth anniversary of *Rerum Novarum*. In the height of the Great Depression, as totalitarian regimes were on the rise, *Quadragesimo Anno* reaffirmed the right to private property while condemning its selfish and arbitrary use. It also introduced the principle of **subsidiarity**.

Mater et Magistra (Mother and Teacher): On Christianity and Social Progress

POPE JOHN XXIII, 1961

Pope John XXIII wrote the encyclical *Mater et Magistra* on the seventieth anniversary of *Rerum Novarum*. He taught that the state must sometimes intervene in the areas of health care, education, and housing. He also stressed the need to work toward authentic community among people as a way to promote human dignity.

Pacem in Terris (Peace on Earth): On Establishing Universal Peace in Truth, Justice, Charity, and Liberty

POPE JOHN XXIII, 1963

Pacem in Terris was the first to address "all people of good will," and it was favorably received by Catholics, other Christians, and non-Christians as well. One of its major contributions is to list basic human rights and the responsibilities that go along with them. It reiterates the importance of the **common good** and addresses the problems with the arms race.

Gaudium et Spes (Pastoral Constitution on the Church in the Modern World)

SECOND VATICAN COUNCIL, 1965

Gaudium et Spes focuses on the human person as the foundation of society and all its structures—familial, cultural, economic, and political. It emphasizes the importance of the Church in dialogue with the world.

Populorum Progressio (On the Development of Peoples)

POPE PAUL VI, 1967

Populorum Progressio builds on *Gaudium et Spes*'s teachings on economic and social life. It teaches on the progress of humans in all their capacities—not just economic and technological but also cultural and social capacities, most especially the capacity to know God. It also encourages international relations.

Octogesima Adveniens (Eightieth Anniversary)

POPE PAUL VI, 1971

Octogesima Adveniens, an apostolic letter written on the eightieth anniversary of *Rerum Novarum*, focuses on issues such as urbanization, the condition of young people, the condition of women, unemployment, discrimination, emigration, population growth, influence of social communications, and ecological problems. It teaches that ideologies are not enough to answer these problems.

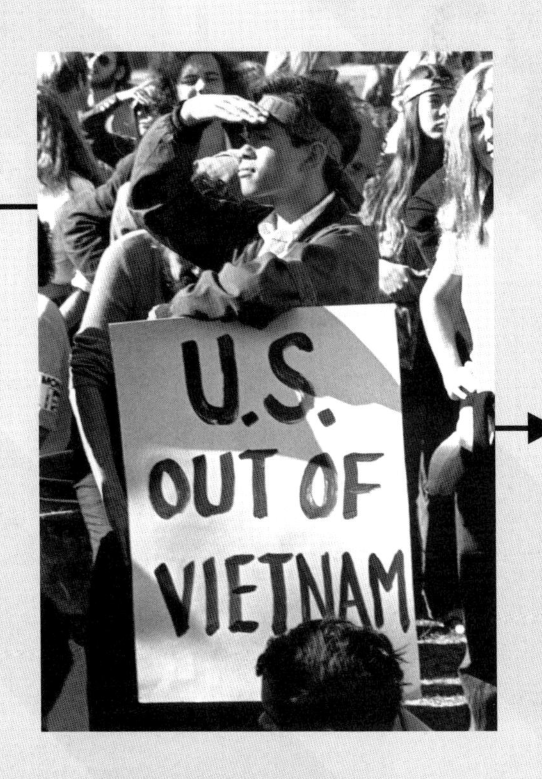

subsidiarity A social principle that stipulates that social matters should be taken care of at the lowest, most local level of authority possible.

common good The collective well-being of society as a whole, particularly in matters related to social justice.

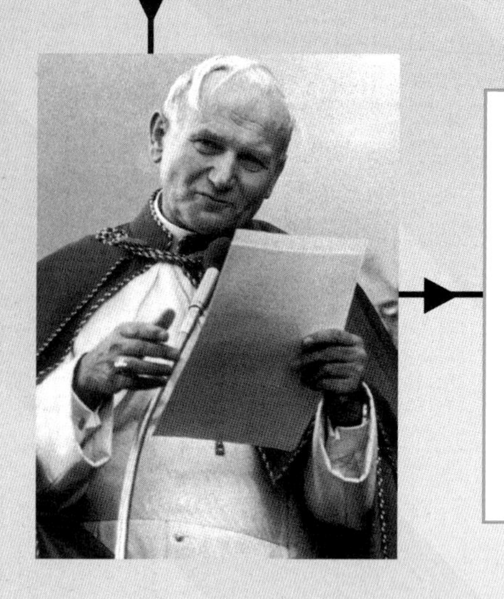

Laborem Exercens (On Human Work)
POPE JOHN PAUL II, 1981

Laborem Exercens, on the ninetieth anniversary of *Rerum Novarum*, shows how work can dehumanize but also can be an important way for humans to participate in God's ongoing creation. The encyclical stresses that work is a fundamental expression of the human person and explains that because work has dignity it helps to fulfill the human vocation.

Sollicitudo Rei Socialis (The Social Concern)
POPE JOHN PAUL II, 1987

Written on the twentieth anniversary of Pope Paul VI's *Populorum Progressio*, *Sollicitudo Rei Socialis* points out that many of the hopes of *Populorum Progressio* have not been fulfilled, especially the lessening of the disparity of wealth between nations. Pope John Paul II calls attention to the "structures of sin" within nations, condemning the West for materialism and the East for offenses against human dignity.

Centesimus Annus (The Hundredth Year)
POPE JOHN PAUL II, 1991

In commemoration of the one hundredth anniversary of *Rerum Novarum*, Pope John Paul II reaffirms the essential teachings of the original encyclical. Written after the collapse of communism in Eastern Europe and the Soviet Union, *Centesimus Annus* points out both the flaws in Marxist communism and the weaknesses of modern market capitalism and consumerism.

The Challenge of Peace

UNITED STATES CONFERENCE OF CATHOLIC BISHOPS, 1983

The Challenge of Peace is a pastoral letter that addresses just war principles, focusing on modern moral questions involving war, including the buildup of nuclear armaments.

Write a prayer for peace in the world. Cite specific examples in both your own community and in the world at large in need of peace.

Dutch anti-nuclear weapons and anti-war poster

Economic Justice for All

UNITED STATES CONFERENCE OF CATHOLIC BISHOPS, 1986

The intention of this pastoral letter is to apply the Christian vision of economic life to the American economy. *Economic Justice for All* issues a challenge to examine the inequalities of income, consumption, power, and privilege and their impact on the poor.

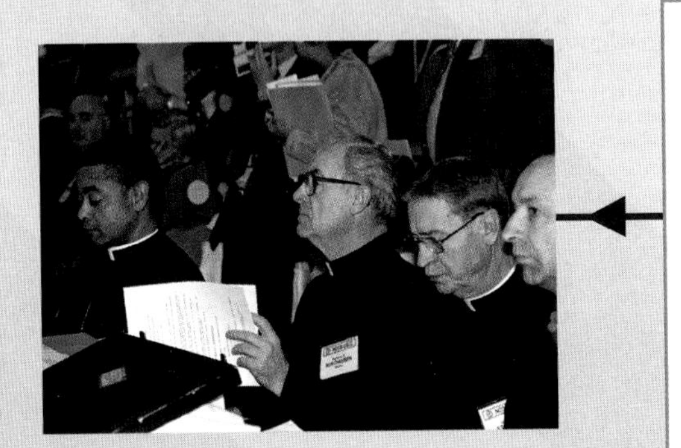

encyclicals make up the official body of modern *Catholic social teaching* today. What is meant by Catholic social teaching? It is the teaching of the Church that lays out and explains God-given doctrine about the truth of human dignity, human solidarity, and the moral principles of justice and peace. This teaching attempts to understand how societies work and then makes moral judgments about economic and social matters in light of revealed truth and the demands of peace and justice.

Pope Leo XIII's Legacy

Pope Leo XIII is sometimes known as the "encyclical pope" because he wrote eighty-four general letters beyond *Rerum Novarum* to the entire Church. His strong personality led to the Church intervening in social issues in several nations and to a greater centralization of the power of the Church.

Regarding modernism, Pope Leo did not condemn the modern world. *Rerum Novarum* was written with a sense of coming to an understanding of the forces of modernism and the forces of industrialization. Pope Leo was also successful in negotiating an end to the *Kulturkampf*, the cultural war in Germany that negatively impacted the Church (see "Liberalism Leads to the Creation of New Nations" in Chapter 7, Section 3).

The Seven Principles of Catholic Social Teaching

The seven principles, or themes, of Catholic social teaching are drawn from a 1998 document of the United States Conference of Catholic Bishops titled "Sharing Catholic Social Teaching: Challenges and Directions." They are:

1. Life and dignity of the human person
2. Call to family, community, and participation
3. Rights and responsibilities
4. Option for the poor and vulnerable
5. Dignity of work and the rights of workers
6. Solidarity
7. Care for God's creation

ASSIGNMENT

Explain each of the seven principles of Catholic social teaching. Write three sentences summarizing each after reading the short descriptions at the USCCB website under "USCCB > Beliefs and Teachings > What We Believe > Catholic Social Teaching > Seven Themes of Catholic Social Teaching."

SECTION ASSESSMENT

NOTE TAKING

Use the key words you recorded to help you answer the following items.

1. What does the universal destination of goods for all people have to do with the common good?
2. Explain the meaning of subsidiarity related to social justice.
3. According to *Quadragesimo Anno*, what are the stipulations on owning private property?

COMPREHENSION

4. Why was the world in need of a reform of capitalism following the Industrial Revolution?
5. What is meant by Catholic social teaching?
6. What tenet of communism did *Rerum Novarum* condemn?

APPLICATION

7. Explain how the seven principles of Catholic social teaching emanate from Jesus' teachings in the Gospels.

SECTION 2

The Church Responds Directly to Modernism

MAIN IDEA

As the twentieth century began, Pope Pius X and the Church responded forcefully to the challenges of modernism and to the world's reluctance to abide more fully by the Church's teachings.

In contrast to his predecessor Pope Pius IX, Pope Leo XIII (1878–1903) saw that the Church had to come to terms with a new age. *Rerum Novarum*, his encyclical on social justice, was forward-looking and prophetic. He encouraged Catholic scholars by setting up a biblical commission and opening up the Vatican Library for historical research. He worked diligently to defeat Germany's anti-Catholic *Kulturkampf* policies, as well as similar policies in Switzerland. He was also able to restore diplomatic relations with Brazil, Colombia, and Russia and was successful in getting anticlerical legislation removed in Chile and Spain. With Leo XIII's diplomatic skills, the Church became less defensive and more willing to dialogue with modernists.

However, Pope Pius X (1903–1914), Pope Leo XIII's successor, looked more critically at the developments of modernism. His main interest was reflected in his motto: "To restore all things in Christ." His major contributions involved Church life. For example, he reformed liturgical music, restoring Gregorian chant to the Mass. Pope Pius X also encouraged frequent reception of Holy Communion and permitted children to receive the Eucharist at the age of reason (around the age of seven) rather than make their First Communion around the age of twelve. He issued a new catechism and undertook a reform of canon law,

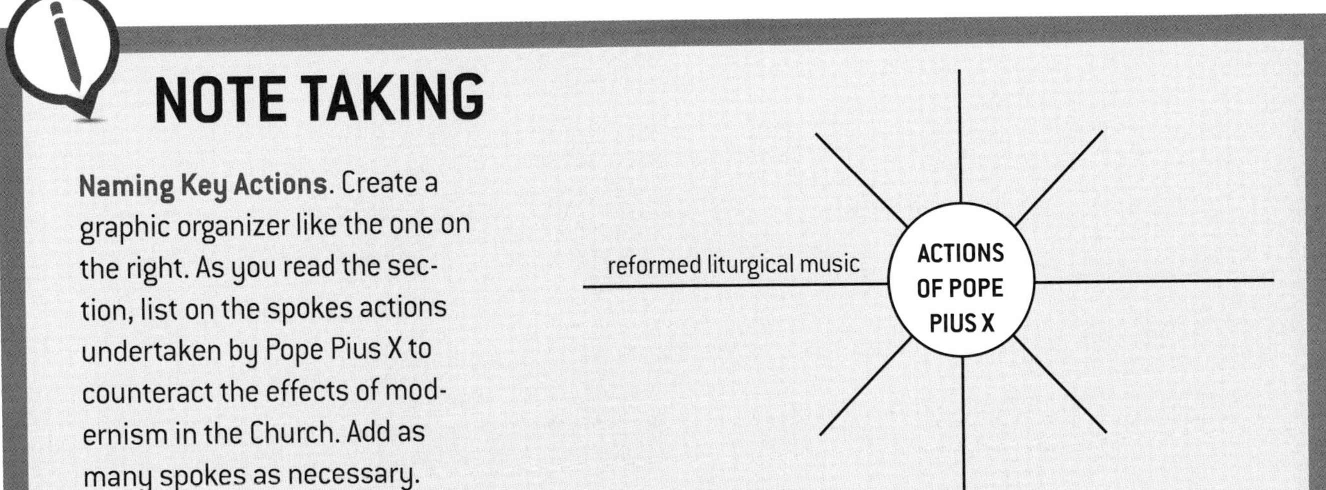

a task only completed and published after his death. In addition, he promoted a lay movement known as Catholic Action, which was dedicated to doing works of charity among poor people, combating anti-Christian elements in society, and defending and supporting the rights of the Church and God wherever possible.

Pope Pius X and Faithfulness to Church Teaching

Pope Pius X lived a holy, pious, and warmly inspiring life that led to his canonization in 1954. During his pontificate, he engaged with certain progressive Catholic theologians of his day known as modernists. Influenced by liberal Protestants, modernists employed critical and historical methods of theological research in their attempt to conform to contemporary philosophies. They began to reject the scholastic thought patterns of traditional Catholic theology, including Thomism. Unfortunately, some modernists uncritically accepted the thinking of evolutionists, historical skeptics, and scientists who excluded all supernatural considerations. Some questioned and even denied traditional Church teaching, while others did not see much value in Church authority, especially in scholarly matters.

Pope Pius X was greatly disturbed by theologians who deviated from Church doctrine, questioned traditional ways of teaching, and challenged the need for scholars to follow the teachings of the hierarchy. He called modernism "the synthesis of all heresies." In response to modernism, Pope Pius X issued in 1907 both a decree (*Lamentabili Sane*) and an encyclical (*Pascendi Dominici Gregis*) that condemned the approaches and conclusions of the modernists. He also required teachers in Church institutions and priests to take an antimodernist oath. Finally, he established a secret network of informers known as the *Sodalitium Pianum* (the Sodality of St. Pius V) that advised him on questionable seminary professors in dioceses around the world.

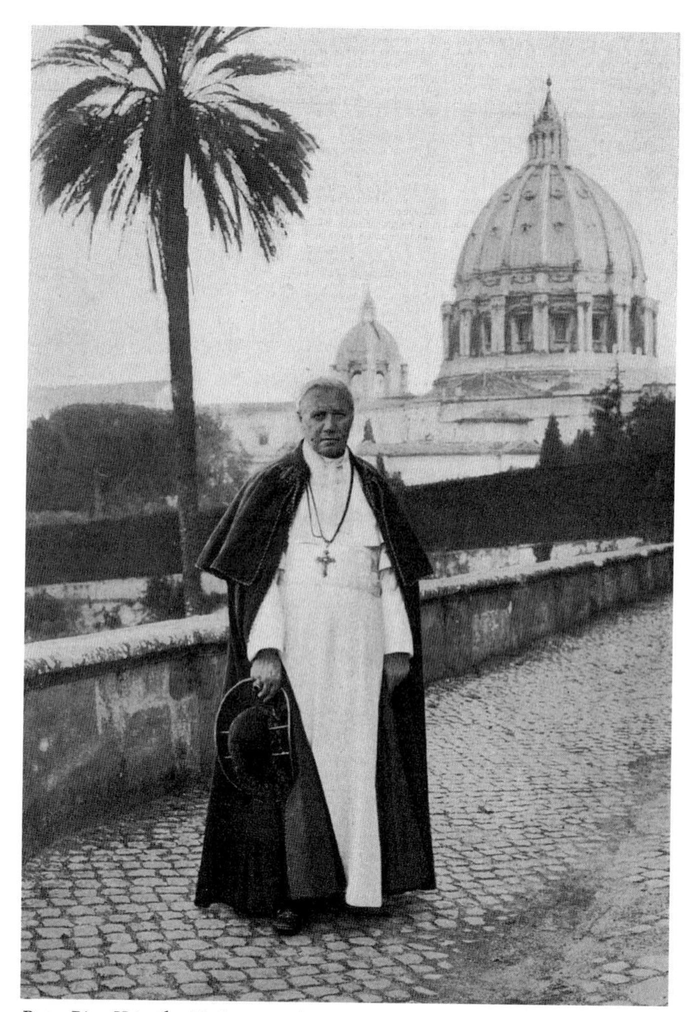

Pope Pius X in the Vatican gardens, 1911

These decisive actions contained the modernist crisis. Antimodernist efforts preserved the Church from dangerous, heretical ideas that undermined and even destroyed traditional dogmatic teaching. Some modernists did, in fact, teach heretical views. For example, the French Scripture expert Alfred Loisy used the techniques of rational criticism to study the Bible. He treated books of the Bible simply as historical texts rather than as inspired documents. He also ignored Church teaching on how to interpret Scripture in light of Divine Revelation. Ultimately, he ended up denying the Resurrection and the divinity of Jesus Christ.

However, a negative effect of *Sodalitium Pianum* was that Catholic intellectual inquiry cooled for decades, especially in areas such as Scripture scholarship. The careers of some innocent men suffered. (When he became pope, Pope John XXIII learned, to his surprise, that he himself had been suspected of modernism by one of the antimodernist watchdog groups.) Some scholars identified as modernists were faithful to the Church and sincere in their attempts to update Church scholarship, especially in the area of biblical studies.

In 1942, Pope Pius XII issued an encyclical, *Divino Afflante Spiritu* (*Inspired by the Spirit*): *On the Promotion of Biblical Studies*, that approved new translations of the Bible from its original languages, initiating an increase in Catholic biblical scholarship carried out under the auspices of the Magisterium and in acknowledgment of the books of the Bible as divinely revealed and inspired.

SECTION ASSESSMENT

NOTE TAKING

Use the graphic organizer you created for this section to help you complete the true-false items below. Rewrite to make true any false statement(s).

1. True or False: Pope Pius X believed children should be older and better trained to receive the Eucharist, so he moved the age of First Holy Communion to twelve.
2. True or False: Pope Pius X was dedicated to works of charity, and he created a clerical movement known as Catholic Action to further this work.
3. True or False: Many modernists rejected scholastic thought approved and preferred by the Church, including Thomism.
4. True or False: Pope Pius X instituted a transparent organization known as *Pianum* to keep track of outstanding seminary professors.
5. True or False: When he became pope, Pope John XXIII found out that he had been suspected of being a modernist.

COMPREHENSION

6. Summarize the objections the Catholic Church of the early twentieth century had to modernism.
7. How was Pope Pius XII's 1943 encyclical *Divino Afflante Spiritu* a sign that the Church was becoming more open to modernism?

CRITICAL THINKING

8. How did social and political challenges brought on by the Industrial Revolution further contribute to the problem of modernism?
9. How is modernism related to the philosophical errors that arose during the Enlightenment?

SECTION 3

The History of Catholics in the United States

MAIN IDEA

The growth of the Church in the United States in postcolonial times was marked by prejudice and discrimination as waves of new immigrants came to America.

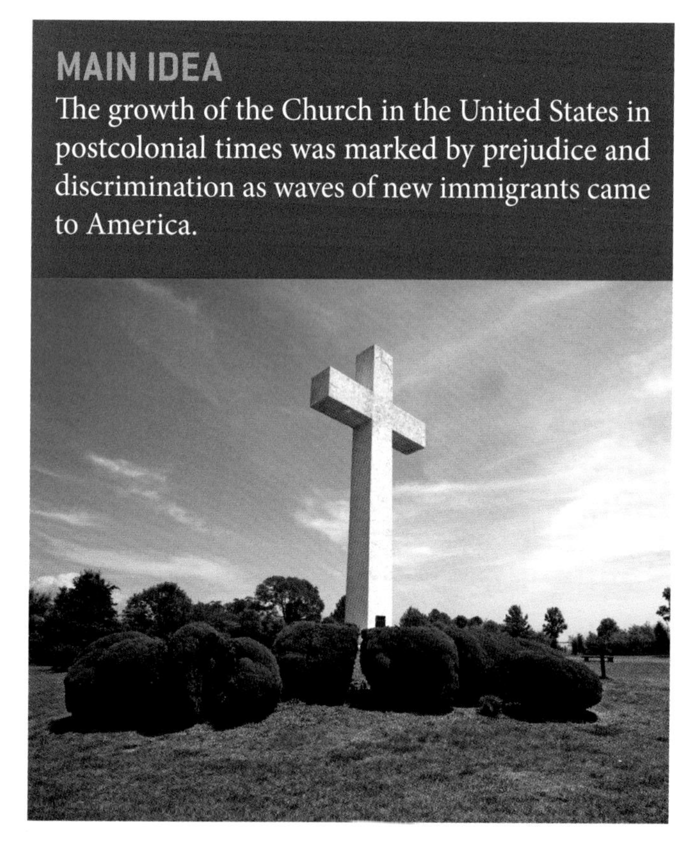

In Chapter 5, you learned about how European settlers and missionaries, particularly from Spain, England, and France, settled in the Americas in great numbers from the late fifteenth through the seventeenth centuries. French-speaking Catholics and explorers, as well as Jesuit missionaries (such as the martyrs St. Isaac Jogues, St. Jean de Brébeuf, and their companions), evangelized regions in the northeastern United States and Canada.

Meanwhile, Spanish-speaking Catholics such as St. Junípero Serra (1713–1784) were evangelizing the Southwest and what is now California. In fact, Junípero Serra, who was canonized by Pope Francis in 2016, established many of the California missions, and to this day, many prominent cities in California still bear very Catholic Spanish names:

- Los Angeles ("The Angels," an allusion to "Our Lady, Queen of the Angels")
- Sacramento ("Sacrament")
- San Diego ("St. Didacus" [of Alcalá])
- San Francisco ("St. Francis" [of Assisi])

At this point in the narrative of Church history, it's important to update the history of Catholics in America. The period from 1815 to 1900 can be considered the "age of immigrants" in the United States, and the majority of immigrants were Catholics. In 1850, Catholics made up only 5 percent of the total United States population; by 1900, Catholics were 17 percent of the population—fourteen million Catholics out of a total population of eighty-two million. Many of these Catholic immigrants worked in the factories

NOTE TAKING

Timeline of Events. Create a timeline to mark key events in American Catholic history from the seventeenth century to the early twentieth century. As you read the section, fill in key events to match the dates listed below.

1624 — 1634 — 1649 — 1773 — 1776 — 1789 — 1829 — 1834 — 1856 — 1875 — 1928 and sweatshops that came with the Industrial Revolution. Their lives were directly impacted by abuses of this period, including prejudice.

This section surveys the Catholic Church in the United States from colonial times until the early twentieth century.

Maryland Becomes a Refuge for Catholics in the Thirteen Colonies

The settlers of the original thirteen colonies were predominantly Protestant. This included Puritans in New England, Quakers in Pennsylvania, and Anglicans in Virginia and other mid-Atlantic states. By and large, Catholics were neither extensive in number nor afforded much consideration within early American society.

In 1624, four years after the first English settlers arrived in New England, Englishman George Calvert, who was a member of the British Parliament (a legislative body akin to the present-day American Congress), converted to the Catholic faith. Since he was already in the favor of the English king James I, Calvert was not directly persecuted for being a Catholic in a country where the Anglican Church exerted its dominance. Calvert was granted permission to establish a colonial settlement in the Americas; he desired a place where Catholicism could be practiced openly, without fear of suppression, if not outright oppression. When George Calvert died, his son Cecil was given the responsibility of settling the region of southern Maryland.

The *Ark* and the *Dove* were the ships carrying a total of approximately two hundred people (around twenty of whom were Catholic) from England to the Americas. Soon after departing England on November 22, 1633, the two ships were separated during a violent storm in the Atlantic. However, weeks later, they were reunited near the island of Barbados in the Caribbean

Fr. Andrew White celebrated the landing of the first settlers in Maryland on March 25, 1634.

Sea. From there, they sailed along the East Coast of North America and eventually up the Chesapeake Bay, landing on what is now St. Clement's Island on March 25, 1634. Fr. Andrew White, a Jesuit priest, offered a Mass to give thanks for the settlers' safe arrival in this new colony. Fr. White was instrumental in learning the language of and evangelizing the Native Americans of the area, which was named St. Mary's (and soon thereafter deemed the first capital of the Maryland colony).

In the midst of discord with Protestant settlers, Governor Leonard Calvert (the son of Cecil Calvert and grandson of George Calvert) pressed for the recognition by the other colonies of the **Maryland Toleration Act of 1649** to afford religious liberty to Catholics in Maryland. The act passed; however, religious freedom for Catholics in Maryland was in place only until 1654, when the colonial government, controlled by Puritans and Anglicans, stripped the Catholic Church of her rights, making it illegal for the Catholic Church to own property or operate schools and for individual Catholics to vote or hold public office in Maryland. This practice remained in effect until the Declaration of Independence was signed on July 4, 1776.

Archbishop John Carroll, First Bishop of the United States

Archbishop John Carroll

John Carroll was born in 1735 in Upper Marlboro, Maryland. The Carroll family, which was well established in Prince George's County, Maryland, had recent Irish ancestry and remained connected with Europe. For example, John and his cousin Charles studied for a time in France. Charles Carroll was perhaps the richest man in America and a leading revolutionary. The Continental Congress sent Charles with Benjamin Franklin to Canada on a delicate but unsuccessful mission to win the Canadians' support for the American Revolution. Charles Carroll also signed the Declaration of Independence, adding "of Carrollton" with pride to let the king know which Carroll was the signee. Another cousin, Daniel Carroll, influenced the writing of the Constitution by arguing for the election of the president by the people, not by Congress. Daniel was also instrumental in choosing the site of the nation's capital, on a large plantation he once owned along the Potomac River.

When Charles returned to the United States after his studies, John stayed in France, where he was ordained as a Jesuit priest and began teaching in various locations throughout Europe. In 1773, during the period when the Jesuits were suppressed in Europe prior to the French Revolution, Fr. Carroll took his ministry back to Maryland just in time for the onset of the American Revolution.

Maryland Toleration Act of 1649 Legislation passed by the assembled representatives of the Maryland colony that permitted free religious practice.

During the American Revolution, Fr. Carroll collaborated with some of the American **Founding Fathers**, including Benjamin Franklin, who were opposing English rule and seeking international support, especially from France. Following America's independence from Britain, Fr. John Carroll took a strong leadership role in the Church in the United States. Fr. Carroll and the Jesuits in Maryland petitioned Pope Pius VI for a bishop to shepherd the Catholic flock of the United States. Pope Pius VI eventually allowed the Jesuits to elect their own bishop, and on May 18, 1789, they chose Fr. Carroll and submitted his name to Rome. Pope Pius VI approved of Fr. Carroll's election and appointed him the first bishop of the United States; Pope Pius VII later elevated him to archbishop.

As bishop and later archbishop, Carroll established various Catholic educational institutions, including Georgetown College in Washington, DC (1789), St. Mary's Seminary in Baltimore (1791), and Mount St. Mary's College in Emmitsburg, Maryland (1808). He also helped to settle a chronic problem of the expanding Church: the problem of **lay trusteeism**. Lay trusteeism included the practice of incorporating Church property in the name of the laity, a practice that was necessary in the early years of the republic because some states had laws against the Church holding property in its name. Lay involvement had its positive features, but it also led to some abuses.

Founding Fathers The leading American men, including philosophers, politicians, and writers, who bridged the colonial era and the Revolutionary era, whose ideas shaped the structure of early American government, and whose legacy is still cited today.

lay trusteeism The historical practice in American Catholicism in which lay (nonclerical) parishioners assumed numerous duties within the administration of their parishes, including naming and dismissing their parish's pastor. The First Provincial Council of Baltimore (1829) ended the practice of lay trusteeism.

Carroll permitted limited lay trusteeism, but he refused to give the laity the right to hire or fire priests. Some laypeople tried to do this when foreign-born priests came into their parishes. Unfortunately, some of these priests did not bother to learn the customs or languages of their parishioners, often leading to needless squabbles and divisions. Eventually the First Provincial Council of Baltimore (1829) condemned lay trusteeism. This decision reduced the voice of lay Catholics in Church affairs until the Second Vatican Council.

As he grew older, Archbishop Carroll emphasized more the authority of the bishop as a symbol of unity and uniformity. Carroll was a giant in American history, held in high esteem by early American leaders such as George Washington and Thomas Jefferson.

Growth of the American Church and Anti-Catholic Attitudes

In the first period of American Church history, the Catholic population had grown from thirty-five thousand in 1790 to two hundred thousand at Archbishop Carroll's death in 1815, but even more impressive growth in America's Catholic population would come through immigration in the nineteenth century.

The second period of American Church history is the "age of immigrants," and it extends from roughly 1815 to 1920. During the Irish Potato Famine years around the mid-1840s, approximately one million Irish immigrants arrived in the United States. Consider that from 1860 to 1890, the Catholic population tripled in size while the national population only doubled. During this period, German Catholics began to equal the number of Irish immigrants. Later, from 1890 to 1920, large populations of Italians and Eastern Europeans came to America. More than two million Catholics immigrated in the first decade of the twentieth century.

This anti-immigrant political cartoon shows two men, an Irish immigrant and a German one, stealing a ballot box in front of a rioting crowd at a polling place. Nativism was a social and political movement that opposed immigration of Catholic Irish, non-Protestants, and non-English speaking peoples.

This rapid growth posed great problems of assimilation into the American way of life. The Church had her hands full ministering to an increasing population and meeting other challenges of the nineteenth century, including the problem of anti-Catholicism. Immigrant Catholics had to face the suspicion of their Protestant neighbors. Their foreign accents and social and religious customs made Catholic immigrants suspect. Furthermore, many immigrants were poor and unskilled laborers willing to compete in the economic marketplace for low wages. Fear, suspicion, and prejudice caused **nativism**, the belief that America should be preserved for "native-born Americans"—white Anglo-Saxon Protestants (called WASPs) who had been in the country for a while.

Outbursts of nativist anti-Catholic violence were especially strong between 1830 and the Civil War. There were feuds over the use of Protestant Bibles in public schools, burning of convents, riots, and destruction of Church property. One notorious outbreak of anti-Catholic violence took place in 1834 in Charlestown, Massachusetts, near Boston, when a bigoted mob burned down an Ursuline convent. The mob violence also spread into an Irish neighborhood, where homes were torched. Venomous anti-Catholic literature also peaked during this period with the publication of Maria Monk's *Awful Discourses*. This infamous fabrication alleged unspeakable crimes committed by nuns and priests in convents. It was later proven that the author had never been a nun and that the lies were fabricated by virulent anti-Catholic Protestant ministers who profited from the large sales the book garnered (three hundred thousand copies before the Civil War).

In the 1850s, the Protestant-sponsored American Party (nicknamed the *Know-Nothings* because members would respond, "I know nothing," when questioned about the group) spewed out hateful literature calling into question the patriotism of Catholics. One of their major charges was that Catholics only gave allegiance to the pope who, they claimed, was planning to invade the United States. The Know-Nothings incited riots in Louisville, fired shots into a St. Louis cathedral, fixed elections in Baltimore, and harassed convents in Massachusetts. Know-Nothing bigotry was especially bitter during the election of 1856. Abraham Lincoln was quoted as saying,

> When the Know-Nothings get control, it will read "all men are created equal, except Negroes, and foreigners, and Catholics." When it comes to this I should prefer emigrating to some country where they make no pretense of loving liberty—to Russia, for instance, where despotism can be taken pure, and without the base alloy of hypocrisy. ("Letter to Justin F. Speed")

The Catholic press in America was founded to counteract the attacks of anti-Catholic bigots. Bishop John England of Charleston founded the *U.S. Catholic Miscellany* (1822–1861) especially for this purpose. It was the first of many Catholic newspapers established in the nineteenth century.

nativism An anti-Catholic cultural push in the early to mid-nineteenth century in which preference in social, employment, and political matters was given to Protestant Americans who had been in the United States for multiple generations, as opposed to Catholics who had immigrated to the United States more recently.

Catholics, Slavery, and the Civil War

Concerning the enslavement of African Americans prior to the Civil War, Catholics in general reflected the same attitudes as Protestants: some Catholics were for the institution of slavery, others against it. Although Pope Gregory XVI condemned the slave trade in 1839, neither the popes nor the American bishops issued an official teaching on the institution of slavery itself. Some bishops did not oppose slavery until it was officially abolished. Some Catholics owned slaves.

In spite of their mistreatment, there were many African American Catholics of the nineteenth century who furthered the mission of the Church. For example, Mother Mary Lange founded the Oblate Sisters of Providence in Baltimore in 1829 despite various setbacks and a severe lack of funding. The Healy family of Macon, Georgia, was another prominent Catholic family of the

Mother Mary Lange

time. The patriarch, Michael Healy, was an Irish immigrant while his wife had been a slave. One of their sons, James Healy, became the first African American bishop of the United States as the bishop of Portland, Maine, in 1875. Another son, Patrick Healy, became the president of Georgetown University in 1874.

When the Civil War came, Catholics fought on both sides of the conflict. General William Sheridan, a Catholic, was a commander for the Union; General P. G. T. Beauregard, a Catholic, led a Southern army. Church leaders could also be found on both sides of the conflict. Bishop John Hughes of New York traveled to Europe at President Lincoln's request to explain the Union position. Meanwhile, Bishop Patrick Lynch of Charleston went to Rome to defend the Confederate side. Priests also served as chaplains while more than five hundred sisters from more than twenty different orders heroically ministered to the wounded on both sides. President Lincoln singled out the Catholic sisters, praising them for their hospital service during the war. The loyalty and sacrifice of Catholic soldiers impressed their fellow citizens. Their heroism and devotion momentarily put to rest nativist charges that Catholics were unpatriotic.

Prejudice against Catholics Extends into the Twentieth Century

Although Catholic participation in the Civil War quieted anti-Catholicism for a time, it emerged again in the 1880s as new Catholic immigrants streamed to America. The American Protective Association was a largely rural society founded in Iowa that was made up of many Irish Protestants. Its goals were to restrict Catholic immigration, make the ability to speak English a prerequisite for citizenship, and remove Catholics from teaching in public schools and participating in public offices.

Church leaders spoke out against these prejudices. Catholic bishops were often at the forefront of encouraging social justice within the United States. For example, Bishop John Hughes (1797–1864) of New York spoke out against anti-Catholic discrimination. He supported immigrant communities through various service-oriented initiatives. Other leaders, such as Cardinal James Gibbons (1834–1921), who served as archbishop of Baltimore for more than four decades, followed in Bishop Hughes's footsteps by implementing many of the Church's teachings regarding workers' rights and labor unions, in line with Pope Leo XIII's proclamations in *Rerum Novarum*. Following the Great Depression that struck the United States between 1929 and 1939 and impacted the world by extension, the Church continued to labor for those in poverty within American society.

Nativism survived into the twentieth century as well. Because of the increasing number of Catholic immigrants from southern and eastern Europe, anti-Catholic legislation was enacted to limit immigration in the 1920s. The Ku Klux Klan, a nativist group opposed to African Americans, Catholics, and Jews, was active in this decade but mostly in rural areas where the Catholic population was sparse. Bigotry also figured in the defeat of Catholic Al Smith in the 1928 presidential election. A widely circulated rumor leveled at Smith was that if he won, the pope would take up residence in the White House and Protestants would lose their citizenship.

Despite the fact that Catholics were generally part of mainstream America by the 1950s and the fact that he was a popular war hero, John F. Kennedy, the first Catholic president, also had to overcome the concern that his patriotism and religion would conflict. Protestants feared that the pope would control the presidency. In the 1960 campaign, Kennedy had to confront anti-Catholic sentiment directly. In a famous speech to Southern Baptist leaders, Kennedy reassured them he would be answerable to the American Constitution, not the pope. He declared, "I am not the Catholic candidate for President [but the candidate] who happens also to be a Catholic. I do not speak for my Church on public matters—and the Church does not speak for me." Kennedy's words reassured many, but his margin of victory was slim, less than half a percent margin. Surveys conducted after the election revealed that anti-Catholic prejudice had contributed to the closeness of the race.

SECTION ASSESSMENT

NOTE TAKING

Use the timeline you created for this section to help you answer the following items.

1. What role did the Calvert family play in bringing Catholicism to the United States during the colonial era?
2. Why was Maryland seen as a refuge for Catholics in the thirteen colonies?
3. Identify the roles of John, Charles, and Daniel Carroll in American history.
4. Detail the prominent role Catholics played in the "age of immigrants" from 1815 to 1900.
5. How have African American Catholics contributed to the history of Catholicism in the United States?
6. Identify the following groups: Know-Nothings, American Protective Association, Ku Klux Klan.
7. What were concerns of the American non-Catholic populace regarding the candidacies of Al Smith and John F. Kennedy for president?

VOCABULARY

8. What was called for by the *Maryland Toleration Act of 1649*?
9. Define *lay trusteeism*.
10. What were the causes of *nativism*?

CRITICAL THINKING

11. What are advantages and disadvantages of the assimilation of Catholics into the mainstream American way of life?

SECTION 4

The History of Catholic Education in the United States

MAIN IDEA

The system of Catholic schools in the United States is a lasting legacy in both Church history and American history. For generations, Catholic schools have existed in order to instill Gospel values into a well-rounded academic curriculum.

Prior to the middle of the nineteenth century, most Catholic children in the United States who attended school (since not every child went to school) went to public schools. Most school boards and curricula at the time had a Protestant bias. In fact, textbooks—especially history textbooks—were frequently explicitly anti-Catholic, ridiculing the Catholic Church and the papacy, as well as downplaying the role that Catholics played in earlier American history. Bishops and other Catholic community leaders worked to establish a network of Catholic schools in order to accommodate this need to bring the Catholic faith into the educational sphere—not only at the elementary level but also at the secondary and university levels.

St. Elizabeth Ann Seton and the Founding of American Catholic Education

A key figure in the development of the Catholic school system in the United States was St. Elizabeth Ann Seton, the first American-born person to be canonized. Born Elizabeth Ann Bayley in 1774 in New York, Elizabeth came from a wealthy and prominent Episcopalian family. Elizabeth received a high-quality education;

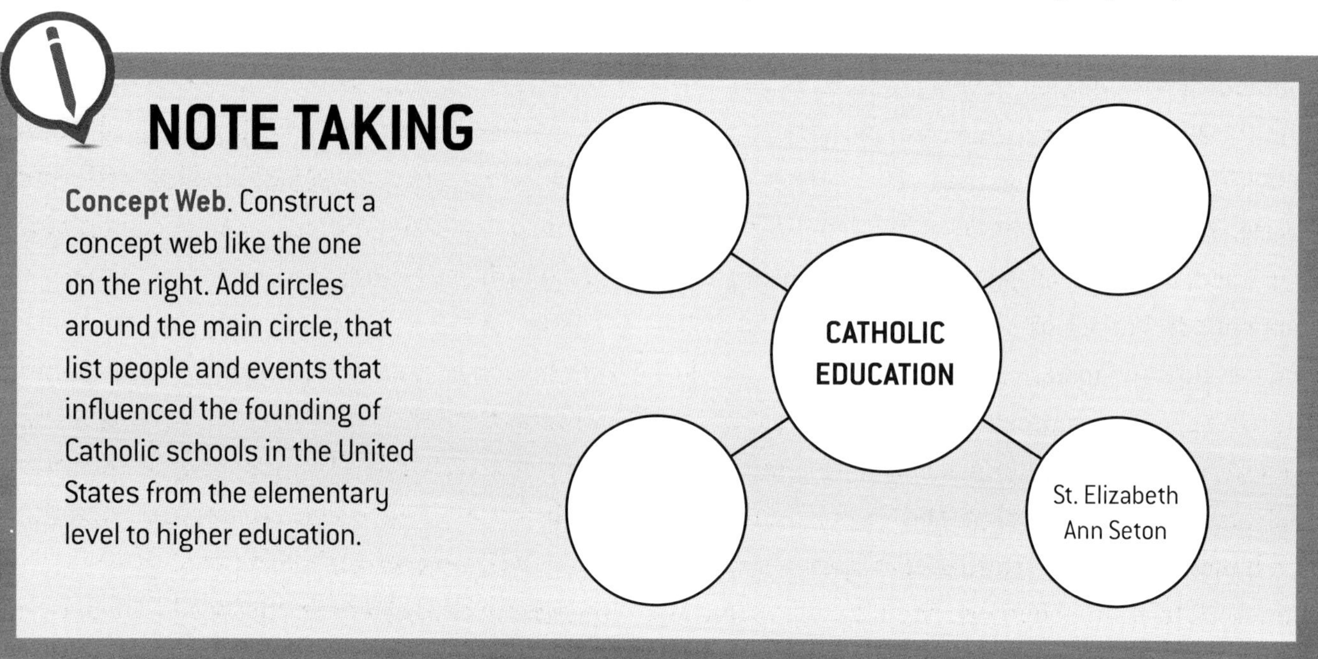

NOTE TAKING

Concept Web. Construct a concept web like the one on the right. Add circles around the main circle, that list people and events that influenced the founding of Catholic schools in the United States from the elementary level to higher education.

National Shrine of Saint Elizabeth Ann Seton, Emmitsburg, Maryland

she would later encourage Catholics to have similar opportunities for advanced study.

In 1794, Elizabeth married William Seton. The couple had five children. Throughout the years, William's health declined, and his physician recommended that he undertake a trip by sea to Italy in order to recuperate. While they were in Italy, William's condition worsened, and he died in 1803. But something else happened in Italy prior to William's death: Elizabeth and her eldest daughter, Anna Maria, visited Catholic churches and were exposed to the beauty and depth of the Catholic faith. They were so impressed that upon their return, both converted to the Catholic faith. Elizabeth made a number of attempts to open a school in New York to educate her own children and others as well, but the efforts failed. Anti-Catholicism was strong during that period.

In about 1806, a Sulpician priest, Fr. Louis William Dubourg, invited Elizabeth to come to Maryland to support the education of Catholic girls. In 1809, Archbishop John Carroll provided Elizabeth with land in Emmitsburg, Maryland, to open a Catholic school. The Sulpicians encouraged Elizabeth to found a religious community of women dedicated to education. They helped her recruit members to the community, known as the Sisters of Charity of St. Joseph, which was patterned after the Daughters of Charity in France. The Sisters of Charity were committed to charitable works, including serving the impoverished and those who were in need of more extensive education. Despite setbacks, the Sisters of Charity overcame these obstacles and their community thrived.

Mother Seton, as she had come to be known, died in 1821, but her labors for the American Catholic Church bore much fruit, and the parochial schools established in the decades following her death were largely modeled on the schools that she formed as part of her ministerial efforts through the Sisters of Charity. St. Elizabeth Ann Seton was canonized by Pope Paul VI in 1975.

The Third Plenary Council of Baltimore and Parochial Schools

Cardinal James Gibbons, a native of Baltimore, was named archbishop of Baltimore in 1872. In 1884, Pope Leo XIII called on Cardinal Gibbons to oversee the Third Plenary Council of Baltimore, a gathering of bishops from around the nation. The Catholic parish was already the center of social life for American Catholics. A decision made at this council was that every Catholic parish should have its own **parochial school**. But the decision was not reached without strong debate; in fact, it came despite an opposing strain of thought within the Church known as *Americanism*, the belief that Catholics should adapt themselves to the best of American culture rather than isolate themselves as a minority. Cardinal Gibbons himself was a prominent Americanist.

The Debate over Americanism

Americanists supported public schools and the separation of Church and state. They also favored cooperative efforts with Protestants, emphasizing common beliefs rather than stressing issues that divide. Americanism seemed to call for the suppression of traditional Catholic virtues in favor of the secular values of America, such as democracy and the separation of Church and state.

The debate over Americanism and the formation of parochial schools stirred up controversy in the United States. For example, because they came to America before the Germans and because they spoke English, Irish bishops and priests rose to dominate the American Church. German Catholics resented being forced to conform to Irish customs. They felt that Irish bishops and Irish Catholics had a disproportionate influence. They wanted their own German parishes with German priests serving them, especially in places such as Cincinnati, St. Louis, and Milwaukee, known as the German Triangle. German immigrants were especially strong supporters of a separate Catholic school system, one that would help pass on the Catholic faith and, at the same time, preserve their German language and customs. They feared Americanism and were supported in this by the Jesuits and by two important Irish bishops: Archbishop Michael Corrigan of New York and Bishop Bernard McQuaid of Rochester, New York, both strong supporters of a separate Catholic school system.

At first, it looked as though the Vatican would side with the Americanists on the subject of Catholic schools, but after a time the Vatican came out in support of separate parochial schools. Pope Leo XIII was not in favor of Americanism as it had become another form of modernism; in fact, he condemned Americanism in a letter he sent to Cardinal Gibbons. The Third Plenary Council of Baltimore was the first official ruling of the Unites States' hierarchy of bishops for a national parochial school system. The council taught that bishops are "exhorted to have a Catholic school in every parish, and the teachers should be paid from

parochial school A Catholic school—typically an elementary and middle school—affiliated with a parish community. The word *parochial* means "affiliated with a parish."

the parochial funds." These parochial schools served as alternatives to the public schools and non-Catholic private schools that were essentially the only options available for Catholic students up to that point.

Catholic Schools and the *Baltimore Catechism*

By 1900, nearly four thousand Catholic schools had been established around the country, serving Catholics of all social classes. Catholic schools played a vital role in introducing young immigrants to the American way of life by teaching English and the democratic values that form the framework of American government. They also led students to better understand the broad tenets of Catholicism as well as the specific contributions of Catholics in American history. The Catholic faith that students learned at school was typically reinforced by what they learned at home.

St. Katharine Drexel

Throughout the nineteenth century and into the twentieth, various other figures contributed to the formation of youth—both Catholic and of other faiths—through the system of Catholic schools in the United States. St. John Neumann (1811–1860) was born in southern Germany but came to the United States in 1836 and was a priest for the Redemptorist congregation. St. John Neumann became the bishop of Philadelphia, where he began the first diocesan school system in the country. St. Katharine Drexel (1858–1955), born and raised in Philadelphia, Pennsylvania, had a special devotion to serving ethnic minorities throughout the United States. Katharine came from a prominent family and used her wealth to establish schools to serve Native American and African American youth in particular.

Catholic schools have greatly contributed to serving those living in urban settings. St. Frances Cabrini (1850–1917) and her community, the Missionary Sisters of the Sacred Heart, came to New York from Italy in 1889. Beyond their work in hospitals and orphanages, Mother Cabrini and her sisters also helped establish Catholic schools for Italian immigrants.

Another prominent outcome of the Third Plenary Council was the publication of the *Baltimore Catechism* in 1885. The *Baltimore Catechism*, which Cardinal Gibbons approved, featured a question-and-answer format (with 499 total questions covered) that provided clear, cohesive, and consistent information about—and formation in—the Catholic faith. The *Baltimore Catechism* was used in Catholic schools and other religious education settings from its publication in 1885 through the reforms that followed the Second Vatican Council (1962–1965).

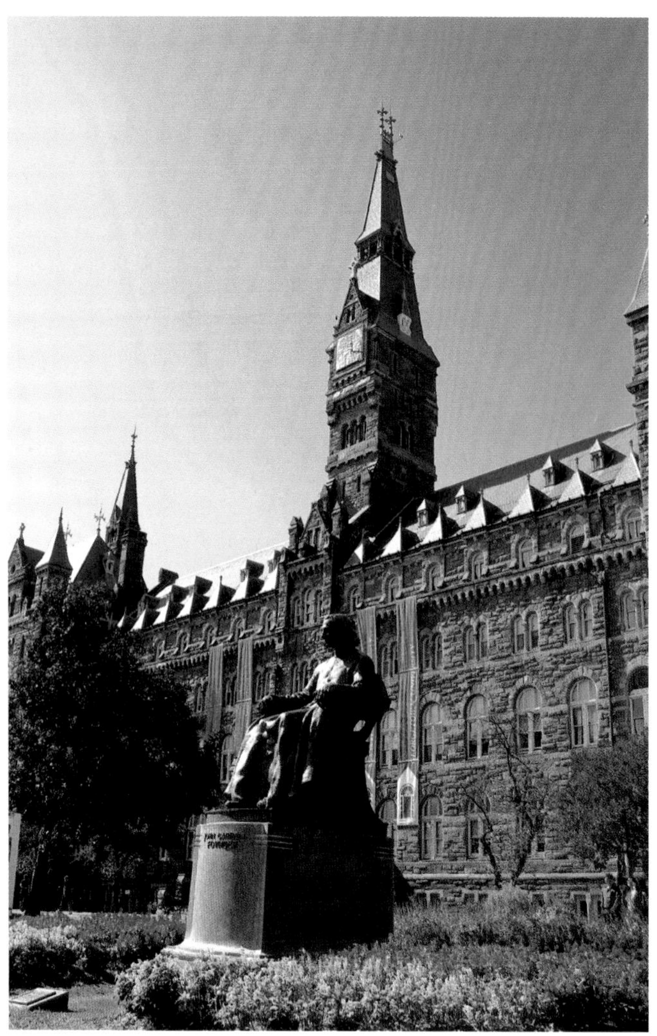

This John Carroll statue stands in front of Healy Hall at Georgetown University.

American Catholic Colleges and Universities

Both Catholic parochial (typically elementary/middle) and high schools and Catholic colleges and universities have a prominent place in both American history and Church history. Recall that Georgetown College (now Georgetown University) was the first Catholic college in the United States, founded in 1790 by Archbishop John Carroll in Washington, DC. After the Third Plenary Council of Baltimore, Cardinal Gibbons helped establish The Catholic University of America in Washington, DC, in 1887. It is the only Catholic university sponsored by the United States Conference of Catholic Bishops. It began offering undergraduate education in 1904. Xavier University in Louisiana, established in 1915 by St. Katharine Drexel, is the only historically African American Catholic college or university in the United States. In 1989, the theological faculty of Franciscan University of Steubenville in Ohio became the first Catholic faculty members in the United States to declare an "Oath of Fidelity" to Catholic magisterial teachings and thereby receive the ***mandatum*** from the local bishop.

> ***mandatum*** "An acknowledgment by Church authority that a Catholic professor of a theological discipline is teaching within the full communion of the Catholic Church" (*The Application of Ex Corde Ecclesiae for the United States*, article 4, 4, e, i). *Mandatum* is Latin for "command" or "mandate."

Today, Catholic schools—from elementary schools through institutions of higher education—continue to fill a critical role in forming future generations. Catholic high schools have historically high rates of both graduation and acceptance into college. As of 2016, approximately nine hundred thousand undergraduate and graduate students were enrolled in 261 Catholic colleges and universities in the United States. Many national leaders of all faith traditions have attended Catholic schools, and Catholic education has been a leading factor in catapulting those in poverty into the middle or even upper classes. Catholic education is an important feature of both American and Church history, and the collective mission of American Catholic schools remains unchanged: to lead students to knowledge of the Kingdom of God and encourage students to bring the Good News of Jesus Christ into the world.

SECTION ASSESSMENT

NOTE TAKING

Use the concept web you created to help you answer the following items.

1. What were aspects of the public school system of the nineteenth century that caused Catholics to seek a parochial school system?
2. Name two incidents from St. Elizabeth Ann Seton's life that led to her opening a Catholic school in Emmitsburg, Maryland.
3. Why was the Third Plenary Council of Baltimore important for Catholic education?
4. What is the *Baltimore Catechism*? What was its role in Catholic religious education?
5. How did St. Katharine Drexel use her financial resources to support Native American and African American communities?
6. How do Catholic colleges and universities contribute to society?

COMPREHENSION

7. What was *Americanism*? What did it have to do with the founding of a parochial school system in the United States?

VOCABULARY

8. Define *mandatum* as it relates to Catholic higher education.

ANALYSIS

9. Write about someone you know who has been positively impacted by Catholic education. Be specific.

Section Assignments

Focus Question

What world events of the nineteenth and early twentieth centuries led to the development and application of modern Catholic social teaching?

Complete one of the following:

- Research and report on how the following Catholics offered a response (see hints in parentheses) to the Industrial Revolution in the United States based on the principles of *Rerum Novarum*: Fr. John A. Ryan (living wage), Cardinal William O'Connell (subsidiarity, rights of the family), and Mother Jones (labor leader).

- Compile a list of five inspiring quotations on social justice from at least three of the social justice documents listed under "Key Documents in Support of *Rerum Novarum*" in Section 1. These documents can be accessed at either the Vatican (www.vatican.va) or the United States Conference of Catholic Bishops (www.usccb.org) website.

- Catholic schools have a long history of serving students from all socio-economic backgrounds. Research and report on the mission of a school (not your own) in your diocese and how its scholarship and financial aid program and offerings support its mission.

INTRODUCTION

The Industrial Revolution Brings New Challenges

Write three paragraphs summarizing key historical events leading up to the Industrial Revolution and how these events combined with industrialization impacted families at that time.

SECTION 1

Pope Leo XIII and Catholic Social Teaching

Write two paragraphs summarizing the main teaching of one of the social justice documents listed under "Key Documents in Support of *Rerum Novarum*." Include at least one quotation from the document itself to support your summary.

SECTION 2

The Church Responds Directly to Modernism

In one or two paragraphs, write a definition of *modernism* in your own words. What effect did modernism have on Catholic scholarship in the first half of the twentieth century? Cite one or more references to support your response.

SECTION 3

The History of Catholics in the United States

Research and write a short biography of an American Catholic from the nineteenth or early twentieth century.

SECTION 4

The History of Catholic Education in the United States

Research and write a three- to four-paragraph history of a parochial elementary school in your area. Include its founding date, influential leaders, religious orders who staffed the school, famous alumni, and its current mission statement.

Chapter Assignments

Choose and complete at least one of the three assignments to assess your understanding of the material in this chapter.

1. Interview with a Nineteenth-Century Factory Worker

Based both on what you have learned within this chapter and on additional research, reflect on the working conditions of a factory worker from the nineteenth century. Take on the role of a Catholic factory worker from that period. Dressed in appropriate period clothing, share a five- to seven-minute description of your life on the job and at home. Include answers to the following questions:

- How many hours do you spend working per day?
- What are the physical conditions in your factory?
- How often do you get to see your family?
- Do you make enough money to be able to support your family?
- If you have concerns with your working conditions, whom do you turn to?

As a conclusion to your presentation, comment on solutions to the conditions you described, referencing at least two passages from Pope Leo XIII's encyclical *Rerum Novarum* (see www.vatican.va). Ask a classmate or family member to videotape your presentation. Save it on a video-sharing platform and provide your teacher with the link. Alternatively, your teacher may ask you to do the presentation live in class.

2. Catholic Immigration in the Nineteenth and Early Twentieth Centuries

Chart two sets of statistics about Catholic immigration from approximately 1800 to 1920. Choose line graphs, bar graphs, histograms, or pie charts to chart statistical information for each of the following:

- total Catholic immigrants by decade (or twenty-year periods)
- total Catholic immigrants by originating nation (e.g., Ireland, Germany, Italy, and Mexico)

Also, color code two blank United States maps state by state—one from 1850 and one from 1920—with the Catholic population by ethnicity of the originating nations listed above.

For each graph and map, write a one-paragraph summary of the data. You should have four total summary paragraphs.

3. Catholic Colleges in the United States

An up-to-date alphabetical and geographic listing of Catholic colleges is archived on the United States Conference of Catholic Bishops website (www.usccb.org) under "USCCB > Beliefs and Teachings > How We Teach > Catholic Education > Higher Education > Catholic Colleges and Universities in the United States." Research several colleges that appeal to your academic, regional, religious, and other interests. Choose a college that requires an essay as part of its application process. Write the essay per the college's directions. Submit the essay to your teacher with this additional information:

- the name of the college
- what interests you about the college
- the name of the main chapel at the college
- the times for daily and Sunday Eucharist
- the day and times to celebrate the Sacrament of Penance
- two student offerings of the campus ministry office
- the general theology course requirements for all students

Prayer

Prayer for Religious Liberty

O God our Creator, from your provident hand we have received our right to life, liberty, and the pursuit of happiness. You have called us as your people and given us the right and the duty to worship you, the only true God, and your Son, Jesus Christ. Through the power and working of your Holy Spirit, you call us to live out our faith in the midst of the world, bringing the light and the saving truth of the Gospel to every corner of society. We ask you to bless us in our vigilance for the gift of religious liberty. Give us the strength of mind and heart to readily defend our freedoms when they are threatened; give us courage in making our voices heard on behalf of the rights of your Church and the freedom of conscience of all people of faith. Grant, we pray, O heavenly Father, a clear and united voice to all your sons and daughters gathered in your Church in this decisive hour in the history of our nation, so that, with every trial withstood and every danger overcome—for the sake of our children, our grandchildren, and all who come after us—this great land will always be "one nation, under God, indivisible, with liberty and justice for all." We ask this through Christ our Lord. Amen.

—United States Conference of Catholic Bishops

9

THE SECOND VATICAN COUNCIL FOLLOWS TWO WORLD WARS

WORLD WAR II CHAPLAIN RETURNS HOME

Nearly seventy-five years after his death in the attack at Pearl Harbor, the remains of Fr. Aloysius Schmitt, the first chaplain killed in World War II, were identified and shortly afterward returned to his alma mater, Loras College in Dubuque, Iowa, for burial.

Fr. Aloysius Schmitt

When the ship he was aboard, the USS *Oklahoma*, was hit by Japanese torpedoes and capsized on December 7, 1941, Fr. Schmitt gave up a chance to save his own life and instead pushed twelve other men to safety through a small porthole.

"Try to imagine the drive for self-preservation that automatically kicks in at such a time when life is threatened, and then try to imagine what it would take to deny that impulse out of love for God, love for country, love for others," said Archbishop Michael Jackels in his homily at Fr. Schmitt's funeral Mass at Loras College in October 2016.

Not only had Fr. Schmitt's remains been identified but also his chalice was recovered from the wreckage of the USS *Oklahoma*. Archbishop Jackels used the same chalice at the funeral Mass.

Hundreds of family members, an American Legion honor guard, and military personnel were on hand for the funeral. Raye Jean Plehn came from Las Vegas to participate in the Mass. Her late father, Raymond John Turpin, a twenty-year-old Marine on the USS *Oklahoma* on the day of the attack, was one of the last people to see Fr. Schmitt alive. As Fr. Schmitt pushed men through the porthole of the sinking ship, Turpin helped to pull them out the other side to safety.

Prior to her father's death in 2009, Plehn said, he had told her about the heroic actions of the man he simply referred to as "the chaplain." When she heard that Fr. Schmitt's remains had been discovered, she knew she wanted to attend the funeral. "It's so nice that people are taking interest in his story even after all these years," she said. "He was a true American hero."

(http://catholicphilly.com/2016/10/news/national-news/world-war-ii-chaplains-remains-laid-to-rest-in-dubuque-archdiocese)

FOCUS QUESTION

How did **CONFLICT, WAR,** and **MODERNISM** shape the **CHURCH'S RESPONSE** to the world at the Second Vatican Council?

Chapter Overview

INTRODUCTION

The Church Faces the Challenges of the Twentieth Century

MAIN IDEA

The world faced two global wars, but the Church remained steadfast as she consistently endeavored to share the Gospel in these times while fostering a sense of enduring hope.

As the twentieth century progressed, the Catholic Church was a voice for peace, stability, and reconciliation in a divided world that would face two world wars within fifty years. Following Pope Pius X (1903–1914), three papacies spanned and responded to a turbulent time:

- During World War I, Pope Benedict XV (1914–1922) offered a seven-point peace plan.
- The pontificate of Pope Pius XI (1922–1939) covered the era between World War I (1914–1918) and World War II (1939–1945). Pope Pius XI officially cut ties with both the fascist Italian dictator Benito Mussolini (in 1931) and the Nazi German dictator Adolf Hitler (in 1937).
- Pope Pius XII (1939–1958) reigned during World War II. He opposed Nazism and made efforts to protect Europe's Jews during the **Holocaust**. In the aftermath of the horrors of World War II, a ray of hope gleamed in 1950, when Pope Pius XII officially proclaimed as dogma the Assumption of the Blessed Virgin Mary, which had been professed since the early centuries of the Church.

After World War II, the world and the Church were impacted by the influence of atheistic communist governments in the Soviet Union and China. Their communism led to a "Cold War" of tense relations with the Western nations, while their atheism distanced the people of the Soviet Union and China from the Church and all religion. The nuclear arms race was also fully underway, with the Soviet Union and China adversarial to the democratic Western nuclear powers of the

Holocaust Also known as the *Shoah*; the attempt by the Nazi forces under Adolf Hitler, by way of a system of concentration camps, to obliterate the presence of the Jewish people and other non-Jewish civilians from areas under Nazi control from 1933 through 1945, resulting in the deaths of more than six million Jews.

NOTE TAKING

Summarizing the Section. After reading the section, write a one-paragraph summary of the Church's role in the twentieth century through the Second Vatican Council. Use one of the following titles as a heading for your paragraph:

- **Facing the Modern World**
- **Rocky Relationships**
- **Preparing for the Future**

The Second Vatican Council met from October 11, 1962, to December 8, 1965, in Saint Peter's Basilica in Rome.

United States, Great Britain, and France. It was onto this global stage that Pope John XXIII stepped when he opened the Second Vatican Council (1962–1965) in an effort to reengage the Catholic Church with the world.

Introducing the Second Vatican Council

The Second Vatican Council ushered in monumental efforts to lead the Catholic Church into greater dialogue with the world while maintaining her irreplaceable role in spreading the Gospel to all people. The Second Vatican Council was called by Pope John XXIII (1958–1963), but upon his death soon after the Council was convened, his successor Pope Paul VI (1963–1978) carried on his legacy by putting the weight of his resources behind the development and implementation of the decisions of the Council.

Following the Second Vatican Council, the West in particular found itself caught up in a *sexual revolution*, a loosening of social norms and an increasing disregard for the institution of marriage that resulted in a multitude of sexual and social sins. The rise of **contraception** in particular was a dilemma that troubled Pope Paul VI so significantly that he wrote the encyclical *Humanae Vitae* (*On the Regulation of Birth*), which was ahead of its time in detailing the problems within a society that becomes too beholden to contraception and promiscuity.

In the years immediately following the Second Vatican Council, the Church encountered a new set of challenges, many of which she continues to address today. These challenges included how to properly implement the teachings of the Second Vatican Council, the role of Sacred Scripture in the Church, how to involve the laity in the life of the Church, how to improve catechesis, how to enhance efforts at evangelization around the globe, and how the Catholic Church is expected to relate to Eastern Churches. This chapter goes into further detail regarding these and other situations and the Church's response.

contraception A chemical or object, such as a birth control pill or a condom, specifically used to ward off the possibility of pregnancy.

UPDATING CHURCH RELATIONS WITH VARIOUS NATIONS

Recall from Chapter 7, Section 3, that the German *Kulturkampf*, a cultural war against the Church, placed religious schools under the German government, among other oppressions, until it finally came to an end in 1887. As the twentieth century began, the Church continued to deal with the lingering effects of earlier conflicts, including schism, political revolutions, and colonialism.

CATHOLIC-ANGLICAN DISCORD

By the middle of the nineteenth century, Anglicans and Catholic leaders in France broached a cause for reconciliation between the Catholic Church and the Church of England. The subject was the validity of ordination of Anglican priests. Pope Leo XIII received the matter with prayerful interest and spent some time in personal study of it, researching the statements of other popes since the original schism. He came to the determination that the nature of the Anglican priesthood, due to differences in the intention of its form, was unlike the sacrificing nature of the Catholic priesthood, which is graced in the Sacrament of Holy Orders. In an 1896 papal bull, *Apostolicae Curae*, Pope Leo XIII declared the Anglican priesthood "null and void" dating from the sixteenth century. More recently, other issues have complicated any reunification around the validity of ordination of Anglican priests, among them the Anglicans' ordination of women.

THE CHURCH IN FRANCE

At the start of Pope Leo XIII's pontificate in 1878, he sought to restore relations between the Church and the French government, which had been damaged during the French Revolution. However, the French government of the early twentieth century persisted in fostering anti-Catholicism. The Church was viewed as opposing personal freedom. In 1905, the Chamber of Deputies of the French government enacted a law officially separating the state from the Church. Catholicism was no longer the state religion of France. This law had many ramifications; it required civil marriage, allowed work on Sundays, abolished public prayer at government meetings, and forbade the military from participating in Church processions. This law and its practices remain in effect through today.

THE PERSECUTION OF THE CHURCH IN MEXICO

Fr. Miguel Pro before his execution

Various Mexican governments had mostly been hostile to Church authority since Mexico gained independence from Spain in 1810. In 1857, Mexico adopted a constitution that took away the property rights and possessions of the Church. This and other persecutions continued well into the twentieth century.

During the most severe years of the persecutions, public worship was punishable by death. In the 1920s, Mexicans were imprisoned for wearing religious medals or even for saying "Adiós" in public. *Adiós* literally means "to God." In 1926, the Church went underground. Bishops closed the churches. A wave of protest among Catholics (95 percent of Mexican citizens were Catholic) erupted into what is known as the *Cristero Rebellion*. Nearly fifty thousand soldiers for the Church fought against federal troops. One of the heroes of the movement was Fr. Miguel Pro, a Jesuit priest who, along with his brother, was arrested and falsely accused of plotting to kill the Mexican president. Prior to his execution by firing squad, Fr. Pro extended his arms in the shape of a cross and yelled, "Viva Cristo Rey," Spanish for "Long live Christ the King." Pope John Paul II beatified Miguel Pro in 1988. In 2000, Pope John Paul II canonized twenty-five other Mexican saints and martyrs from the period. In 2005, Pope Benedict XVI canonized another thirteen Mexican martyrs, including José Luis Sánchez del Río, a fourteen-year-old Cristero who refused to renounce his faith in Christ.

In 1940, enforcement of the laws against the Church (and all religions) was lessened, but it was not until 1992 that the Church again received legal status in Mexico.

The Church and PEACE AROUND THE GLOBE

On a 2012 pastoral visit to Mexico, Pope Benedict XVI met with some schoolchildren. Part of his message to them was:

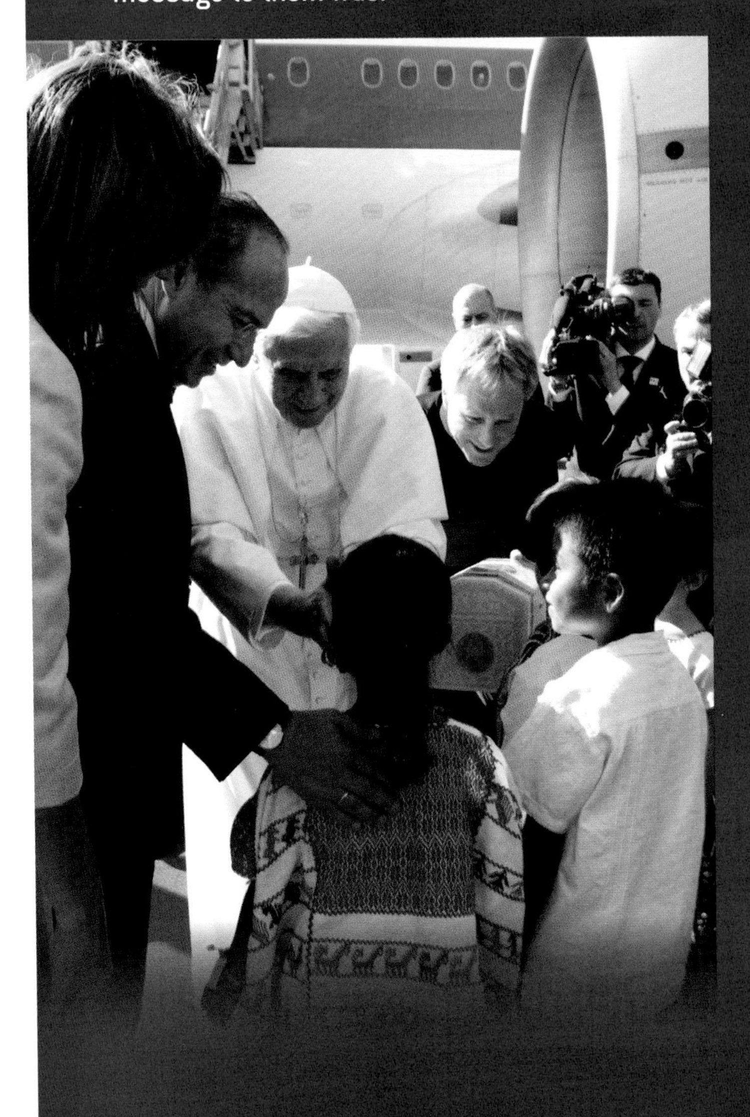

> You, my young friends, are not alone. Rely on the help of Christ and his Church to lead a Christian lifestyle. Attend Sunday Mass, catechesis, some apostolate groups, seeking places of prayer, fraternity and charity. It was so that the blesseds Cristobal, Antonio, and Giovanni, the young martyrs of Tlaxcala, lived who, getting to know Jesus, at the time of the first evangelization of Mexico, discovered that there is no greater treasure than him. They were little like you, and from them we can learn that there is no age to love and serve. (May 24, 2012)

In this message, Pope Benedict offered suggestions for living a Christian lifestyle: (1) attend Sunday Mass; (2) attend catechesis; (3) attend apostolate groups (e.g., youth ministry or service groups); (3) seek places of prayer, fraternity (friendship), and charity (love). Write three paragraphs explaining practical ways you will attend to each of these suggestions.

SECTION ASSESSMENT

NOTE TAKING

Refer to your summary paragraph to help you answer the following questions.

1. How were the Church's conflicts with France and Mexico at the turn of the twentieth century different from the conflict emanating from England?
2. What was occurring in Western society in the 1960s that led Pope Paul VI to warn humanity about what would happen if it continued?

COMPREHENSION

3. Name the three popes following Pope Pius X and one highlight of their papacies.
4. What was Pope Paul VI's role at the Second Vatican Council?
5. Why is it accurate to say that Pope Paul VI's encyclical *Humanae Vitae* was ahead of its time?
6. Explain the rationale of Pope Leo XIII's *Apostolicae Curae* related to its declaration of the Anglican priesthood as null and void.
7. What was the Cristero Rebellion a response to?

REFLECTION

8. After studying the first nineteen centuries of Church history, how would you rate the challenges faced by the Church in the twentieth century in comparison?

SECTION 1

World War I and Its Devastating Aftermath

MAIN IDEA

The start of World War I in 1914 marked the beginning of a period of more than thirty years during which the world was either at war or under threat of war. This period also saw the rise of *totalitarianism*, a political system in which all authority is held by the state. Pope Benedict XV and Pope Pius XI voiced the Church's opposition to both war and totalitarian governments.

An important date in world history is August 4, 1914, the start of World War I—exactly two weeks prior to the death of Pope Pius X. Historians acknowledge *supernationalism*—"my country right or wrong"—as a major cause of the war, summing up the belligerent attitude of combatants on both sides. The war—termed the "war to end all wars"—was a novelty in human history. It was a total war, involving conflict on land, on the sea, and in the air. It involved deadly weapons—including poison gas—that enabled combatants to kill their enemies from a distance, without ever meeting face-to-face. And it involved not only all of Europe and North Africa but also countries in the Western Hemisphere, such as the United States and Canada. Like many European wars of the past, World War I confronted the Church with a dilemma: How should it respond when Catholics fought on both sides of the conflict, all claiming theirs was the moral cause?

Pope Benedict XV Voices the Church's Response to World War I

After the death of Pope Pius X, Giacomo della Chiesa, archbishop of Bologna, Italy, was chosen as his

NOTE TAKING

Summarizing Church Documents. Create a chart like the one below and list the documents of Pope Pius XI introduced in this section. In the second column, write a brief summary of the subject of each document, and also specify the main audience it was intended for.

DOCUMENT	SUBJECT
Lateran Treaty	
Non Abbiamo Bisogno	
Mit Brennender Sorge	
Divini Redemptoris	

Pope Benedict XV, cardinals, and the faithful praying for peace in Europe

successor. Pope Benedict XV's election was unexpected. An aristocrat, he was myopic and physically frail, and he possessed a congenital condition that caused him to stoop. But he was a moral giant during the conflict, the soul of generosity, who used all his diplomatic skills to foster peace both inside and outside the Church. In internal Church affairs, for example, he toned down the harsh methods used against the modernists.

Pope Benedict XV also deplored the war. He refused to take sides and condemned it as unjust. During the war he engaged in significant humanitarian efforts such as organizing army chaplains and arranging for prisoner exchanges. In 1917, he offered visionary peace proposals and volunteered to mediate the conflict. He presented the following seven-point peace plan to the international community:

1. Freedom of the seas
2. The limitation of weaponry
3. The formation of an international tribunal
4. A peaceful accord between the territories of Belgium, Britain, and Germany
5. Specific economic regulations
6. Resolutions to the boundary disputes between France and Germany, as well as between Austria and Italy
7. A resolution of disputes between Poland and other nations

However, Pope Benedict XV's proposals were met with criticism from the political powers and were generally ignored. Interestingly, many of Pope Benedict XV's proposals were part of American president Woodrow Wilson's famous Fourteen Points, which

On April 2, 1917, President Woodrow Wilson addressed Congress to declare war on Germany.

eventually helped to bring a resolution to World War I, though not lasting peace.

Pope Benedict XV had offered a Christian solution to the war: peace won through compromise. The warring nations, however, settled for nothing less than unconditional surrender. Pope Benedict XV was not invited to help negotiate the terms of peace after the war ended in 1918. This was unfortunate because the Treaty of Versailles of 1919 did not bring a lasting peace. Some of its misguided provisions resulted from vengeful motives and were responsible for crippling Germany's economy in the 1920s. In the devastation of the Great Depression, Germans would succumb to the Nazi political party and one of humanity's truly evil men—Adolf Hitler—to help restore their pride as a nation.

History has judged Pope Benedict XV more favorably than his contemporaries did. His work for reconciliation was admirable. For example, he worked to smooth relations between the Church and the Italian state, which were strained by the confiscation of the Papal States in 1870. He encouraged Catholic politicians to serve in the Italian government. This eventually prepared the way for an amicable compromise on the role of the Church in Italian affairs under his successor, Pope Pius XI. Pope Benedict XV also organized relief efforts for the starving and homeless after the war. His charity knew no bounds as he emptied the Church's coffers to help those in need. His work for peace inspired Cardinal Joseph Ratzinger to choose the name Benedict XVI at the time of his election as pope in 2005 as the world again faced war on a global basis.

Initial Devastation after the War

World War I devastated Europe physically, psychologically, economically, and spiritually. It is estimated that eight and a half million people died. Another twenty-one million were wounded. Vast areas of northeastern Europe were in rubble. France, on whose soil many of the battles were fought, was left with a destroyed infrastructure. To add to the misery, in the middle of 1918, the devastating Spanish Flu hit the world, with an estimated twenty-five million deaths resulting in Europe alone. In America, an estimated 675,000 people died of influenza, ten times as many as died in the war.

Also, the 1917 Russian Revolution resulted in a Marxist state—the Union of Soviet Socialist Republics (USSR) under Vladimir Lenin. Inspired by an atheistic, materialistic, and anti-Christian philosophy, Lenin and his successor, Joseph Stalin, ruled their country as totalitarian dictators. They ruthlessly eliminated dissidents and did everything possible to suppress Christianity, both Russian Orthodoxy and Roman Catholicism. Within seventeen years, the Communist Party destroyed 5,300 Catholic churches and chapels. Clergy were dismissed, churchgoers harassed, and Catholics forbidden to join the Communist Party. Two hundred thousand Catholics, including every Catholic bishop, simply disappeared in the first eight years of the Bolshevik Revolution.

In light of all the war, death, and destruction, people worldwide became disillusioned and cynical. Some turned to the new science of psychology to make sense of their world. The ideas of Sigmund Freud were influential, though they were hostile to religion, claiming that religion was a control mechanism society used to keep people in line. Freud taught that religious belief was childish and that God was simply a wish projected by the unconscious mind. Others turned to the morally lax and hedonistic lifestyle that became popular during the Roaring Twenties in Western countries or sought refuge in accumulating wealth as a hedge against hard times. Foolhardy capitalistic ventures abounded, leading to unstable financial markets that eventually crashed, setting off the Great Depression.

Vladimir Lenin, shown here addressing a crowd, was the first head of government of the USSR.

The Rise of Fascism and Communism

In 1922 Pope Pius XI (1922–1939) succeeded Pope Benedict XV. In the same year, Benito Mussolini took absolute control of Italy. He was a dictator who created a new form of totalitarianism called **fascism**. Fascism developed in the aftermath of World War I's revenge-filled peace treaties, political turmoil, fear of communists, and economic turbulence. Like communism, fascism controlled all aspects of people's lives—personal, political, and economic—in trying to create the perfect state. It was marked by oppressive, dictatorial control. Mussolini, Adolf Hitler in Germany, and Francisco Franco in Spain were dictators who mobilized

> **fascism** A governmental system typified by authoritarianism and dictatorship, in which individual rights are suppressed by the will of those in power.

> Pope Pius XI instituted the Solemnity of Christ the King, saying,
>
> **Nations** will be **reminded** by the **annual celebration** of this feast of **Christ the King** that not only **private individuals** but also **rulers and princes** are bound to give **public honor** and **obedience to Christ**. It will **call** to their **minds** the thought of the **last judgment**, wherein Christ, who has been **cast out** of public life, **despised**, **neglected** and **ignored**, will most severely **avenge these insults**; for his **kingly dignity demands** that the **State** should take **account** of the **commandments of God** and of **Christian principles**, both in **making laws** and in **administering justice**, and also in **providing** for the **young** a **sound moral education**.

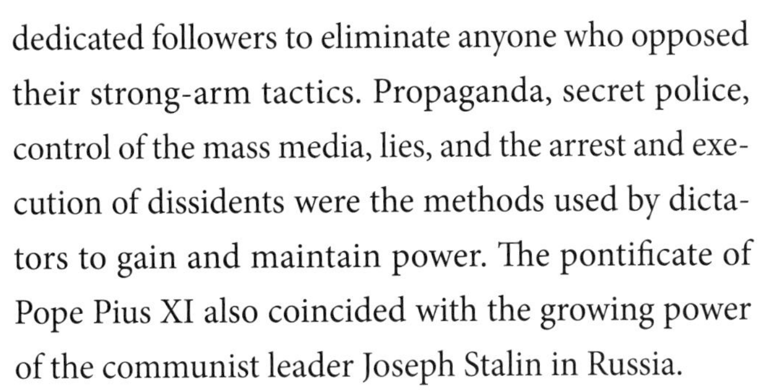

dedicated followers to eliminate anyone who opposed their strong-arm tactics. Propaganda, secret police, control of the mass media, lies, and the arrest and execution of dissidents were the methods used by dictators to gain and maintain power. The pontificate of Pope Pius XI also coincided with the growing power of the communist leader Joseph Stalin in Russia.

A former librarian and mountain climber, Pope Pius XI was a hard working, disciplined, stern man born in Desio, near Milan, Italy. By lending some initial support to Mussolini who, like the Church, hated communism, Pope Pius hoped to reconcile the Vatican to the Italian state. His strategy paid dividends in the Lateran Treaty (1929). This treaty finally settled the long-standing problems between the Church and Italy caused by the confiscation of the Papal States in the nineteenth century. Mussolini gave the pope a large sum of money for the Papal States in exchange for the Church's surrendering all claims to land in Italy. The Italian government also recognized Vatican City as a sovereign state and gave the Church privileged status in Italy.

Pope Pius XI Condemns Fascism

The forging of the Lateran Treaty typified the way Pope Pius XI dealt with dictators. His policy was to make formal agreements with the dictatorial governments to guarantee certain rights for the Church. These rights included the prerogative of the pope to appoint bishops and freedom for Catholic laypeople to participate in Catholic Action lay movements, of which Pius XI was a strong supporter. In 1931, Pius XI harshly condemned

Mussolini for his attempt to disband Catholic organizations, especially Catholic Action groups. He issued an antifascist encyclical, *Non Abbiamo Bisogno* (*We Do Not Need*), that insisted on the right of Catholics to organize and that condemned fascism's "pagan worship of the state." Mussolini, needing Catholic support to remain in power, backed down. Thus, it is accurate to report that the Church helped curb Mussolini's totalitarian power.

In Germany, Hitler—a lapsed Catholic who embraced a strange mixture of Aryan racial superiority, astrology, and the anti-Christian philosophy of Friedrich Nietzsche—ignored *Non Abbiamo Bisogno* and began to persecute the clergy and dissolve Catholic organizations. In a bold move in 1937, Pope Pius XI snuck a hard-hitting encyclical titled *Mit Brennender Sorge* (*With Burning Concern*) into Germany. It condemned various Nazi crimes, saying in part:

> Whoever exalts race, or the people, or the State, or a particular form of State, or the depositories of power, or any other fundamental value of the human community—however necessary and honorable be their function in worldly things—whoever raises these notions above their standard value and divinizes them to an idolatrous level, distorts and perverts an order of the world planned and created by God; he is far from the true faith in God and from the concept of life which that faith upholds. (*Mit Brennender Sorge*, 8)

Pope Pius XI instructed all German priests to read *Mit Brennender Sorge* from the pulpits of their churches, which infuriated Hitler, leading him to suppress the Catholic Church, particularly the clergy and religious.

Pope Pius XI Condemns Communism

To the very end of his pontificate, Pope Pius XI feared communism even more than fascism. He saw its avowedly atheistic claims and program of violent worldwide revolutions as more dangerous than fascism. Many Catholics agreed with the pope's assessment, seeing communism, a worldwide movement, as a threat to universal peace. On the other hand, many believed fascism to be dangerous only in the countries that had adopted it. Pope Pius XI issued another encyclical in 1937, *Divini Redemptoris* (*On Atheistic Communism*), a few days after his anti-Nazi encyclical. In it, he unequivocally condemned communism:

> Communism is intrinsically wrong, and no one who would save Christian civilization may collaborate with it in any undertaking whatsoever. Those who permit themselves to be deceived into lending their aid towards the triumph of communism in their own country, will be the first to fall victims of their error. And the greater the antiquity and grandeur of the Christian civilization in the regions where communism successfully penetrates, so much more devastating will be the hatred displayed by the godless. (*Divini Redemptoris*, 58)

Pope Pius XI died in February 1939 while preparing a speech extremely critical of fascism. A few short months later World War II broke out.

SECTION ASSESSMENT

NOTE TAKING

Use the chart you created to help you match the names of the following documents with their primary subjects.

1. *Mit Brennender Sorge*
2. *Non Abbiamo Bisogno*
3. Lateran Treaty
4. *Divini Redemptoris*

A. recognized Vatican City as a sovereign state
B. unequivocally condemned communism
C. condemned fascism's "pagan worship of the state"
D. condemned various Nazi crimes

COMPREHENSION

5. What response did Pope Benedict XV offer after the outbreak of World War I?
6. What happened to the Church in Russia in the first years after the Russian Revolution?
7. Why did Pope Pius XI fear communism more than fascism?

VOCABULARY

8. Define *fascism*.

FURTHER RESEARCH

9. Compare Pope Benedict XV's seven-point peace plan with the Fourteen Points offered by President Woodrow Wilson. What were specific points taken by Wilson from Pope Benedict's plan?

SECTION 2

The Church and World War II

MAIN IDEA

Devastating crimes against humanity and against the Church in particular accompanied the run-up to World War II and the war itself. The Church undertook several efforts to minimize human suffering and oppression during the war. After the war the Church responded to issues brought by the proliferation of godless governments and societies.

In 1933, following contentious presidential elections in Germany, Adolf Hitler was appointed German chancellor. His Nazi party promised to restore Germany's infrastructure, economy, and pride following Germany's losses during World War I. At first the Catholic Church and many governments of the West did not recognize the threat from Nazism because Nazism promised to oppose communism, which had already infiltrated the USSR. However, as the years progressed, the Nazis' views—inspired by Hitler—became increasingly extreme, and their immoral practices and principles, such as anti-Semitism, racial supremacy, and eugenics, were exposed. Easily the worst manifestation of the Nazi philosophy came in the form of the genocide known as the Holocaust, or by its Jewish name, the *Shoah*.

Meanwhile, the communist government continued to oppress the people of the Soviet Union. The violations of human rights in Germany and the Soviet Union portended what was to come. Europe was about to be the scene of another global conflict that eclipsed even World War I in extent and destructiveness.

NOTE TAKING

Chronicling Responses. Create a chart like the one below. As you read the section, note the key incidents named in the left column. In the right column, write a paragraph summarizing how the Church responded to them

INCIDENT	HOW THE CHURCH RESPONDED
Nazism	
The rise of communism	
Historical and scientific study	

The Church and Nazism

When Nazi Germany under Hitler invaded Poland on September 1, 1939, Europe was catapulted into another world war barely twenty years after the conclusion of the first in 1918. Pope Pius XII (1876–1958), born Eugenio Pacelli, was elected as pope on March 2, 1939, mere months before the outbreak of World War II. Pope Pius XII was an opportune choice for pope, having served in a diplomatic capacity, including as the Vatican's secretary of state.

From the beginning, Pope Pius XII opposed Nazism and did what he could against it while isolated within the Vatican by Mussolini's forces. In the decades since World War II, some critics have accused Pope Pius XII of timidity for failing to condemn more strongly Hitler's crimes. Hitler was systematically targeting Catholics, in addition to other groups, for extermination. Most notably, three million Polish Catholics and 20 percent of Poland's Catholic clergy perished at the Auschwitz concentration camp. Besides being physically confined to one place, Pope Pius XII had other good reasons for taking the approach of working behind the scenes:

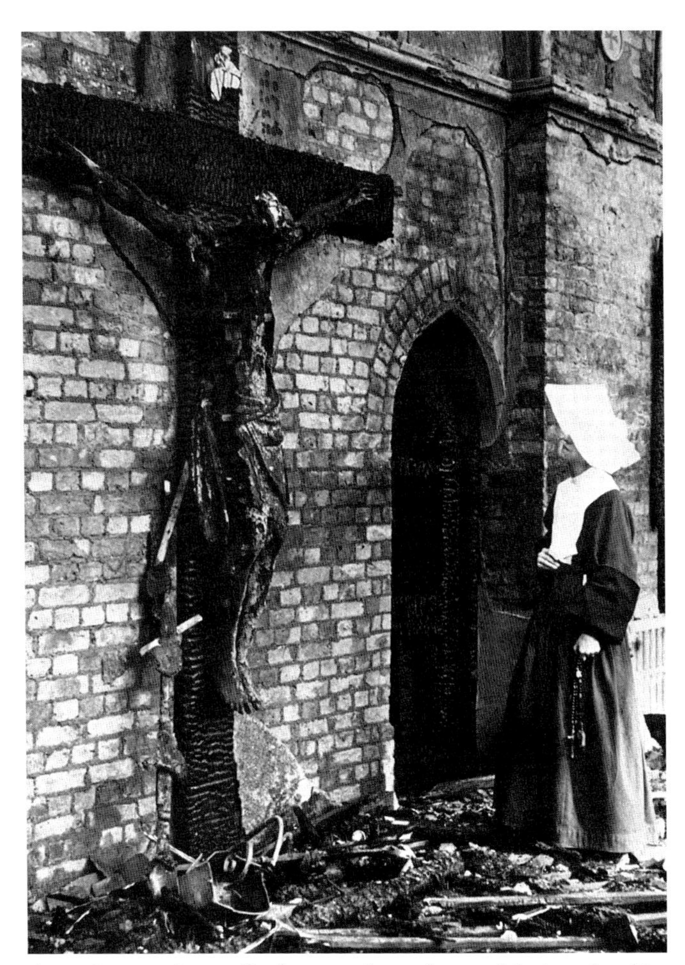

A nun inspects the crucifix that was almost destroyed during a bombing raid by Nazi planes in the Church of Our Lady of Victories in London, England.

- First, Pope Pius XII believed that if he spoke out, Hitler would be even crueler than he already was. This happened in Holland when, in 1942, the Dutch bishops, at the pope's urging, publicly deplored the Nazi deportation of the Jews. In retaliation, the Nazis sped up their roundup of Jews, including seizing all Jewish converts to Catholicism, and deported them to Auschwitz. (Among the imprisoned who perished there was the brilliant convert St. Edith Stein, the Carmelite sister Teresa Benedicta of the Holy Cross, canonized a saint in 1998.) On Christmas Day in 1942, over Vatican radio, Pope Pius XII did strongly speak out. He condemned the extermination of people on the basis of race. The forty-five minute talk spoke of human rights and a civil society.
- Second, he believed that he could do more for the Jews in a clandestine way without arousing the suspicion of the Nazis. He did, in fact, help many Jews escape persecution, providing them with shelter and giving them homes. In 1967, Pinchas Lapide, an Israeli diplomat, reported in his book *The Last Three Popes* that Pope Pius XII was instrumental in saving as many as 860,000 Jews, a number estimated to be a full 30 percent of the world's Jews who survived Hitler's *Final Solution*, the Nazi plan to exterminate all those of Jewish descent. Rabbi Israel Zolli, chief rabbi of Rome, was so moved by the sterling character of Pope Pius XII and his devotion to religious brotherhood that he converted to Roman Catholicism in 1945 and took Eugenio as his baptismal name.

A Catholic church in the town of Laxenburg, Austria, flying the Nazi flag during World War II

World War II ended on September 2, 1945, but this was only after one of the most controversial acts in history: American forces dropped atomic bombs on the Japanese cities of Hiroshima (August 6) and Nagasaki (August 9), killing or gravely injuring nearly 250,000 Japanese, most of whom were civilians. After the war, it took years for Europe and Japan to rebuild from the war and return displaced persons, or refugees, to their homelands.

It was within this setting that the America-based **Catholic Relief Services** (CRS), whose work still helps to alleviate poverty and situations of political instability around the globe, had its origins in 1943. The world, in a crisis of faith and skepticism, needed true hope, which only the Lord could provide (cf. Jn 14:27) through works as those facilitated by CRS.

The Aftermath of World War II

After the war, Pope Pius XII continued to speak for Christian values against the godless forces of the modern age. For example, through his preaching he helped to mobilize world opinion against atheistic communism, which oppressed the Catholic Church and other Christian churches in the countries the Soviets controlled.

When the Soviet Union set up communist governments in Hungary, Yugoslavia, East Germany, Bulgaria, and Romania, Catholics were systematically persecuted. Priests were exiled, imprisoned, or forced to work in labor camps. Church schools and properties were confiscated. Public worship was outlawed. The Church went underground in many Eastern European nations, only to emerge triumphant with the collapse of the Soviet Union in 1989–1990. Cardinal Stefan Wyszynski in Poland and Cardinal József Mindszenty of Hungary were two brave witnesses who, despite persecution, served as beacons of hope to the Catholics in communist-dominated countries.

With the ascent to power of Mao Zedong in China in 1949, the People's Republic of China also became a communist nation. It imprisoned or exiled foreign missionaries, killed professing Catholics, and forced others to go underground. Today, there are an estimated twelve to fifteen million Catholics in China, a very small part of a population of 1.3 billion people. Officially, they are allowed to worship openly, but they must be part of a nationalized Catholic Church that is registered with the government. In 2006, the Chinese

Catholic Relief Services A humanitarian relief organization established in 1943 by the bishops of the United States. Catholic Relief Services (CRS) originally helped replenish war-torn Europe and house its refugees. Today, CRS continues to focus on service to the poor overseas, using the Gospel as its guiding mandate.

national church ordained new bishops without the Vatican's approval, risking excommunications. In 2016, Pope Francis welcomed a Chinese delegation to Rome as part of a conference on the environment. Some observers speculated that this brief meeting could lead to negotiations between Rome and the Chinese government to settle disputes between the Church, the government, and the underground Catholics living in China.

Pope Pius XII helped the Church plant many seeds of renewal that would find fruition in the Second Vatican Council. In his encyclical *Divino Afflante Spiritu*, he supported the modern historical and scientific study of the Bible. Another encyclical, *Mystici Corporis Christi* (*On the Mystical Body of Christ*), taught the value of each member of the Church in the Mystical Body of Christ (including the laity) and the universal call to holiness. Pope Pius XII laid the theological groundwork for the liturgical renewal that would come after the Second Vatican Council with the publication of his encyclical *Mediator Dei* (*On the Sacred Liturgy*) in 1947.

Pope Pius XII at the Proclamation of the Dogma of the Assumption of the Virgin Mary into Heaven

The scholarly Pope Pius XII also wrote on important topics such as medical ethics and addressed the world frequently on peace issues. He declared 1950, the year he defined the doctrine of the Assumption of Mary into heaven by his encyclical *Munificentissimus Deus* (*Defining the Dogma of the Assumption*), a holy year. Millions of Catholics made a pilgrimage to Rome to celebrate this momentous occasion.

Pope Pius XII died in 1958. His successor was an aging compromise candidate, Angelo Roncalli, who took the name Pope John XXIII. This rotund, peasant-like priest became one of the twentieth century's most admired men. He was canonized a saint by Pope Francis in 2014. His greatest achievement was convoking the Second Vatican Council. Because of Pope John XXIII's optimistic, joyful vision, the Church confronted and embraced the modern world head on at the Second Vatican Council.

SECTION ASSESSMENT

NOTE TAKING

Use the chart that you completed at the beginning of this section to help you answer the following questions.

1. Why did Pope Pius XII respond to Nazism behind the scenes?
2. What aid organization began to address the human suffering that was a consequence of World War II?
3. Why was the Church forced to go underground in Eastern Europe following World War II? What was the ultimate result?

COMPREHENSION

4. Why was Pope Pius XII confined to the Vatican during World War II?
5. Briefly trace the Church's relationship with the Chinese government after World War II.
6. Summarize the subjects of the three encyclicals written by Pope Pius XII in proximity to World War II.

FURTHER RESEARCH

7. Research and report in two paragraphs on the life of St. Edith Stein. Optional: Research and report in two paragraphs on St. Maximilian Kolbe, another saint of World War II.

SECTION 3

The Second Vatican Council: The Church Engages the World

MAIN IDEA

Pope John XXIII convoked the Second Vatican Council (1962–1965) with the goals of renewing the Church through dialogue with the world and working to repair Christian unity.

A month shy of his seventy-seventh birthday, Cardinal Angelo Roncalli was already elderly when he was elected pope in 1958. Most observers thought he would be an interim pope who would not serve long or accomplish much. However, Pope John XXIII's warmth, sense of humor, and kind heart, which contrasted sharply with the often aristocratic bearing of his predecessor, quickly won over the entire world. One of his first official acts was to visit prisoners in Rome, telling them, "You could not come to me, so I came to you." One of his famous jokes was his response to a question from a reporter: "Holy Father, how many people work in Vatican City?" The pope responded, "About half of them."

Pope John XXIII claimed that the idea to call the Second Vatican Council—the first ecumenical council since the First Vatican Council ninety years earlier, which came to an abrupt end due to the political turmoil surrounding the collapse of the Papal States—came to him like a ray of blinding light, an inspiration from the Holy Spirit. When he announced the Council to a gathering of eighteen cardinals in January 1959, they were dumbfounded. Days later, they voiced their reservations, but Pope John XXIII insisted that the Church lived in a new age.

The Catholic Church was no longer just a European community but a worldwide Church embracing many people. Moreover, the Church needed to engage with the fast-changing world of politics, economics, science, technology, and so forth. This council would be unlike previous councils that were called in times

NOTE TAKING

Identifying Main Ideas. As you read, create an outline like the one started for you below to record the main points and subpoints about the Second Vatican Council that are detailed in this section.

I. Setting the stage for the Council
- A. *Mater et Magistra*
- B. Potential subjects
  - 1. Enhancement of Catholic social teaching

II. Pope John XXIII opens the Council
- A. Overarching goals

III. Documents of the Second Vatican Council

of crisis and heresy. It would be a pastoral council, one of mercy and hope, one that would reach out to the modern world and invite people around the world to consider the joyfulness of the Gospel. Pope John XXIII famously gave this as his reason for the Council: “I want to throw open the windows of the Church so that we can see out and the people can see in.” The Italian term for this invitation is ***aggiornamento***.

Setting the Stage for the Council

In 1961, leading up to the start of the Council, Pope John XXIII issued his encyclical *Mater et Magistra*. This encyclical was written on the seventieth anniversary of *Rerum Novarum* (see “Key Documents in Support of *Rerum Novarum*” in Chapter 8, Section 1) and was intended to remind nations of their responsibility to promote human dignity and care for their citizenry in areas such as health care. Pope John XXIII’s vision for the Second Vatican Council was to discuss ways in which the Church should direct her efforts to spread the Good News of Christ in a world of increasingly fast-paced socioeconomic changes, political volatility, scientific research, technological advancement, and other factors.

The following subjects broached in the Church in the preceding decades gave some indication of what the Council would address:

An enhancement in direct instruction on Catholic social teaching by way of Church documents from the pontificate of Pope Leo XIII up through that of Pope John XXIII.

aggiornamento Italian for “bringing up to date,” the term used by Pope John XXIII to describe the process by which the Church was called to reengage with the world, as inspired by the spirit of the Second Vatican Council.

An increase in lay participation in the Church in areas such as missionary activity and charitable works, particularly in the wake of World War II. Pope Benedict XV instructed his bishops to look out first and foremost for the welfare of people in mission lands rather than that of the colonial interests attempting to exploit those territories. He also promoted priestly vocations among the native peoples.

Reengaging the laity in the sacramental and liturgical life, as through Pope Pius X’s initiatives. Some bishops and Church scholars prior to the Council promoted renewal of the liturgy, stressing that sacraments should be signs people could understand. Their efforts prepared the way for the use of the vernacular in the liturgy and the renewal of all the sacraments.

A return to serious biblical scholarship, such as the devotion to Scripture that Pope Pius XII promoted in *Divino Afflante Spiritu*.

More ecumenical efforts between Catholics and other Christians as well as interreligious dialogue with non-Christians. For example, the Council would publish *Unitatis Redintegratio* (*Decree on Ecumenism*), the landmark work of theological commissions.

Theological renewal, which welcomed the contributions of Catholic theologians of the 1940s and 1950s, some of whom had periodically received rebukes for their writings. Nevertheless, theologians such as Jesuits Karl Rahner, Henri de Lubac, John Courtney Murray, and Dominican Yves Congar all served as theological consultants to the bishops at the Council.

The Second Vatican Council Opens

Pope John XXIII officially opened the Second Vatican Council on October 11, 1962, by way of his speech titled *Gaudet Mater Ecclesia* ("Mother Church Rejoices"), which began with these compelling words: "Mother Church rejoices that, by the singular gift of Divine Providence, the longed-for day has finally dawned when—under the auspices of the Virgin Mother of God, whose maternal dignity is commemorated on this feast—the Second Vatican Ecumenical Council is being solemnly opened here beside St. Peter's tomb."

In his opening address, Pope John XXIII also asked the bishops to trust the Holy Spirit, to be hopeful, and not to look for the worst in the modern world. He talked about reading the "signs of the times," trying to find God's presence in ordinary life. He said the Council was meeting not to suppress false teaching but to find new and better ways to present Church doctrine to people of modern times. The pope pointed out that the Church "desires to show herself to be the loving mother of all, patient, full of mercy and goodness."

Once the Second Vatican Council was underway, Pope John XXIII remained in the background, encouraging the bishops to have an open exchange regarding matters concerning the Church in the twentieth century. However, the pope did clearly remind the attendees of his two overarching aims for the Council:

The Church should engage with the modern world with the goal of Church renewal.

Pope John XXIII is carried through a large crowd gathered in front of Saint Peter's Basilica, prior to the opening of the Second Vatican Council.

The Church should lead and encourage efforts for Christian unity.

Some cardinals in the Curia, fearing too much change, tried to control the agenda of the Council. However, their efforts eventually failed. As Pope John XXIII said, the Holy Spirit had blown open the windows of the Church to let in some fresh air. There was no going back.

While Pope John XXIII expressed his hopefulness about the proceedings, his health was in decline, and it was revealed that he was suffering from stomach cancer. Even in his condition, Pope John XXIII was able to issue his last encyclical, *Pacem in Terris*, two months before his death.

Pope John XXIII died on June 3, 1963. Although he died less than a year after opening the Second Vatican Council, his efforts were not in vain. The work of the Council proceeded. Pope John XXIII was canonized by Pope Francis in April 2014.

Pope Paul VI and the Continuation of the Second Vatican Council

Following the death of Pope John XXIII, Cardinal Giovanni Battista Montini, the archbishop of Milan, was elected pope; he took the name Paul VI. Pope Paul VI was eager to continue the work of his predecessor and was likewise content to allow the Council to proceed without a great deal of interference. Pope Paul VI was canonized by Pope Francis in October 2018.

The Second Vatican Council met in four separate sessions over the course of about three years and produced sixteen documents. The most authoritative are four constitutions, which are summarized here:

- *Sacrosanctum Concilium* (*Constitution on the Sacred Liturgy*) emphasized that the liturgy is the pinnacle of the Church's activity, stressed the vital importance of the Eucharist, and permitted the use of the vernacular languages in the liturgy, instead of only Latin. (December 1963)
- *Lumen Gentium* (*Dogmatic Constitution on the Church*), perhaps the most important Council document, updated the Church's self-image by emphasizing the mystery of the Church as a community, as the People of God, and as a sacrament or sign of God's presence in the world. *Lumen Gentium* also reminded Catholics that everyone in the Church—clergy and laity alike—is called to holiness and stressed collegiality between the bishops and the pope. (November 1964)
- *Dei Verbum* (*Dogmatic Constitution on Divine Revelation*) encouraged the faithful—especially the laity—to read the Bible more extensively and also reinforced the close relationship between Sacred Scripture and Sacred Tradition. It emphasized Revelation as God's self-disclosure. (November 1965)
- *Gaudium et Spes* (*Pastoral Constitution on the Church in the Modern World*) underscored the importance of social justice from the Gospel and reminded Catholics that they should look at their role in the world with joy (English for *gaudium*) and hope (English for *spes*). The document also reminded Catholics to read the signs of the times in light of the Gospel in order to be effective instruments of the Gospel in their daily lives. (December 1965)

The Second Vatican Council also produced three declarations and nine decrees. One of the decrees, *Unitatis Redintegratio* (*Decree on Ecumenism*), while reaffirming that the Catholic Church is entrusted with the fullness of the means of salvation, committed the Church to the ecumenical movement and affirmed the many positive qualities of other religions. This topic was in line with one of Pope John XXIII's central goals. The Council concluded on December 8, 1965 (the Feast of the Immaculate Conception of the Blessed Virgin Mary).

The Second Vatican Council was closed by Pope Paul VI during a solemn ceremony on the steps of the St. Peter's Basilica.

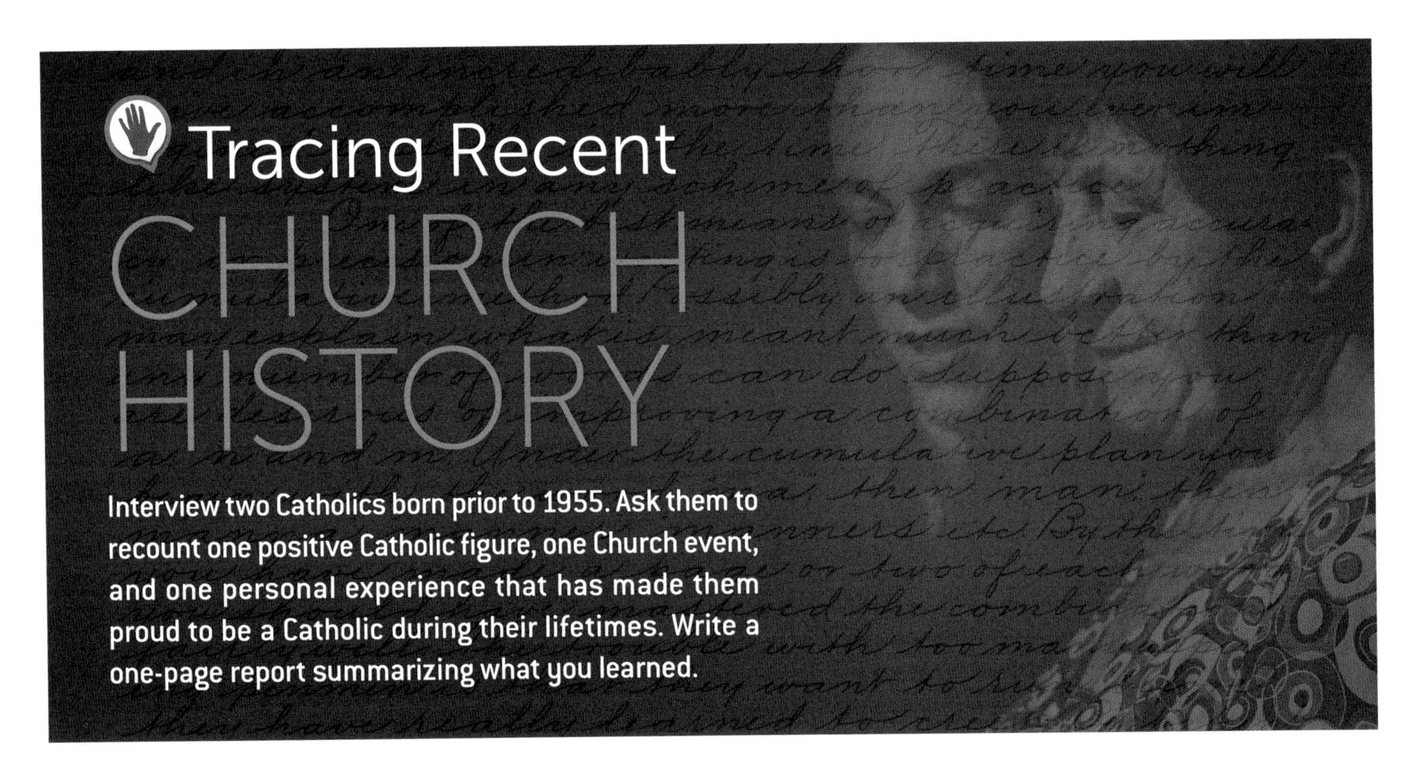

Tracing Recent CHURCH HISTORY

Interview two Catholics born prior to 1955. Ask them to recount one positive Catholic figure, one Church event, and one personal experience that has made them proud to be a Catholic during their lifetimes. Write a one-page report summarizing what you learned.

SECTION ASSESSMENT

NOTE TAKING

Use the outline you created to help you answer the following questions.

1. What was the main subject of *Mater et Magistra*?
2. What were three subjects introduced prior to the Second Vatican Council that made their way onto the agenda?
3. What were Pope John XXIII's two overarching aims for the Second Vatican Council?
4. Which of the four constitutions of the Second Vatican Council is considered to be most important? What is its subject?

COMPREHENSION

5. Why was the Second Vatican Council unlike previous Church councils?
6. Name four theologians who served as consultants at the Second Vatican Council.
7. What role did Pope John XXIII take once the Council was underway?
8. When was the close of the Second Vatican Council?

VOCABULARY

9. Define *aggiornamento* in the context of the Second Vatican Council.

ANALYSIS

10. From your interviews for the feature "Tracing Recent Church History" with people who were raised prior to the Second Vatican Council, briefly describe what you imagine the faith life of an American Catholic teenager in the 1950s to be like.

SECTION 4

The Post–Second Vatican Council Era

MAIN IDEA

After the Second Vatican Council closed, the Church not only had to implement conciliar decisions but also had to address several social concerns while reminding the faithful of their call to follow Christ and obey the Church's teachings.

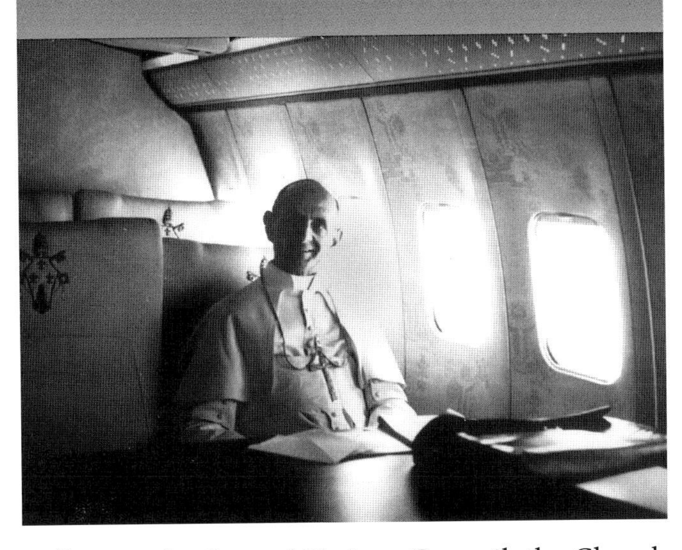

Following the Second Vatican Council, the Church was both different and the same. There were changes in pastoral initiatives, and the laity had a more active role. The Church boldly proclaimed her nature for Catholics and non-Catholics alike. There were greater efforts at unity among all Christians and with non-Christians. In sum, the Church remained in dialogue with the modern world yet preserved her irreplaceable sanctifying role, keeping in mind the words of St. Paul: "Do not conform yourselves to this age but be transformed by the renewal of your mind, that you may discern what is the will of God, what is good and pleasing and perfect" (Rom 12:2).

The world also was both different and the same. The Second Vatican Council had taken place in the midst of various global conflicts, including the Korean War (1950–1953) and the Vietnam War (1954–1975). The Cold War continued, and since the horrors of World War I and World War II were still fresh in the minds of all, authority and tradition were widely questioned. The so-called sexual revolution was a by-product of speculation about cultural norms that had been taken for granted for generation upon generation.

When the Second Vatican Council concluded in 1965, Pope Paul VI sought to lead the faithful to embrace the decisions of the Council by implementing its teachings through a renewed commitment to various initiatives within the Church, including:

- performing acts of social justice (which the Church had embraced in particular since the pontificate of Pope Leo XIII, and which groups such as Catholic Action continued)
- maintaining religious freedom despite communism and other totalitarian threats
- encouraging scriptural study among the clergy, the religious, and the laity

NOTE TAKING

Key Words. Write three sentences describing some key changes implemented in the Church after the Second Vatican Council. Make sure the following terms and phrases are used at least once.

Synod of Bishops
ecumenism
Humanae Vitae
vernacular
sexual revolution
collegiality
liturgy
Athenagoras I of Constantinople

- fostering greater ecumenism among Christian communities and interreligious dialogue with those of other faiths
- enhancing *catechesis*, or instruction in matters related to the faith, by emphasizing the need for both substantive content and solid formation taught by qualified teachers

As stressed in *Lumen Gentium*, Pope Paul also helped to foster *collegiality* between the pope and bishops. Collegiality is the principle that the bishops of the Church with the pope as their head form a single "college" that succeeds the Twelve Apostles with Peter at their head. This principle holds that the bishops, together with the pope and never without him, have full authority as they interact and collaborate in governing the Church. One way collegiality has been implemented since the Council is through a permanent **Synod of Bishops** that meets periodically to advise the pope on various matters. Pope Paul VI also encouraged the formation of national bishops' conferences. In nations such as the United States, the bishops have been leaders in implementing the Second Vatican Council reforms. For example, the United States Conference of Catholic Bishops has issued important pastoral letters on many topics of current concern, including peace and war, abortion and bioethics, and the economy.

Pope Paul VI: A Pope of Stability in Tumultuous Times

Pope Paul VI had the fortitude the Church needed to implement the decisions of the Second Vatican Council. He was a personal advocate for greater efforts at social justice, for seeking peace in the midst of international tensions, for ecumenism (particularly with Orthodox Churches and the Eastern Catholic rites), for modernizing church architecture, and for greater lay participation in liturgical celebrations and parish life. Pope Paul VI reminded the laity of the Second Vatican Council's emphasis on the universal call to holiness—that is, that every state of life leads to holiness as long as a person is open to God's grace.

The Council had left the Church directions for fostering ecumenism, and Pope Paul VI personally modeled this effort by traveling extensively in order to meet with representatives of other faith communities throughout the world. Travel was a hallmark of Pope Paul VI's pontificate. For example, in 1964, while the Second Vatican Council was still underway, he traveled to the Holy Land, becoming the first pope since 1802 to travel outside of the Italian peninsula during his pontificate. It was during this trip that he met with Patriarch Athenagoras I of Constantinople, and the two lifted the mutual excommunications between the Roman Catholic Church and the Orthodox Church that had been in place since the Great Schism of 1054. The two leaders met again in 1967 when Pope Paul VI visited Istanbul, becoming the first pope to visit the former Constantinople since the Great Schism. On that occasion, they spoke of a joint commission to study theological differences and of the future of holy places in Jerusalem. In a similar vein, Pope Paul VI strengthened the Church's relationship with the Eastern Catholic rites. He emphasized the importance of Eastern Catholic hierarchies in such a way that they are able to contribute substantively to the rich liturgical life of the broader Catholic Church.

Among other travels, Pope Paul VI journeyed to New York City in 1965, met with President Lyndon Johnson, and spoke to the full body of the United

Synod of Bishops A periodic meeting of various bishops from around the world with the pope for the purpose of holding theological discourse and advising the pope on matters related to the faith.

Pope Paul VI delivered an address to the United Nations General Assembly in New York City on October 4, 1965.

Nations. He was not only the first pope to visit the United States but the first pope to travel to the Western Hemisphere. He also traveled to India, the Philippines, and other nations, continuing to promote social justice by calling on local governments and international organizations to serve those living in poverty and on the margins of society. It was also at this time that Pope Paul VI reminded the world that "the hungry nations of the world cry out to the peoples blessed with abundance. And the Church, cut to the quick by this cry, asks each and every man to hear his brother's plea and answer it lovingly" (*Populorum Progressio,* 3).

Liturgical Changes Following the Second Vatican Council

Some of the most visible changes that occurred following the Second Vatican Council involved the celebration of the Mass. Formerly, the Mass had been exclusively in Latin, and the priest and the congregation faced God and the altar together. After the Council, increasingly both the Liturgy of the Word and the Liturgy of the Eucharist were celebrated in the vernacular, allowing people to participate in their own languages. The altar was moved closer to the people, and the priest faced the people. Many new songs were introduced in this era; some were similar to folk music, accompanied by guitars and other instruments. It is important to note that many of these new practices were not mandated by the Council; for example, the usage of Latin at Mass was retained in many places and continues to be used at Mass today.

Mass attendance declined during this time. This was not necessarily a response to the changes in the liturgy but more a reflection of a society that was increasingly consumerist, secularized, and otherwise worldly. Similarly, the number of vocations to the clergy and religious life fell in Western Europe and North America. Some who had taken vows no longer felt that they

Humanae Vitae

Confronts the Sexual Revolution

During this time, sexual norms were loosening throughout Western cultures, and there was a push from powerful cultural icons to accept immoral sexual practices as normal and harmless. In 1968, Pope Paul VI issued a groundbreaking encyclical called *Humanae Vitae* (*On the Regulation of Birth*). At its core, *Humanae Vitae* directly opposed the increasingly permissive culture of the Western world. In *Humanae Vitae*, Pope Paul VI emphasized and reinforced the Church's age-old teachings as they relate to both the sacredness of human life and the importance that must be placed on respecting God's plan for human sexuality within the covenantal bond of marriage. Pope Paul VI underscored that the marital union of a husband and wife should be faithful and open to new life, meaning that the "conjugal act" (sexual intercourse) should not be interfered with through the use of artificial contraceptives such as condoms, birth control pills, or other impediments to the conception of new life.

Many lay Catholics ignored the message of *Humanae Vitae*, interpreting it as yet another attempt by the Church to impose outdated moral teachings on a society where "free love" was the rule of the day. There was even some resistance from misguided Catholic theologians who thought that Pope Paul VI would endorse the sexual behavior the world increasingly claimed was benign and harmless. However, the pope remained steadfast and courageously reiterated the long-held Christian position that respect for human life and traditional sexual morality—intercourse reserved for marriage—are required by God's plan for marriage (see, for example, Matthew 19:1–12 and Mark 10:1–12).

ASSIGNMENT

Humanae Vitae was not intended to be a prophetic encyclical, but Pope Paul VI did share some warnings for society if artificial birth control became widely practiced. Read paragraph 17 of *Humanae Vitae* at www.vatican.va. Create a chart like the one below that names some of Pope Paul's warnings. In the second column, list a current example from the news of how this warning has been realized.

WARNING	EXAMPLE FROM TODAY
1. Marital infidelity and moral decline	Marital infidelity has risen from approximately 9 percent in the 1950s to 29 percent in the 1960s to affecting more than 50 percent of couples today.
2.	
3.	
4.	

After the Second Vatican Council, new worship music and new instruments for worship were introduced.

could live up to them and left their ministries after the Second Vatican Council, while not as many families fostered vocations. Meanwhile, in Africa, Asia, and Latin America, vocations were on the rise.

The Remaining Years of Pope Paul VI's Pontificate

Following his issuance of *Humanae Vitae* in 1968, Pope Paul VI was noticeably shaken by the response of many otherwise faithful Catholics who did not abide by God's plan for marriage. However, he remained steadfast in leading the Church with pastoral charity. In 1971, he issued his apostolic letter *Octogesima Adveniens* (1971), a celebration of the eightieth anniversary of Leo XIII's *Rerum Novarum*. In the 1970s, the world faced economic troubles, and it was important for the Church to persevere in its commitment to serving and providing for those living in poverty.

Ten years after the close of the Second Vatican Council, Pope Paul VI extended, by way of his 1975 apostolic exhortation *Evangelii Nuntiandi* (*On Evangelization in the Modern World*), an invitation to the faithful to spread the Good News. In *Evangelii Nuntiandi*, Pope Paul VI promoted synods of bishops by asserting that "the Second Vatican Council recalled and the 1974 Synod vigorously took up again this theme of the Church which is evangelized by constant conversion and renewal, in order to evangelize the world with credibility" (*Evangelii Nuntiandi,* 15).

Pope Paul VI died on August 6, 1978. He was succeeded by Pope John Paul I. In his homily at Pope Paul VI's canonization in October 2018, Pope Francis compared him to St. Paul the Apostle:

> Like [St. Paul], Paul VI spent his life for Christ's Gospel, crossing new boundaries and becoming its witness in proclamation and in dialogue, a prophet of a Church turned outwards, looking to those far away and taking care of the poor. Even in the midst of tiredness and misunderstanding, Paul VI bore witness in a passionate way to the beauty and the joy of following Christ totally.

Pope Paul VI remains an example of faithful witness to Christ in the midst of worldly adversity.

SECTION ASSESSMENT

NOTE TAKING

Use the sentences you completed at the start of this section to help you complete the following items.

1. What was significant about Pope Paul VI's trips to the Holy Land and Istanbul?
2. Name another way the liturgy changed after the Second Vatican Council besides the introduction of the vernacular.
3. How did the formation of a Synod of Bishops contribute to collegiality between the pope and the bishops?

COMPREHENSION

4. Name two ways Pope Paul VI promoted social justice efforts following the Second Vatican Council.
5. What was historic about Pope Paul VI's trip to the United States?
6. Summarize the teachings of *Humanae Vitae*.
7. According to *Evangelii Nuntiandi*, how is the Church herself evangelized?

CRITICAL THINKING

8. Why do you think vocations decreased in developed nations and increased in developing parts of the world following the Second Vatican Council?

REFLECTION

9. What do you think would have happened in society if there had been more openness to what Pope Paul VI asserted in *Humanae Vitae*?

Section Assignments

Focus Question

How did conflict, war, and modernism shape the Church's response to the world at the Second Vatican Council?

Complete one of the following:

→ Research the life of Bl. Franz Jägerstätter or another Catholic saint or hero associated with World War II. Write a one-page report that explains how his or her life intersected with the turmoil around the war.

→ In 1950, in the aftermath of the tragic era of the two world wars, Pope Pius XII declared the dogma of the Virgin Mary's Assumption into heaven. Review the term *ex cathedra* (see the subsection "Papal Infallibility" in Chapter 7, Section 4). How did this proclamation on the part of Pope Pius XII serve as an inspirational moment during such worldly turmoil? Formulate your answer in a one-page essay.

→ The Second Vatican Council called for greater participation on the part of the laity in the life of the Church. Interview a layperson who is employed in professional ministry in the Church. This person may be the parish director of religious education, a youth minister, a parish or regional director of a Catholic social justice agency, or another position. Report on the following: (1) how the person felt called to his or her ministry; (2) the training that was necessary; (3) the duties of the position; and (4) the rewards of the position. You may share this report in a one-page essay or videotape the interview and save it at an Internet location approved by your teacher.

INTRODUCTION

The Church Faces the Challenges of the Twentieth Century

Pope John XXIII was a charismatic figure in the Church of the twentieth century. Look up and share one quotation of Pope John XXIII that you find interesting. Explain why you find it so.

SECTION 1

World War I and Its Devastating Aftermath

Research and report on three major outcomes of the Lateran Treaty. What was its long-term effect for the Church?

SECTION 2

The Church and World War II

In *Mediator Dei*, what did Pope Pius XII write was the "nature and object" of sacred liturgy? See paragraph 171.

SECTION 3

The Second Vatican Council: The Church Engages the World

Read paragraphs 1–8 of *Lumen Gentium*. Make a list of several images of the Church named in that section of the document.

SECTION 4

The Post–Second Vatican Council Era

Though many in the Church anticipated that the Church might change her position on artificial birth control, *Humanae Vitae* reaffirmed the immorality of the artificial means of birth regulation. Read "On the 40th Anniversary of *Humanae Vitae*" by Bishop Thomas G. Wenski at www.usccb.org. What was courageous about Pope Paul VI's stance?

Chapter Assignments

Choose and complete at least one of the three assignments to assess your understanding of the material in this chapter.

1. Addressing the Issue of War

The twentieth century was marred by two devastating world wars and many smaller regional wars. The world today is subject to terrorist attacks. To address the issue of war and how the Church calls world leaders and you yourself to respond, do each of the following:

- List the strict conditions for a nation to use "legitimate defense by military force." This is also called the *just war* doctrine. Its essential points can be found in paragraph 2309 of the *Catechism of the Catholic Church*.
- Answer this question: What should a Catholic in the military do if he or she believes a particular war to be unjust and he or she is required to participate in that war? This is called *conscientious objection*. To help formulate your response, read an answer to this question at the United States Conference of Catholic Bishops website (www.usccb.org) under "USCCB > Issues and Action > Human Life and Dignity > Military > Conscientious Objection."
- Write a paragraph explaining what you think leads to aggression among teenagers, which often leads to acts of violence. Then offer a list of practical strategies to reduce tension, conflict, and aggression among teens. Suggest ways to apply these strategies among peers at your school.

2. Situating the Second Vatican Council in Contemporary History

The Second Vatican Council occurred at a tumultuous time (1962–1965) in history. Consider these events that took place during the three years of the Council:

- John F. Kennedy, president of the United States, was assassinated.
- The United States and the Soviet Union almost went to war over the Cuban Missile Crisis.
- John H. Glenn Jr. became the first American to orbit the earth.
- "I Left My Heart in San Francisco" by Tony Bennett was the record of the year.
- *Lawrence of Arabia* won the Oscar for best picture.
- The Selma to Montgomery civil rights march took place.

In the midst of all this, Pope John XXIII was named *Time* magazine's "Man of the Year."

Create a poster in collage form displaying photos of the Second Vatican Council interspersed with photos of other contemporary events. Write at least four two-paragraph captions to attach to your poster. Caption subjects: (1) biography of Pope John XXIII; (2) who attended the Second Vatican Council (research item); (3) major documents/decisions of the Council; (4) reaction of American Catholics to the Council (research item).

3. Great Catholic Writers of the Twentieth Century

Several of the great writers of the twentieth century were Catholic. In many if not all of their works, Christian doctrine and theology are important to the plot. Do *one* of the following:

- Write a three-paragraph biography of each of these twentieth-century writers: Flannery O'Connor, J. R. R. Tolkien, G. K. Chesterton, and Evelyn Waugh. Include in their biographies the importance of Catholicism to their lives.
- Write a three-paragraph biography of one of the Catholic authors listed below and a one-page book report on one of their short stories. You can report on one of these stories or one you choose on your own:
    - Flannery O'Connor ("A Good Man Is Hard to Find")
    - J. R. R. Tolkien ("Leaf by Niggle")
    - G. K. Chesterton ("The Invisible Man")
    - Evelyn Waugh ("Out of Depth")

  These short stories are available online in most cases or at the library.

Prayer

Opening Prayer for Every Session of the Second Vatican Council

We stand before you, Holy Spirit,
conscious of our sinfulness,
but aware that we gather in your name.
Come to us, remain with us,
and enlighten our hearts.
Give us light and strength
to know your will,
to make it our own,
and to live it in our lives.
Guide us by your wisdom,
support us by your power,
for you are God, sharing the glory of Father and Son.
You desire justice for all;
enable us to uphold the rights of others;
do not allow us to be misled by ignorance
or corrupted by fear or favor.
Unite us to yourself in the bond of love
and keep us faithful to all that is true.
As we gather in your name, may we temper justice with love,
so that all our discussions and reflections
may be pleasing to you, and earn the reward
promised to good and faithful servants.
We ask this of you who live and reign with the
Father and the Son, one God, for ever and ever.
Amen.

THE CHURCH IN THE TWENTY-FIRST CENTURY

Pope Francis Names the FIRST CARDINAL FROM BANGLADESH

Following his noon Angelus prayers offered in St. Peter's Square at the Vatican on Sunday, October 9, 2016, Pope Francis announced that he would be elevating thirteen clergymen (mostly archbishops) to the rank of cardinal during his consistory to be held at the Vatican on November 19. Among those named to be elevated was Archbishop Patrick D'Rozario of the Archdiocese of Dhaka in Bangladesh.

Cardinal D'Rozario is a member of the Congregation of Holy Cross. Holy Cross missionaries, working in cooperation with the Vatican and inspired by the founder of Holy Cross, Bl. Basil Moreau, were sent to spread the Good News in Bangladesh in the mid-nineteenth century. Cardinal D'Rozario was first elevated to the episcopate by Pope John Paul II on September 12, 1990, and he is widely regarded by his brother bishops as a prudent and judicious shepherd for his flock in Bangladesh. His ecumenical efforts have been exemplary, and he has been a champion for facilitating dialogue among Christians, Muslims, and Hindus in Bangladesh. In fact, with the pope's announcement, Cardinal D'Rozario received an outpouring of congratulations from the Muslim and Hindu communities in Bangladesh. "This is a real gift for the country of Bangladesh," the new cardinal said, "not just the tiny Christian minority."

Pope Francis's elevation of Archbishop D'Rozario and the twelve other bishops from around the world served as an indication of his interest in ensuring that the College of Cardinals is reflective of the Church's truly global reach.

Cardinal D'Rozario called his selection both "a blessing and a grace." He said that it is "a recognition of the Church in Bangladesh, a recognition of the 'smallness' of the Church, but a Church that's vibrant in faith, and a witnessing Church in society through our works."

FOCUS QUESTION

As the Church enters the **TWENTY-FIRST CENTURY**, what are signs that the **GOSPEL** is being **SHARED AND PRACTICED** throughout the world?

Chapter Overview

INTRODUCTION

The Church in the Current Age

MAIN IDEA

The Church is not a staid or sedate institution locked in the past. Rather, even as society evolves at a rapid pace into the twenty-first century, the Church keeps its eternal commitment to preaching and living the Gospel of Jesus Christ.

This last chapter covers the current era in Church history. However, before discussing the contributions of figures such as Pope John Paul II to spreading the Good News, it is first vital to fathom how different the world is today from the early days of the Church's history.

Consider the rapid pace of advancement in technology. In fact, it would be unwise for a current textbook to mention examples of advancement, as new discoveries are made each day. But do consider that there are many adults who grew up without the Internet, the global source of information you are used to having at the touch of a finger. You might also briefly reflect on advances in transportation. Can you imagine how different the world of travel was at the start of the twentieth century? Most people were limited to spending their entire lives within a radius of a few hundred miles. There are countless other examples of the fast pace of development in medicine, communications, environmental and space science, and more over the past century.

In this era of advances in technology and other areas of society, the Church is sometimes portrayed as being stopped in time and rooted in the past rather than moving into the future. This is an inaccurate portrayal. As stated in *Gaudium et Spes*, the Church "has always had the duty of scrutinizing the signs of the times and of interpreting them in the light of the Gospel" (4). The Church closely follows what is going on around the world; she perpetually endeavors to share the unchanging Gospel of Jesus Christ in new ways to make it more comprehensible to the changing world. The message of the Church is not always a popular one or one that is easily received, but the Church offers a significant, irreplaceable gift to humanity. The Church never shirks from her duty to proclaim and live the Good News.

This chapter examines the Church's entrance into the third millennium through a study of the pontificates of the era.

The Year of Three Popes

Pope Paul VI's death on August 6, 1978, set in motion a whirlwind two-month period that would mark 1978 as the "year of three popes." Cardinal Albino Luciani, who took the papal name of John Paul to honor his two

NOTE TAKING

Connecting with the News. Research and list in your notes a technological advance in society that is currently in the news—for example, in science, medicine, space, transportation—and how the Church has responded to it.

Two New Popes in the "Year of Three Popes"

Pope John Paul I

Born Albino Luciani

- October 17, 1912
- Forno di Canale, in the Veneto region of Italy

Episcopate/Cardinalate

- Named Bishop of Vittorio Veneto by Pope John XXIII in 1958
- Created Cardinal of San Marco (Venice) in 1973 by Pope Paul VI

Papacy

- Elected pope on August 26, 1978, the second day of the conclave
- Known as the "smiling pope" for his warm personality; sometimes also known as the "September pope"
- Died on September 28, 1978, after only thirty-three days as pope

Quotation

We wish to continue to put into effect the heritage of the Second Vatican Council. Its wise norms should be followed out and perfected. We must be wary of that effort that is generous perhaps but unwarranted. It would not achieve the content and meaning of the Council. On the other hand, we must avoid an approach that is hesitant and fearful—which thus would not realize the magnificent impulse of the renewal and of life. (*Urbi et Orbi* radio address, August 27, 1978)

Born Karol Wojtyla

- May 18, 1920
- Wadowice, Poland

Pope John Paul II

Before Ordination

- After the Nazis closed the University of Kraków in 1939, worked in a quarry and then a chemical factory to avoid deportation to Germany
- Entered clandestine seminary in Kraków in 1942; was also an actor and an organizer of the underground Rhapsodic Theatre

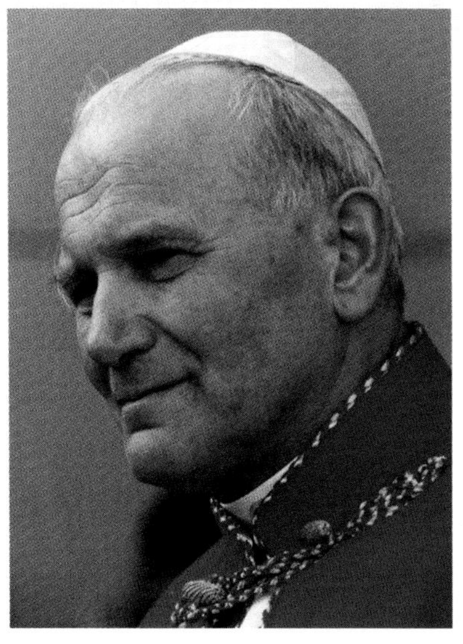

Episcopate/Cardinalate

- Named auxiliary bishop of Kraków on July 4, 1958, by Pope Pius XII
- Appointed archbishop of Kraków on January 13, 1964, by Pope Paul VI
- Created cardinal on June 26, 1967, by Pope Paul VI

Papacy

- Elected pope on October 22, 1978
- Made 146 pastoral visits in Italy, including to 317 of 322 parishes
- Authored fourteen encyclicals, fifteen apostolic exhortations, forty-five apostolic letters, and five books; also commissioned and helped oversee the publication of the *Catechism of the Catholic Church* (1992)
- Canonized 482 saints
- Received more than 17.6 million pilgrims at his Wednesday general audiences
- On May 13, 1981, while riding around in St. Peter's Square, was shot at close range in an attempted assassination by Turkish-born Mehmet Ali Ağca, suffering severe blood loss. Ağca was immediately apprehended and later given a lengthy sentence by the Italian court system. Pope John Paul II went on to make a full recovery. In 1983, Pope John Paul II went to visit Ağca in the Italian prison where he was being held and personally forgave him. Though beset by mental illness, Ağca (and his family) remained indebted to and in friendship with Pope John Paul II for the rest of his life.

Death

- Died on April 2, 2005, the vigil of Divine Mercy Sunday, which he had instituted
- Struggling to breathe, uttered his last words six hours before he passed away: "Let me go to the house of my Father" (in Polish)

immediate predecessors, served as pope from August 26 to his sudden death on September 28. His thirty-three-day pontificate was one of the shortest in history. The third pope of the calendar year was elected after the second conclave in two months. Cardinal Karol Wojtyla of Kraków became the first non-Italian pope in 455 years on October 16, 1978. He was inaugurated on October 22 and took the name John Paul II.

Pope John Paul II was the third-longest-serving pope in history; his papacy extended over twenty-six years until his death on April 2, 2005. His canonization by Pope Francis on April 27, 2014, hints at the depth and breadth of his life and his role in leading the Church into the twenty-first century. His era and accomplishments and those of his successors, Pope Benedict XVI and Pope Francis, are the focus of this chapter.

SECTION ASSESSMENT

NOTE TAKING

Use the recent advance and the Church's response to it that you researched and listed in your notes to help you complete the following item.

1. Briefly summarize the advance you researched and the Church's response to it. Then, answer: How was the Church's response beneficial to society?

COMPREHENSION

2. Why was 1978 an important juncture in Church history?
3. Why was Pope John Paul I commonly referred to as the "smiling pope"?
4. What is significant about the date of Pope John Paul II's death?

CRITICAL THINKING

5. How is the Church's place in contemporary society different than it has been in other historical eras? How is it the same?

REFLECTION

6. Briefly share your vision and understanding of how the Church should respond to the current age.

SECTION 1

The Influential Life of Pope John Paul II

MAIN IDEA

Pope John Paul II was one of the most influential people of the twentieth century. His nearly twenty-seven-year pontificate was marked by devoted worldwide pastoral care, much theological writing, and great personal holiness.

The man who would one day be Pope John Paul II was born Karol Wojtyla on May 18, 1920, in Wadowice (a town near the city of Kraków) in Poland. At an early age, Karol experienced a great deal of suffering: his mother died of organ failure when Karol was only eight years old; this loss was followed four years later by the death from scarlet fever of his older brother, a medical doctor. Years earlier, before his birth, Karol's older sister had died at only a few days old. Following these tragedies, Karol moved with his father in 1938 to Kraków, where he enrolled at the University of Kraków to study world literature and foreign languages; he also became very involved in theater. By the time of his pontificate, he was fluent in ten languages in addition to Latin, the official language of the Church.

Turmoil came in 1939 when the Nazi regime under Adolf Hitler invaded Poland. The Nazis closed down the University of Kraków, and Karol was forced to perform grueling manual labor in lieu of being deported to Germany. It was at this time that Karol acted on a call to seek ordination to the priesthood. He studied the writings of the saints (particularly St. Teresa of Avila and St. John of the Cross), performed in theatrical productions, and most importantly, undertook studies for the priesthood. All of these things were forbidden by the Nazis and done in secret. When the war was over, Karol Wojtyla was ordained a priest on

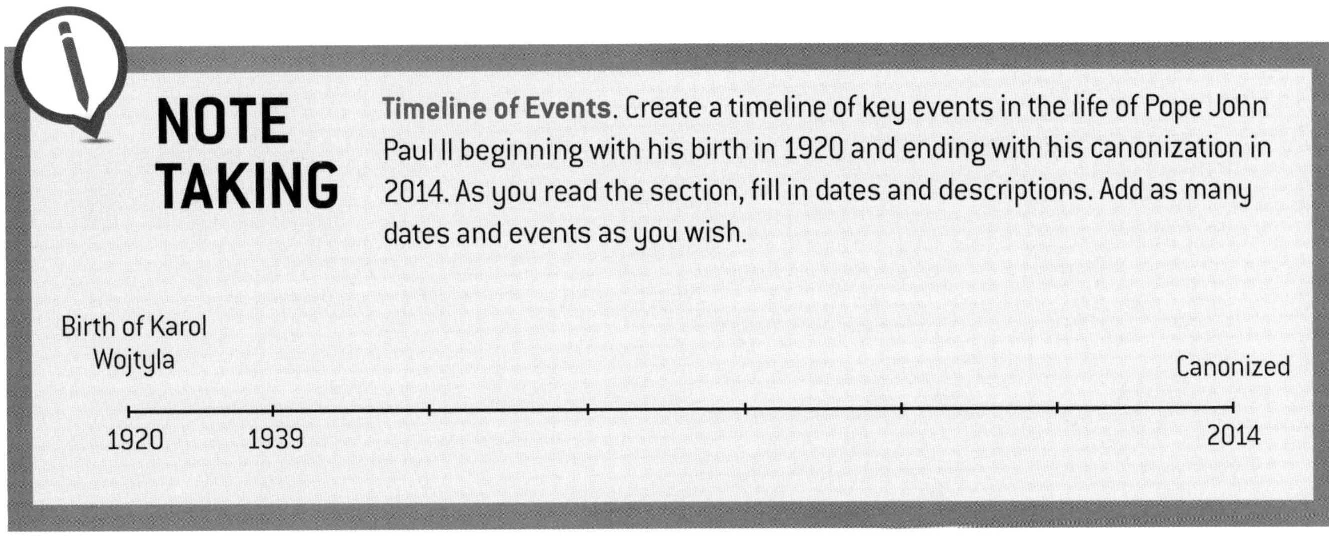

NOTE TAKING

Timeline of Events. Create a timeline of key events in the life of Pope John Paul II beginning with his birth in 1920 and ending with his canonization in 2014. As you read the section, fill in dates and descriptions. Add as many dates and events as you wish.

November 1, 1946, after which he was sent to Rome for doctoral studies in theology and philosophy.

Karol Wojtyla as Priest, Archbishop, and Cardinal

Fr. Wojtyla served numerous roles after his ordination: parish priest, university professor and chaplain, youth mentor, and journalist. He was active as an outdoorsman and as a performing actor; he skied, hiked, participated in plays, and delivered poetry. Fr. Wojtyla's appreciation for the humanities, along with his youth spent around many kinds of people from all different walks of life, contributed greatly to his ability to relate to people from a variety of backgrounds.

When Fr. Wojtyla was only thirty-eight years old, Pope Pius XII named him bishop, and only a few years later, he was able to attend some of the sessions of the Second Vatican Council (1962–1965). He made valuable contributions to the early drafts of *Gaudium et Spes*. Bishop Wojtyla was highly regarded by Pope Paul VI, who relied heavily on Wojtyla's groundbreaking book *Love and Responsibility* (1960) when writing his 1968 encyclical *Humanae Vitae*. Bishop Wojtyla also participated in five Synods of Bishops prior to becoming pope.

Bishop Wojtyla was named archbishop of Kraków in 1963 and was elevated to the College of Cardinals in 1967. This was a particularly difficult time for Poland and other countries under Soviet control because of the suppression of several freedoms, including the freedom to practice religion. Nevertheless, Archbishop Wojtyla was steadfast in his opposition to communism while continuing to serve the Church in Poland in various capacities, even ministering secretly when necessary in order to subvert the antireligious tactics of the communist government. Later, in 1979, upon returning home to Poland for the first time as pope, he first kissed the ground and then exhorted the Polish people "to form your own culture and civilization." He reminded them that the measure of their lives is not their "utility to the state, but their dignity before God."

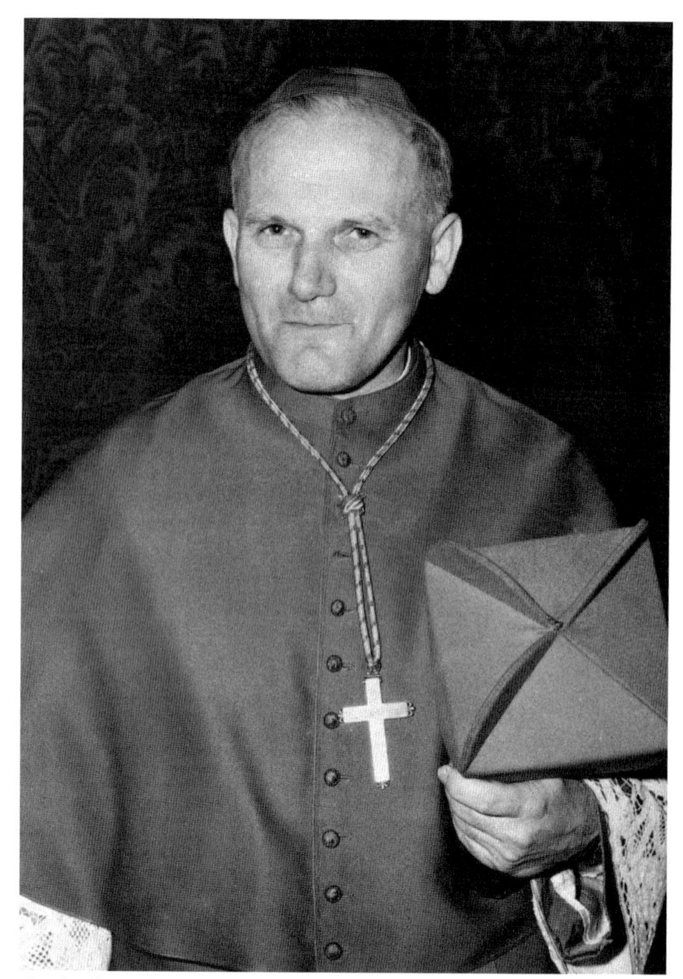

Cardinal Karol Wojtyla, archbishop of Krakow, 1968

Cardinal Wojtyla Becomes Pope John Paul II

When Cardinal Karol Wojtyla was elected pope on October 16, 1978, he chose the name John Paul II in homage to his immediate predecessor, who became known as Pope John Paul I thereafter. Pope John Paul II was the first non-Italian pope since the Dutch-born Pope Adrian VI, who reigned from 1522 to 1523.

A recurring theme throughout Pope John Paul II's pontificate was "Be not afraid," which he would reiterate to his adoring audiences, particularly the

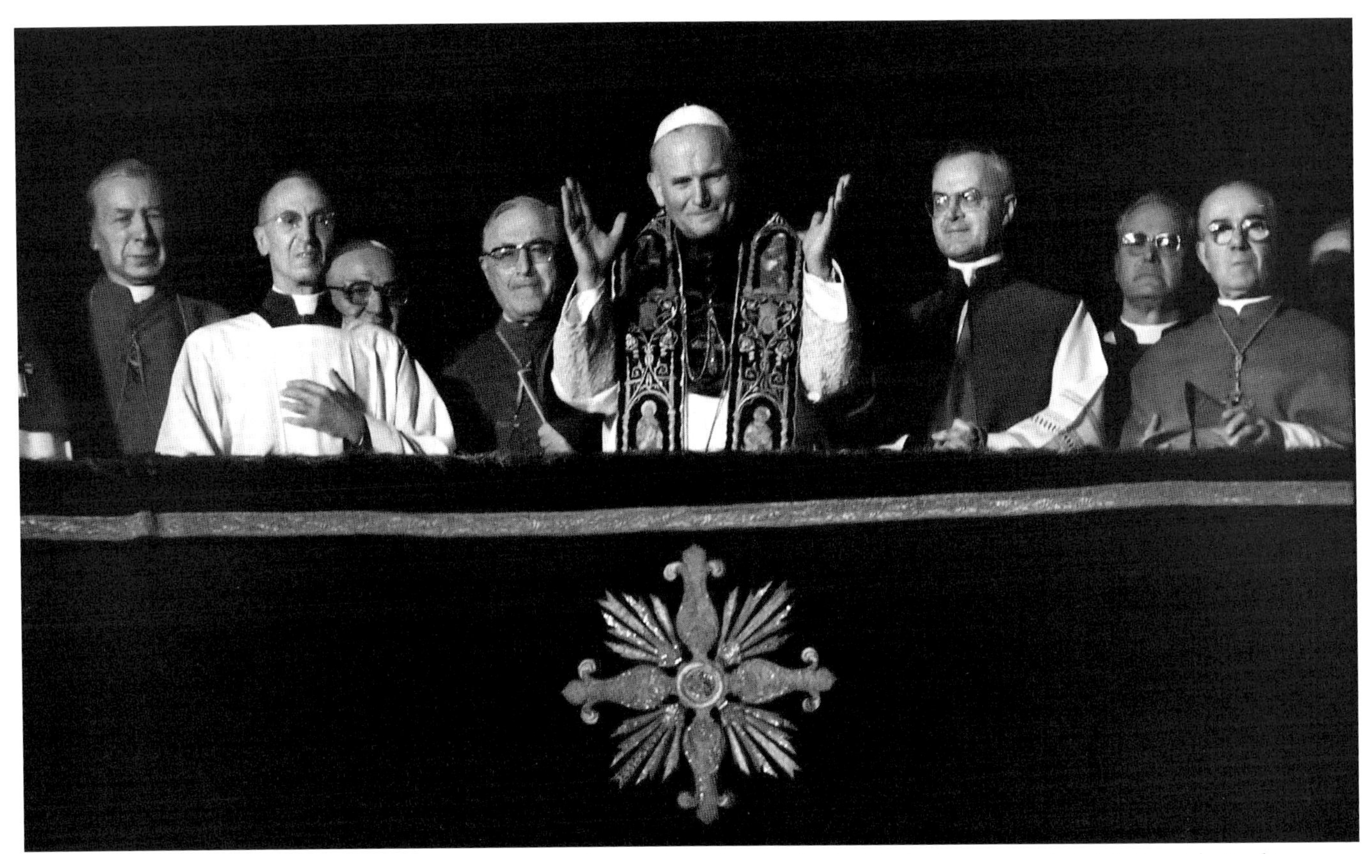

Pope John Paul II greets the cheering crowd from the balcony of St. Peter's Basilica shortly after his election to succeed the late Pope John Paul I.

youth. These words of Christ's occur frequently throughout the Gospels, and Pope John Paul II used them to remind the faithful to remain courageously righteous as they strove to live for the Lord. The pope also had a deep devotion to the Blessed Virgin Mary. The Mother of God figured prominently within his spiritual framework, especially since he lost his own mother at a young age. His papal motto was the Latin phrase *Totus Tuus* ("All Yours"), expressing his deep personal devotion to Mary. He concluded his opening address as pontiff this way:

> In this grave hour which gives rise to trepidation, we cannot do other than turn our mind with filial devotion to the Virgin Mary, who always lives and acts as a Mother in the mystery of Christ, and repeat the words "*Totus tuus*" which we inscribed in our heart and on our coat of arms twenty years ago on the day of our episcopal ordination. We cannot but invoke Saints Peter and Paul and all the saints and blesseds of the universal Church. (*Urbi et Orbi* radio address, October 17, 1978)

Reminiscent of the global voyages of Pope Paul VI, Pope John Paul II was, right from the beginning, an extensive traveler, both within the Italian peninsula and around the world, making 104 international trips during his pontificate. Pope John Paul II spread the Good News wherever he went and engaged in a "Dialogue of Salvation" with those of all different faiths around the world, presenting the truths inherent to Christ and the Church while consistently valuing the contributions of other faith communities.

Later Years of Pope John Paul II's Pontificate

In addition to his own writings, Pope John Paul II was instrumental in commissioning and overseeing the development of the universal *Catechism of the Catholic Church*, which was finalized and published in 1992. Thirty years after the start of the Second Vatican Council, the pope issued his apostolic constitution *Fidei Depositum* (*Deposit of Faith*) to introduce the *Catechism*. Pope John Paul II's other avenues for pastoral outreach included his Holy Thursday letters to the priests of the world and his 129 Wednesday audiences between 1979 and 1984 that became known as his Theology of the Body lectures. During these talks, Pope John Paul II reflected extensively on the Book of Genesis and on the meaning of God's plan for marriage, human sexuality within God's covenantal bond of husband and wife, and the embrace of chastity.

Throughout his pontificate, Pope John Paul II was a world leader, particularly in the West's struggle to peacefully dismantle the Soviet Union (which was finally achieved in 1991). He was also a champion of interreligious dialogue, ecumenism, and human rights, as well as a fierce opponent of **moral relativism**, secularism, and dissent from Church teaching. Following a steady decline in his health, Pope John Paul II died on April 2, 2005. To acclaim from the faithful around the world, he was canonized by his successor, Pope Benedict XVI, only nine years later, on April 27, 2014. Pope John Paul II was a popular pope whose long pontificate was a bridge between the twentieth and twenty-first centuries and a holy man who inspired more than one generation to take more seriously the demands of the Gospel of Jesus Christ.

moral relativism The problematic ethical stance that claims that there are no moral absolutes and that morality can only be considered from the individual's perspective.

WORLD YOUTH DAYS

Pope John Paul II initiated World Youth Day in 1985, and the first international event was held in Buenos Aires, Argentina, in 1987. These gatherings have occurred, every two or three years, in various cities throughout the world, ever since. Featuring clergy, religious, and lay faithful devoted to calling older teenagers and young adults to spread the Good News and embrace holiness, World Youth Days are widely popular and have invigorated the faith lives of those who have attended.

Search online and review information at the official World Youth Day website. Write your responses to the following questions:

- Where will the next World Youth Day be held?
- Who is invited?
- When will it occur?
- What are two events at World Youth Day that you would be most interested in? Why?
- Name the locations of every World Youth Day since 1986.
- Summarize one positive testimony of a person who attended the most recent World Youth Day.
- Offer two or three reasons why you might wish to attend a World Youth Day in the future.

A Glimpse at the Writings of POPE JOHN PAUL II

Pope John Paul II had many gifts with which he evangelized; one of them was his powerful mind for philosophy and theology. He had an impressive level of academic experience, and his writings have greatly added to the Church's collective knowledge. Pope John Paul II wrote several books and many encyclical letters, postsynodal apostolic exhortations, and other papal documents. Common themes in his writings are an emphasis on human dignity and the common call to participate in the **New Evangelization**. Listed below are some of Pope John Paul II's most prominent encyclicals, most of which add to the Church's social teaching:

Laborem Exercens (On Human Work) (1981)

emphasizes the importance of work and of human dignity. It is reflective of Pope Leo XIII's *Rerum Novarum*.

Sollicitudo Rei Socialis (The Social Concern) (1987)

was written to mark the twentieth anniversary of Pope Paul VI's *Populorum Progressio*.

Centesimus Annus (The Hundredth Year) (1991)

commemorates the one-hundredth anniversary of *Rerum Novarum*.

Veritatis Splendor (The Splendor of Truth) (1993)

emphasizes the Church's key role in providing the world with foundational moral teachings.

Evangelium Vitae (The Gospel of Life) (1995)

is a declaration of the importance of defending all human life, especially from direct threats such as abortion, **euthanasia**, and capital punishment.

Fides et Ratio (Faith and Reason) (1998)

underscores the necessary balance between faith and reason, which the Church has emphasized especially since the Middle Ages.

New Evangelization An initiative within the Church to spread the Gospel to all nations as well as to invite those already in the Church to a renewed commitment to their faith.

euthanasia The purposeful killing, through lethal injection, starvation, or other means, of someone whose life is not deemed worthy of continuing.

SECTION ASSESSMENT

NOTE TAKING

Use the timeline you created on the life of Pope John Paul II to help you answer the following questions.

1. What happened to Karol Wojtyla in 1939?
2. What concessions to World War II did Karol have to make during his seminary training?
3. What was a significant contribution Bishop Wojtyla made to the Second Vatican Council?
4. What motto for his pontificate did Pope John Paul II reveal at his opening address in October 1978? What does it mean?
5. What did the topic of Pope John Paul II's Wednesday audiences between 1979 and 1984 come to be known as?
6. Where was the first international World Youth Day held? What year did it take place?

COMPREHENSION

7. Name two things Karol Wojtyla did during the Nazi occupation of Poland.
8. What were the main subjects of Pope John Paul II's Theology of the Body lectures?

VOCABULARY

9. What is meant by the *New Evangelization*?

CRITICAL THINKING

10. How was Pope John Paul II's theme of "Be not afraid" especially applicable to the people of Poland? How did he communicate this message to the Polish people on his first trip back to Poland as pope in 1979?

SECTION 2

The Complementary Pontificates of Pope Benedict XVI and Pope Francis

MAIN IDEA

Pope Benedict XVI, a theologian of supreme intellect, continued the legacy of Pope John Paul II by encouraging the faithful to embrace holiness. Thereafter, Pope Francis led with a warmth that drew people of good will to accept and celebrate the Lord's mercy and compassion.

Following the death of Pope John Paul II, the College of Cardinals elected Cardinal Joseph Ratzinger, a prominent theologian, as the next successor of St. Peter. Cardinal Ratzinger chose the papal name Benedict XVI in order to, among other considerations, emphasize his desire to re-evangelize Western Europe, (as St. Benedict of Nursia had) as well as other traditionally Catholic areas of the world in which the practice of the Faith had fallen into decline.

Writings and Other Achievements of Pope Benedict XVI

Pope Benedict XVI, was the first pope with German roots since Pope Adrian VI (though born in the Netherlands region, Pope Adrian also had German ancestry). Benedict had been the archbishop of Munich prior to 1981, when Pope John Paul II named Cardinal Ratzinger as the new prefect for the Congregation for the Doctrine of the Faith. In essence, this role meant that Cardinal Ratzinger was the chief enforcer of the Church's doctrines and was responsible for overseeing the Church's condemnations of heresies when they arose. Cardinal Ratzinger relied on his rich intellect to explain the Church's position on any number of topics, while embracing a pastoral approach to supporting the clergy and the lay faithful alike.

NOTE TAKING

Researching and Summarizing Facts. Use the format of the informational feature on Pope John Paul I and Pope John Paul II (see "Two New Popes in the 'Year of Three Popes'" in the Introduction to Chapter 10) to accumulate basic notes on Pope Benedict XVI and Pope Francis. From material in this section and additional research, compile a simple table that includes information on birth date, birthplace, episcopate/cardinalate, papacy (election date), and key achievements.

In addition to the three apostolic exhortations and three encyclicals he wrote as pope, Pope Benedict XVI published sixty-six books between 1963 and 2013.

Pope Benedict XVI created an extensive library of deep theological writing, some of which he authored before he became pope. Among the more noteworthy writings that he completed during his pontificate are the following:

- *Deus Caritas Est* (*On Christian Love*) (2005) is a reflection on the different categories of Christian love and how all of human love has God as its origin.
- *Sacramentum Caritatis* (*The Sacrament of Charity*) (2007) underscores the Lord's gift of the Eucharist and reminds the faithful that the Eucharist is the source and summit of Christian life.
- *Spe Salvi* (*On Christian Hope*) (2007) details the ways in which the believer in Jesus Christ has a hope that cannot be matched. "The one who has hope lives differently; the one who hopes has been granted the gift of a new life" (2).

During his pontificate, Pope Benedict XVI also composed the three installments of his now classic *Jesus of Nazareth* book series. The pope wrote this in-depth, three-volume series under his name Joseph Ratzinger, the theologian, rather than as Pope Benedict XVI.

Pope Benedict XVI had other notable accomplishments in his pontificate. For example, he furthered ecumenism, including through his dialogue with those of the Eastern Catholic rites, and with the Oriental Orthodox and Eastern Orthodox Churches, as well as with Protestant groups. Benedict XVI also extended the interreligious efforts of Pope John Paul II by fostering good relations with those of the Jewish faith and other faith communities. Pope Benedict XVI's pontificate will also be remembered for his staunch opposition to moral relativism. In his last homily before being elected pope, he described a world that is ruled by a "dictatorship of relativism":

> Today, having a clear faith based on the Creed of the Church is often labeled as fundamentalism. Whereas relativism, that is, letting oneself be "tossed here and there, carried about by every wind of doctrine," seems the only attitude that can cope with modern times. We are building a dictatorship of relativism that does not recognize anything as definitive and whose ultimate goal consists solely of one's own ego and desires.
>
> We, however, have a different goal: the Son of God, the true man. He is the measure of true humanism. An "adult" faith is not a faith that follows the trends of fashion and the latest novelty; a mature adult faith is deeply rooted in friendship with Christ. It is this friendship that opens us up to all that is good and gives us a criterion by which to distinguish the true from the false, and deceit from truth. (*Mass for the Election of a Pope*, April 18, 2005)

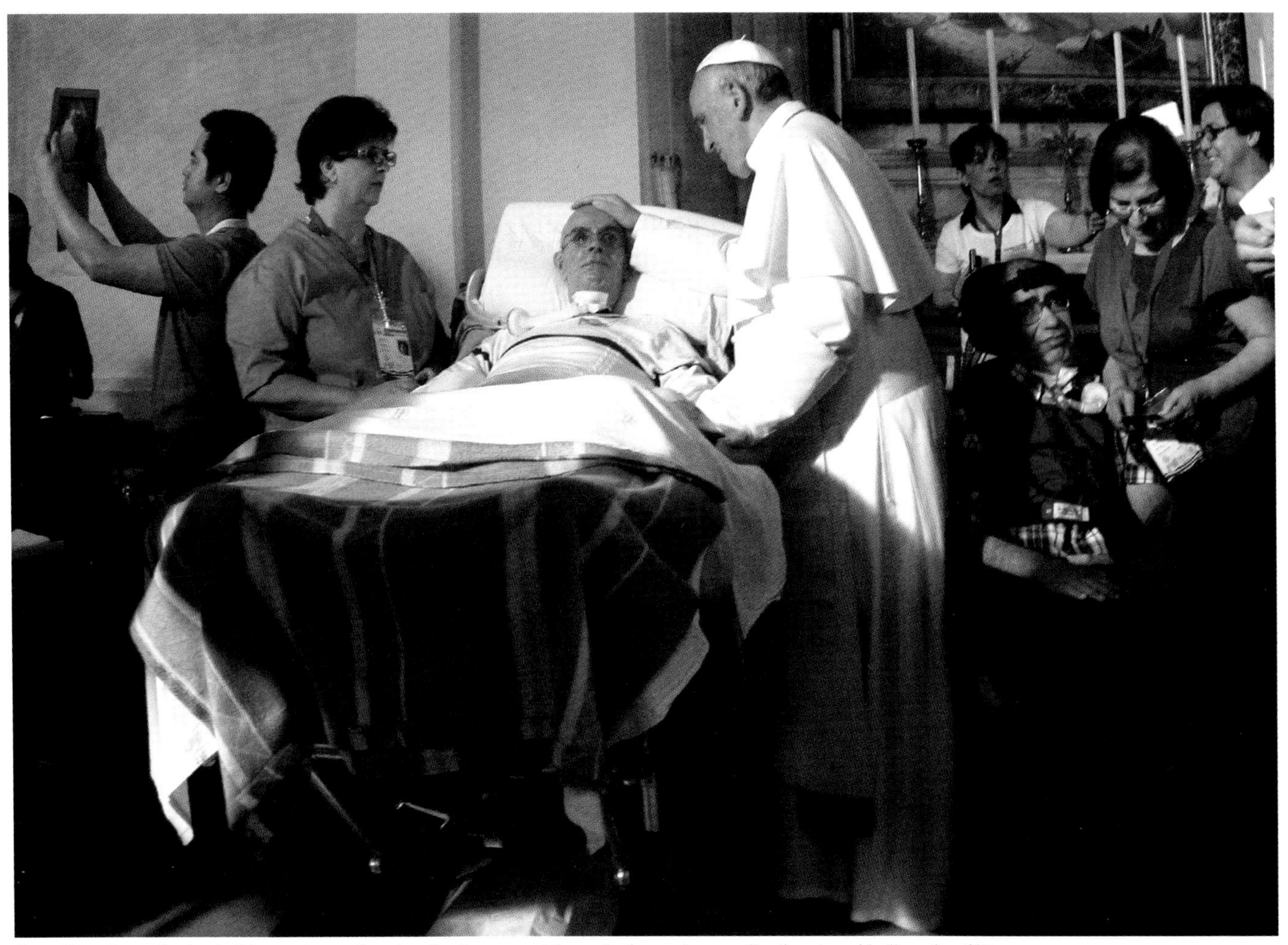

Pope Francis made charitable service and caring for the poor, sick, and others who are disadvantaged hallmarks of his papacy.

Pope Benedict XVI was also concerned about the need to infuse faith into cultures and civilizations in order to facilitate their stability in an increasingly secularized world.

Pope Francis and the "Francis Effect"

In February 2013, Pope Benedict XVI stunned people in the Catholic Church and throughout the world by announcing that he was retiring, citing old age and declining health. This made him the first pope to resign his position in nearly six hundred years, since Pope Gregory XII in 1415. Thereafter, he became known as Pope emeritus Benedict XVI.

In March 2013, the College of Cardinals elected the archbishop of Buenos Aires, Cardinal Jorge Mario Bergoglio, to succeed Pope Benedict. Cardinal Bergoglio chose the papal name Francis. "Right away, with regard to the poor, I thought of St. Francis of Assisi, then I thought of war," Pope Francis said. "Francis loved peace and that is how the name came to me."

A native of Argentina, Pope Francis was the first pope ever from the Americas, North or South. His father, Mario, was born in Italy, and his mother, likewise of Italian descent, was born in Buenos Aires. Hence, although Argentina is a Spanish-speaking country, Pope Francis grew up speaking the Italian language as well, which prepared him for his future life at the Vatican.

Francis was also the first Jesuit pope. Since he was a member of the Society of Jesus, his priestly life was marked by living out the Jesuit charism. From the time he was a priest up to his role as the archbishop of Buenos Aires, Pope Francis had a particular concern for outreach to alienated communities, going out to them to serve them and to call them to faithfully follow the Lord as disciples. Pope Francis described his vision of a Church "that is poor and for the poor." This was very much in the spirit of several Church documents on service to the poor, including the 1986 pastoral letter of the United States Conference of Catholic Bishops, *Economic Justice for All* (see the feature "Key Documents in Support of *Rerum Novarum*" in Chapter 8, Section 1), which has become a pillar of the Church's social teaching.

Pope Francis became known for charitable service to others—whether those living in poverty, the unborn, the elderly or infirm, or those in other circumstances—with his service based on Jesus' Gospel commands. As a sign of his commitment to simplicity and solidarity with the poor, the pope chose to live in a Vatican guesthouse rather than move into the papal apartments.

Pope Francis's first encyclical, *Lumen Fidei* (*The Light of Faith*), emphasized the role of faith in the life of a Christian. This encyclical was partially written by Pope Benedict XVI as the completion of a trilogy of encyclicals; the first two covered the other two theological virtues of love and hope. In 2015, Pope Francis released his second encyclical, *Laudato Si'* (*Praise Be to You*): *On Care for Our Common Home*. In this encyclical the pope offered a critique of consumerism and societal development that takes place without regard for the poor. He also wrote clearly of our need to protect the earth and of the dangers of human-caused climate change.

Pope Francis was immediately viewed by Catholics and non-Catholics alike as a breath of the fresh air of humility, patience, and openness to dialogue and pastoral care. Pope Francis inspired many fallen-away Catholics and non-Catholics to take a new look at the Church; this was known as the "Francis effect." More concretely, in 2015, Pope Francis declared a worldwide Extraordinary Jubilee of Mercy, during which the faithful were called to seek reconciliation and ongoing conversion, both in light of the Lord's abundant mercy.

CONSIDERING MERCY

In his prayer for the Extraordinary Jubilee Year of Mercy, Pope Francis prayed in part in remembrance of the compassion and mercy Jesus exhibited when through his "loving gaze [he] freed Zacchaeus and Matthew from being enslaved by money; the adulteress and Magdalene from seeking happiness only in created things; made Peter weep after his betrayal, and assured Paradise to the repentant thief."

ASSIGNMENTS

- **Reference one additional example from the Gospels where Jesus offers compassion and mercy to another.**
- **Share a time when you showed compassion and mercy to another.**
- **Share a time when someone showed compassion and mercy to you.**

SECTION ASSESSMENT

NOTE TAKING

Use the information you recorded about Pope Benedict XVI and Pope Francis to help you complete the following items.

1. Name one key achievement of Pope Benedict XVI and Pope Francis before each man became pope.
2. Name a key theme each pope addressed in his writings.

VOCABULARY

3. Define *moral relativism*, and explain why it is problematic from an ethical standpoint.

COMPREHENSION

4. Why did Cardinal Ratzinger choose the papal name Benedict?
5. Pope Francis's election brought with it two firsts in the long history of popes. What were they?
6. What is the subject of Pope Francis's encyclical *Laudato Si'*?

REFLECTION

7. What are some situations people face that would make them open to Pope Francis's offer of forgiveness and mercy as represented by his Extraordinary Jubilee Year of Mercy?

SECTION 3

The Church Addresses Current Challenges and Concerns

MAIN IDEA

The twenty-first century has brought new challenges that were unknown in previous eras. The Catholic Church responds with calls for justice, peace, and love, reinforced by the Gospel. The Church remains part of human history yet she also transcends time.

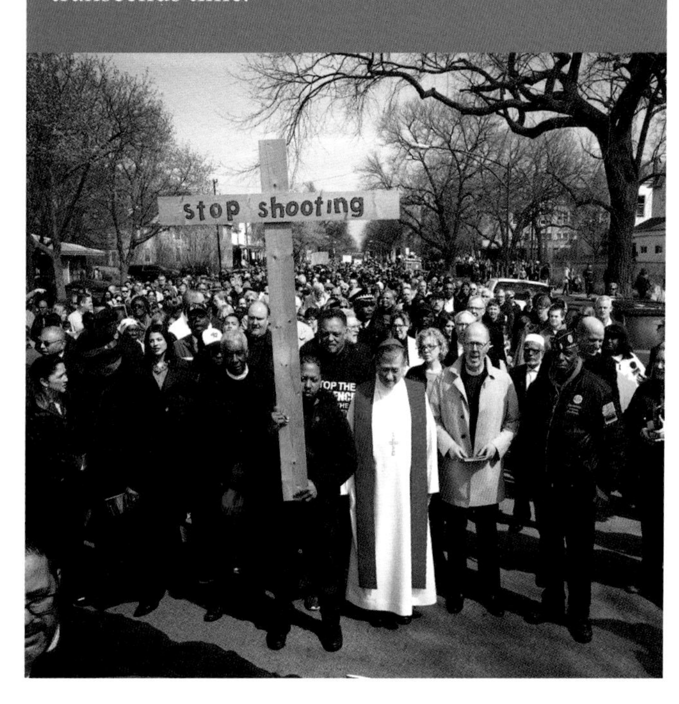

In this recent era, the Church is addressing contemporary challenges and areas of concern, including the following:

- the destructive forces of a **culture of death** that sanctions legalized and rampant abortion and euthanasia
- the aftermath of a devastating scandal known as the *priest sexual abuse crisis*, which tainted the Church's image globally
- the effect of rapid secularization on Mass attendance and priestly and religious vocations
- a problem of dual religious illiteracy—regarding one's own faith and the faith of others—that has led to religious intolerance, sometimes manifested in acts of terrorism in the name of or against a religion

This section addresses some areas of concern in more detail and identifies ways the Church has responded and continues to respond to them. Always remember that though the Church is part of human history, she also

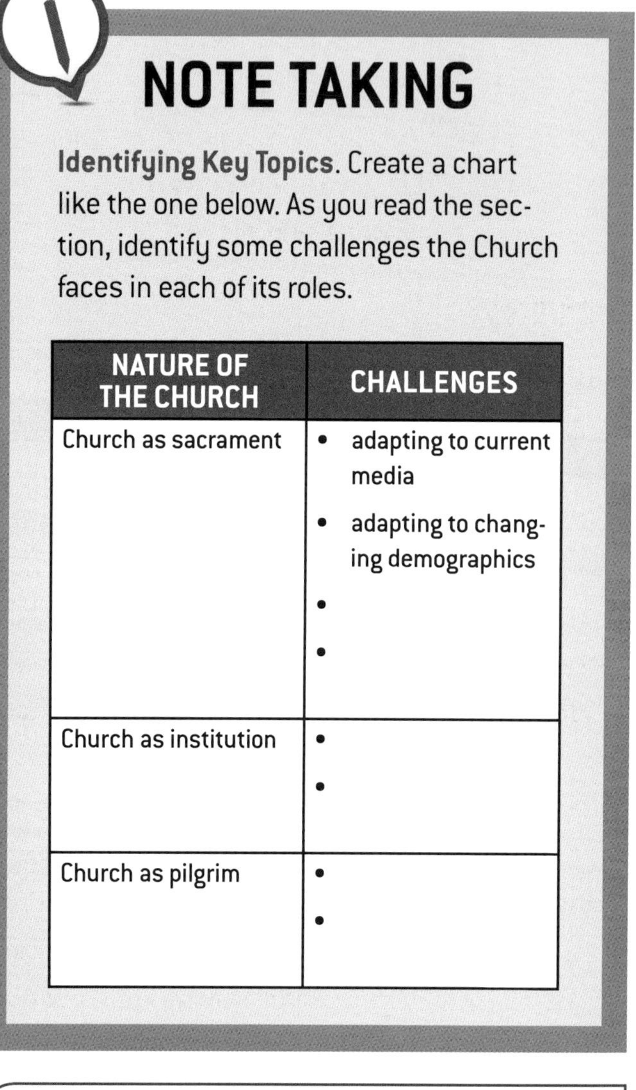

NOTE TAKING

Identifying Key Topics. Create a chart like the one below. As you read the section, identify some challenges the Church faces in each of its roles.

NATURE OF THE CHURCH	CHALLENGES
Church as sacrament	• adapting to current media • adapting to changing demographics • •
Church as institution	• •
Church as pilgrim	• •

culture of death The state of society in which human life, especially the most innocent and vulnerable (such as the unborn, the elderly, and the terminally ill), is not given its proper dignity and recognition.

transcends history, surpassing human comprehension of her mystery. Only in faith can you see the Church as a bearer of divine life within her place in history and understand how the Church deals with the challenges of human history. The Church's definitions as *sacrament*, *institution*, and *pilgrim* provide ways to measure her response to these challenges as the future unfolds.

The Church Today as Sacrament

The Church is the sacrament of Jesus Christ in the world, a union of the divine and the human. To remain a universal sacrament of salvation, the Church must continue with her fourfold task of *message*, *community*, *service*, and *worship*. Some future concerns in each of these areas are described below.

Message

In her role as herald of the Gospel, the Church must propose the Good News in solidarity with those to whom the Gospel is being preached rather than impose on them extraneous elements of a foreign culture. Perhaps the major challenge facing the Church's evangelization efforts in the twenty-first century is to find an authentic way to adapt the Gospel to the profoundly spiritual African cultures, the fastest-growing Catholic community in the world. In the past generation, Catholics have almost tripled in number in Africa. Past experience has taught the Church to use caution in evangelizing non-European peoples. Imposing European culture in mission territories is not a necessary adjunct to preaching the Good News of Jesus, but some deeply ingrained African customs such as polygamy are at odds with Church teaching.

A second challenge for the Church is to develop new ways to preach the Gospel to a tech-savvy generation. Surveys show that many Catholics lack basic **religious literacy**. Many are ignorant about fundamental

doctrines and what is required for the practice of the Faith. Popes, bishops, pastors, and catechists are becoming more adept at using current media, including social media, to proclaim the Gospel. Evangelists worldwide work to stay current with the tools of modern media. Marshall McLuhan, a communication theorist who converted to Catholicism, famously said that "the medium is the message." This means that the *form* of media (book, television, phone) dramatically influences the message being communicated. The Church must continue to investigate essential forms for communicating the Gospel.

religious literacy The familiarity with the basic tenets of various mainstream faiths that allows meaningful and peaceful dialogue with those of other faiths.

Community

The Church is the People of God, the Body of Christ. Demographically, the Church of the future will not be Eurocentric. By 2025, an estimated 80 percent of the world's Catholics will be African, Asian, and Latin American. This means that future Catholics will be less Caucasian and younger than the members of today's Church. Many will also come from countries where there is a severe shortage of priests (for example, Latin America). Thus, the Church will have to develop new ways for Catholics of the future to experience the fullness of the Body of Christ.

Service

All Christians are called to service. One of the Second Vatican Council's positive outcomes was its encouragement of laypeople to embrace their baptismal call to holiness and service:

> The laity are called in a special way to make the Church present and operative in those places and circumstances where only through them can she become salt of the earth. (*Lumen Gentium*, 33)

Catholics today are asked to witness to the Gospel wherever they are and in whatever they do. Homemakers, lawyers, teachers, tech workers, accountants, truck drivers, and everyone else are called to witness to the Lord in their everyday lives by performing works of mercy—feeding the hungry, educating the ignorant, comforting the elderly, healing the sick, reforming the prisons, caring for the homeless, and finding jobs for the unemployed. In addition, the rich body of the Church's social justice teaching gives the laity a blueprint of how to combat the sinful structures in society that keep people from receiving justice.

Worship

The Church must be a worshipping community that assembles around the table of the Lord. The Eucharist is the heart of Catholic life. Pope Francis has reminded Catholics that taking part in the Eucharist "conforms us in a unique and profound way to Christ." The gift of the Eucharist, he said, "is a foretaste of full communion with God in heaven. It is such a great gift and that is why it is so important to go to Mass on Sundays."

While in the West, with its increasingly secular culture, church attendance has decreased, Catholic congregations in Africa, Asia, and Latin America have grown.

Recent trends, however, are alarming. Mass attendance in many Western nations is at an all-time low. For example, a recent survey from Georgetown University found that slightly more than 20 percent of American Catholics born after 1960 reported attending Mass at least once a week. Mass attendance in the United States has not trended noticeably upward due to the "Francis effect." Internationally, the numbers are just as disappointing: for example, only 12 percent of French Catholics and 24 percent of Australian Catholics attend Mass once a week or more often.

It is ironic and sad that now that the liturgy is more pastorally sensitive and in the vernacular, fewer Catholics are participating on a regular basis. The Church must battle the forces at work in the secular, materialistic, pleasure-seeking, consumerist world. The Church must find new ways to invite Catholics to worship as a vital Christian community. Catholics cease to be Catholics without the Eucharist to sustain them and nourish them spiritually.

The numbers are dramatically better in Africa, however: 92 percent of Nigerian Catholics, for example, attend Sunday Mass.

The Church Today as Institution

In an age that is disrespectful of authority in other areas, the Church encourages Catholics and others to pay attention to the Magisterium, the teaching office of the Church. It is the Magisterium's task to authentically interpret the Word of God in both Scripture and Tradition. As a teaching body, the Magisterium addresses the faithful in a pastoral way, careful to explain the reasoned depth of the Church's teachings.

Catholics are asked to accept many teachings that they may find difficult. The teaching against contraception is one example. And currently, with many nations sanctioning same-sex unions as marriage, Catholics often find themselves as a minority voice in opposition. The Magisterium must carefully and thoughtfully explain why marriage cannot be redefined to include two men or two women.

The Church must also address and communicate the truth of her teaching to Catholics and non-Catholics in several other areas, including the following:

- combating poverty
- protecting life from conception to natural death
- protecting the environment
- welcoming and caring for migrants
- checking unbridled consumerism
- promoting interreligious dialogue
- encouraging peaceful resolutions of conflict

The Holy Spirit continues to help the Church fulfill her mission. The human Church is filled with good people trying their best to live and share the Gospel, but even good people fail and sin. It is the divine energy of the Holy Spirit that empowers the Church to thrive as an institution.

The Church Today as Pilgrim

With the historic global travels of popes since Pope Paul VI, the Church has come to understand her role as pilgrim more clearly than ever. Papal visits have not only taught the nations of the world about Christ's love but have also served as opportunities for the Church to learn from various cultures. The Second Vatican Council's *Gaudium et Spes* instructs Catholics to be open to all the good the world has to offer while prioritizing the Church's faithfulness to Jesus Christ, her biblical foundations, and her own history as Christ's presence in the world.

With the rest of the world, the Church follows very closely the political debates over the growing population in poor countries, the dwindling resources of the planet, and ecological crises such as global warming.

THE EXTRAORDINARY JUBILEE OF MERCY, also referred to as the Year of Mercy, was first announced in Pope Francis's papal bull *Misericordiae Vultus*. Beginning December 8, 2015, and ending November 20, 2016, the Extraordinary Jubilee of Mercy was a time for remission of sins and universal pardon with a special focus on forgiveness and mercy. "Missionaries of Mercy" were available in dioceses throughout the year to absolve sins that normally only the Apostolic Penitentiary can address.

She pays very close attention to developments in bioethics. She is very willing to learn about the scientific and technological advances that will transform our lives in ways that we can only imagine today.

The Church does not retreat into a fortress: she engages the great problems confronting humanity. As a pilgrim, the Church must point out to all of God's people the eternal destiny that awaits each human being. Therefore, armed with the Gospel entrusted to her, the Church addresses everything that threatens human dignity, diminishes the essential equality of human beings, and weakens the solidarity God intends for his children. As a follower of the Prince of Peace, the Church remains a strong voice for peace and reason, especially in the face of multiplying threats of terrorism.

The Church is openly ecumenical, knowing well that to have peace among the nations there must be peace among religions. Christian unity, especially with Orthodox Christians, has been a strong goal of the post–Second Vatican Council popes, and it will remain so in the future. A few steps forward and a few steps back have been the course with other Christian groups, especially Anglicans and Lutherans. Ecumenical efforts will continue among Christians, and joint efforts in areas of social justice will be more evident. Great strides have been made in Jewish-Catholic relations: In January 2016 Pope Francis became the third pope to visit a synagogue in Rome. In his address there, he noted the unique and special bond between Jews and Christians due to their common roots. "Jews and Christians must therefore feel as brothers, united by the same God and by a rich common spiritual patrimony," the pope said.

For many observers the biggest question of the future is how the Catholic Church will relate to Islam, the fastest growing of the world religions. A barrier effecting Catholic-Muslim relations is Islamic fundamentalism, which has turned violent and is engaging in a battle for world domination. At the rise of the terrorist group identified as the Islamic State in Iraq and Syria (ISIS), Pope Francis was quick to dissociate this extreme fundamentalist group from the tenets of Islam. "Not all Muslims are violent," he often pointed out. Yet how will the Church approach Islam on an international level, especially given that it does not have a central authority figure such as the pope? The future will undoubtedly reveal answers.

The Church remains true to her mission of preaching the whole of Christ's truth to "cafeteria Catholics" in the United States, who are called this because they select only certain beliefs and practices from the "menu" of Church doctrine, and nominal Catholics in European countries such as France, who have become increasingly secular and even hostile to traditional Catholic teaching. Pope Francis's proclamation of the Extraordinary Jubilee of Mercy was in part to call lapsed Catholics back home to the Church.

Faithful Catholics may look at the future and feel overwhelmed at the problems the Church faces. However, a study of Church history reveals that the Church has always been confronted with problems: persecutions, doctrinal debates that turned violent, corrupt leaders, tepid faith in her members, outside political pressures, crises brought on by new discoveries, and so forth. It is a marvel, explainable only with the eyes of faith and the gift of the Holy Spirit, that the Church has survived into her twenty-first century.

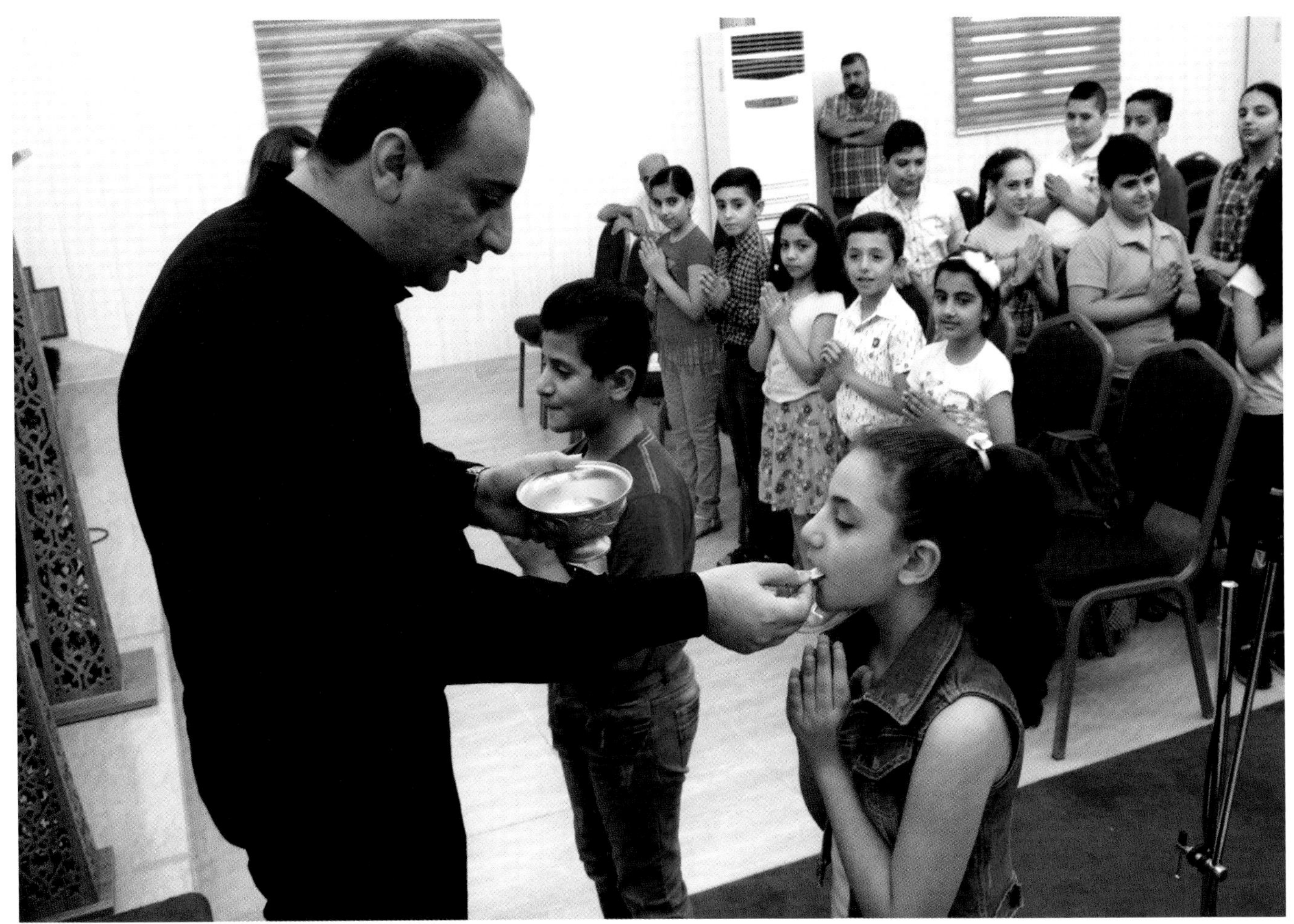

Holy Communion preparations with unconsecrated hosts of the New Syriac Catholic Church in Dohuk, Northern Iraq

SECTION ASSESSMENT

NOTE TAKING

Use the chart that you created at the beginning of this section to answer the following questions.

1. Name a challenge the Church faces when evangelizing non-European peoples.
2. What is meant by "the medium is the message"? How does this statement apply to how the Church shares the Gospel?
3. What is the Magisterium's role in the Church?
4. What challenges does the Church face in her ecumenical efforts?

COMPREHENSION

5. How will the Church's demographics change by the middle of the 2020s?
6. What has been the result of the "Francis effect" on Mass attendance?

VOCABULARY

7. What is meant by the *culture of death*?

FURTHER RESEARCH

8. How have Christians around the world been threatened by terrorism and other forms of religious intolerance?

CRITICAL THINKING

9. Why do you think there are so many people who call themselves Catholics yet do not regularly attend Sunday Mass? How might the Church respond to this problem?

SECTION 4

The Church as a Sign of Hope

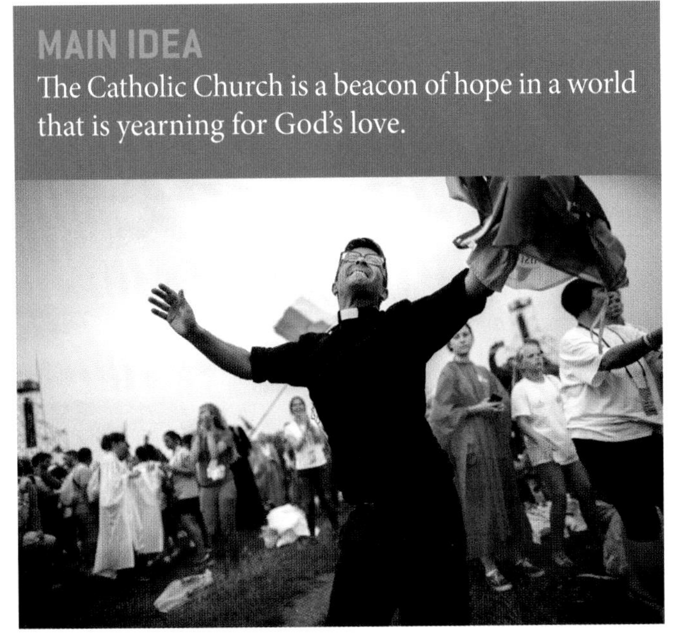

MAIN IDEA

The Catholic Church is a beacon of hope in a world that is yearning for God's love.

Section 3 identified some of the challenges the twenty-first-century Church is facing, but despite those, there are still many reasons for hope.

Pope John Paul II left a lasting legacy within the Church, particularly for the youth, who were encouraged by his very personal leadership style as well as his efforts at the New Evangelization. One way Pope John Paul II made the Catholic faith more inviting to a wider audience during his pontificate was through the publication of the *Catechism of the Catholic Church*, an orderly and accessible presentation of the tenets of the faith. Today, the *Catechism of the Catholic Church* is accessible online at no cost.

It was also during Pope John Paul II's pontificate that the Church became prominent in promoting a *culture of life*—that is, spreading the message of the pro-life movement by pushing back against the culture of death. Millennial Catholics and millennials in general support pro-life causes in greater numbers than the generations before them. A recent Gallup poll survey found that 51 percent of eighteen- to twenty-nine-year-olds believe abortion should be illegal in most circumstances, in comparison to 36 percent of people that age who answered the same way in 1991. Many Catholic youths travel from great distances to join the nearly five hundred thousand people who protest each year at the March for Life in Washington, DC, against the 1973 *Roe v. Wade* Supreme Court decision that legalized abortion in the United States.

Beyond teaching against abortion, euthanasia, and the death penalty, the Church advocates for **adult stem cell research**, which is not only a successful

adult stem cell research A scientific procedure that involves the collection, manipulation, and study of adult human stem cells, as opposed to embryonic stem cell research, which leads to the unnecessary destruction of innocent human life. Adult stem cell research is approved by the Church and has a positive success rate for finding solutions to illness and disease.

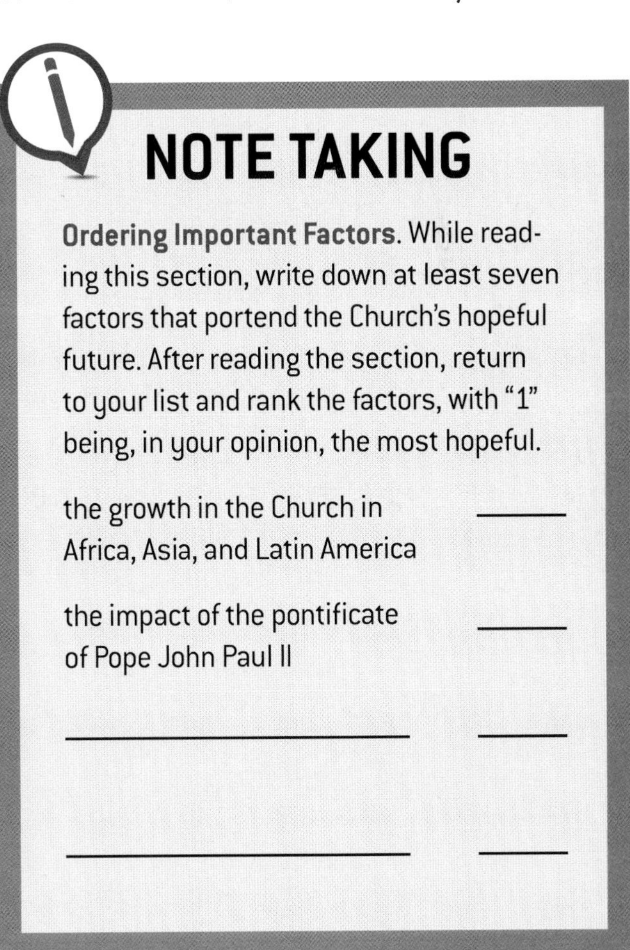

NOTE TAKING

Ordering Important Factors. While reading this section, write down at least seven factors that portend the Church's hopeful future. After reading the section, return to your list and rank the factors, with "1" being, in your opinion, the most hopeful.

the growth in the Church in Africa, Asia, and Latin America ______

the impact of the pontificate of Pope John Paul II ______

______________________ ______

______________________ ______

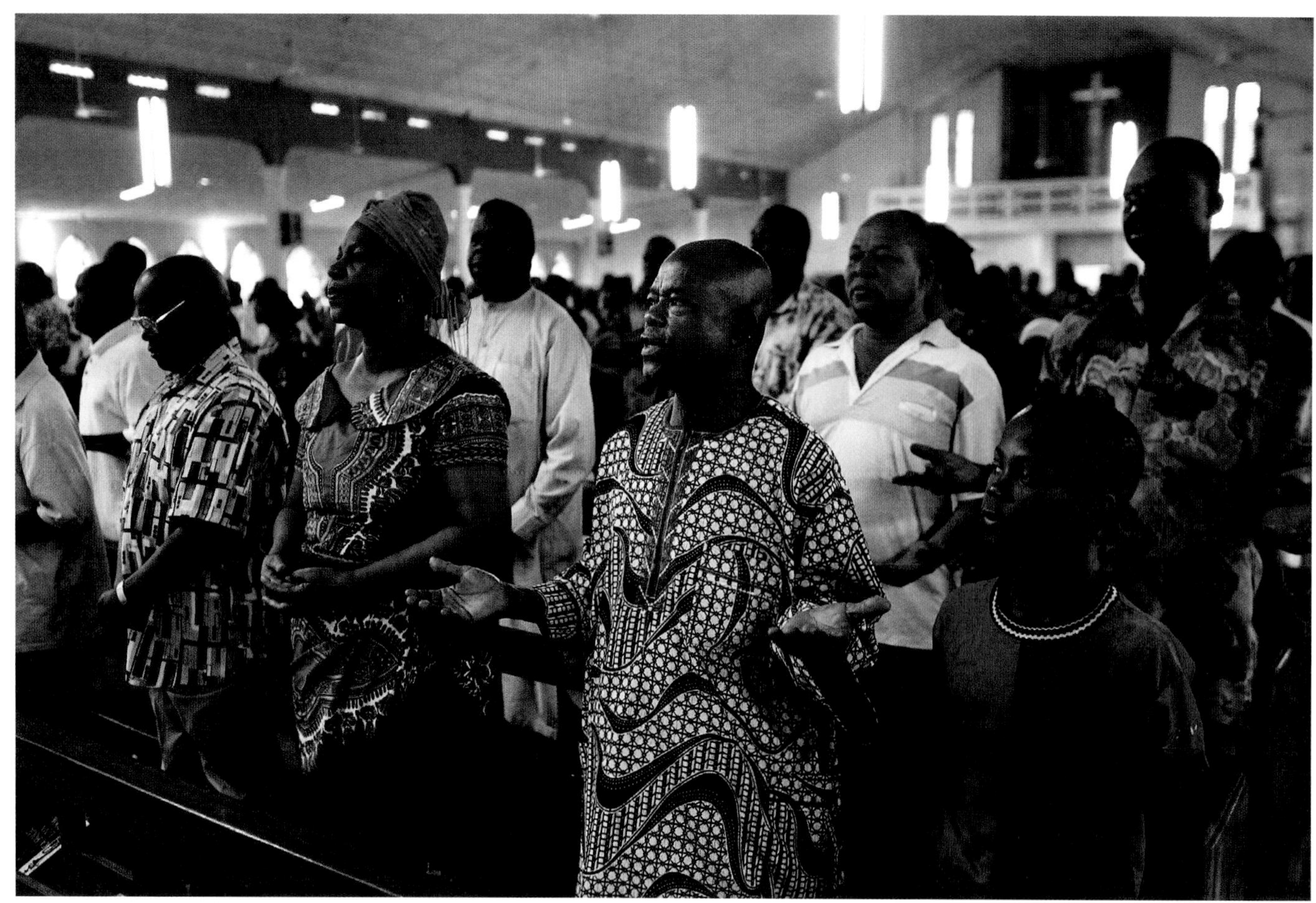

Nigerian Catholics celebrate morning Mass in Kano, Nigeria.

method of scientific research but also one that provides a life-affirming alternative to embryonic stem cell research, which ends a human life in its embryonic stage. No cure or successful treatment of disease has been attributed to embryonic stem cell research; in contrast, more than seventy cures and treatments—for illnesses ranging from cancer to autoimmune diseases to liver diseases as well as for wounds and injuries—are attributed to adult stem cell research.

The Young Church of the Present and Future

The influx of voices of the millennial generation—many of them inspired by the engaging words and actions of the popes of their lifetime—and the great influx of new Catholics in Asia, Latin America, and Africa provide much hope for the Church and the world as the century unfolds.

When examining the "young Church" worldwide, it's appropriate to begin in Africa, where, as mentioned in Section 3, the Church is growing rapidly. Note the following statistics:

- Since 1980, Africa's Catholic population has increased by nearly 240 percent.
- There are nearly two hundred million Catholics in Africa.
- It is estimated that by 2040, approximately one in four Africans will be Catholic.

By the numbers, Africa holds the keys to the future of the Catholic Church. In fact, priests from Africa are sent to parishes in the West in order to re-evangelize the very communities that brought the faith to Africa centuries ago. Consider these remarks from Pope John Paul II regarding the special role of the Church in Africa: "God's salvific plan for Africa is at the origin of the growth of the Church on the African continent. But since by Christ's will the Church is by her nature missionary, it follows that the Church in Africa is itself called to play an active role in God's plan of salvation" (*Ecclesia in Africa*, 29).

Meanwhile, today in the United States more than half of millennial Catholics are Hispanic. Two-thirds of Catholics under age thirty-five are Hispanic as well. The first diocesan Hispanic youth and young adult coordinator in Shreveport, Louisiana, Marcos Gonzalez Villalba, shared his enthusiasm for a bright future for the Church in the United States: "The seeds that have been planted are starting to sprout. More people in our Hispanic community are excited about their faith and share their love for God within their own culture."

This enthusiasm among young Catholics has spread among all nations, races, and cultures, much of it due to the success of the New Evangelization and centered around national and regional extensions of the World Youth Days. Attending a gathering of more than fifty thousand young people from twenty-three countries at the Asian Youth Day in Korea in 2014, Pope Francis reminded them that "as young Christians you are not only a part of the future of the Church, you are also a necessary and beloved part of the Church's present. You are the present of the Church."

Vocations and Mission

Pope Francis emphasized that the youth are the present of the Church, whether they are at work, are in school, have begun a career, or have answered a call to marriage, religious life, or the priesthood. Particularly, there is hope that young people will listen to God's voice and respond to a call to help to alleviate a shortage of priests and religious. In some areas of the world, particularly in Africa and in Asia, vocations to the priesthood and religious life are flourishing. The revitalization of seminaries and the work of religious communities will continue to be signs of hope for the Church. In the United States, ordinations in 2015 increased by 25 percent from the previous year, with a total of 595 men ordained.

Some religious communities also see evidence of an increase in vowed vocations. One example is the Sisters of Life (founded in 1991), whose charism is to promote the Church's teaching of the importance of all human life, from conception through natural death. Another is the Missionaries of Charity, founded by St. Teresa of Calcutta (1910–1997), who dedicated her adult life to serving the poorest of the poor around

Sisters of Life (top) and Missionaries of Charity (below)

the world, particularly in India. The Missionaries of Charity are made up of religious sisters, brothers, and priests. At the time of Mother Teresa's death in 1997, there were 3,194 sisters and 363 brothers serving the poor. In 2016 at the time of her canonization, the Missionaries of Charity had 5,161 sisters and 416 brothers. They are in 139 countries worldwide.

Responsibility for the Church's outreach and mission is not dependent solely on priests and religious. In his apostolic exhortation *Christifideles Laici*, Pope John Paul II encouraged laypeople to build the Kingdom of God by re-evangelizing the world through authentic Christian living. He stressed that everyone—young and old—has a role to play in turning the world toward Christ and being Christ for others. He warned against separating one's Christian life from one's secular life.

Pope John Paul II also commended various lay associations and organizations that had begun or were reorganized after the Second Vatican Council. He was a strong supporter of certain groups in particular, including the **Focolare Movement**, founded in 1943. Its goal is world unity achieved by putting Gospel love into action.

Focolare Movement A movement founded by Chiara Lubich in 1943 with the goal of world unity achieved through putting the Gospel love of Jesus Christ into action.

Spanish Inquisition A bureau or commission that had branches in most of the larger dioceses of Spain that was empowered to call on civil authorities to help weed out heretics. Once the heretics were discovered, the Church authorities conducted a trial with those accused presumed guilty and required to prove their innocence.

The Church of the Future: Moving Forward in the Midst of Challenges

How can it be said that the Church is holy and a guardian of truth when her history has included events such as the Crusades, the **Spanish Inquisition**, the

Discerning Vocation Facts

Here are some recent statistics from the National Religious Vocation Conference on women and men who choose a religious vocation:

WOMEN

- The average age of entrance is thirty-two.
- Women are most likely to hear about their religious institute through the recommendation of a friend.
- Women who attended a Catholic primary school are three times as likely to consider being a religious sister as those who did not.
- Women tend to consider a vocation prior to the age of fourteen.

MEN

- The average age of entrance is thirty.
- Men are most likely to encounter their religious institute in a school or other institution served by the congregation.
- Men who attended a Catholic secondary school are more than six times as likely to consider a vocation as those who did not.
- Men who consider a vocation tend to do so during their college years.

DISCERNMENT SURVEY

In a quiet space, reflect on the questions posed in a discernment survey that is either provided to you by your teacher or referenced by the United States Conference of Catholic Bishops (see "USCCB > Beliefs and Teachings > Vocations > Discernment Tools" at www.usccb.org). Write short answers to the following:

- What did you learn about yourself from taking the survey?
- Name a religious community that you find interesting and worth learning more about. Explain why.
- On a scale of 1 to 10, how interested are you in exploring a religious vocation (with 10 being the most interested)? Explain.

Young people like you are the future of the Catholic Church.

persecution of Jews, the Galileo trial, and the priest sexual abuse crisis? The short answer is to say that some humans have acted unjustly while carrying the banner of the Church and that their actions have tainted the public's perception of the Church as a whole. Pope John Paul II and other Church leaders have formally apologized on various occasions for the sins that some within the Church—such as those who carried out the Crusades and the Inquisition—have committed throughout Church history.

It is also important to consider the historical context within which many of these offenses occurred. People of previous epochs dealt with perceived threats differently than modern people; sometimes Christians of those times resorted to actions that were common within their societies but would be unacceptable to Christians today. Thus it would be unreasonable to judge figures in history as harshly we might judge people committing the same acts today.

Although the human members of the Church are prone to sin, the Church herself is sinless and holy. Thus, despite the sins of individuals within the Church, even including the ordained clergy, God has entrusted the Church with the grace and truth of the Good News of salvation. The Church serves as the source of holiness and the path to holiness for all people, according to God's design. Many within the Church have lived lives of enduring holiness and heroic sanctity, as can be seen through their countless sacrifices—frequently to the point of martyrdom, which has taken place in every era of Church history. Whether or not a saint is a martyr, this person's holy life validates the truth and power of the sacraments and teachings of the Church.

No one can predict exactly what the future holds for the Church on earth. What is certain is that the Church has persisted for nearly two thousand years since its founding by Christ, who promised his followers that "the gates of the netherworld shall not prevail against it" (Mt 16:18b). No matter what the future brings, the Church will do what she has done for going on two millennia: draw souls closer to the Lord Jesus Christ and his salvation by exercising the virtues of faith, hope, and love for the greater glory of the Kingdom of God.

SECTION ASSESSMENT

NOTE TAKING

Use the ranking you made of hopeful factors for the Church's future to help you answer the following questions.

1. What did you name as the most hopeful factor for the Church's future? Why do you find it so?
2. Generally, on a scale of 1 to 10, with 10 being the most hopeful, how hopeful are you for the Church's future? Explain your ranking.

COMPREHENSION

3. What evidence is there that the millennial generation is a "pro-life generation"?
4. Why does the Church condemn embryonic stem cell research?
5. What is the focus of the ministry of the Missionaries of Charity?
6. What did Pope John Paul II stress as key responsibilities for laypeople in the Church?

CRITICAL THINKING

7. How would you respond to a person who challenges the holiness of the Church based on the sinful actions of some of her members?

REFLECTION

8. Discuss what you believe is the greatest challenge the Catholic Church will face in the twenty-first century.

Section Assignments

Focus Question

As the Church enters the twenty-first century, what are signs that the Gospel is being shared and practiced throughout the world?

Complete one of the following:

- Read the apostolic constitution *Fidei Depositum*, which can be found online or at the beginning of a print edition of the *Catechism of the Catholic Church*. According to Pope John Paul II: (1) What is the purpose of the *Catechism*? (2) What was the process for drafting the text? (3) How was the material arranged? (4) What is the doctrinal value of the text? Respond to the questions in a one-page essay.

- Using information from the United States Conference of Catholic Bishops website (www.usccb.org) under "USCCB > Issues and Action > Cultural Diversity," prepare a table, graph, or display to share and compare relevant information about the demographics of African American, Asian American, Pacific Islander, Hispanic/Latino, and Native American Catholics in the United States. Write a two-paragraph introduction to the information that expresses the positive nature of cultural diversity in the Church in the United States.

- Reflecting on the last approximately two thousand years of Church history, what era do you find the most fascinating, and why? What can the Church of today and the future learn from the issues of the era you chose and the Church's response to those issues? Address these questions in an essay long enough to respond to them in detail.

INTRODUCTION

The Church in the Current Age

- Examine the website of your parish or another local parish. Imagine you are a non-Catholic looking for information about the Catholic faith. Write two paragraphs that (1) tell about the information you found and (2) rate how effective the website was at presenting the information.

SECTION 1

The Influential Life of Pope John Paul II

Write down one event or characteristic that typified Pope John Paul II's holiness at each of these stages of his life: prior to ordination, as priest and bishop, and as pope.

SECTION 2

The Complementary Pontificates of Pope Benedict XVI and Pope Francis

In *Laudato Si'* Pope Francis wrote, "Young people demand change. They wonder how anyone can claim to be building a better future without thinking of the environmental crisis and the sufferings of the excluded" (13). Respond to Pope Francis's words in three paragraphs. Detail the type of change you would like to see in the world during your adult years.

SECTION 3

The Church Addresses Current Challenges and Concerns

Make a two-column chart. Label the left column "culture of death" and the right column "culture of life." List at least three corresponding examples from the world today that fit under each title.

SECTION 4

The Church as a Sign of Hope

Read Matthew 16:13–20. Write about two things in this passage that offer you hope for the future.

Chapter Assignment

You will be assigned to a small group of five to eight students and asked to research, discuss, and record your group's answers to one of the sets of questions listed below. Make sure to answer all of the questions in your set.

Set 1

→ *Leadership.* How can the bishops strengthen their credibility among laypeople? How can they exercise their authority in a consultative and collegial way? How can they most effectively share the best of America's cultural and societal values with the universal Church?

→ *Parish life.* How can the Church reanimate the person in the pew through a better appreciation of the Eucharist? How can the Church better support laypeople in their family and work lives? How can she affirm life and family concerns more effectively and teach respect for the beauty of human sexuality?

Set 2

→ *Immigrants.* How can the Church in America best embrace the fast-growing number of Hispanic Catholics? Will an English-speaking Church impose her customs on them, or will she respect the cultural and linguistic diversity of this important Catholic community? How can the Church help other Catholic immigrants adjust to American society? How should she better embrace the contributions of African Americans, Asian Americans, Pacific Islanders, Native Americans, and other cultures?

→ *Ecumenism.* How can the Church repair differences with other Christian denominations? What can be done by the Church to highlight the common ancestry of faith that Catholics share with the Jewish people? How can the Church reach out to people of other faiths, including Islam?

Set 3

→ *Vocation crisis.* How can the Church call and train priest leaders to provide vision for the laity, who will assume even greater roles of leadership? How can the Church form priests to lead worship and preach God's word most effectively to an educated and increasingly secularized laity? How can the Church mobilize the laity to support priests and those in religious life in their difficult ministries?

→ *Women.* What role should women have in the Church? How can the Church best meet their needs and desire to serve God's people? How can the Church aid women facing crisis situations of unwed pregnancy, single parenthood, and abuse of any kind? How can the Church help women embrace and live out well their role as mothers?

Set 4

Religious education. How can the Church most effectively reach out to disaffected Catholics—those who have dropped out—particularly young adults? How can the Church appeal to Catholics who subscribe to the American values of individualism and consumerism, rather than to Christ's call to community and responsibility? How can the Church win over the minds and hearts of those Catholics whose attitudes toward abortion, stem cell research, cloning, and sexual ethics mirror those of their non-Catholic fellow citizens?

Schools. What is the future of Catholic schools on all levels—elementary, secondary, and collegiate? How should Catholic schools differ from their public school counterparts? How should they be similar? What is their specifically *Catholic* identity and mission?

Set 5

Gospel witness. How can American Catholics remain true to the vision of Jesus in a pluralistic and increasingly secular society that accepts behaviors and lifestyles contrary to the Gospel as normal and legal? How can the Church challenge national leaders to work for peace in just ways in a world beset by violent conflict? How can the Church best use her material resources (for example, her sponsorship of medical facilities and social services through Catholic Charities) to help the poor and needy?

Self-identity. How can the Catholic Church in America remain faithful to the universal Roman Catholic Church in her life and witness in the pluralistic American culture? How can the Church in America be *American* and yet *Catholic*? How can the Church in America best be the servant of Jesus Christ?

Group Presentation Formats

After your group has answered the questions, plan a group presentation to share your answers with the rest of the class. This may be done in one of the following ways or, with your teacher's permission, you may choose another.

Debate. Divide your group in half. One side presents the answers researched and formulated and agreed to by the majority of the group. The other side presents different or dissenting answers in response.

Presentation. Allowing every member a chance to speak, the group summarizes the answers to each question.

Role playing. The group develops a short skit with a fictional but reality-based scene that helps to summarize the topic and the questions. One option is to share questions and answers in a "man on the street" interview format.

 *Interview.* Half the group members are interviewers, and the other half are interviewees in a panel format. The interviewers address the questions, which the interviewees answer. The interviewers can also ask follow-up questions.

Media presentation. The group gives its answers in a media presentation that can be shown in the classroom.

Prayer

A Prayer for Vocations

Merciful and holy Lord,
continue to send new laborers
into the harvest of your Kingdom!
Assist those whom you call
to follow you in our day;
contemplating your face,
may they respond with joy
to the wondrous mission
that you entrust to them
for the good of your people
and of all men and women.
Amen.
—Pope John Paul II

APPENDIX
CATHOLIC HANDBOOK for FAITH

Beliefs

From the beginning, the Church expressed and handed on its faith in brief formulas accessible to all. These professions of faith are called creeds *because their first word in Latin,* credo, *means "I believe." The following creeds have special importance in the Church. The Apostles' Creed is a summary of the Apostles' faith. The Nicene Creed developed from the Councils of Nicaea and Constantinople and remains in common between the Churches of the East and West.*

Apostles' Creed

I believe in God,
the Father almighty,
Creator of heaven and earth,
and in Jesus Christ, his only Son, our Lord,
who was conceived by the Holy Spirit,
born of the Virgin Mary,
suffered under Pontius Pilate,
was crucified, died, and was buried;
he descended into hell;
on the third day he rose again from the dead;
he ascended into heaven,
and is seated at the right hand of God the Father Almighty;
from there he will come to judge the living and the dead.

I believe in the Holy Spirit,
the holy catholic Church,
the communion of saints,
the forgiveness of sins,
the resurrection of the body,
and life everlasting. Amen.

Nicene Creed

I believe in one God,
the Father almighty,
maker of heaven and earth,
of all things visible and invisible.

I believe in one Lord Jesus Christ,
the Only Begotten Son of God,
born of the Father before all ages.
God from God, Light from Light,
true God from true God,
begotten, not made, consubstantial with the Father;
through him all things were made.
For us men and for our salvation
he came down from heaven,
and by the Holy Spirit was incarnate of the Virgin Mary,
and became man.

For our sake he was crucified under Pontius Pilate,
he suffered death and was buried,
and rose again on the third day
in accordance with the Scriptures.
He ascended into heaven
and is seated at the right hand of the Father.
He will come again in glory
to judge the living and the dead
and his kingdom will have no end.

I believe in the Holy Spirit, the Lord, the giver of life,
who proceeds from the Father and the Son,

who with the Father and the Son is adored and glorified,
who has spoken through the prophets.

I believe in one, holy, catholic and apostolic Church.
I confess one Baptism for the forgiveness of sins
and I look forward to the resurrection of the dead
and the life of the world to come. Amen.

How to Become a Catholic

After taking this course and participating in the life of a Catholic school, you may wonder how a person who is your age and not a Catholic might join the Catholic Church. The following steps offer a guide and are numbered, but their order can certainly vary from person to person.

1. Pray. Ask God to be with you as you consider inquiring about the Catholic Church.
2. Read the Bible (especially the Gospels), a life of a saint you are interested in and find inspiring, and the *Catechism of the Catholic Church*. Do the best you can on your own to familiarize yourself with Jesus Christ and his teachings by reading the Gospels. Consider choosing a saint who was also a convert to the Church. Read the table of contents of the *Catechism* and peruse topics in each section to uncover key Church teachings.
3. Contact your campus minister, a priest, or a theology teacher. Tell the person of your interest in the Church. You will probably be directed to a precatechumenate process, which may either informally or formally ask you to attend Mass and open a regular dialogue with a priest. *Catechumenate* is a word that means "instruction."
4. Start your education process. This is known as the Rite of Christian Initiation for Adults (RCIA). It culminates in your reception of the Sacraments of Initiation—Baptism, Confirmation, and Eucharist—and formal entrance into the Catholic Church. Its steps are briefly outlined here:
   - *Catechumenate.* This step may take a full year or longer. You take instruction in a special class, typically at a parish. You are accompanied by a sponsor who answers your questions. You do service work in the community and participate in the Mass through the time of the Liturgy of the Word. The season of Lent begins your final time of preparation. On the first Sunday of Lent, you travel to the diocesan cathedral, where the local bishop enrolls you in the Book of the Elect, which records the names of all in the diocese who will receive the Sacraments of Initiation.
   - *Purification and enlightenment.* This step also takes place during Lent. On the Sundays of Lent, rituals known as the *scrutinies* help you look deeply at—scrutinize—your life and do penance for your sins. You are given the Lord's Prayer and the Creed and asked to make a promise to keep these central to your life. As in early Christian times, this period culminates with the reception of the Sacraments of Initiation at the Easter Vigil Mass. This Mass begins in literal darkness, representing the darkness of Christ's Death. The Easter candle is then lit, followed by several readings tracing the entirety of salvation history.
   - *Mystagogia.* As a new Catholic, you are called a *neophyte*. You continue to meet with your sponsor and RCIA group after Easter, at least up until Pentecost.

The length of the period of inquiry about the Church varies by person, often dependent on age. Also, the RCIA process is for people who have never been baptized in either the Catholic Church or another Christian denomination. If you have been baptized and are now seeking full initiation into the Catholic Church by reception of the Sacraments of Confirmation and Eucharist, the process will be somewhat different. However, if you have interest in becoming Catholic, the first three steps listed above are valid no matter what your circumstance is: pray, read, and talk to a knowledgeable Catholic with whom you are comfortable.

GLOSSARY

accommodation The method by which religious missionaries, such as the Jesuits, adjust their evangelization methods to match the cultural and linguistic elements of the group whom they are evangelizing.

adult stem cell research A scientific procedure that involves the collection, manipulation, and study of adult human stem cells, as opposed to embryonic stem cell research, which leads to the unnecessary destruction of innocent human life. Adult stem cell research is approved by the Church and has a positive success rate for finding solutions to illness and disease.

aggiornamento Italian for "bringing up to date," the term used by Pope John XXIII to describe the process by which the Church was called to reengage with the world, as inspired by the spirit of the Second Vatican Council.

Albigensianism A heresy that falsely taught that all matter is evil and the spirit is inherently good (with the two being therefore opposed to each other). Albigensianism spread throughout much of France in the thirteenth century.

apologists Christian writers who defend the Church against anti-Christian writings or heresies through the use of reason and intellectual defenses. An apologist "speaks in one's defense."

Apostles Jesus' twelve specially chosen and commissioned disciples, as well as other figures such as St. Paul; they earned this designation when they were sent forth to evangelize. The word *apostle* originates from the Greek for "to send forth."

apostolic succession The handing on of the teaching, preaching, and office of the Apostles to their successors, the bishops, through the laying on of hands.

apparition A supernatural appearance. A Marian apparition is an appearance of the Blessed Virgin Mary to a person, typically to deliver an important message. In order for an apparition to be considered authentic, it must be verified by the Vatican.

Arianism A heresy of the fourth century that took its name from Arius, a priest from Alexandria. The heresy denied the divinity of Jesus, claiming that he was like the Father except that he was created by the Father.

Ascension The event that "marks the definitive entrance of Jesus' humanity into God's heavenly domain" (*CCC*, 665). It is from heaven that Christ will come again.

Baroque An artistic movement or dramatic style in art, architecture, and music originating around 1600 that, among other goals, sought to emphasize the truth of Catholic doctrine through direct emotional connection. The word *baroque* has origins in a Portuguese term that means "rough or imperfect pearl." The French etymology of the word is also associated with "odd."

bourgeoisie A term for the middle class, often used to denote the rising French middle class particularly in the centuries following the Middle Ages.

caesaropapism The political theory often practiced when Christianity was legalized that held that a secular ruler could also have authority over the Church, including in matters of doctrine.

canon The official list of inspired books in the Bible. The Catholic canon lists forty-six Old Testament books and twenty-seven New Testament books.

capitalism An economic and sociopolitical system with limited governmental control, centered upon the free market and with an emphasis on private property, sometimes resulting in economic inequality.

catechumens People who are undergoing a period of study and spiritual preparation before receiving the Sacrament of Baptism.

Catholic Reformation Also known as the Counter-Reformation, the response of the Catholic Church to the protests of Martin Luther and others who had separated from the Church. It consisted of an effort to clarify and re-present the teachings and pastoral practices inherent to Catholicism.

Catholic Relief Services A humanitarian relief organization established in 1943 by the bishops of the United States. Catholic Relief Services (CRS) originally helped replenish war-torn Europe and house its refugees. Today, CRS continues to focus on service to the poor overseas, using the Gospel as its guiding mandate.

charism A special gift or grace of the Holy Spirit that directly or indirectly builds up the Church, helps a person live a Christian life, or serves the common good.

Christendom A time of great achievement in the Middle Ages when the Church and Western society were one. It refers to a group of nations in which Catholicism was the established religion of the state. In a wider sense, the term refers to a larger territory where most people are Christian.

Christology The systematic contemplation within the Church on the Divine Person and work of Jesus Christ. In short: Who is Jesus? What salvific work did he do and why does this matter?

Church Fathers Those men from the first through eighth centuries AD who were given this title based on their monumental contributions to the Church, especially their extensive teaching and writing about the Faith in order to help it growand develop.

Codex Vaticanus From the early fourth century, the oldest complete copy of the Bible in existence; it features the forty-six books of the Old Testament and the twenty-seven books of the New Testament.

colonization The process by which a nation establishes a prominent presence by exerting an element of power or control in an area beyond their original borders.

common good The collective well-being of society as a whole, particularly in matters related to social justice.

communism A socioeconomic and political system that aims to bring about a utopian society on earth as envisioned by Karl Marx. This theory includes the government's unrestrained control of citizens' property, the suppression of free speech and assembly, the oppression of religion in public life, and other denials of democratic values.

conciliarism An erroneous idea, popular in the Middle Ages, that an ecumenical council of the Church had more authority than the pope and could depose him if they so desired.

conquistadors Spanish for "conquerors"; those explorers who left Spain to conquer new faraway territories and claim them in the name of the Spanish crown.

contraception A chemical or object, such as a birth control pill or a condom, specifically used to ward off the possibility of pregnancy.

covenant The partnership between God and humanity that God has established out of his love. The New Covenant is offered through Christ; the blood that Christ shed on the Cross is a sign of the New Covenant.

Crusades A series of military expeditions made according to a solemn vow to return holy places to the possession of the Church from the Muslims.

culture of death The state of society in which human life, especially the most innocent and vulnerable (such as the unborn, the elderly, and the terminally ill), is not given its proper dignity and recognition.

Deism A philosophical position that developed in the Enlightenment, it is the belief that while God does exist and did create the world, he refrains from any kind of interference or direct participation in his creation.

deities Higher beings or gods based on the belief system of a particular religion.

Deposit of Faith "The heritage of faith contained in Sacred Scripture and Sacred Tradition, handed down in the Church from the time of the Apostles, from which the Magisterium draws all that it proposes for belief as being divinely revealed" (*CCC*, Glossary).

Desert Fathers Christians of about the fourth century who withdrew into the desert to live an ascetic life of prayer, fasting, and abstinence. Their teachings had a profound impact on the theology and spirituality of the Church and the development of monasticism.

ecumenical councils Meetings of Catholic bishops from around the world, typically convened in order to discuss and resolve pressing theological topics.

Edict of Milan A joint declaration by the Roman emperor Constantine and Licinius in the East in 313 that legalized the practice of Christianity and other religions throughout the Roman Empire.

Eucharistic species The Real Presence of Jesus' Precious Body (under the mere appearance of the bread) and Jesus' Precious Blood (under the mere appearance of grape wine), accompanied by the fullness of his soul and divinity, after the bread and wine have been consecrated by the priest at Mass.

euthanasia The purposeful killing, through lethal injection, starvation, or other means, of someone whose life is not deemed worthy of continuing.

evangelical counsels Vows of personal poverty, chastity (understood as lifelong celibacy), and obedience to a bishop or superior of a religious community.

faith Both a gift from God that can only exist with God's preceding grace and an act of a person's intellect, an assenting to the divine truth by command of the will that has been moved by that grace. Though only possible by grace and the interior helps of the Holy Spirit, faith is truly a human action. "Trusting in God and cleaving to the truths he has revealed are contrary neither to human freedom nor to human reason" (*CCC*, 154).

fascism A governmental system typified by authoritarianism and dictatorship, in which individual rights are suppressed by the will of those in power.

feast day The day on the liturgical calendar commemorating a saint's entry into heaven, typically celebrated on or close to the day when a saint died.

feudalism The governing system that prevailed in Europe in the Middle Ages in which a superior or lord granted land to a vassal in return for military services of that vassal.

Filioque Latin for "and from the Son"; a phrase added to the Nicene Creed by the Western Church without the agreement of the Eastern Church to specify that the Holy Spirit proceeds from both the Father *and the Son*; it became a point of contention within Eastern Orthodoxy.

First Council of Nicaea The first ecumenical council; a meeting of three hundred bishops that took place in 325, most importantly to provide a response to the Arian heresy and a common profession of faith.

Focolare Movement A movement founded by Chiara Lubich in 1943 with the goal of world unity achieved through putting the Gospel love of Jesus Christ into action.

fortitude The courage that Christians are called to embrace and rely on in order to evangelize and live their faith openly; also, one of the four cardinal virtues (along with temperance, justice, and prudence).

Founding Fathers The leading American men, including philosophers, politicians, and writers, who bridged the colonial era and the Revolutionary era, whose ideas shaped the structure of early American government, and whose legacy is still cited today.

heresies Incorrect and otherwise errant understandings or teachings about certain doctrinal matters or dogmas; they are opposed to right teaching (orthodoxy).

Holocaust Also known as the *Shoah*; the attempt by the Nazi forces under Adolf Hitler, by way of a system of concentration camps, to obliterate the presence of the Jewish people and other non-Jewish civilians from areas under Nazi control from 1933 through 1945, resulting in the deaths of more than six million Jews.

humanism A cultural and intellectual movement of the Renaissance that emphasized the rediscovery of the literature, art, and civilizations of ancient Greece and Rome.

hypostatic union From a Greek term (*hypostasis*) employed to describe the union of the human and divine natures of Jesus Christ, the Son of God, in one Divine Person. The First Council of Ephesus (431) used this term, and it was expanded and affirmed at the Council of Chalcedon (451).

Immaculate Conception The dogma that states that Mary, in view of the merits of Jesus Christ, was preserved free from the stain of Original Sin from the moment of her conception.

indulgences The remission before God of the temporal punishment still due to forgiven sins. Indulgences are, as the *Catechism of the Catholic Church* teaches, "closely linked to the effects of the sacrament of Penance" (*CCC*, 1471).

Justinian Code of Law A collection of laws written in Latin that were instituted by the Byzantine emperor Justinian (527–565) and became the basis of European law. Its Christian orientation gave women and children more protection than earlier law, but it still reflected the customs of its times, such as bodily mutilation as punishment for some crimes and repressive measures against non-Christians, including Jews.

Kingdom of God The reign or rule of God. The Kingdom of God began with the coming of Jesus. It will exist in perfect form at the end of time.

Kulturkampf A German term meaning "cultural struggle"; the steady attempts, between 1871 and 1887, of German chancellor Otto von Bismarck to control the Catholic Church in Germany through governmental officials.

lay investiture A practice in the Middle Ages whereby secular rulers chose the bishops for their territories, thus usurping the right of the pope to choose bishops.

lay trusteeism The historical practice in American Catholicism in which lay (nonclerical) parishioners assumed numerous duties within the administration of their parishes, including naming and dismissing their parish's pastor. The First Provincial Council of Baltimore (1829) ended the practice of lay trusteeism.

liturgical year Cycle of the liturgical seasons of Advent, Christmas Ordinary Time, Lent, Triduum, and Easter, organized around the major events of Jesus' life.

Liturgy of the Word The part of the Mass that includes the "writings of the prophets" (the Old Testament readings and psalms) and the "memoirs of the Apostles" (the Gospels and the New Testament epistles), the homily, the profession of faith (Creed), and the intercessions for the world.

Magisterium The bishops, in communion with the pope (the successor of St. Peter), who are the living and teaching office of the Church. The Magisterium authentically interprets the Word of God in the forms of both Sacred Scripture and Sacred Tradition.

mandatum "An acknowledgment by Church authority that a Catholic professor of a theological discipline is teaching within the full communion of the Catholic Church" (*The Application of Ex Corde Ecclesiae for the United States*, article 4, 4, e, i). *Mandatum* is Latin for "command" or "mandate."

martyrs The word *martyr* literally means "witness" in Greek. Martyrs are witnesses to the truth of faith who endure even death to be faithful to Christ.

Maryland Toleration Act of 1649 Legislation passed by the assembled representatives of the Maryland colony that permitted free religious practice.

Messiah From the Hebrew for "the Chosen One" or "the Anointed One"; the role that Jesus filled.

modernism A movement of the late nineteenth and early twentieth centuries that attempted to reduce and/or limit Church teaching to modern advances in history, science, and biblical research.

monasticism Religious life in which men or women leave the world and enter a monastery or convent to devote themselves to solitary prayer, contemplation, and self-denial. After martyrdom became rare, monasticism became the most demanding way to live out a Christian vocation.

Monophysitism The heresy taught in the fifth century that asserted that there is only one nature in the Person of Christ—his divine nature.

Monothelitism The heresy taught in the seventh century that claimed that Jesus has two natures but only one will—his divine will.

moral relativism The problematic ethical stance that claims that there are no moral absolutes and that morality can only be considered from the individual's perspective.

Muhammad The founder of Islam, regarded as a prophet by Muslims.

mystic A morally upright figure who strives to be open to God's direct and transformative presence oftentimes through contemplation, meditation, and prayer.

nativism An anti-Catholic cultural push in the early- to mid-nineteenth century in which preference in social, employment, and political matters was given to Protestant Americans who had been in the United States for multiple generations, as opposed to Catholics who had immigrated to the United States more recently.

Nestorianism The heresy spread by Nestorius, a fifth-century patriarch of Constantinople, that asserted that some of Christ's traits were purely human and others were purely divine.

New Evangelization An initiative within the Church to spread the Gospel to all nations as well as to invite those already in the Church to a renewed commitment to their faith.

New World A term applied to the Americas, as compared to the "Old World" of Europe.

Nicene Creed The foundational statement of Christian belief that was produced by the Church leaders gathered at the First Council of Nicaea in 325.

pagan In earlier times, "pagan" exclusively referred to a person who was polytheistic. Today a broader definition refers to a person holding religious beliefs other than those of one of the major world religions or being polytheistic.

pantheism A false belief that identifies the universe as God or God as the universe.

Papal Inquisition A Church tribunal established in the thirteenth century that was first designed to curb the Albigensian heresy. In collaboration with secular authorities, papal representatives employed the Inquisition to judge the guilt of suspected heretics with the aim of getting them to repent. Unfortunately, before long, many abuses crept into the process.

Papal States The territory in modern-day central Italy that was overseen by the pope from the eighth century until 1870.

parochial school A Catholic school—typically an elementary and middle school—affiliated with a parish community. The word *parochial* means "affiliated with a parish."

Paschal Mystery The redemptive Passion, Death, Resurrection, and glorious Ascension of Jesus Christ, through which Jesus not only liberated humans from sin but also gave them new life.

patriarchs Bishops of one of the five episcopal sees, the name for the places of residence of bishops: the Eastern patriarchates of Jerusalem, Antioch, Constantinople, and Alexandria; and the Latin patriarchate of Rome. In the early Church, the bishop of Rome (the pope) was acknowledged the principal patriarch.

Pentecost From the Greek for "fiftieth day," a Jewish harvest feast occurring fifty days after Passover; the first Pentecost for Christians was when the Holy Spirit appeared to the Apostles in the form of wind and fire fifty days after Jesus' Resurrection.

predestination A belief that one's actions are not only preknown by God but also predetermined, thus denying God's gift of free will. The Catholic position is that God does have knowledge of who will be saved and who will be lost, yet it is God's desire that all will be saved. To this end, he provides graces and helps, which people are free to accept or reject. This means that while God knows certain people will be lost, this is not the choice of God but of those individuals.

Purgatory The final purification of all who die in God's grace and friendship but remain imperfectly purified. Purgatory is the final cleansing away of all sin and of all consequences of sin.

rationalism A philosophy of the Enlightenment that taught that only human reason, separated from religious belief, can bring people into the light of knowledge.

relic The physical remains or personal effects of a saint that are approved by the Church for veneration.

religious literacy The familiarity with the basic tenets of various mainstream faiths that allows meaningful and peaceful dialogue with those of other faiths.

Renaissance A cultural rebirth begun in the Late Middle Ages that rediscovered the ancient civilizations of Romeand Egypt. The Renaissance stressed the natural and the human. It emphasized the pleasures of life, glorified the human body, and celebrated education.

Sacred Heart of Jesus A devotion that recognizes that Jesus, both fully divine and fully human, deeply loves his people with an outpouring of love from his human heart.

salvation history The story of God's action in human history. Salvation history refers to the events through which God makes humanity aware of and brings humanity into the Kingdom of God. It began with the creation of the world and will end with the second coming of Christ.

schism A break in Christian unity that takes place when a group of Christians separates itself from the Church. This happens historically when the group breaks union with the pope.

scholasticism The theological system that arose during the Middle Ages, developed notably by St. Thomas Aquinas, balancing faith and reason and relying heavily on classical philosophy and the Church Fathers.

second coming The final judgment of all humanity when Christ returns to earth. It is also known by its Greek name, *Parousia,* which means "arrival."

simony The controversial practice of selling and buying positions or favor within the Church. The Church condemns this practice.

social Darwinism The theories of Charles Darwin applied to the social realm. For example, the concept of "survival of the fittest" works in economics too, resulting in an image of the economic jungle and so-called laissez-faire economics, or liberal capitalism.

socialism At its core, an economic and sociopolitical theory that advocates for the government or society as a whole to own and administer the production and distribution of goods.

Spanish Inquisition A bureau or commission that had branches in most of the larger dioceses of Spain that was empowered to call on civil authorities to help weed out heretics. Once the heretics were discovered, the Church authorities conducted a trial with those accused presumed guilty and required to prove their innocence.

subsidiarity A social principle that stipulates that social matters should be taken care of at the lowest, most local level of authority possible.

Synod of Bishops A periodic meeting of various bishops from around the world with the pope for the purpose of holding theological discourse and advising the pope on matters related to the Faith.

Thomism Teachings that follow the theology and philosophy of St. Thomas Aquinas, especially from the *Summa Theologiae*. St. Thomas presents five ways by which humans can infer the existence of God through reason. He also teaches that the highest truths are those which are freely revealed by God.

transubstantiation Church teaching that holds that the substance of the bread and wine is changed into the substance of the Body and Blood of Christ at the consecration at Mass.

universal destination of goods The principle that resources and material goods within society should be accessible to humanity as a whole rather than restricted to the private realm.

SUBJECT INDEX

D

E

F

G

H

I

J

K

L

N

Q

R

T

U

V

PRIMARY SOURCES INDEX

Photo Credits

Alamy
p. 3, 5, 47, 49, 66, 80, 87, 89, 94, 108, 111, 148, 168, 189, 196, 197, 199, 200, 204, 209, 233, 234, 235, 236, 237, 238, 243, 248, 263, 267, 268, 269, 271, 274, 276, 283, 285, 295, 298, 300, 303, 313, 319, 321, 339, 352, 359, 362

Associated Press
p. 31, 54, 269, 295, 301, 311, 312, 317, 323, 336, 337, 340, 341, 355, 359

Bridgeman Images
p. 172, 211, 282, 315

Getty Images
p. 1, 3, 4, 7, 8, 13, 15, 23, 29, 35, 37, 39, 40, 42, 45, 48, 49, 61, 63, 66, 67, 68, 70, 71, 72, 73, 74, 75, 76, 78, 83, 84, 93, 101, 103, 107, 108, 109, 111, 112, 116, 117, 124, 125, 126, 131, 134, 135, 143, 145, 151, 152, 153, 154, 156, 157, 160, 164, 168, 169, 170, 171, 179, 183, 184, 186, 187, 191, 192, 194, 200, 201, 202, 205, 206, 209, 217, 222, 223, 224, 226, 228, 232, 236, 241, 244, 245, 247, 250, 259, 260, 265, 266, 286, 292, 299, 306, 307, 310, 319, 331, 333, 335, 336, 343, 345, 346, 347, 350, 352, 354, 357, 358, 360, 361, 369

Granger Historical Picture Archive
p. 325

National Black Catholic Congress, www.nbccongress.org
p. 279

Rev. James Robison, LIFE Today TV
p. 181

Superstock
p. 10, 20, 21, 33, 49, 52, 65, 68, 75, 76, 85, 91, 105, 106, 109, 115, 118, 123, 128, 130, 132, 134, 136, 147, 149, 158, 159, 162, 163, 166, 169, 170, 188, 201, 207, 208, 210, 221, 227, 229, 255, 261, 266, 267, 268, 272, 275, 278, 297, 304, 305, 307, 337

Tonia Borsellino/Catholic News Agency
p. 50

Verbum Dei High School, Los Angeles
p. 257